Foundation ActionScript for Macromedia Flash MX 2004

Sham Bhangal

friendsof

DESIGNER TO DESIGNER™

an Apress® company

Foundation ActionScript for Macromedia Flash MX 2004

Credits

This book is dedicated to the creator of the No Conspiracy Theory.
No sleep, 6:00 in the morning, February 25, 2004.
I've just worked it out. I know who you are.

CONTENTS AT A GLANCE

CONTENTS

ABOUT THE AUTHOR

Sham Bhangal has written for friends of ED on new media since its inception over 3 years ago. In that time, he has been involved in the writing, production, and specification of just under 20 books.

Sham has considerable working experience with Macromedia and Adobe products, with a focus on web design and motion graphics. Creating books that tell other people about his favorite subjects is probably the best job he has had (ignoring the long hours, aggressive deadlines, lost manuscripts, and occasional wiped hard drives). If he was doing something else, he'd probably be losing sleep thinking about writing anyway.

Sham currently lives in the north of England with his longtime partner, Karen.

ABOUT THE TECHNICAL REVIEWER

 **Marlene Spector** is a freelance web designer, Flash animator, and editor who is always looking for interesting new assignments. Her personal website is at www.anthology.us. Marlene has been using Flash since version 3 and is enthusiastic about the changes in the latest version of her favorite development environment. In addition to Flash and ActionScript, she has considerable experience writing HTML and XHTML code, and in creating cool stuff using Photoshop.

Marlene lives in Southern California with her partner, Patrick.

INTRODUCTION

With the release of Flash MX 2004, scripting in Flash has moved from being a desirable asset to an essential power-tool in the world of web design. It has evolved over the last few revisions to become *the* language to learn if you want to produce low-bandwidth, high-impact interactive content on the Web. No longer is ActionScript a provider of simple Flash eye candy; it's now positioned as the number-one tool to create intelligent interfaces, interactive games, and across-the-Web sound/video delivery.

ActionScript is, quite simply, the center of power in Flash, and it's no surprise that most of the advances in Flash MX 2004 are script-centric. So much has changed in this version that ActionScript has finally moved up a revision—we now have ActionScript 2.0, a major step forward in the language that allows us to build larger and more compelling interactive content.

ActionScript is that scary code stuff that programmers do, right? Wrong. ActionScript adds power and potential to your design work. It's not going to turn you into someone who speaks in 1s and 0s, who only comes out after dark, and whose idea of design is a different HTML color. It's going to turn you into someone who finally has the power to achieve his or her web design goals, rather than being hemmed in by frustrating limitations.

If you know nothing or little about ActionScript, this book will take you to a position where you have a real foundation of knowledge from which you can build some awe-inspiring structures.

What you need to know

You've picked up this book, so I guess that you have the Flash basics under your belt. You'll probably have built some basic timeline-based movies with tweens and so on, and you may have read an introductory Flash book such as friends of ED's acclaimed *Foundation Macromedia Flash MX 2004*. If you haven't, I do recommend looking at it; you can find it at www.friendsofed.com.

If you don't have a copy of Macromedia Flash MX yet, you can download a fully functional 30-day free trial from those nice people at www.macromedia.com. You can use either the Standard or Professional edition of Flash with this book. If you're going to use the trial version of Flash with this book, I recommend downloading the Professional version (it has all the features of both versions).

Support: Fast, free, and friendly

Got a problem? Can't get one of the book's exercises to work? Unable to find a bit of code that I've promised you? The folks at friends of ED offer free technical support to make sure that you experience an unhindered path through the pages of this book. So, if you have a problem, don't hesitate to get in touch.

You can reach friends of ED at support@friendsofed.com. Please include the last four digits of this book's ISBN number (3057) in the subject of the e-mail, and even if the dedicated support team is unable to solve your problem immediately, your queries will be passed to the people who put the book together—the editors and authors—to solve.

We'd love to hear from you, even if it's just to request future books, ask about friends of ED, or tell us how much you loved *Foundation ActionScript for Macromedia Flash MX 2004*!

If your question concerns an issue not directly concerned with book content, the best place for these types of questions is the friends of ED message lists at http://friendsofed.infopop.net/ 2/OpenTopic. Here, you'll find a variety of fellow readers and designers, plus dedicated forum moderators from friends of ED.

Finally, you can e-mail me, Sham Bhangal, at boy@futuremedia.org.uk.

FLAs for download

There's a wealth of code and support files available for this book. They're organized by chapter at the Foundation ActionScript page at www.friendsofed.com. Select Flash Titles in the contents area (at the top left of the page), and select the title of this book from the list that appears. While you're there, you can also sample the source files from other titles in the friends of ED Flash series.

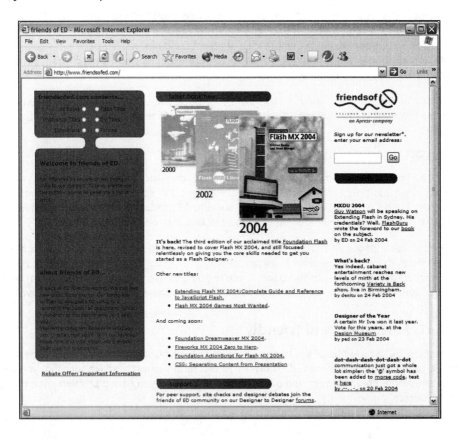

The case study: Futuremedia

Throughout the course of this book you'll create a website called Futuremedia from scratch. You can access a fully functioning version of the website you'll be building as you progress through this book at the URL you'll find on the downloads page (or you can go to www.futuremedia.org.uk for the latest incarnation).

Futuremedia font

The font used in the Futuremedia site at www.futuremedia.org.uk is called Century Gothic. It's a sans-serif font with fairly wide characters that give it a light and modern feel. This is a commercial font, although you may find it already installed on your computer, depending on what other applications you have installed. If you don't have it, other fonts will suffice, including Trebuchet/Trebuchet MS, Verdana, and Arial/Helvetica. At least one font in this list will be already installed on your system. If all else fails, you can use the default Flash sans font, _sans.

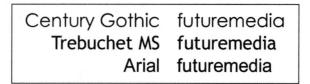

At the end of the book, you may want to customize the look and feel of the Futuremedia site. I recommend you use any sans or techno font.

Centering the Futuremedia site in the browser

When you publish the Futuremedia site, you should use the following settings in the File ➤ Publish Settings ➤ HTML tab:

With these settings, you'll see something like this in the browser (press *F12* to publish the site and view it in your browser):

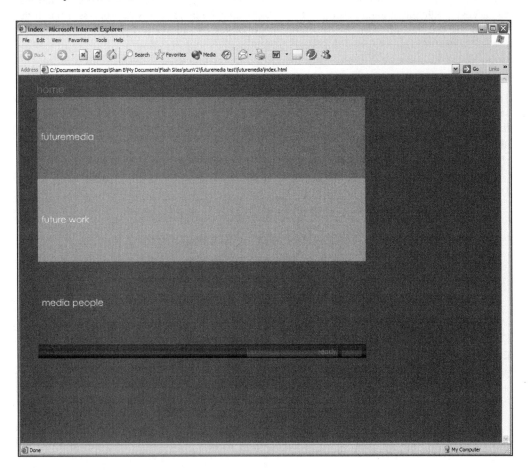

That's fine, but most professional sites center the Flash site in the browser, so it looks something like this instead:

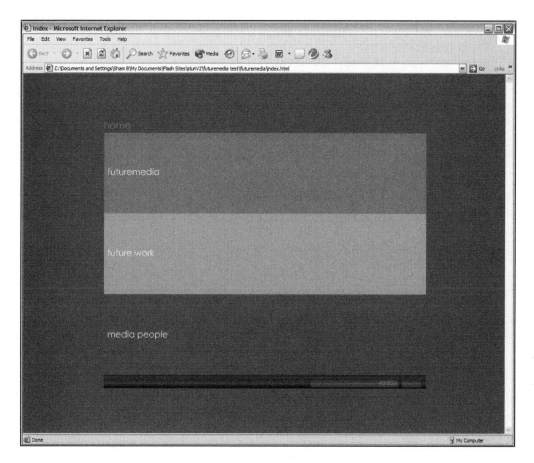

There's no direct way of achieving this in Flash—you have to edit the HTML. To do this, find the HTML file created by Flash (it will be in the same folder as the FLA), and open it in a text editor such as Notepad. You'll see something like this:

```
<!DOCTYPE html PUBLIC "-//W3C//DTD XHTML
➥ 1.0 Transitional//EN"
"http://www.w3.org/TR/xhtml1/DTD/xhtml1-
➥ transitional.dtd">
<html xmlns="http://www.w3.org/1999/xhtml"
➥ xml:lang="en" lang="en">
<head>
<meta http-equiv="Content-Type" content=
➥ "text/html; charset=iso-8859-1" />
<title>index</title>
</head>
<body bgcolor="#666666">
<!-urls used in the movie->
<!-text used in the movie->
<!-
futuremedia
future work
media people
loading:
this is a skip-intro free site
->
<object classid="clsid:d27cdb6e-ae6d-
➥ 11cf-96b8-444553540000" codebase=
➥ "http://fpdownload.macromedia.com/pub/
➥ shockwave/cabs/flash/swflash.cab#
➥ version=7,0,0,0" width="800" height=
➥ "600" id="index" align="middle">
<param name="allowScriptAccess" value=
➥ "sameDomain" />
<param name="movie" value="index.swf" />
<param name="quality" value="high" />
<param name="bgcolor" value="#666666" />
<embed src="index.swf" quality="high"
➥ bgcolor="#666666" width="800" height=
➥ "600" name="index" align="middle"
➥ allowScriptAccess="sameDomain" type=
➥ "application/x-shockwave-flash"
➥ pluginspage="http://www.macromedia.com/
➥ go/getflashplayer" />
</object>
</body>
</html>
```

This is XHTML, so you should really play ball and use CSS and <div> and <span>, and no HTML tables or table horizontal and vertical centering (not least because vertical centering of a table doesn't work in XHTML!). Add the following lines to create a CSS-based centered-in-browser page:

```
<!DOCTYPE html PUBLIC "-//W3C//DTD XHTML
➥ 1.0 Transitional//EN"
➥ "http://www.w3.org/TR/xhtml1/DTD/
➥ xhtml1-transitional.dtd">
<html xmlns="http://www.w3.org/1999/xhtml"
➥ xml:lang="en" lang="en">
<head>
<meta http-equiv="Content-Type" content=
➥ "text/html; charset=iso-8859-1" />
<title>index</title>
<style type="text/css">
<!-
body
{
 margin: 0px
}
#centercontent
{
 text-align: center;
 margin-top: -300px;
 margin-left: -400px;
 position: absolute;
 top: 50%;
 left: 50%;
}
->
</style>
</head>
<body bgcolor="#666666">
<!-urls used in the movie->
<!-text used in the movie->
<!-
futuremedia
future work
media people
loading:
this is a skip-intro free site
->
<div id="centercontent">
<object classid="clsid:d27cdb6e-ae6d-
➥ 11cf-96b8-444553540000" codebase=
➥ "http://fpdownload.macromedia.com/pub/
➥ shockwave/cabs/flash/swflash.cab#
➥ version=7,0,0,0" width="800"
➥ height="600" id="index" align=
```

```
⮕ "middle">
<param name="allowScriptAccess" value=
⮕ "sameDomain" />
<param name="movie" value="index.swf" />
<param name="quality" value="high" />
<param name="bgcolor" value="#666666" />
<embed src="index.swf" quality="high"
⮕ bgcolor="#666666" width="800" height=
⮕ "600" name="index" align="middle"
⮕ allowScriptAccess="sameDomain"
⮕ type="application/x-shockwave-flash"
⮕ pluginspage="http://www.macromedia.com/
⮕ go/getflashplayer" />
</object>
</div>
</body>
</html>
```

> This should work for sites other than the Futuremedia site. You need to change the `margin-top` setting to minus half the height of your Flash stage and the `margin-left` setting to minus half the width of your Flash stage. This will force the top-left corner of the Flash stage to appear at the center of the browser window, offset by half the Flash stage's height and width. Note that the body style also gets rid of any browser gutters.

Layout conventions used in this book

I've tried to keep this book as clear and easy to follow as possible, so I've used the following text conventions throughout.

When you first come across an important word, it will be in **bold** type, then in normal type thereafter.

I've used a fixed-width font for code and `file names`.

Text you need to type in for yourself appears like this.

Sections of code that need to be added to an existing script are additionally highlighted **like this**.

You'll see menu commands written in the form Menu ➤ Submenu ➤ Submenu.

When there's some information I think is really important, I'll highlight it like this:

> *This is very important stuff—don't skip it!*

Exercises are formatted like this:

1. Open Flash.

2. Create a new movie file and add a circle in the middle of the stage.

When I ask you to enter code that spills onto two lines **without** using a carriage return, I'll use a code continuation character, like this: ➡

PCs and Macs

To make sure this book is as useful to you as possible, I've tried to avoid making too many assumptions about whether you're running Flash on a PC or a Mac. However, when it comes to mouse clicks and modifier buttons, I can't generalize. There's no two ways about it: they're different!

When I use the term "click," I mean *left*-click on the PC or simply *click* on the Mac. On the other hand, a *right*-click on the PC corresponds to holding down the CTRL button and clicking on the Mac. I abbreviate this as CTRL-click.

Another important key combination on the PC is when you hold down the CTRL key while you press another key (or click something). I abbreviate this sort of thing as CTRL-click. The Mac equivalent is to hold down the CMD key (also known as the APPLE or FLOWER key) instead, so you'll normally see this written out in the form CTRL/CMD-click.

Here's a quick rundown of the most common commands:

PC	Mac
Right-click	CTRL-click
CTRL-click	CMD-click
CTRL+Z (to undo)	CMD+Z
CTRL+ENTER	CMD+ENTER

All screenshots in this book were taken using the Windows XP style and the Silver color scheme. This is recommended over the default Windows XP appearance, as it's by far the most color neutral and won't detract from your web design color work.

Mac users will find that their Flash scripting environment is interchangeable with the Windows XP environment. All the buttons and panels will be in the same place; only the window styling is slightly different.

OK, now that I've taken care of the preliminaries, let's get to work!

Chapter 1

INTERACTIVE FLASH

What we'll cover in this chapter:

- Introducing ActionScript and the Actions panel
- Using actions to give commands to a Flash movie
- Targeting actions at different things in a movie
- Listening to Flash and handling Flash events
- Writing callbacks so that real-time events can trigger actions
- Using variables as containers for storing information

So, what's this ActionScript business all about? You may well have done loads of great stuff with Flash already, but you still keep hearing people say you've barely scratched the surface because you haven't learned to **program** your movies. On the other hand, programming is supposed to be a strange and highly complex business, practiced by myopic young people with pale skin and peculiar taste in clothes. If you're anything like me, that's a path in life you'd probably rather avoid.

Fortunately, there's some good news. Programming is a bit like mountaineering: there are dedicated full-timers who might spend every waking minute preparing to tackle the north face of the Eiger, even if that means their day-to-day lives come to resemble some kind of hideous training regimen. However, there are plenty more folks who'll just take a few weeks out from "normal life" to join a trek up Mount Kilimanjaro and get back home fit, tanned, and with a whole new perspective on things—not to mention a great big wad of stunning photos!

I'm not going to suggest that learning ActionScript is somehow going to get you fit and tanned. But it can help you to race ahead with making rich, powerful, truly fantastic Flash movies that will leave most non-ActionScripting Flash-meisters wondering how to even begin creating such things. So, to get back to the point, what's this ActionScript business all about? Well, as far too many irritating game show hosts have reminded us over the years, "The clue is in the question." There are two words to consider:

- Action
- Script

We all know what these mean: an action is something you do, and a script is something actors read so that they know what to say and do when they go on stage or in front of a camera. Well, that's really all there is to it. ActionScript is like a script that you give to a Flash movie, so that you can tell it what to do and when to do it—that is, you give it **actions** to perform.

The analogy between ActionScript and film scripts is more than just a metaphor. When writing ActionScript, I often like to assume that I'm writing scripts for human actors, and before I write code, I figure out how I would say what I want to do to a real actor before implementing it in ActionScript. This is actually a very good test—if you find you aren't able to find the words needed, it's probably because you don't really understand your problem, and it's time to turn away from the machine and work it out on paper first.

Giving your movies instructions

Actions are the basic building blocks of ActionScript. It's sometimes helpful to think of them as instructions you give to the movie, or even better, as **commands**. You tell the movie to stop. You tell it to start again. You tell it to go to such and such a frame, and start playing from there. You probably get the idea. Whenever you want to tell your movie to do something that it wouldn't normally do anyway, you can do so by giving it an action.

Since this book is about ActionScript, I'll stick to using the word "actions." If you mention actions to programmers who don't use Flash, though, they may look at you blankly for a moment before saying, "Ah, you mean commands!" In my opinion, it's well worth keeping the idea that actions are the same thing as commands at the back of your mind.

As you know if you've sneaked a look at the ActionScript Dictionary (Help ➤ ActionScript Dictionary), there are stacks of different actions available in Flash, which makes it (a) possible to do all sorts of weird and wonderful things to your movies, and (b) pretty hard to know where to start. Don't worry, though, I have a cunning plan! You'll start off by looking at some simple actions that let you start and stop a movie's main timeline, and then go on to look at jumping about from one frame to another. Nothing too tricky to begin with.

Before you start writing actions, though, I need to make an important introduction. The **Actions panel** will be your partner in crime throughout this chapter, the rest of the book, and your future career as an ActionScript hero. Let's check it out.

> *If you own the Professional version of Flash, you have the ability to open a full-screen ActionScript editor by choosing* File ➤ New *and then selecting* ActionScript File *from the* General *tab of the New Document window that will appear. This editor is actually very similar to the normal Actions panel. The major difference with the full-screen editor is it's just that—there's no stage and no timeline. The full-screen editor is designed for writing a stand-alone ActionScript file, something you'll have the option to use as you build your website. Just because this is a beginner book doesn't mean I'm not going to fully cover the Professional version of Flash as well as the Standard edition, so don't worry, I haven't forgotten you!*

Working with the Actions panel

The Actions panel is where you'll be writing all your ActionScript, so it'll pay for you to know your way around it before you make a proper start. Before you do, though, let's make sure we're all on the same page. Select Window ➤ Panel Sets ➤ Default Layout, and the interface should go back to the out-of-the-box state.

> *If you ever get to a point at which you have many panels open and a generally cluttered screen, this is a good option to select—you don't lose your work in progress by doing it. It's also a good idea to select this option before you start any of the step-by-step tutorials.*

First, you need to open up the Actions panel. As with any panel, there are several ways to do this, but the simplest is to click the panel's title bar, which you should spot near the bottom of the screen.

If you don't see the title bar there, you can always select Window ➤ Actions (or use the keyboard shortcut *F9*) to call it up. Another option is to click the little arrow icon (which Flash uses to represent all things ActionScript) at the far right of the Property inspector. This is how it should look when you open it for the first time:

Let's take a look at what we have here. At the bottom is a little tab that looks like this:

This tab tells you that any actions you add are going to be **attached to** a frame (via the attached to icon). You also know the actions will be attached to a layer called Layer 1, and on frame 1 of that layer via the text Layer 1 : 1 . . . um . . . you also know this must be true because that's the only frame you have at the moment!

Actions are always attached to something—usually a keyframe. (You can also attach a script to a movie clip or button using the Flash 5 style of ActionScript coding, but you will *not* be using that in this book—it's outdated and not recommended anymore.)

> *Flash beginners have* **behaviors** *in Flash MX 2004 to help them create sites that would otherwise require them to write ActionScript. You won't be using behaviors at all in this book, partly because you'll be writing code yourself and partly because behaviors use the aforementioned outdated dialect of ActionScript.*
>
> *Behaviors are cool and fine for designers who don't look at code, but you won't be that sort of designer by the end of this chapter.*

You tell Flash what you're attaching to by selecting it before you start typing in the Actions panel. The tab is very useful because it reminds you what you're attaching to and where it is. Sometimes this may not be obvious (because you have, for example, selected the wrong thing in error), and you should always get into the habit of checking the tab to make sure what Flash thinks it should be attaching to is what you want it to attach the script to. Most scripts will *not work properly* (or at all) if you get this wrong.

Sometimes you'll find that the script you're writing suddenly vanishes. This is one of those "Omygod, I've lost all my stuff! <*add expletive*>!" moments that every beginner has, but not to worry, it usually only means the keyframe you're attaching to has somehow become

unselected, and something on the main stage is now selected instead. Before you start writing it all out again and glare at your cat/dog/coworker for ruining your concentration and/or day, it usually helps to try reselecting the keyframe first.

Once you've selected a frame, you add scripts via the Script pane (the big white area to the right of the Actions panel). This is the where you enter scripts once you've selected the keyframe you want to attach them to. Simply click inside the Script pane and start typing. Try this:

```
// My first line of ActionScript
```

> *Macromedia calls the little windowlike areas within a panel* **panes** *(as in, "The panel is a window, and the bits inside it are the windowpanes.").*

The // tells Flash that this is a **comment** rather than code, and Flash will actually ignore everything after the //. Adding comments to your scripts is a good way to remind yourself what the scripts do 6 months after you've written them and/or 20 minutes after you've written them, depending on how bad a day you're having. Press *ENTER* on your keyboard to start a new line. Your scripts will consist of many such lines, and it's a good idea to *number* them so you know how far down a script you are (this also makes it easier to refer to line numbers later in the book). Select the little pop-up menu icon (at the top-right corner of the Actions panel) and select View Line Numbers in the menu that appears.

OK, let's look at the other goodies. On the left side are two more panes.

You'll notice that there's a little letter "a" above frame 1 on the timeline. This tells you that the keyframe here has a script attached to it. That's fine for small FLAs with not many timelines, but for bigger Flash productions, you need a centralized place that allows you to search out all your stuff that has ActionScript attached to it. The bottom-left pane, called the **Script navigator**, does just that. It consists of two file trees. The top one shows where the currently displayed script (in the Script pane) is within the Flash hierarchy, and the bottom one shows all scripts in the current FLA. Because you don't know much about the timeline hierarchy and how it affects ActionScript just yet, I'll leave further discussion of this pane until later, except to say that the reason the two trees look the same at the moment is because the one script you're looking at is the only one in the FLA.

The top-left panel (the **Actions toolbox**) is a list of little "book" icons, the first of which is called Global Functions. If you click it, the icon will "open" to reveal more books.

If you also open the Timeline Control book inside the Global Functions book, you'll see some icons:

These icons represent **actions**, and the ones in the Timeline Control book are the most basic ones, so you'll be using them soon. The other books contain operators, functions, constants, and other bits and pieces you can use to tie lots of actions together in the way you want. If you hover the mouse pointer over one of them, a tooltip should appear that gives you a brief definition of the book's contents and where it's used.

Don't worry about the details of all these for now, though—you'll learn about them soon enough. This is the Actions toolbox, and it gives you a neat little way to write code in a no-brainer, "building blocks" fashion.

Look down the list of actions in the Timeline Control book and double-click the second-to-last one, stop. This adds a stop() action to your Script pane at line 2:

You now have an action called stop() that is attached to the first frame on the layer called Layer 1. This action will stop the timeline at frame 1. Looking at the rest of the actions in the Timeline Control book, you'll have probably figured out that the play() action makes the timeline start playing, and so on.

Direct typing

Well, you've made a start. All the actions you're ever going to need are stashed away inside those icons, so you could continue using this technique to write all the code you're ever likely to need. What's more, Flash won't let you make any changes to the script that could break it (such as mistyping the stop() action as slop()), so you literally *can't* put a foot wrong along the way.

However, there's another option to consider: you can bypass the books completely and type your scripts directly into the Script pane.

If you have a nervous disposition, this may seem like a worrying step. "It's only the first chapter, but already you're expecting me to type code and get it right first time?" you cry. But honestly, it's not like that at all! Macromedia added so many enhancements to the Actions panel for Flash MX 2004 that there's really no need to use the Actions toolbox. Although searching out the actions and other stuff in the toolbox seems like a safe option (you can't spell them incorrectly if you do it this way, and you have less to remember), it has one problem: it's darn slow! If you take the time to type everything in directly, except for the odd bit of code you can't remember, not only will you work faster, but also you'll get *much* faster with time.

OK, let's try it.

> *Don't worry about the brackets and semicolon (;) at the end of the* stop *for now. Sure, they make the simple* stop *appear a little otherworldly, and they look suspiciously like they were put there by someone with a serious code-fetish, just to scare the non-believers off, but they're actually there for some simple reasons that you'll look at later on in the book.*
>
> *You may have noticed that just after you entered the first bracket, a tooltip popped up showing you the full command, but it swiftly disappeared again when you entered the second bracket. This is another of the Actions panel's helping hands called a* **code hint**. *This is Flash's way of telling you that it's recognized what you're typing, and that all you need to enter now is a closing bracket and a semicolon to finish off the job. It may not look like much now, but when you start looking at more complicated actions later on, you'll begin to find it invaluable. If you ever want to see the code hint again, you can click between the brackets at the end of the action and click the* Show Code Hint *button at the top of the panel.*

First of all, you want something that will tell you if you've made a mistake. Using the Script pane as you would a normal text editor, try changing stop(); to slop(); and you'll see (if you look carefully, particularly if you're using a CRT screen rather than a TFT screen) that the first four letters have changed from blue to black. The Script pane will normally show all action names (or **keywords**) in blue, though you may want to use the Preferences dialog box (*CTRL/CMD+U*) to change this color to a more noticeable shade of blue.

Second, you'll want to fix that "disappearing script" problem I mentioned earlier. Just select frame 10 on the main timeline, add a keyframe (press *F6*), and select the keyframe to see what I mean—look, no more script! Of course, that's not quite true. Your script is still attached to frame 1, but you're looking at the script attached to frame 10, and there currently isn't one. You can see this if you remember to look at the tab at the bottom of the Script pane, though. It has changed:

So what if you want to work on the graphics on the stage at frame 10 while you're looking at the script in frame 1? Easy! Just click frame 1 again, and then click the pushpin button that's just to the right of the text box. This is called **pinning**. The tab won't disappear, even if you select something else. So now you're thinking, "Yeah, I see that, but now I've got *two* tabs that show the same thing!"

The one on the right (the light one) is the one that's pinned, and the one of the left is for the thing you have currently selected. The confusing thing at the moment is that they're both showing the same thing. All becomes clear when you click back on frame 10. The tab on the left will change, and the pinned one to the right will stay as it is.

> *You can pin as many scripts as you need. Pinned scripts will go to the right, and the script for the currently selected item will appear to the left. Some applications with a similar tabbed system work the other way around, which may be confusing to some.*

Pinning is a very useful feature to know about, but only so long as you remember to turn it off when you start trying to add actions elsewhere. Click the pushpin button again to unpin the script, and click back on the first frame. Now you're ready to continue.

One more thing that's well worth knowing at the start about Flash is that it's **case sensitive**. When typing code, you generally have to get both the spelling *and* the capitalization right, otherwise the code may not work.

The Actions panel will lie at the center of all the ActionScript that you'll ever write. You'll explore a few more of its mysteries as you work through the book, but you now have enough information to start and create your first ActionScript-enabled movie.

> *Several more helpful features are built into the Actions panel—you've probably already noticed all the buttons running along the top of the Script pane. You won't examine them right away, though; it will be easier to demonstrate what they do once you have a little more script under your belt.*

Let's start with a simple example that shows how easily you can bypass the usual flow of a movie with just a tiny bit of ActionScript. You can close the current FLA if you wish by clicking the "x" at the top right of the timeline (you don't have to save it).

1. Create a new movie and add a new layer to the root timeline. Rename the original layer as graphics and the new layer as actions. This is a good way to start all your ActionScripted movies.

> *Rather than use the File ➤ New menu option, you can right-click/CMD-click the tabs above the timeline to open/close/save files—this is much quicker!*

Scripts should normally always be attached to keyframes on the topmost layer (if you put them on the bottommost layer, the scripts may not work on the Web because then they'll be loaded before the graphics, and this tends to confuse Flash). It's also a good idea to have only scripts in the topmost layer, which is why you'll call this layer actions—to remind you that that's what this layer contains, and nothing else.

> *A good trick is to always keep the actions layer locked. This stops you from inadvertently placing graphics in this layer, but it doesn't stop you from attaching scripts to it or modifying the frames and keyframes in the timeline panel. Locking a layer simply prevents you from editing the contents of the stage.*

Finally, lock the actions layer (for the reason just noted).

Let's add those graphics now. You don't need any terribly fancy graphics to demonstrate what's going on with the timeline. For simplicity's sake, let's just create a simple motion tween between two points.

2. Select frame 1 on the graphics layer, and use the Oval tool to draw a circle on the left side of the stage. With the Selection tool, select the oval (double-click it on the fill to select both the fill and the outline stroke) and press *F8*. The Convert to Symbol dialog box will appear. Select the Movie clip option and call it ball:

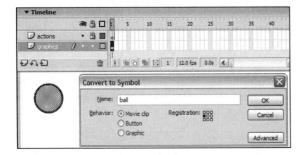

3. Now select frame 20 of the graphics layer and press *F6* to insert a keyframe. Right-click (or *CTRL*-click if you're on a Mac) frame 1, and select Create Motion Tween from the menu that appears.

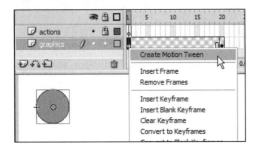

To complete the animation, select the keyframe at frame 20, and then move ball to the right to create a motion tween. If you test your creation with Control ➤ Test movie, you'll see the ubiquitous "ball moves forever from left to right" animation. So much for originality!

The ball's movement depends on the timeline, and you know that ActionScript can be used to control that. Let's prove it.

4. Select frame 1 on the actions layer and take a look at the Actions panel. Make sure the Script pane is active (by clicking in it with the mouse so that the margin turns dark gray; it's a lighter shade when inactive) and you should see the cursor blinking away right next to it. Also, note that the tab at the bottom of the Script pane reads actions : 1. You're about to begin your hand-coding journey, so flex your fingers, crack those knuckles, and type exactly what you saw before:

5. Place the cursor at the beginning of line 1, press *ENTER* to shift the action down to line 2, and fill the now-blank first line as shown here to remind you what your code does with a comment:

As I said before, when the movie runs, Flash will completely ignore all the gray text (everything following the double slash), so you can add as many comments as you like. In fact, I strongly recommend that you do just that!

6. If you take a look at the timeline, you'll see that there's now a little "a" showing in the first frame. This reminds you that there are actions attached to this frame.

Run the movie again and you'll see what a difference your single action has already made. As expected, the circle doesn't move. That's all well and good, but on its own, this isn't really that exciting, let alone useful. You're some way into this chapter, and all you've done with ActionScript is stop your movie from doing anything at all. OK, it's time I introduced a couple more actions before *you* decide it's time to stop.

7. Head back to the Actions panel and delete all the script you've written so far. Replace it with the following lines:

```
// jump to frame 20 and then stop
gotoAndStop(20);
```

Run the movie again, and you'll see once again that the ball is dead still. This time, though, it's dead still on the right side of the stage, because you've told to timeline to go to frame 20 and then stop.

8. Now select frame 20 on the actions layer, press *F6* to insert a keyframe, and attach these lines of script. You don't have to unlock the layer to do any of this, the advantage of this being that if you accidentally on purpose click the stage during this part of the tutorial, you'll see that your keyframe doesn't become unselected (you'll see a pop-up asking whether or not you want to unlock the layer; click No). The beauty of this is that you won't inadvertently get to the "Dude, where's my script gone?" situation.

```
// jump to frame 10 and then play
gotoAndPlay(10);
```

Now you should have a little more action to see on the stage. When the movie starts up, it will see the gotoAndStop() action you've attached to frame 1. This tells it to jump ahead to frame 20 and stop, so it will do just that.

However, attached to frame 20 is an action telling your movie to jump back to frame 10 and start playing again. Even though the movie will have stopped playing at this stage (that is, it won't be moving automatically from one frame to the next), it still has to follow instructions.

> *You can see the movement of the movie in terms of frames if you have the Bandwidth Profiler open during the test (*View ➤ Bandwidth Profiler*).*

So, you see the circle jump back to the middle of the stage and start to move smoothly across to the right. Of course, once you reach frame 20 again, you're sent back to play from frame 10, and so on, and so on, for as long as you care to watch it.

Hmm. That's a little more interesting to look at, but it still doesn't seem like much to write home about. Why not just start the tween from the middle of the stage? Surely the end result is the same. Maybe, but the important thing you've seen here is that you can use a couple of simple actions to *override what would normally happen* in the movie. In this case, you've stopped the root timeline and jumped about from frame to frame.

This is just the tip of the iceberg. There's plenty more in a movie that you can turn to your bidding.

Who are you talking to?

One of the most important things to understand about actions is that they always have a **target**. If you think of them as commands again, it's fairly obvious that each command is directed at someone or something. Thinking back to when my parents would tell me to go clean my bedroom, they might just say, "Get up there and clean that darned bedroom *now*!"

Now that was fine when I was the only person in the room, but if other people were there too, they'd need to say, "*Sham*, get up there and clean that darned bedroom *now*!"

So what's all this got to do with ActionScript? Well, you already know that actions are basically just commands to the Flash movie, telling it to do something. You know that they're always attached to something, and so far that's always been a keyframe on the root timeline. When you attached a simple stop() action to the root timeline, it stopped *the current timeline*, where *current* is the timeline the code is on. That being the case, how do you target an action at something else? What, for that matter, do you do when you want a script to control *two or more* movie clips?

Rather like when we give each other instructions, Flash will sometimes *assume* what our scripts are supposed to control, and sometimes it will need us to tell it via a name.

> The movie clip that a line of script controls by default is called the **scope** of that script.
>
> Although this is a slight simplification of what scope actually is, it's a good approximation to use at this stage.

When you used the stop() action earlier, you used the **assumed** scope—the timeline the code is attached to. As you get into more complicated situations, the process becomes much like human interaction. When you have a *choice* of who to talk to (or you simply want to make it clear), you have to use *names*. ActionScript calls these names **instance names**.

Controlling movie clips on the stage

It's all very well *saying* that, but how do you *do* it? Well, the answer comes in two parts.

First you need to give the movie clip a name. "But it already has a name!" I hear you cry. When you create a movie clip (or any kind of symbol), it appears in the Library panel with a name associated with it, normally "Symbol 1" or something like that, unless you change it

to something else. In fact, this name doesn't mean anything at all to ActionScript; it's just a label that Flash gives the movie clip to make life easier for you when you're making movies. What's more, the items you see in the Library aren't actually part of the movie—it's only when you drag an **instance** of the symbol onto the stage that it becomes a thing you can control with ActionScript.

> One reason you can't use the Library name as the instance name is if you dragged two instances of the same symbol onto the stage, they would have the same name!
>
> Some of you might be wondering at this stage, "How did I control the previous ball animation without giving the ball instance a name?" Well, the simple answer is that you were never controlling the ball. You were controlling the tween on the main timeline (that includes the ball). Because the main timeline was the implied scope of your animation, you could get away with not stating an instance name.

Once you've dragged your symbol onto the stage, the Property inspector gives you a neat little way to christen that instance with its very own unique name. Say you have a movie clip in the Library called Symbol 1, and you've just dragged it onto the stage. This is what the Property inspector might look like:

There's a text box just below where Movie Clip is selected in the drop-down box that holds the following text in gray:

<Instance Name>

No prizes for guessing, but this is where you give your movie clip instance a name. Let's assume for now that you call it myClip_mc:

You'll also soon come to appreciate how useful it is to have the _mc reminder like this, so that when you see it in code, you know immediately that it's referring to a movie clip. What's more, the Actions panel also recognizes _mc instance names as movie clips, so it can prompt you with options that are specifically relevant to movie clips. You'll see the use of suffixes come into play in more detail later in the book, but here's a quick

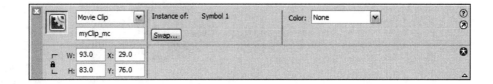

There are a couple of things that you may be worrying about here:

- You may be wondering why you call the movie clip "myClip" instead of "my clip". Computer languages don't like spaces in any names so, although you're allowed to add spaces in the Library name (because it will be read by you only), you can't have spaces in the instance name (because ActionScript uses it). One way around the fact that you can't use spaces is **camelCase**, where you put a capital letter after the point at which you would normally use a space (it's called camelCase because of the hump the change of case causes).

- You may be wondering what the _mc suffix is all about. Why not just call it myClip? Humans have names for boys and girls, so that you can (usually) tell the sex of someone without actually seeing the person. Unfortunately, there are no such names for movie clips, buttons, and all the other things in Flash that can have a name, so the Flash parser (the code that interprets your code) can't tell if the name you give the movie clip is a typical name for a movie clip. The way around this is to use a suffix. The _mc tells Flash "And it's a new, bouncing baby movie clip!" in the same way most of us know that baby John would be a baby boy.

Don't worry if camelCase looks like something it will take a while to get used to—it will be second nature by the time you finish the book, honest!

list of all of the suffixes that Flash recognizes and what they mean:

Suffix	Description
_mc	Movie clip
_btn	Button
_sound	Sound
_video	Video
_str	String
_array	Array
_txt	Text field
_fmt	Text format
_date	Date
_color	Color
_xml	XML
_xmlsocket	XMLsocket (Note that camelCase isn't used here!)

The first two suffixes are the ones you'll use most often, but it's worth knowing what the others are so that you'll recognize them when you see them.

Now that your instance has a name, you can use ActionScript to talk to it. This is where the second part comes in: **dot notation**. The **dot** (aka the **period** or **full stop**) might be the smallest text character going, but when it comes to ActionScript, it's also one of the most important. This is how you use it to tell Flash that you want to stop the timeline of the movie clip instance called myClip_mc:

```
myClip_mc.stop();
```

In terms of the earlier room-tidying analogy, "Sham, go tidy your room!" would be the following in Flash, if there was some ActionScript to force me to do it (luckily, my parents never asked for it via the Macromedia wish-list e-mail, so I don't think there is):

Sham.goTidyRoom(your);

> *The bit before the dot tells Flash who (rather, what) the instruction is directed toward. The bit after the dot is what you want to be done.*

Let's bolt together all that you've learned so far.

Talking to different timelines

In this exercise, you're going to use ActionScript to control a couple of cars. You can find the graphic symbols I've used in the download for this chapter (in the file car.fla), though there's nothing stopping you from creating your own!

1. Open car.fla. Create a new Flash document (File ➤ New) and select File ➤ Import ➤ Open external Library. Drag an instance from the newly opened external Library (it will have the title Library - red car) onto the left side of the stage, and press *F8* to convert it to a movie clip called carRunning.

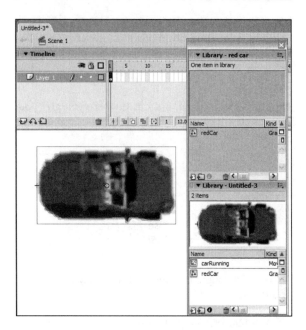

2. Double-click the unnamed instance to edit the movie clip in place. Select frame 2 of the timeline and press *F6* to insert a keyframe. Select the graphic again and use the Property inspector to move it vertically (that is, change its y-coordinate) by 1 pixel. If you run the movie now, you'll see the car shudder slightly up and down, which tells you that the car's engine is running.

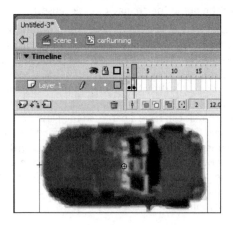

3. Double-click a blank part of the stage to return to the main timeline. Make sure the instance of carRunning is selected and use the Property inspector to set its instance name to myCar_mc.

4. Select frame 50 of the main timeline and press *F5* to insert a frame. Use Insert ➤ Create Motion Tween and hold down *SHIFT* while you drag the car across to the right side of the stage. Run the movie again, and you'll see the car shudder its way across the stage. So far, so good!

Now it's time to add some ActionScript, so create a new layer called actions, lock it, and then select frame 1 in this new layer.

5. Open the Actions panel and enter the following script:

```
// stop the car traveling
stop ();
```

Since you've attached your script to the root timeline, Flash assumes that the stop() action is directed at the root timeline. That's where your car's motion is controlled, so the car should stop traveling.

Test the movie and you'll see this is true. More important, though, while the car may not actually be going anywhere, its engine still appears to be running. That's because the shuddering motion is part of the movie clip, so it's controlled by a separate timeline.

6. One way you could stop the car's timeline would be to open up the movie clip and attach a stop() action to its timeline. That would do the trick, but it would quickly get fiddly if you wanted to do more complex things and found yourself having to switch back and forth between the timelines. There's no point, anyway, since you have a perfectly good way to do the same thing directly from the root timeline. Change your script so that it looks like this:

```
// stop the car's engine
myCar_mc.stop();
```

and try the movie again. You'll now see that the car is moving across the screen, but it's no longer shaking. Someone's either fixed the shaky engine or left it out of gear and forgotten to put on the brake!

In terms of your movie, you've now stopped the myCar_mc timeline but left the root timeline alone. If you stopped both of them, the car wouldn't move at all:

```
// stop the car moving at all
stop();
myCar_mc.stop();
```

The other big advantage of using dot notation and scripting everything from the main timeline is that you can now do different things to different instances. The process of identifying different movie clips for different actions is called **scoping**. The first stop() is scoping the main timeline, and that's what it stops. The second one is scoping myCar_mc, and unsurprisingly, it stops the shuddering animation caused by that timeline.

7. Create a new layer and add a new instance of carRunning called myCar2_mc. You may want to rename these layers as car1 and car2. Make sure your new car is well below the original and re-create the motion tween I described earlier on. Run the movie, and you'll see that the first car is still dead, but the second car is running (even if it's not going anywhere right now).

8. Finally, let's prove that it's not just down to chance that one car is running while the other isn't. Change the last line of your script to read

```
stop();
myCar2_mc.stop();
```

Run the movie one last time, and sure enough, the engine in the first car (myCar_mc) now runs, while the second (myCar2_mc) is motionless.

Arguments

Of course, my parents had an easy time of it with the bedroom-cleaning instructions. I had only one bedroom, so it was obvious which one I had to clean. If I'd been one of the Getty children, my parents might have had to say, "John-Paul, get up to bedroom number seven this instant or it's no rum truffles for you!"

My parents didn't need to add extra details about *which* room they meant, because it was obviously *my* room. John-Paul's parents had to add an extra bit of information: *which one* of his bedrooms he had to clean.

This extra piece of information that qualifies the initial command is called an **argument**. No, this doesn't mean that John-Paul refused to clean his room and started a family fight. It's just a name we give to values that help to determine what an action does for us.

So, to tell me to tidy my room via a line of ActionScript I would have (as you saw earlier) this:

> *sham.goTidyRoom(your);*

Most people have only one room, so in most cases, the room you have to clean is implicit—yours. This implicit argument is often assumed in many actions if you give no argument as the "*default* argument." For example, this:

> *Sham.goTidyRoom();*

would mean the same thing as the previous line of ActionScript.

For young John-Paul, the situation is slightly different. If you wanted him to clean bedroom number 7, you might use

> *johnPaul.goTidyRoom(7);*

The argument here becomes important because John-Paul has no default bedroom.

Finally, if I wasn't bad enough to have to tidy my room, but was due for a temporary grounding, I might be told to simply go upstairs:

> *sham.goUpstairs();*

Here, no argument is needed because what I have to do is simple: go upstairs and make myself scarce. Notice that even here I use the parentheses ( ), even though nothing is expected inside them. This is because the *instancename.action(argument);* code structure is *standard;* you must always use it even if some of it isn't required, rather like a period isn't always needed for total comprehension (like at the end of this sentence), but you put one in anyway.

Further, sometimes I'll be the only misbehaving kid in the room, so the "sham" part isn't needed—there's no confusion in omitting the name, because everyone knows I mean "the ornery child in this room":

> *goUpstairs();*

This all goes some way toward explaining

- Why you always have stop() rather than simply stop. You *must* have the parentheses ( ) because they're part of the basic structure of the language, irrespective of whether any arguments are ever actually needed.

- Why you sometimes have stop() (meaning the timeline this action is attached to, and there's only one of those, so you don't need to say anything else) and you sometimes have myClip_mc.stop() (because you don't want to stop the default timeline, but another one, which you have to name).

- Why some actions *always* have an argument, such as gotoAndPlay() (an argument is always needed because there's no implied frame to goto; you always have to say, for example, gotoAndPlay(7);).

Listening to what your movies are telling you

So far, all the ActionScript you've looked at has been fairly predictable and not terribly exciting. That's because you've figured everything out in advance—before you even run the movie, you know exactly what actions you want to give your movie and exactly when you want them to kick in.

When you think of Flash, you probably think of **interactivity**. Whoever ends up watching your movie should be able to react to what they see and hear, and make things happen in the movie spontaneously. That's probably why you're here in the first place, learning how to add some more of that interactive power to your designs.

Interactivity is a two-way process, though. As well as giving out commands, you need some way to respond to what's going on when the movie runs. You need some way to **trigger** actions whenever some event happens while the movie is running—for example, when the movie finishes loading, when the user clicks a button, when the hero of your adventure game catches all the magic artichokes before the villain's bomb goes off . . . I think you probably get the idea.

When I was a child, I was given a cuckoo clock as a present. Well, actually, a cuckoo clock only in the loosest sense, given that it was in the shape of a cartoon lion with a swinging tail as a pendulum. Every time the clock struck the hour, the lion would wake up, open his mouth, and growl. He could act as an alarm clock, too, and give an almighty roar when the alarm went off.

As I've said, there were two things that set my lion into action:

- When the clock reached the beginning of the hour, it was time to growl.
- When the alarm time arrived, it was time to roar.

So, in this case there were two **events** that the lion was waiting for. As soon as either occurred, the lion would perform the appropriate **action** (a growl or a roar).

In fact, the magic word here is **event**. You need a way to write ActionScript that can react to events that happen during the course of the movie. That is, "Whenever *this event* happens, perform *these actions*." Or, to be more succinct, "If *this* happens, do *that*."

ActionScript is called an **event-driven language**, *which sounds like complicated programming-speak until you realize that, just like the lion, it's set up to wait for something to happen and then react to it— nothing more complicated than that.*

Events in Flash

So what sort of event happens in a Flash movie? Well, it could be something obvious that happens externally— say, the user clicking a button on your website or typing on the keyboard. An event can also be something less obvious that happens internally within Flash, like loading a movie clip or moving to the next frame on the timeline.

Whether you're dealing with an internal event or an external event, you can write a sequence of actions (called an **event handler**) that will run whenever that event occurs.

In the real world, you can see all sorts of event/event handler pairs around you. For example, your electric kettle waits for the water to start boiling (the event) and has a special circuit that switches the power off (the event handler) when this occurs. Another example would be your central heating. When the air in your apartment falls to a certain temperature (the event, in which this temperature is decided by how you've set the thermostat), your heating kicks in (the event handler) to make things warm and toasty again.

External events

Back in the Flash world, let's consider the simplest event/event handler partnership: a button click.

- The button push_btn sits there waiting for some user interaction.
- The user clicks push_btn, and this shows up as a Flash event called onPress.
- Flash looks for an event handler that's been assigned to that particular event on that particular button: push_btn.onPress.
- If Flash finds one, it runs the ActionScript inside it; otherwise, it does nothing.

The most important thing to notice about events is that they're very specific to the thing that generated them. Say you have another button called red_btn. If you click it, it also generates an onPress event, but it doesn't trigger anything unless you specifically define an event handler for red_btn.onPress.

Yes, the dot notation gets everywhere! Don't panic, though, the rules are similar to what I covered before: the bit before the dot tells Flash where the bit after the dot is *coming from*. It's really just as it was with actions, except that it's telling you *where an event came from* rather than *where an action is going*.

Internal events

This event/event handler relationship is fairly easy to spot when we're talking about external events such as a button click. However, internal events aren't always so obvious, since movies generate them automatically. Probably the easiest one to get your head around is the onEnterFrame event, which is generated every time a timeline's playhead enters a new frame. Yeah, but what does this mean in practical terms? Well, it means that it's easy to write a bit of script that Flash will then run for *every* frame.

Say you want to make the timeline run at double speed. _currentframe refers to the number of the frame you're currently on, so you could write an onEnterFrame event handler that contains the action gotoAndStop(_currentframe+2):

1. The movie starts, generating an onEnterFrame event.
2. This triggers gotoAndStop(1+2), sending you to frame 3.
3. This generates another onEnterFrame event.
4. This triggers gotoAndStop(3+2), sending you on to frame 5.
5. And so on. . . .

Basically, you skip every other frame, so the movie appears to run at twice the normal speed. If you did the same thing using gotoAndStop(_currentframe-1),

you could even make the movie run backward, as every time the playhead enters a frame, it would be told to go to the frame before the one it's currently in, where it would find the same command again.

OK, this may not seem like particularly useful stuff just at the moment, but that's just because you're still fooling around with the timeline. Once you've tackled a few more actions, you'll start to realize just how powerful this onEnterFrame business really is.

Before doing that, though, let's get down to business and look at how you actually write these fabled event handlers.

Introducing callbacks

Earlier on, I described event-driven programming in these terms: "Whenever *this event* happens, perform *these actions*."

You now know that *this event* might be something like push_btn.onPress and that *these actions* are what you call the event handler. You can express that in ActionScript like this:

```
push_btn.onPress = function() {
// actions here make up the event handler
};
```

Hmm. It's not nearly as intuitive as stop() and play() were—I confess, there's a bit more to this one than I've talked about so far. But before you shrug your shoulders and start checking the index for what = and function are all about (because I know you want to know!), just stop for a moment. You'll move on to all that soon enough. All that matters here is this:

> *Whatever actions you write between the curly braces { and } will be run whenever someone clicks the button called* push_btn.

The technical name for this wee beastie is a **callback**, and while it may look a bit intimidating at first, you'll forget all about that once you've used it a couple of times—callbacks will almost always look much the same.

Nesting spiders—argh!

I hate anything that has lots of brackets and commas and dots and stuff. Rather like some people hate spiders because they have too many legs, I just hate lines with too many brackets. I managed to get my head around this with ActionScript when I realized that these aren't the sorts of brackets that require you to reach for a calculator and start thinking; they're just there to help arrange things into groups, like this:

- All small dogs (including dachshunds and terriers) should go to the tree on the left, but all other dogs (including beagles and Alsatians) should go to the tree on the right.

I'd say that this looks a *lot* less frightening than

$$s = \tfrac{1}{2}(u+v)t + 5(a+20c) - 1$$

Ugh! Spiders! I know a lot of the stuff coming up will look like that awful equation, but it's not as bad as all that. Most of the time, it's just a shorthand way of writing the "dogs and trees" sentence. When any sort of math gets involved, it's usually of the 2 = 1 + 1 variety.

Let's get over any apprehension about callbacks as quickly as possible, and put them through their paces. You're going to base this example on the earlier FLA you made with the racing cars going across the screen, so either open your own copy or grab the file called therace.fla from this chapter's download folder.

You're going to begin by adding some buttons to the stage, so you may want to close the Actions panel for the time being.

1. Create a new layer called controls, and place it above the car layers.

2. Now, rather than creating buttons from scratch, pull some good-looking ones from the Macromedia Buttons Library (Windows ➤ Other Panels ➤ Common Libraries ➤ Buttons). Open the Circle Buttons folder and drag one "forward" and one "back" button onto the stage.

3. Drop the buttons at either side of the stage, and add a horizontal line between them:

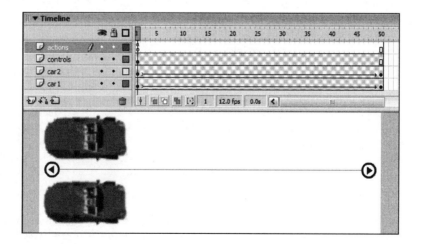

4. Select the left button and pop down to the Property inspector to give it the instance name back_btn. Do the same for the right button, calling it forward_btn. Any guesses for what they're going to do?

5. OK, it's time to open the Actions panel again. Make sure that frame 1 of the actions layer is selected (so that the bar at the top of the panel reads Actions for Frame 1 of Layer Name actions), delete the existing script, and enter the following:

```
// stop the cars traveling
stop();
// callback for onPress event on
➥'back' button
back_btn.onPress = function() {
   // goto the previous frame and stop
   gotoAndStop(_currentframe-1);
};
// callback for onPress event on
➥'forward' button
forward_btn.onPress = function() {
   // goto the next frame and stop
   gotoAndStop(_currentframe+1);
};
```

That looks a bit intimidating, but actually, there's less script there than it might seem, mainly because of all the comments I've put in. Let's consider it one piece at a time.

You begin by telling the root timeline to stop in its tracks. Otherwise, the cars would zoom straight across the stage and there would be nothing for you to do.

Next, there's a callback, which listens out for an onPress event coming from the "back" button. If it picks one up (as it will if someone clicks the button), then you use the gotoAndStop() action to jump to the previous frame.

The next callback is pretty much the same, except it listens out for an onPress event coming from the "forward" button and jumps to the next frame on picking one up.

Each time you write a callback, you'll notice that after you type the first { brace, Flash will start to indent your script. Likewise, just as soon as you

type the closing brace }, it will automatically "out-dent" back to where it started. This incredibly useful feature is called **auto-formatting**, and it can be a real lifesaver, especially later on when you start putting braces inside braces.

6. Now run the movie, and you should see a couple of motionless cars. Been there, done that. So what? Try clicking the "forward" button, and you'll see both cars inch forward. Then click the "back" button and both cars will move back again.

Yes, with just a couple of really-not-so-scary callbacks, you've wired up a couple of buttons that give you complete control over the movie's main timeline. Not bad, eh?

Now you may feel the need to point out that with both cars covering exactly the same ground, it's really not much of a race. Yes, the foolish and shortsighted approach I used for animating the cars (two motion tweens on the same timeline—d'oh!) doesn't really do the movie any favors.

What if there was a quick and simple way to separate them? (Preferably involving ActionScript and not too many long words. . . .)

Animating movie clips with ActionScript

OK, this isn't strictly part of the chapter's storyline, but I'm not going to leave you wondering for the sake of a lesson plan. After all, this is supposed to be fun!

So far, you've done all your animation using tweens, and all your actions have been aimed at one timeline or another: stopping, starting, jumping about the place, and so on. That's a pretty good place to start if you're already quite familiar with Flash, since you're mainly tackling things you're already aware of.

> If the formatting of your code ever goes a bit awry for some reason, you can easily bring it back into line by clicking the Auto Format button in the Actions panel.

Now that you've begun to grasp ActionScript stuff like targeting actions at movie clips and wiring up event handlers, I can start to reveal the truth.

> *You don't need the timeline to animate a movie clip.*

Rather than explaining that statement, I'm going to show you the alternative.

1. Back at the races, click frame 50 in the actions layer and drag down to frame 2 in the car1 layer, so that frames 2 to 50 are selected on every one of the four layers:

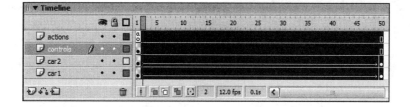

2. Now right-click (or *CTRL*-click) the selection to call up a menu, and select Remove Frames to get rid of everything following frame 1. Yes, that's right, you want to lose *everything* except the contents of frame 1 in each layer.

3. Select frame 1 in the actions layer and open the Actions panel. You'll need to make the following highlighted changes to get the first set of buttons working:

```
// stop the cars traveling
stop();
// callback for onPress event on
➥'back' button
  back_btn.onPress = function() {
  //move myCar_mc horizontally -10 pixels
  myCar_mc._x -= 10;
};
// callback for onPress event on
➥'forward' button
forward_btn.onPress = function() {
  //move myCar_mc horizontally +10 pixels
  myCar_mc._x += 10;
};
```

Test the movie now, and you'll find that the top set of buttons controls the top car, while the bottom car sits still. Let's fix that.

4. Now add the following script to the end of what's already there:

```
// callback for onEnterFrame event
onEnterFrame = function() {
// move the myCar2_mc across to
➥mouse position
  myCar2_mc._x = _xmouse;
};
```

This lets you control the second car using the mouse. Just as _currentframe refers to the current frame number, _xmouse refers to the mouse's current x-position, and you use this to update the car's position. Because it's inside the onEnterFrame callback, it's updated 12 times every second, which keeps the position up to date.

Run the movie again. Now you can use the two sets of controls to maneuver each car separately.

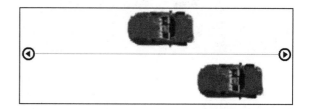

This animated effect is far more advanced than anything you've done thus far in this chapter—it's truly interactive. The original car race movie just moved the cars from left to right, and that's all it will ever do. This time, you can control the cars using buttons and the mouse.

Even simple interactivity like this opens up fantastic possibilities that you didn't have before. With a little imagination, you could replace each of the cars with a bat, and bounce little squares back and forth across the screen, just like one of those old TV video-game consoles.

Tennis, anyone? Take a look at pong.fla in this chapter's download to see how easy it is to create an interactive bat.

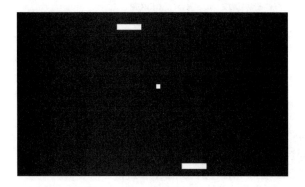

As another option (perhaps just a *little* more exciting), you could change one of the cars into a spaceship, so it could be The Lone Crusader on a mission to save the world from the evil alien hordes.

This time, your Starfleet SpaceCruiser has to dodge alien plasma bolts. *Save those cities, young pilot!* Have a look at spaceinvaders.fla from the download if you want to see this screen moving.

I'm afraid you're not yet *quite* advanced enough to start adding alien hordes or the associated "bloolly bloolly bloolly blooop" sound effects just now. But hey, you've only been learning this stuff for about 20 minutes!

Remember that all this movement comes from just a few lines of ActionScript. Even better, they're the same lines of ActionScript every time, and the whole thing is only one frame long. You're already up to the maximum interactivity offered by the home computer entertainment systems available when I was a kid—just think what you could achieve with another few frames and 40 more lines of ActionScript.

This is why it pays to know ActionScript. It's so much more versatile and dynamic than plain Flash that it quickly leaves traditional Flash animation standing in the corner feeling sorry for itself!

Summary

In this chapter, you've gone quickly through the basic concepts behind event-driven programming. You started off by looking at how to attach script to the root timeline, and then you saw how to write **actions** that control the timeline. Along the way, you learned about **targets** and **instance names**.

After that, I introduced the idea of **events** and **event handlers**. Instead of writing plain actions that Flash will run regardless, you can enable a movie to trigger off scripts while it's running. By writing **callbacks** that wire up event handlers to button events, you can even give users a way to control what's going on in real time while the movie runs.

Don't worry if you didn't understand every single detail of what this chapter discussed; you've covered a lot of ground in a short time. Also, at this stage, a lot of the topics may seem a little abstract and theoretical because you don't have all the tools in place to try out all the possibilities this stuff opens up.

As long as you got all the exercises up and running, though, you should be able to cope just fine with what's coming up. From here onward, you'll be moving through the surrounding concepts in greater depth, but at a much more leisurely pace.

Chapter 2

MAKING PLANS

What we'll cover in this chapter:

- Planning your design project with the client in mind
- Building your ActionScript step by step to create the effect you want and to make your code easy to change if necessary
- Structuring the flow of your ActionScript within individual effects
- Introducing the first half of a case study describing the design and creation of a fully functional website

> *I've been involved in programming and design for some time now. My original discipline was engineering, and I've been close to computers in one form or another since the late 1980s. My engineering discipline has taught me a lot about computers and coding, and there's one fundamental rule that I've carried over with me into multimedia design:*
>
> *If it doesn't work on paper, it won't work when you code it.*

In this chapter, I'd like to show you how, as I'm setting out on a design project, I've learned to define the overall problem, split it into manageable sections, and structure my ActionScript so that it gives me exactly what I need in a way that's easy to change if I need to.

I'll round off the chapter with a little reminder that web design isn't just a cold-coding process. I'll introduce you to Futuremedia, a website project that you'll work on as you progress through the book. By following Futuremedia's development, you'll learn how to plan usable interfaces and brew up cool vehicles to show off your cutting-edge ActionScript skills.

The best place to start is always the beginning, and that beginning is where you define what you need to do.

Defining the problem

If this book were a textbook on writing novels, this chapter would be all about defining your **plot**. Without plot, your characters would have no motive and your audience would quickly realize your book was going nowhere.

The same holds true for ActionScript coding. If you don't have a good idea of what you want to achieve, you're stuck. Most designers love to play around with ideas and end up with a toolbox of little demos and cool effects that they can put together later to build a full website. Even this organic way of working (which is

the way I work) requires you to think about how your effects will fit together and what your aim actually is for a website. You should have a fair idea of direction *before* you start.

In real life you have a further complication that thwarts your ideas and clean, structured designs. That complication is **the client**. A good plan is a safety net that helps you guard against those little requests: "Can we just move everything half a pixel to the left?" or "No, we can't use that—didn't I tell you we wanted an advertising banner to go on top?" *("Uh, no you didn't. . . .")* or the all-time classic "That's great, and I know we go online in 2 days, but here's a list of 35 minor changes that Bob and I would like."

The driving force of design must be managing the client's **expectations** and discussing (and finding) the client's **real needs** (as well as, of course, getting everything in writing so Bob and his boss don't feel like they can have a second redesign for free!). Formulating the project beforehand and getting agreement early on goes some way toward solving this. It also allows you to go back to the client and ask for costs if they start changing the project partway through (in the world of business, this is called a "variation on the contract" and you should always be in a position to be able to charge for this).

All the same, I'd be making false promises if I told you that, in a typical project, your design objectives wouldn't change at least once! This is something you just have to live with, and you should make sure that your design is defined well enough to let you go backward as well as forward, and branch out onto a new path if the client (or technical problems) force you to do so.

Your plans will help you through this, so you can point to them and say things like "Well, if you want to make that change, this will have to go, this will have to move here, and that will go there. Is that OK?" without having to take the time to actually do it first to see what it looks like. This is a fact of web design, and though you may not experience it until you've finished a few paid jobs, you'll be glad of your plans when you do.

> As I've implied here, design is partly creative, but designers also have to build commercial and legal factors into the design process, and there are many issues behind a successful site other than just technical design and aesthetics. Although it's beyond the scope of this book to discuss these issues in detail, you can have a look at the following links for more information on how to do some of the other things that fall under the general topic of "design" (or, more correctly, "managing a design project").

Writing a web-design contract. The following are a number of sample standard contracts, ranging from the basic to the verbose. Note that some of them cover issues that you may not at first think of as important when writing the contract, such as browser compatibility and other gotchas that the client may come back to you with.

- www.scottmanning.com/services/contract: Scott Manning, Freelance Flash web designer. A typical basic contract. I wouldn't recommend using this contract as is, although it forms a good base.

- www.glasseyeweb.com/contract.html: Glass Eye Web. A long contract, but one that addresses most technical loose ends. This contract assumes a technically-minded client.

- www.emmtek.com/contract.asp: EMMtek. A brief contract that is close to one I would typically create. It's short, but it covers most of the big issues without getting too technical.

Costing a website. This is one of the thorniest issues for a new designer. Check out the following links. Also be aware that many web-design houses charge different rates for different parts of the job, and scripting (including ActionScript) can command some of the highest rates once you have a good portfolio. Don't be shy!

- www.webdevbiz.com/article.cfm?VarArtID=5: WebDevBiz. This is a general article on costing a website. Although I disagree that you shouldn't give estimates to some potential clients, it's a good overview on how to cost a site (assuming that you've already decided on an hourly rate).

- www.proposalkit.com: Proposal Kit. This company sells a complete proposal and contract management collection of documents and templates for small-scale web developers. The kit contains templates for proposals, agreements, and related documents, and estimating and costing spreadsheets.

Note: The other route to "per hour" costing is to charge per item created (typically per image, area of formatted text, menu, etc.). This isn't usually done by small design houses/freelancers, so we won't consider it. As a freelance ActionScript person, you would typically give only an estimate of hours and the rate you charge per hour.

Keep your ideas in a safer place than your head

Working in a field that requires me to think creatively doesn't mean that I'm instantly creative. By the time I need some ideas, they're usually all gone. We all get good ideas, but most of us forget them with the passage of time. I now keep a hardbound book of lined paper for these transient ideas and a book of black card pages (black because it makes things much easier to scan into a computer) where I keep pictures that have caught my eye.

I have a big collection of images in my book now, from Polish Nightclub advertisements to stylized, textless instructions for inserting camera film told through icons. It's all great reference material. For example, I kept the edge of an old paycheck from a few years ago, one that was obviously printed by a big, fast, industrial computer printer. It has those funny sprocket holes in it, some print registration marks, and some optical character-recognition numbers. I would normally have put this straight in the trash can, but one day it struck me that it had a real made-by-computer feel, so I kept it. Several years later, I used it for the opening titles of a graphic novel I wrote and illustrated, which has an intelligent supercomputer as a main character.

You can see the progress from the grubby bit of paper on the left to the finished article on the right. You may think that it looks similar to the data animations from *The Matrix*, but mine was based on a scrappy bit of paper and not an expensive computer animation!

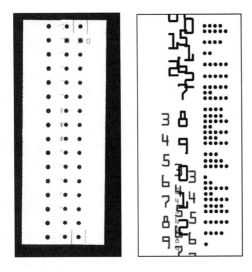

So, you've talked to the client, and you've gathered a collection of ideas from things that you see every day and perhaps any assets (sound, music, video clips) that will play a part in your final site design. The next step is to tie down these ideas to form a concrete shape that shows you how you need to implement the site design.

There are a number of ways you can do this:

- Write down the essence of the site in plain English.
- Quickly code a basic sample site and discuss it with the client if possible.
- Storyboard the site, perhaps as a set of static Photoshop or Paint Shop Pro mock-ups, and present it for approval.

In fact, you'll most likely use a mixture of all the above. I find the storyboarding option the most useful, both in terms of communicating with the client and for my own use, to see how the site develops stage by stage.

Storyboarding

Storyboarding is a good way to get a preliminary feel for what you want. It allows you to define navigation, visualization, and style early on in your site design. The term is a throwback to the film industry; it refers to the sequence of pictures drawn by cartoonists to plan how characters will move during an animation.

Some people may ask, "Why waste time creating static sketches when you could just as easily start drawing in Flash?"

I find that the little extra work I put into storyboarding really lifts a presentation and allows me to fully explore my creative ideas before I need to concentrate on developing and animating them in Flash.

A rather well-kept secret is that it's easy to import a Photoshop PSD image into Flash, complete with layers. Export the PSD one layer at a time as PNG files from Photoshop, and you'll find that the Photoshop per-layer alpha channels are exported as well as the pixel information. Import the PNGs into Flash. If you place the PNGs in the correct order using Flash layers, you can easily re-create your Photoshop image in Flash, but this time around you can also animate it using either tweens (or, if you know what you're doing, ActionScript). Although this doesn't of course lead to a web-optimized Flash site, it is a quick and dirty way of transferring a Photoshop storyboard to Flash, for the purposes of showing the basic design to a prospective client.

A storyboard can be whatever you want: a sketch on the back of a drink coaster just for your own use or a full-blown presentation of the site from beginning to end to show to the client. I've seen complex storyboards showing a full website mocked up, with arrows and typed notes saying how everything will work. My advice is to find the middle ground between those two. I rarely do more than a few sketches and perhaps a preliminary mock-up of one page in Photoshop to get the feel of the site. The client is paying you for the finished site and not the intermediate artwork, so make the storyboarding functional and don't go overboard—

it isn't a finished product in its own right. Also, remember that a complete storyboard isn't something that you want to give to a client just so the client can give it to another designer! Keep the storyboard content that you give to a client to no more than a couple of pages.

The following is the kind of sketch that I begin my work with (assume that the client hasn't requested to see it). This sketch is for part of a site I designed in which you can select from a number of different band names and download available (and, I hasten to add, legal) MP3 files.

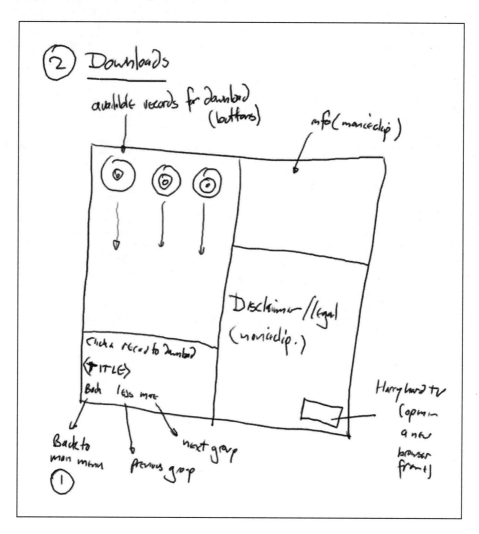

This sketch probably took me a maximum of 10 minutes to draw, but if you look at the final page (below) based on it, then you can see that the final interface is very true to the initial sketch. Having a sketchbook near the computer so you can draw a few rough ideas is always a good thing.

Trying to fit everything into Flash without an initial goal would have taken a lot longer, so you can see how this initial storyboarding saved time.

Storyboarding also gives you an opportunity to start figuring out how to begin coding effects for particular

areas of the site. On the music site, I had to deal with the fact that the user might choose to skip the intro before the essential components of the main site had downloaded. To cater to this, I needed something to show viewers how long they would have to wait and keep them amused for this short time.

I thought a VU meter would be quite a novel way of showing this, with the needle flickering up the meter to show the percentage loaded. As you can see (below), in this part of the storyboarding and sketching, I'm already starting to think about how the needle needs to be animated by ActionScript.

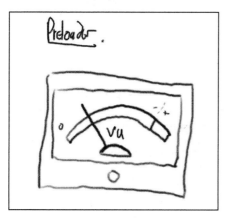

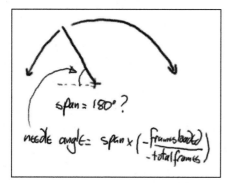

A volume unit (VU) meter is a common audio measuring device. It displays the average volume of a sound. Just the thing for a music website's preloader!

Here's the final work. Again, it's quite close to the initial 10-minute scrappy sketch.

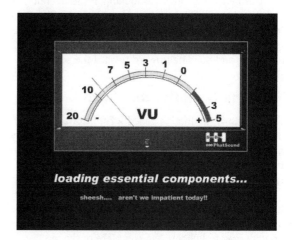

It's worth reiterating that Flash isn't necessarily the best environment for you to develop your initial ideas. Playing around within graphics packages like Photoshop or Paint Shop Pro, along with making your own sketches, can be a much richer way of working. Twenty minutes at the beginning of your project with a sheet of paper and a pen planning the interface and storyboarding how the ActionScript will work is time well spent.

Once you've sketched what you want to do with your ActionScript, you can again save yourself a lot of time by staying away from your monitor just a little longer and not diving headfirst into that Actions panel. Take some time to plan in more detail how your code will be structured to fit with your designs.

Building your ActionScript

As you begin to think in ActionScript terms, you're always starting from the same point: you know how you want your designs to work. What you need to think about is the best way to get there. There are two main ways of breaking down programming problems: top down or bottom up.

A **top-down** design involves looking at the overall task and breaking the problem down into smaller and smaller chunks, whereas a **bottom-up** design means starting by looking at the basic building blocks, adapting them, and building upward toward the solution.

Thinking from the top down

The top-down method is called a **functional** method, because it looks at the functions that you have to carry out, or *what you have to do at every stage*, to perform the solution. You begin by looking at the aim in general terms or **high-level requirements**. Then you break up each of those general stages into separate steps that become easier and easier to manage. These are the individual **requirements** that you can deal with in turn on your way to building the complete package.

Sound strange? Let's say that you're looking at breaking down the high-level requirement of making a cup of tea with an electric kettle, a tea bag, milk, and water. If you take the top-down approach, you'll first define the top-level design statement, which is

Make a cup of tea and then break it down by one level to its main stages.

1.0 Start boiling some water by filling the kettle with water and switching it on.

2.0 Put some sugar and a tea bag into a cup.

3.0 If the water in the kettle has boiled, pour some of the water into the cup.

4.0 After 2 minutes, remove the tea bag, add some milk, and stir.

Breaking the task down to this level is called the **first iteration**.

You'll then look at each of these tasks and break them down even further:

1.0 Start boiling some water by filling the kettle with water and switching it on.

    1.1 Fill the kettle with water, two-thirds full.

    1.2 Switch on the kettle.

2.0 Put some sugar and a tea bag into a cup.

    2.1 Add one teaspoonful of sugar to the cup.

    2.2 Add one tea bag to the cup.

3.0 If the water in the kettle has boiled, pour some of the water into the cup.

    3.1 Wait until the kettle has boiled.

    3.2 Pour some water from the kettle into the cup, until the cup is three-quarters full.

4.0 After 2 minutes, remove the tea bag, add some milk, and stir.

    4.1 Wait 2 minutes.

    4.2 Remove the tea bag from the cup.

    4.3 Add milk to the cup until the cup is seven-eighths full, and then stir.

This is the **second iteration**.

*You might be thinking that this looks suspiciously like a table of contents (or a **TOC** as we call it in the publishing field). Well, that's exactly what it would become in a major project. This is the basis for a TOC for a top-down specification document for the making tea software project. Section 4.2 would (for example) introduce what the process is and perhaps provide further specifications about what removing a tea bag actually entails.*

Although this might sound trivial, section 4.2 would actually be a rather long section if a robot was making the tea. There would be technical drawings of the tea bag telling you how tightly the robot could grip the tea bag and where to do it from (you don't want it to burst in the tea), how the robot should find the tea bag in the tea, and all sorts of other clauses and subclauses.

Graphically, we can represent the top-down approach as a chart something like this:

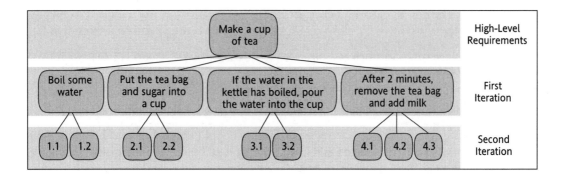

The second iteration would link to charts that further break down the problem.

> A common question for the beginner is "When do I stop iterating?" Well, it's a bit of a black art, but a general answer would be when you've broken down the problem so that it's easy to see how you would code each of your iterations at the lowest current level in the chart.

The top-down approach fits well when you're dealing with a tightly defined problem. A tight definition eliminates the need for too many iterations, or breaking the task down again and again, and makes each stage easy to change if necessary. For anything more complex, though, it throws up some pretty basic problems. The most important of these is that if the high-level requirement changes, that change must filter down through all the iterations, making you think about what you do at every stage all over again.

For example, if you prefer coffee, you'll have to start at the beginning all over again with a new top-level design statement:

Make a cup of coffee.

And you'll need to modify all the instructions at every stage below that, changing **tea bag** references to **spoonful of instant coffee**, taking out that **wait 2 minutes** stage (because now you don't need to wait

for coffee to brew), and so on. You may think that this isn't such a big job in this domestic real-world example, but if your top-level design statement reads

Build a navigation computer system for a combat helicopter with satellite positioning systems, radar, and weapons management facilities.

you'd have a bit more of a problem changing things around when the Navy changed its mind about what it wanted its helicopter to do. You'd have to look at all 10,000 requirements for the system and see what the impact of the change that the Navy was asking for was on each requirement. This could take an extremely long time (I know, I've been there in similar civil projects!) and even longer if you have to prove that you did the analysis of the changes properly (of course, this ignores the fact that the Navy will invariably want something different from the seaborne version!).

Experience has taught me to go for the easier option when I can. Speaking of which . . .

Thinking from the bottom up

Making a change in a bottom-up design is nowhere near as difficult as in a top-down design. Taking the bottom-up approach involves looking at the problem, splitting it up into very general areas, and asking, "What are the basic building blocks here?" You look for basic structures within your problem and write general solutions for them before adding specific details to these general solutions to make them suit the problem that you're dealing with.

31

Going back to the tea example, the general building blocks of the problem are as follows:

- Moving things from one container (such as a sugar bowl) to another container (such as a cup)
- Measuring quantities
- Waiting for particular processes to complete (such as boiling the water in the kettle)

If you were tackling this in ActionScript, you'd begin to create actions based around these general building blocks.

You could start with a **moving** action, adding details of whichever containers and substances were involved:

```
move(fromContainer, toContainer, thing)
```

Then you could add a **measuring** action, in which you could display "how much" of "what substance" you want measured:

```
measure(quantity, substance)
```

Next, you could add **switching the kettle** action, using basic on/off commands:

```
kettle (on)
kettle (off)
```

and a conditional structure that allows you to do something (switch the kettle on or off) only when certain conditions are met (the water is boiling):

```
if (water boiling) {switch kettle off}
```

You could then look at the problem and see how to build up to making a cup of tea using these structures. For example, to fill the kettle you'd want to use the move routine to fill it with water from the tap, so

- fromContainer is the tap.
- toContainer is the kettle.
- thing is the water.

The thing isn't just any amount of water, but two-thirds of the kettle, so you can express it as follows:

```
measure(water, TwoThirdsOfTheKettle)
```

So the full statement to fill the kettle would be this:

```
move(tap, kettle, measure(water,
TwoThirdsOfTheKettle))
```

Taking it all in this way, the basic solution might look like this:

```
move (tap, kettle, measure(water,
TwoThirdsOfTheKettle))
kettle (on)
move (sugarbowl, cup, measure(sugar,
OneTeaspoon))
move (teacaddy, cup, teabag)
repeat {
}
until (event (kettleBoiled))
move (kettle, cup, measure(water, measure
➥(water, TwoThirdsCup))
repeat {
}
until (event(teaBrewed))
move (cup, trashBin, teabag)
move (milkContainer, cup, measure(milk,
➥OneEighthCup))
stop
```

The two repeats will make you wait (repeatedly doing nothing) until the event you've specified has been detected.

This looks suspiciously like ActionScript already! You've lost the timings like "wait 2 minutes" from the previous top-down version. Why? Because it doesn't matter! You've moved away from the initial problem to the extent that what didn't really matter dropped out of the problem. You never even considered it. This method can save you a little work and is also useful when the main problem or design aim is likely to change frequently, which could happen more often than you think. You use a move routine to fill the kettle with water from the tap. Once you've written that general routine, you can use it over again, with just minor changes for several other actions, including.

```
move (teacaddy, cup, teabag)
```

With the top-down solution, wanting coffee instead of tea caused you a major problem and you had to look again at the whole process. If you're faced with that problem here, the basic building blocks stay the same; you just have to change a few minor details again, and you can substantially reuse the existing code:

```
move (coffeejar, cup, coffeepowder)
```

That's much easier. Because the bottom-up design didn't just look at the top-level problem (making tea), you generalized the problem, or **abstracted** it. So, you don't care whether it's tea or coffee or crude oil—you can still use your basic move() and measure() building blocks again, and you won't have to change them when you do. Bottom-up design digs the foundations before building on top of them, whereas top-down just puts itself down in any old way. When the winds of change blow, you can guess which one stays standing longer.

This bottom-up design method can be much harder to understand than the top-down alternative because, as adults, I guess we all prefer to think **functionally**. Common sense says that bottom-up design shouldn't work, but it seems to work rather well. It really comes into its own with problems that can be reduced to a few types of building blocks, which means that it works particularly well with animation and graphic interfaces.

Graphic interfaces tend to have very few building blocks. For example, you can build a basic Flash site using only three building blocks: movie clips, buttons, and graphic symbols.

A while back, I provided technical support for another friends of ED book series called *New Masters,* in which Flash designers such as Yugo Nakamura wrote about their work and showed how they had put together some pretty impressive effects. It struck me that all the designers featured were, without exception, using a bottom-up approach to their ActionScripting. This was despite the fact that these were all creative people at the very top of their field who had taught themselves ActionScript—in other words, the type of people you might expect to find using a top-down approach.

The work that you'll do in the final few chapters of this book will be based on a bottom-up style, as it looks like a required approach for those of you who want to be in the future volumes of *New Masters of Flash*! When you code in Flash, matters aren't usually as clear-cut as a straight choice between a top-down and a bottom-up approach. Most ActionScript structures will require a mix of the two. I'll talk about what approach to take with different ActionScript structures later. The aim of this section is to enable you to look at a problem and start to think about the best way to code it.

You've just taken a look at the type of general approach you might want to take in your coding. Next, you're going to have a look at a way of presenting a coding problem graphically that might help put you in a better position when you come to coding.

Flowcharting

You've got an ActionScript problem—not necessarily with your whole site, but probably just the ActionScript for a single frame. You can't describe what you want to do to, say, the first iteration of a top-down design process. Your problem can't be easily defined, so you might consider sketching the problem as a flowchart.

Thinking and looking before you jump straight into coding will mean that your ActionScript changes from a "keep coding until it works" mind-set to something altogether more elegant in thought and design.

To build an ActionScript flowchart, I use three kinds of flow symbol:

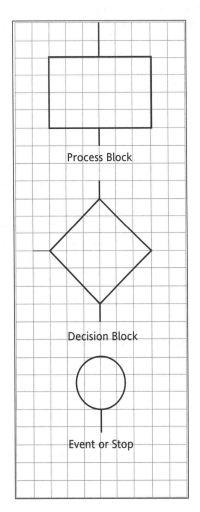

Process Block

Decision Block

Event or Stop

- The **process block** represents a set of linear actions that occur one after the other.

- The **decision box** is like an intersection where you can continue down one of two paths, depending on whether the answer to your question is true or false (yes or no).

- The **event or stop** circle represents the event that starts or finishes a particular flowchart.

Let's look at how this would work if you wanted to build a menu of buttons that allows the user to control how a movie clip plays, just as if it were a videocassette in a video player. Once you create a set of buttons a bit like these, you'll want to attach some ActionScript to each of them. I'll show you how you can use flowcharts to help define what each button does.

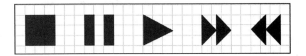

As you begin to plan, you'll make a note of some main points:

- You're interested in two main properties of the movie clip: _currentframe and _totalframes.

- The _currentframe property describes the frame that Flash is currently playing.

- The _totalframes property is the total number of frames within the movie clip (which is, of course, equal to the number of the last frame).

- The first frame is when _currentframe = 1.

With these points in mind, let's build some flowcharts.

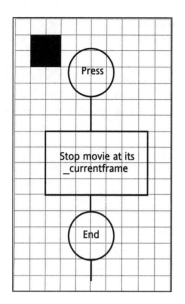

The Stop button is fairly straightforward. When the user clicks it, you want the movie to stop. The flow-chart shows that when a press event is detected on the Stop button, you need to have some ActionScript that stops the movie exactly where it is, at its _currentframe.

The Pause button is slightly more complicated. When the user clicks it, you need the movie to stop just where it is, as if the Stop button had been clicked. But you also need to set the movie playing again when the Pause button is released. So, you have two events in the flowchart:

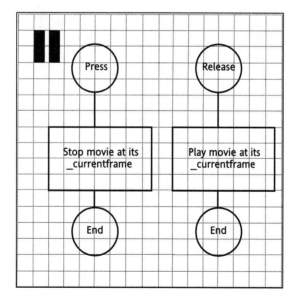

When the user clicks the FastForward button, you need the movie clip to advance at a much faster rate than normal. To make it move at, say, five times the normal rate, you ask it to go to _currentframe + 5 every time the user clicks FastForward.

Houston, we have a problem. If you click FastForward when you're within five frames of the end of the movie, that means that you're asking the movie to go beyond the last frame. Unfortunately, the Flash player won't let you do this. It will probably come to rest in the last frame, but introducing an anomaly like this is never a good idea, as it might just break your movie. You should always try to ensure that your code is free from

quirks like this that could introduce avoidable glitches. You therefore need to make sure that you don't ask your script to take you further than the end of the clip. So, your ActionScript needs to make a decision. If the _currentframe is within five frames of the last frame, you want the movie to go to the last frame. If it isn't, you want the movie to go to _currentframe + 5 as normal.

If you draw a flowchart for this, you can see that you need to build in code to check whether _currentframe is greater than or equal to (>=) _lastframe - 5 and create two routines to tell the movie clip what to do depending on the answer:

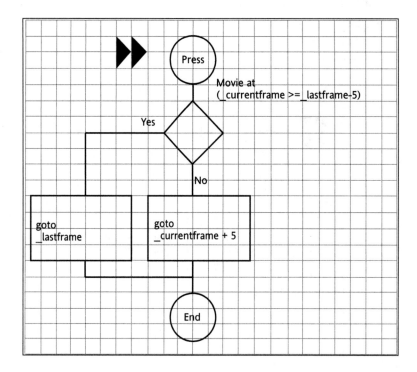

These diagrams show how you can help yourself to work out the advanced level of logic that the final code must have, using a simple graphical tool. You could very quickly sketch these diagrams on a piece of scrap paper before you begin to build the ActionScript behind each button to give yourself some pretty useful visual clues.

Don't go overboard, though. Flowcharts are useful, especially for designing a single event handler that consists of lots of decisions or loops, or both, but they do have their limitations. If you try to flowchart really long sections of ActionScript, you'll quickly run out of paper. You may even discover that the flowcharts become more difficult to produce than the code itself!

I use flowcharts to get a simplified bit of ActionScript going. Then, once it's working, I forget about flowcharts and slowly start building up the ActionScript itself. For example, with the FastForward button, the simple structure that you saw in the flowchart is fine as a beginning, but if things were left this way, users would find that they have to click the button over and over again to keep the movie playing FastForward.

The solution for this would be to build a **toggle** mechanism into the button, something that makes it continuously alternate between two actions each time it's clicked. The first time the user clicks it, it's set to run on FastForward and continue running until it's clicked again, when it's set to stop.

*Flowcharts are traditionally used when a solution is essentially **linear**, which means you do things in a defined order, such as calculating the average of 100 numbers. In **user interface** (UI) design, things work in the order specified by the user, which makes flowcharting difficult. You'll also find that flowcharts don't really tell you much about the way a Flash site will look and feel, so you can only go so far with flowcharts. Although most programming courses aimed at beginners sell flowcharts heavily, I can report that they're actually hardly used at all other than for setting up simple code structures.*

Let's put some of this theory into practice. It's time to introduce the book's case study.

Book project: Introducing the Futuremedia site

Let's begin putting some of your newly acquired ActionScript skills into practice by creating the interface for the Futuremedia site.

In the download for this chapter, you'll find an HTML file called index and a number of other files. Place these in the same directory (or on your desktop). Open the HTML file in a browser. As long as all the files are in the same place as the HTML, you will see the Futuremedia site in the browser:

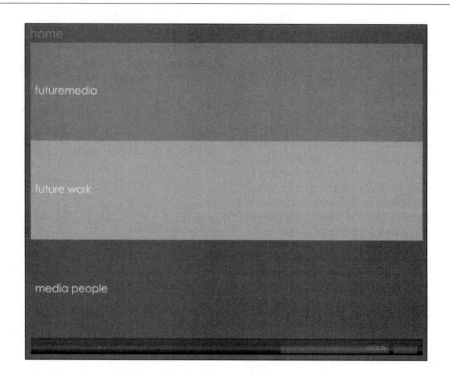

There are three areas to look at. The top left text indicates where you are now. As you move through the site, it keeps track of your current position in the site hierarchy.

At the bottom is a *visual* representation of the same thing. The pages change color as you move through the site, and this is reflected in the lower black strip, called the **back button strip**. It's sometimes also referred to as a **breadcrumb trail** because it's reminiscent of a person dropping breadcrumbs to mark a trail so that he can retrace his path.

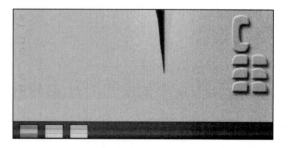

The back button strip contains a small icon of the pages you have visited. Clicking any of the icons will take you back to a previous page with the same color scheme.

The back button strip shows an important feature of the compact or integrated UI: not only are the colors pretty, but also they're a critical part of the UI. The color coding is used to allow you to recognize the back path. There are no bells and whistles in a compact UI design. Everything has something to do with navigation, and put together, all these little cues and pointers (hopefully) create that elusive beast: a website that needs no instructions because its interface is totally stripped down and **intuitive**.

Finally (if you haven't worked it out yet), you can navigate the site simply by clicking the strip you want to go to next. The selected strip zooms and pans to fill the browser window, and if there are further pages to visit in the current navigation, it will split into strips again. It's one of those sites that's far more difficult to describe than to actually use.

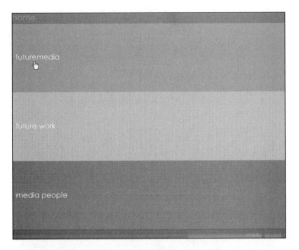

Click the navigation once or twice and it should all immediately (and intuitively) make sense. Not mentioned here is the *way* it moves. The navigation transitions are smooth, as are the color fades and transformations (shown right).

Right, that's what you'll design from scratch.

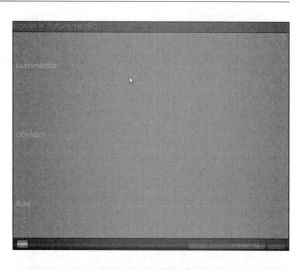

Of course, seeing the final site before you start is a bit of a cheat, but this is a learning exercise, so I can shortcut a little and show you the final piece at the beginning. In real life, this introduction would be replaced by the vision you have in your head. I hope you have the same vivid imagination as most web designers—you'll need it!

The next question is *how do you start?*

Deconstructing the problem

The most important thing in any competition is to know your enemy, and the next important thing is to know how to beat them, and the best way to do that is divide and conquer (although I have a book by Sun Tzu on my desk that has some other cool tips as well). Um . . . anyway, you'll also do a bit of dividing and conquering as you move through this project. You will

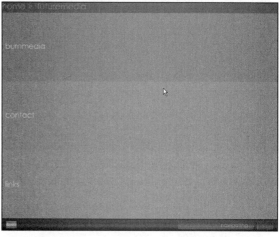

1. Work out what the problem actually is, so you know your enemy.

2. Subdivide the problem into easy-to-beat parts, so you can tackle each one on its own, which is something that gives you a much better fighting chance.

You can think it all through, but that tends to hide practicalities. Let's instead construct the method behind what the Futuremedia site does manually, but within Flash, to make a working sketch of what you need to achieve.

The following walk-through is an "edited highlights" taken from my design notes that traces exactly how I worked out how the final site should operate *before* I coded it.

This part of the project will hopefully show how far you can move a coding task onward through the initial conceptual stages without even touching or thinking about the code. After the initial afterglow of the brainstorming session you went through to come up with an idea that may (or may not) be solvable with ActionScript, the following exercise is the sort of thing you have to do to prove to yourself that your design is actually feasible and can stand up to the nemesis of any creative person: **achievable reality (AR)**.

1. Open a new Flash document. Select View ➤ Rulers to show the rulers. Click-hold-drag the horizontal and vertical rulers to drag out four ruler guidelines as shown here:

Copying the screenshots exactly isn't important in this exercise.

2. The middle rectangle represents the viewable browser area. In this area, draw out a light gray rectangle as shown, making it cover about one-third of the inner rectangle.

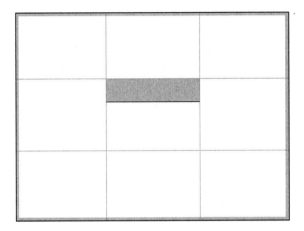

3. This is one of the three strips in the final site. Select it and make it a movie clip by pressing *F8*. Call it strip.

Why do you make it a movie clip? Why not leave it as it was? Well, the UI uses color changes as part of its operation, and this only works for a movie clip because only a movie clip can be made to have a variable attribute called color. That is because the movie clip is a **class**, but if you want to see proof that you can't change the color of a raw graphic, here's the lowdown.

4. With the movie clip strip selected, open the Properties panel. The Color drop-down menu currently says None. Change it to Tint. By varying the sliders that will now appear, you can vary the color of strip.

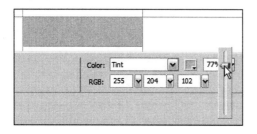

In the final site you'll have Flash varying the color via the Color class (a part of the ActionScript language), and you'll use it to create all those funky but subtle color transitions via code. For now, though, convince yourself that the Color object can't be used with a raw graphic by drawing another square, and this time don't make it into a movie clip. Notice that when you select it, the Properties panel doesn't show the Color drop-down menu. This is because the raw graphic doesn't have the properties that allow the Color class to work with it.

5. Delete the graphic so you end up with only the strip movie clip on the stage. Select the movie clip and return the Color drop-down menu on the Property inspector to None to bring the clip back to its original color.

You have your strip movie clip and are happy that there's a reason for it to be a movie clip and not anything else.

> *The ball, tennis racquet, and Starfleet SpaceCruiser in Chapter 1 were movie clips for the same reason: they had properties and an instance name, which Flash needs before it can control them with ActionScript. Flash just doesn't have the capability to control raw graphics in this way, and that's why ActionScript sites use movie clips all the time.*

6. Now open the Library panel (CTRL/CMD+L) and drag another two instances of the strip movie clip onto the stage to emulate the Futuremedia site's tricolor (shown below). If your strips are too big or too small, you can either scale them to fit or simply change the ruler lines around them.

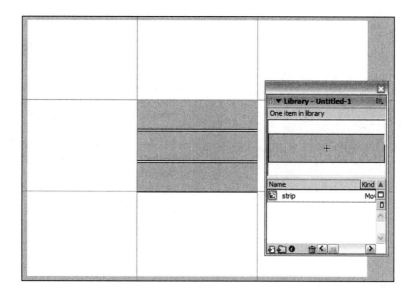

7. So how do you scale this? Well, suppose you click the bottom strip. Flash will scale it and the other strips up as it zooms in to it. Let's try it manually.

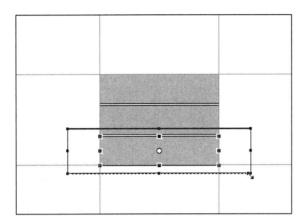

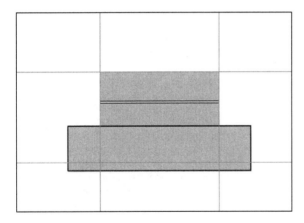

Whoops. There are two problems straight away.

One problem is that as the page starts to grow, it goes offscreen. The final site always keeps the selected strip onscreen as it grows. That's something your code will have to watch: *the selected strip must never be allowed to go offscreen.* Rather, it has to "push" the unselected strips offscreen to make room. The other problem is that only the selected strip does anything. The other strips just sit there, and the selected strip will eventually cover them. Now, these issues are actually the two critical problems of the whole site UI, because the site navigation relies on them working in some other way.

How do I know that this is the critical problem? Some of you might be thinking, "You know because you're a programmer, and I wouldn't get that insight because I'm not a programmer." Well, that does my ego a lot of good, but it isn't actually the truth. The truth is that I gained this "insight" by thinking about the design for a day. A whole freakin' day!

There's no magic point at which you become a New Master of Flash and just know. The thing about New Masters is that they have the courage and conviction to keep thinking about a problem until it's solved. As you progress you will, of course, realize that there are some routes that tend to work in Flash and some that tend not to (and you get a feel for what is a problem and what isn't), but all creative design is about taking leads and following them until one works, using judgment, creativity, and cunning in the process.

A lot of the process is knowing when something won't work rather than when it will work, and identifying it as such.

Time and thought is the main resource, though.

Solving problem 1

Let's have a look at the *"the two strips don't move when I scale the third"* problem first. There are three possible solutions:

- Implement some sort of collision detection, so that you can detect when the expanding tricolor begins to overlap something else.
- Move all three strips proportionally so that they always keep the same relative distance apart and they'll never overlap.
- Cheat.

All the existing similar sites use the first or second solution, but I always have a soft spot for the third item when I see a problem like this. I know this is one of those problems that's a **performance bottleneck**. Moving all three strips together in some controlled way will be a brain-wringer for Flash because it has a lot of things to do. It would be better if it all worked in some automatic way that required no coding.

The following step is *so* simple in hindsight, and it solves the problem with no coding at all. As a coder, you will learn to *love* such solutions, because they make your job all the easier!

1. Press undo (*CTRL/CMD+Z*) until you get back to the three equally sized strips. Select each in turn so you have them all selected (hold down *SHIFT* while you select), and then press *F8* to make them into a new movie clip.

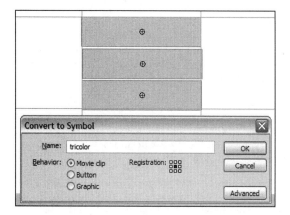

2. Call the movie clip `tricolor`, because that's what it is: a movie clip with three strips in it.

3. OK, now try to scale the bottom strip. See that? This time all the other strips scale as well *because they're embedded in the same movie clip!*

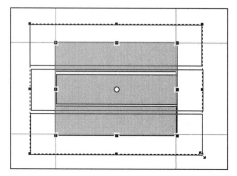

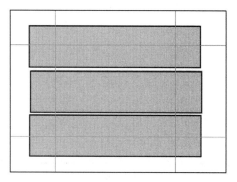

Cool! So now the movie clips never overlap, and you don't have to do anything highfalutin like collision detection (or, for that matter, write *any code at all*) to achieve this!

Solving problem 2

You want the bottom strip to stay onscreen as it scales (zooms) by moving it so that it never overlaps the ruler guidelines. This will keep it onscreen by **panning** so that it always stays on the visible screen. The best way to make something do *what you want* in programming, if the solution isn't immediately obvious, is to look at *what you don't want to do*.

What makes the strip go offscreen? Well, you drag with the cursor and the tricolor moves off all four edges. If you look at the finished site, you'll see that you don't seem to care about the right edge—it's the left, top, and bottom edges that concern you. A strip scales when you select it and grows off the right side of the screen. It doesn't go offscreen on the other three edges as it grows. Once it has filled the screen, it stops.

So the final site does something different: it scales the tricolor, but at the same time moves the selected strip so that its top, left, and bottom-left corners never go offscreen.

You can model this by doing it yourself with a little Flash sketch:

1. Starting with the original tricolor, suppose the bottom strip is clicked. You need this strip to scale so that it fills the screen, but as soon as you begin to scale it, you get the following situation, in which the whole tricolor goes offscreen on all four edges. Try this yourself, scaling the tricolor by a small amount.

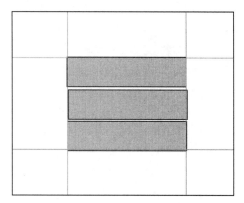

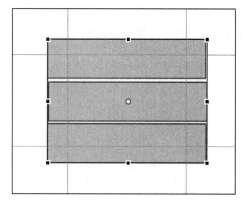

2. What you actually want to happen is this. Move the tricolor so that it occupies a position as shown. The left edge is kept at the screen edge, and the selected strip is prevented from going off the bottom.

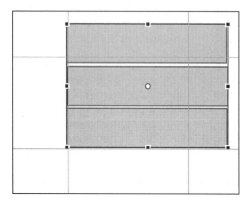

3. If you keep doing this, you'll eventually end up with the strip hitting the top edge of the screen. Its color now fills the screen.

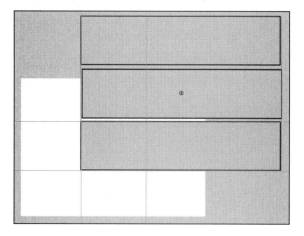

So that's how the final code does it! The three strips are actually a single movie clip that forms a tricolor. In addition to this, because the three strips are separate movie clips within the bigger tricolor, you can still access them individually to make color changes.

OK, so what happens next? Well, have a look at the final site design again.

You're halfway through a transition. You have one strip that now fills the screen, and two strips that are offscreen and can't be seen. Although the nonselected strips are offscreen, Flash still has to draw them, so you need to do something about them, or you have another performance bottleneck looming. You also need to change the one strip so it changes into the tricolor again. You're stuck!

Although you're seeing lots of problems in the walkthrough here, this is a good thing, because you'll know about all the pitfalls up front when you come to code it. If you saw this new problem after you had already coded the zoom/pan functionality, you may have found that you would have had to discard the coding so far to overcome the new problem.

A good programmer always plays about with the ideas before committing to coding because it uncovers the potential problems further on.

A good motion-graphics programmer will do a bit more and take the animations manually through a dry run as you're doing here, because it uncovers issues that would be missed if you drew sketches or just thought about it. Doing it for real manually has several advantages, the main one being that it injects a healthy dose of AR into your ideas!

So you've solved problems 1 and 2, but you now have two new ones. That's not unusual, and not a worry. You know this because your overall solution has moved *forward*. You're now looking at new problems further on in the process.

Time to look at the options:

- Split each strip into another tricolor, so your original tricolor has further tricolors already embedded in it.
- Redraw the pages using the drawing API (you may have heard about this; you'll look at it in more detail in a later chapter) so that they can be redrawn to look like three strips again . . . or something intense like that.
- Get Flash to somehow physically delete the extra offscreen strips.
- Cheat.

All the options are actually either inflexible or difficult, except my favored way forward.

Guess which option I chose?

Solving problems 3 and 4

In all the best detective novels, the culprit is someone who was innocuously introduced early in the story. Nobody suspects the blind flower girl in the opening chapter, but that was the fatal mistake, for it was she who killed the countess (and she was only pretending to be blind).

I introduced the solution early on: changing color. Use the by now oversized tricolor from the last part.

1. To see how this is done, you have to make this little test look more like the final site. Leave the tricolor in the same place and position it's currently in on the screen. You need to make sure there are no gaps between the strips within the tricolor. Edit the tricolor in place (double-click tricolor to enter this mode) to move all the strips so they just touch:

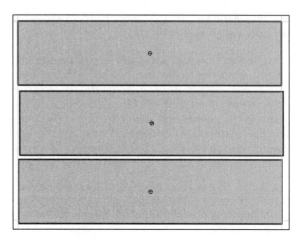

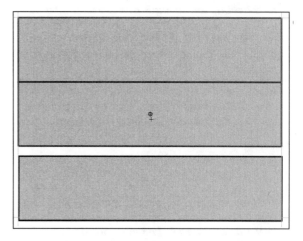

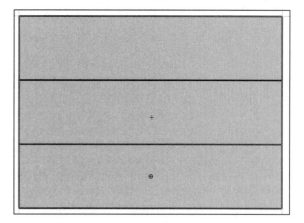

2. Change the color of the lowest strip instance via the Properties panel as you did before, to blue. Note that you still have to be inside the tricolor clip editing in place, or you'll tint all three strips.

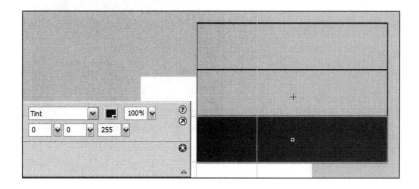

3. Give the other strips different colors. You can choose them yourself—the values aren't important as long as none of them is blue, for reasons that will soon become clear.

4. Let's recap. Only the blue strip is onscreen at the moment, and you want to somehow get rid of the other two strips that are offscreen. The cheat is that you don't get rid of them. You bring them back onscreen.

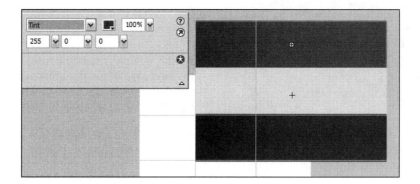

5. Change the color of all the nonblue strips to the same blue as the bottom strip.

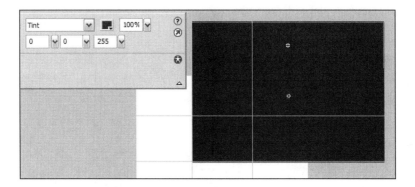

6. Now, here's the really cunning part. Get out of edit in place mode and *scale the tricolor* back to where it was at the start of the whole thing. Because the three strips are all the same color, the user won't notice this *and won't see the fact that you've brought the missing strips back onscreen,* because the user can't see what's going on offscreen.

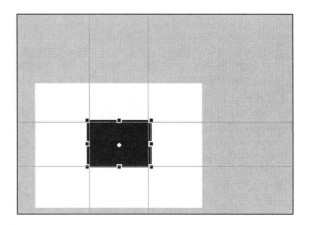

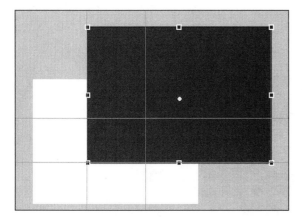

All you do now is fade the blues toward the colors of the next page in the hierarchy, and users think they've gone to a new page because you've zoomed in to a strip, which then split into three new strips.

You've done no such thing! What you've actually done is zoomed out and then sneakily swapped back to the *same tricolor,* but with different colors. You don't constantly zoom in at all—it's a trick!

What's more, you're now almost at the starting point, with all three strips onscreen, so you can start the whole fake-zoom process again *using the same code*.

This is the difference between motion-graphics programmers (including programmers of PlayStation games and film special effects, as well as Flash web design) and other programmers—*we're always cheating*. The 3D in *Quake* isn't really 3D (it's on a 2D monitor screen, for a start), and the X-wing fighters in *Star Wars* are really 12-inch models or nothing but data in a computer. We cheat like heck. In fact, the bigger and subtler your cheats, the better you are as a motion-graphics programmer!

Of course, others call this *"approximation,"* but I know different. Have another look at the Futuremedia site to get a feel for what is *really* happening when you click a strip and "zoom in" to a new page. Play about with it until you can see all the wires and mirrors and how the lady is really not sawed in half at all.

Parting shots

You've learned the first important rule in Flash motion graphics: *know what you want to code before you start*. You've addressed all the problems in the navigation you'll be using, and you've solved them in principle by running through the animations and transitions *manually*. You're much better off doing this by manually

updating the graphics in real time than just dry-running it on paper, because motion graphics is, by definition, about *animation*. By doing it this way, you get some insight into what Flash has to do, and some shortcuts and approximations that you can make in your motion graphics, while still maintaining the desired effect.

This is what creative ActionScript is all about. So far in the project, you haven't touched ActionScript at all, but I hope that already you're beginning to see something important: the *mind-set* that creates all that cool and impossible Flash stuff on the Web.

Best of all, Flash problem solving and coding isn't about math. It's about creating cool effects and stuff for other people to see, and I hope you're beginning to see the fun of it all—our problems aren't those of database programs or other serious applications. Flash programming is all about color, movement, and creating something that's cool and fun to interact with.

Summary

You've seen how planning is a crucial first step in designing a Flash site. It's particularly important when you're trying to develop something novel or new (such as the Futuremedia user interface) so that you can not only plan what you want to do, but also determine whether it's feasible!

Chapter 3

MOVIES THAT REMEMBER

What we'll cover in this chapter:

- Introducing variables as containers for storing information
- Understanding different types of variables: numeric, string, and Boolean
- Using expressions to generate values to be stored in variables
- Taking user interactivity beyond button clicking, using input and output text
- Using arrays to deal with complex, related information

So far, all our ActionScript has dealt with what's going on in the present, for example, what the *current* frame is or where the mouse pointer is *at this moment*. Of course, technology hasn't progressed far enough to let us peer into the future—not even with Flash! But looking at what's happened in the past isn't a problem. The only reason that all our movies so far have been stuck in the present is that they have no **memory**.

The advantages of having memory might not be obvious right away. After all, there's plenty you can do in Flash already, and you've seen how a little bit of ActionScript manages to raise the bar on that. What do you need memory for?

Once again, the answer has everything to do with inter-activity. If you want to create a movie that makes users feel they're really involved with what's happening on the screen, you need to ensure there's a bit of continuity to the experience. For example, take the Starfleet SpaceCruiser game you looked at in Chapter 1 and think about how much less fun it would be to play if you couldn't give it any kind of scoring system.

> In short, there's nothing wrong with movies that have no memory, just as there's nothing wrong with movies that don't use ActionScript at all. It's just that there's a whole lot more you can do with it than without it!

Having memory means having a place to store **information**, or **data**. Once Flash has stored a piece of data, it can keep the data there for as long as it likes and call up the data whenever required. Flash can still *respond instantly* to whatever's going on (as you saw in the last chapter), but once it has memory, it can choose *not to*, and respond whenever it chooses.

Even more important, once Flash has somewhere to *store* data, users can send it much more interesting messages (like text and numbers) than they'd ever manage by clicking a button.

Virtually all your ActionScript-enabled movies are going to use some kind of data, and it's fairly normal to find that you'll want to change it from one moment to the next. For precisely that reason, the ActionScript

"containers" you use for holding data are designed so that it's extremely easy to vary their contents—that's why they're called **variables**.

Here's an official-sounding definition:

> *A variable is a named memory location for holding data that's prone to frequent change and required to be accessible rapidly.*

In the first part of this chapter, we'll take a look at what this definition really means and see how Flash uses variables to keep track of what's going on, to make decisions and predictions, and to perform calculations.

Does it sound like you're in for some heavy math? No, and don't let the idea of math put you off! Variables don't need to be used to contain things like the speed of light squared—they can just as easily be used to specify how high you want your cartoon Flash character to jump. It's not math; it's just a powerful way to get Flash to do the fun things you want it to.

So, without further ado . . .

Introducing variables

A **variable** is a named "container" that you can use to store data that you need to use several times (and possibly change) during the course of a movie. Whenever you need to use the data, you give Flash the variable name, and Flash will look in the right place and retrieve it for you. If you've never wrangled with code before, this concept may be confusing, so let's consider it in nonprogramming terms.

Your wallet is designed specifically to hold money (hopefully you have some to put in it!). At any given time, the wallet will contain a particular amount of money, which will increase and decrease as you visit ATM machines and stores full of cool and tempting goodies. The wallet itself probably isn't worth much; it's the money inside that defines its value. Whatever you paid for it, your local superstore isn't going to accept an empty wallet as payment for produce!

To put it another way, the wallet is a container that you recognize as holding your money. When you hear the word "wallet," you know that what you'll find inside is money—never socks or frozen pizza. You also know that the amount of money in the wallet won't stay the same for long.

Of course, you might use other containers to store money too. You might have a tin in the kitchen to store cash to pay for coffee, tea, and chocolate cookies. You might have a piggy bank or a bottle into which you throw all your small change throughout the year. (If you're like me, you might spend that big bottle of money on a small bottle of something else at Christmas.) You have different containers because you need separate places to store money that's set aside for different purposes.

So I have three different storage places, each holding separate quantities of money that fluctuate constantly:

- My **wallet**, containing my day-to-day money
- My **tin**, containing money for tea
- My **bottle**, containing my Christmas beer money

You can think of these storage places as being my "variables": each contains a different value that may change at any time. My first variable is `wallet`, and the value it contains is the amount of money that I have to spend on everyday items. I also have a `tin` variable that holds tea money, and a `bottle` variable that holds beer money.

An important aspect of my high-level financial management is that I keep money for the right purpose in the right variable. Imagine the tragedy of confusing my `tin` variable with my `bottle` variable, so that at the end of the year I have enough cash to buy tea for the whole of China, but only $2.50 for a glass of beer on Christmas Eve!

Hopefully, I'm not very likely to confuse physical items like a tin, a bottle, and a wallet, but we don't have that luxury when we're programming. To ward off potential tragedy, I'll have to stick labels on the front of my containers, or name my variables so that I know what each one holds.

Even with labels, you can still get lost. You can have containers that have the same name, but in different places. For example, I might have a bottle in the kitchen labeled "Christmas," for buying a Christmas drink or two, and a piggy bank in the living room labeled "Christmas" that contains savings for gifts for my friends and family. In the same way that I can have containers for Christmas money in two rooms, I can have variables on different timelines. Obviously, I therefore have to know where each of my containers is as well as the name of the container. If not, my friends might be a bit annoyed when they see me at Christmas and I'm very drunk, having spent all the money meant for their gifts on beer!

The location of a variable is called its **scope**, and it can sometimes be as important as the variable's name. The scope is basically the area that the variable exists in (or where it's visible to the code). You'll look at scope closely in later chapters.

Values and types

In the real world, you're surrounded by different kinds of storage spaces designed to hold different things:

- Your wallet is designed to store money.
- Your refrigerator is designed to store food.
- Your closet is designed to store clothes.

In ActionScript too there are different kinds of values that you might want to stow away for later use. In fact, there are three such **value types**:

- **Strings**, which are sequences of letters and numbers (plus a few other characters) such as *Sham*, or *Hello*, or *a1b2c3*. String values can be any length, from a single letter to a whole sentence, and they're especially useful for storing input from visitors to your site.
- **Numbers**, such as 27, or −15, or 3.142. As I'll discuss later, putting numbers in variables can be useful for keeping track of the positions of things in your movies and for controlling how your ActionScript programs behave.

- **Booleans**, which are "true" or "false" values. These can be useful for making decisions.

Some programming languages can be very fussy when it comes to storing different types of data, forcing you to work with variables that can store only one kind of value. If this were true in the real world, you'd discover it was physically impossible to hide chocolate at the back of the bedroom closet or put your jeans in the refrigerator. And what a cruel world that would be!

ActionScript lets you decide whether or not you want it to be fussy. By default it's an **untyped language**, which means that you don't have to specify what sorts of values a variable will hold when you create it. If you use this default, ActionScript variables can hold different kinds of data at different times. In most cases, Flash can work out for itself what the type is. Flash isn't infallible, though, so this flexibility sometimes means you need to exercise a little strictness yourself, which in turn means that there's the potential for *you* to get it wrong and fool Flash into making mistakes.

Sometimes it's important to be strict with Flash and tell it what sort of data to accept—like telling your kids not to leave their shoes in the refrigerator. When you use Flash this way, you're creating code that's **typed** (also called **strictly typed**). Writing code this way forces you to always consider the type of each variable when you use it, and Flash will warn you when you get it wrong. Although code written this way takes longer to produce, it's less likely to be wrong.

You'll look at some examples of untyped and typed code later on in this chapter, although for much of the book you'll be using the one that creates the more robust code: typed.

> *Always try to work with the value type that's most appropriate to the particular problem you're solving. For example, we'd all like to be able to converse with machines in a language like the one we use to talk to each other. Strings are useful here, because they represent a friendly way for Flash to communicate with users. On the other hand, strings are no good for defining a complex calculation; for this, you'd want to use numbers.*

Creating variables and using them with literals and expressions

Shortly, you'll look at some examples that will start to demonstrate just how useful variables can be. When you get there, you'll find that Flash gives you quite a lot of help, but it's often nice to know what to expect.

The easiest way to store a value in a variable is to use an = sign like this:

```
variable = value;
```

Whatever value (whether it's a string, a number, or a Boolean) you specify on the right gets stored in the variable you've named on the left.

Note that = here isn't the same as "equals" in math. You are *not* really equating the left side to the right side (although if you assume that you are, nothing untoward will happen to convince you otherwise); rather, you're **storing** the value in a container (or location) called variable. Programmers sometimes call this process **assigning**—you assign the value to the variable.

Naming variables

In Flash, you can name a variable however you like, *so long as Flash isn't likely to confuse it with something else*. Built into Flash are numerous names and symbols that are important to its correct operation, so you can't use them for your own purposes. These are called **reserved names**, and they include the following:

- **Actions** and other parts of ActionScript that might be mistaken as *part of an action*, including {}, ;, and (). Examples of reserved names that can be used within actions are break, call, case, continue, default, delete, do, else, for, function, if, in, new, on, return, set, switch, this, typeof, var, void, while, and with.

- Of course, actions themselves can't be variables. Basically, if it shows up in dark blue when you type it, then it's a reserved word and you can't use it. Obviously, don't start your variable name with //, because then it just becomes a comment!

- **Spaces** in a variable name will confuse Flash into thinking the name has finished before it actually has. For example, sham bhangal = "author" will look to Flash like a variable called sham that's followed by a string of random gibberish.

- Variable names that **begin with numbers** (such as 6pic) won't work either. Use pic6 instead. p6ic is also OK for Flash (although it looks a little cryptic to us!).

- **Operators** such as +, -, *, and / should be avoided. Otherwise, Flash may try to treat your variable as a sum to occur between two variables.

- The period character . is actually another operator (though you may not have realized it), so you should steer clear of using it in your variable names as well. However, as you'll see shortly, this character plays an important role in how you **locate** variables.

Also, Flash is case sensitive, so although the variable names mycat, MyCat, MYCAT, MY_CAT, and myCat are all possible, it's a good idea to pick a naming system; otherwise, you'll become very stuck very quickly. For example, if you name a variable as myCat and later use mycat, Flash will treat them as two separate variables without telling you anything is wrong. You will, of course, know something is wrong (your code most likely won't work), but it will be difficult to see what has gone wrong—the difference between "c" and "C" isn't much when you're looking through a 400-line script!

The standard naming strategy used in the Flash community—and, for that matter, in most scripting languages (oh, and in this book too)—is as follows:

- Start normal variables with a lowercase letter everywhere you start a new word and an uppercase letter wherever you would normally have a space. Your chosen standard variable name would thus be myCat. As explained in Chapter 1, this format is known as **camelCase**, so named after the humps it creates because of the change in case (who says programmers don't have imagination?).

- Create all variables that you don't want to change in value once they've been assigned (constants) in UPPERCASE. When you want to add a space to a constant, add a _ (underscore) instead. So, if you want a variable that holds the name of your cat (which isn't likely to change), you use the variable name MY_CAT.

- Don't use any of the other available permutations of the possible variable names. Flash won't raise an error if you do; it's just that you're more likely to make mistakes as you write your code if you mix naming styles.

With these provisions in mind, some example valid and recommended variable names are

- cow
- cowPoke
- menu6
- label7
- off

Examples of invalid and not recommended names are

- on, because Flash will expect it to be part of an onEvent action.

- label 7c, because Flash will see 7c as garbage because of the space before it.

- 6menu, because it starts with a number.

- my-toys, because it contains a minus operator, so Flash will assume you actually want the difference between the two variables my and toys.

- play, because ActionScript has an action called play().

- TOP_menu, because it doesn't fit into this variable naming system. Although Flash won't complain, you're likely to get the variable name wrong at least once in any long piece of code, and it's tough to find the mistake (I know—I've been there!).

There's one slight complication: suffixes. Rather like your operating system uses file extensions such as .exe, .hqs, and .zip so that it (for example) knows that flash.exe is an executable file, Flash has a system of suffixes that let the Actions panel know what the type of each variable is.

For a string variable, use the suffix _str. For Booleans or numbers, leave them as is. A good string variable name would be myVariable_str rather than myVariable, which by implication would be either a number or a Boolean.

Creating variables

You have two ways of creating variables in Flash. First, you can simply start using them, and if Flash sees a variable name it doesn't recognize, it will create a new one to suit. The following line will create a new variable called myVariable and assign it the value 10:

```
myVariable = 10;
```

Second, you can define a variable with the var action. Both of the following are acceptable (and do the same thing).

```
var myVariable;
myVariable = 10;
```

or

```
var myVariable = 10;
```

Now you might be thinking, "Heck, both of these are longer than the myVariable = 10; line. Why go the extra mile here?" Well, using var allows you to create *much* more structured code. In the myVariable = 10; line, it isn't obvious that you're creating a new variable, so it may be hard for you to see what's going on 6 months down the line. Using var is a signpost to you that says "I'm creating a new variable here."

> *The other good reason for using* var *is that it allows you to more fully define the variable, rather than leaving Flash to its own devices and just taking what it offers you. Using* var *enables you to do clever things with scope and type, as you'll see.*

In this book, I'll always define a new variable with var because it's a good programming habit to get into.

Once you've obeyed these rules to keep Flash happy, the important thing is that your variable names keep you happy too. You don't want to spend time figuring out what types they contain or what values they're meant to hold, so be as efficient as you can. Make sure that the names say something about what the variables hold.

For example, if I have three variables holding my three amounts of money, I could name them dayMoney, teaMoney, and beerMoney. This will really make debugging a lot easier. As you become more experienced, you may find there are times when you need to use variables of the same name in different places. As long as you're clear on the reasons why you need to do that, it's fine.

The easiest way to specify what you want to store is to use a **literal value**. Let's see what that means.

Literal values

Imagine you want an ActionScript variable called myName_str. If I wanted to store my own name in this variable, I might do it like this:

```
var myName_str;
myName_str = "Sham";
```

Here, "Sham" is a **string literal**. The string value that you want to store in myName_str is **literally** what appears between those two quotation marks. Why do you need the quotes? Simply because Flash is too dumb to know which part of your code is the string literal and which part is code. Code, after all, is simply text. Quotes always enclose string literals so Flash can make the differentiation.

It's important to include the quotation marks in a string literal. Without the quotes, Flash will think that you're referring to another variable. Say you have this:

```
var myName_str;
myName_str = Sham;
```

Instead of setting the value of myName_str to the word "Sham," Flash will go looking for a *variable called* Sham because it assumes the "Sham" part of the line is *code* rather than a literal value. If such a variable existed, it might contain any number of different things—probably not what you want, though! You always need to use the right syntax to tell Flash what you want it to do, and for literal string values, that means using quotes.

Similarly, you could have another variable called myAge. To create this variable and store a value in it, you might use a **numeric literal**, like so:

```
var myAge;
myAge = 35;
```

After these two lines, the variables myName and myAge can be used in your code as direct replacements for the values they contain. Although your code can't change the literal values "Sham" and 35, it *can* alter the values of the variables myName and myAge—they can be made to contain something else later. That might not sound like much now, but you'll soon see just how much versatility this can provide.

Expressions

The next way of generating values to be stored in variables is through the use of **expressions**. As you'll see in the exercises, this is where programming starts to look a bit like math, because expressions are often sequences of literals and variables linked together by mathematical symbols. For example, you might have something like this:

```
var myAge, myResult;
myAge = 35;
myResult = myAge - 10;
```

Flash would calculate the mathematical expression 35 − 10 to reach the answer 25 and store this new value in result (or *assign it to* result).

It's when you start to use expressions like this that you have to think carefully about the types of data being stored by your variables. The price you pay for the ease of using your untyped variables is that it's **your responsibility** to keep track of what they're holding. If you get it wrong, you run the risk of using a value in the wrong place and producing incorrect results.

Think back to your high school algebra. You can plan an equation like $a + b = c$ and be sure that it will work even before you know what the exact values of a and b are. Whatever happens, they're both numbers, and you know that two numbers added together will give you another number. Easy.

Programming is only slightly more complex. Variables don't always hold numbers; as you know, they can contain other things such as letters and words. You have to be aware of the types of data and make sure that you don't try to mix two different types together.

If variable $a = 2$ and variable $b = 3$, you could add a and b to get a value for c that makes sense to a math-savvy person, because $2 + 3 = 5$ (well, except to a physicist, who might tell you that it equals 6 because you're using a heavy 2).

You can also use expressions with strings. If variable a = "mad" and variable b = "house", you can add a and b to get a value for c that makes sense: "mad" + "house" = "madhouse".

When you mix up variables, though, you can get some unexpected results. For example, if variable a = "mad" and variable b = 3, and you add them together, the value for c is unlikely to make sense, because "mad" + 3 = "mad3".

To make variables work for us, we have to manipulate types separately and not mix them together. As a rule, if you input all numbers, then you can expect the result to be a number as well. If you input a string, then you can expect the result to be a string. If you mix a number and a string, then the result will be a string too. If this doesn't happen the way you expect it to, it's important that you know why, because this can be one of the most subtle and difficult errors to find if you aren't expecting it (and you'll see a way around this almost immediately when you look at strict typing). One simple error is assuming that because a string consists of only a number, then Flash will treat it as a number, but this isn't the case. For example, if you have the following expression:

```
myAge = 33 + "3";
```

you might expect the answer to be 36 (33 + 3), but Flash sees that you defined the second value as a string, and as you just learned, a string plus a number gives a string as the result, so Flash would set myAge to be a string value of "333". Now imagine that the second value was a variable that you'd set to a string somewhere else in the movie, possibly by mistake, and you can see how easy it is to get confused.

> *Note that if you kept to the game plan and used the variable name myAge_str if you actually wanted a string value in the age variable, you would have smelled something fishy about the preceding line—the variable myAge doesn't look like it should be assigned a string value.*

Determining and defining the type of a variable

Wouldn't it be handy if you could just ask Flash what type a variable was? Well, luckily you can. You'll use the preceding example as your starting point.

1. Open a new Flash document and type the following lines into the Actions panel for the first frame:

   ```
   var myAge;
   myAge = 33 + 3;
   ```

   The first line creates the variable myAge, with the var action, but doesn't give it a value. The second

line is an expression that sets your newly created variable to some value.

2. Press *CTRL/CMD+ENTER* to test-run the movie. As you'd expect, there's nothing on the screen, but Flash has stored your variable away in its memory. To see this, go to the Debug menu and choose List Variables. You should see a box like this appear:

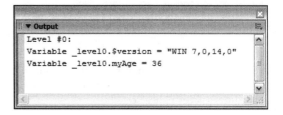

As you can see, the final entry contains your variable (don't worry about the first two entries or the _level0 bit for now). You can clearly see that your variable is set to be the number 36.

3. Now go back to the Actions panel and change the line so that it reads as follows (forgetting for a moment that you should really be using the variable name myAge_str):

   ```
   var myAge;
   myAge = 33 + "3";
   ```

   Now when you test your movie and look at the variables, you should see this:

   ```
   Level #0:
   Variable _level0.$version = "WIN 7,0,14,0"
   Variable _level0.myAge = "333"
   ```

You can see that your variable is now a string (notice the double quotes) and that it's set to the value "333".

Well, that's one way of checking. Once you start building more complicated movies, though, it will become much harder to find the variable you're looking for in this list. That doesn't make this technique useless, though—in fact, should you ever need to do this, you'll find a handy Find command hidden away in the Output window's Options menu, which allows you to search the entire contents of the Output window for whatever it is you're looking for. To test this, go to Options ➤ Find and type in myAge. Click Find Next, and the variable will be highlighted for you.

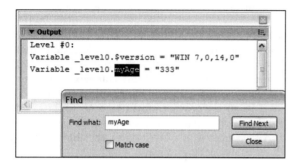

Note that the Find window allows you to match case. Clearing the Match case *check box is a good way to find any variable names that have been entered incorrectly—for example,* myage *instead of* myAge.

Close the SWF window and go back to the Actions panel. Add the following line just after the first two:

```
var myAge;
myAge = 33 + "3";
trace(myAge);
```

The trace command is one of the most useful commands in Flash to help you debug your ActionScript. If you run the movie now, you'll see that the Output window appears with just the contents of your variable in it:

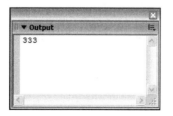

This is helpful enough as it is, but it's not all you can do. To the casual observer, that still looks like just a number. Let's see if you can be a bit more explicit.

Go back to the Actions panel and alter your third line as follows:

```
var myAge;
myAge = 33 + "3";
trace(typeof (myAge));
```

Be careful with the brackets here—if you put in too many (or too few), Flash will generate an error.

The typeof command tells Flash that you want it to give you the type of the variable that you've supplied as an argument. The whole of this expression is still taking place within the trace command, so it will still output whatever the result is.

If you test the movie now, you should get the following:

Now you can definitely see what type the variable is!

4. Try changing the variable back to how it was originally:

```
var myAge;
myAge = 33 + 3;
trace(typeof (myAge));
```

Then test your movie and see if the Output window contains the expected results.

So, you can now find out what type a variable is when things go wrong, but wouldn't it be better if there were a way you could prevent things from going wrong in the first place? Well, there is—if you tell Flash the type of your variable when you define it.

1. Change the first and last line of the code as follows:

```
var myAge:Number;
myAge = 33 + 3;
trace(myAge);
```

This time, you define the type of myAge as well as its name when you define it—you want it to contain numbers only. So what happens if you try to get Flash to store a string in myAge? Only one way to find out. . . .

2. Change the second line of your code as shown:

```
var myAge:Number;
myAge = 33+"3";
trace(myAge);
```

When you run this code, Flash will realize that you've tried to store something in myAge that it wasn't defined to hold and will raise an error. Although the code here is less flexible—you can't store the string value "thirty five" in myAge, for example—it does stop you from creating code that would place a string value in myAge by mistake.

Next up, you'll investigate more ways in which you can use your newfound variable friends—more specifically, by using them to increase user interaction.

Input and output

So far, I've talked only loosely about what variables are and the kinds of values they can store. It's about time you had a proper example of using them, so that you can start to see what they can do for your movies and websites. You'll begin by using them to store strings, since the practical benefits here are most obvious.

The act of storing strings is closely associated with **input to** and **output from** Flash, simply because users generally prefer to interact with a computer using text rather than raw numbers. Most complex interactions with computers are done using text of some kind, from filling in an online order form to entering keywords into a search engine. Both are much more involved than, say, entering numbers into a calculator, and this is where string variables shine.

Creating an input field

If you're going to use a variable to **store** a string that the user has entered, you need to enable the user to input a string.

1. Open a new movie and select the Text tool. Now turn your gaze to the Properties panel and make sure that Input Text is selected in the drop-down menu on the far-left side:

2. Select the Text icon in the Tools panel. Now click the stage to create a text field. If you've only worked with static text before, then you'll notice that two things are different:

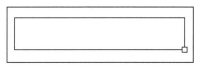

First, a static text box has a circle at the top-right corner, whereas the **input text field** has a square at the bottom right.

Second, a static text box will always start its life one character long and grow as you add more text to it. An input text field, on the other hand, immediately comes up with room enough to enter several characters. There won't be any text placed into it until after you've published the movie, so until then Flash needs to make a rough guess as to how much text you might need to enter.

The default size is Flash's best guess; you can make the field longer (or even make room for more than one line of text) by dragging the little square on the bottom right of the text field.

3. Look at the Properties panel again. Now that you've assigned this box as an input field, Flash knows that you'll probably want to store that input in a variable for later use. To make this easy for you, it's provided a text box (labeled Var) where you can give it a name for that variable. Since this is your first input box, let's call it input_str.

Also, while you're at it, click the Show Border Around Text icon (the icon immediately to the left of Var). Flash will draw a box around the text area's limits. Since this area will be used for inputting text, users will want to click it and make sure it's selected before they type anything in. The border will show users where to click.

The way you're using text fields at the moment isn't the normal way of using text fields in Flash MX 2004. It is, however, the best way to show how variables work. You'll learn the proper way to use text fields (using event-driven code and the text *property of text fields) when the time comes.*

4. Now make sure that the text color isn't set to white. This may sound like a really obvious thing to do, but it's easy enough to forget, and annoying if you run the movie and can't think of why you don't see any text appear in the text box.

5. Test the movie. You should see an empty rectangle on the stage. Click inside it, and a text-entry cursor will appear. Type in whatever you want. If you type in more than the box can fit, it will scroll to accommodate your input as you type. You can use BACKSPACE, normal copy and paste keyboard combinations, and most of the other keys you'd expect, though you can't use ENTER to finish your input:

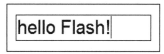

Now it may appear that Flash isn't doing anything when you type, but it's actually storing whatever goes in your text field inside your input_str variable. At this point, you could look up input_str in the variables list and find (sure enough) that input_str contains the string literal "hello Flash!".

63

Creating an output field

1. Bring up the Properties panel and change the top drop-down menu to Dynamic Text. This time, make sure the Show Border Around Text and Selectable icons are **not** selected:

You deselect these icons because the field that you're about to create is for use by Flash, not the user. It's being used as a display area, so the user won't need to see it drawn or be able to select it.

2. With the Text tool, add a new text field directly below the existing one, and set it to your variable name, input_str. Whereas for the input field the variable name tells Flash to take whatever is in the text field and put it into your variable, for the dynamic text field the variable name does the opposite: it takes whatever is in the variable and displays it in the text field.

3. Now test the movie. You'll see the same empty rectangle, until you start entering some text. When you do that, the dynamic text field will begin to "echo" what you've entered.

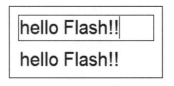

You'll also see, though, that it's of fixed length, and it won't scroll in the same way as the input box to display everything that you type in:

Let's see more
hello Flash!! Let's

The update speed of both text fields is determined by the frame rate specified for the movie. At the default frame rate of 12 frames per second (fps), the speed of text entry and its echo should look immediate. If you go and change the frame rate via Modify ➤ Document to 1 fps, you'll see a marked change in the update rate when you test the movie again. When you're done experimenting, return the frame rate to 12 fps.

At the moment, Flash is displaying a copy of what you type into the input box in real time, as soon as you type it in. If you make a mistake, Flash displays it for the world to see. You need a way to make Flash wait until you've finished entering your text and are happy with it before considering it the finished article. The easiest way to give you this extra feature and expand on what you've got is to create an enter button.

4. Select the lower text field (the output box), and change its variable to output_str:

5. Next, add a button next to the input text field and use the Properties panel to give it the instance name enter_btn. You should know how to create your own buttons by now, so I'll leave the details to you (or you can use the download file inputOutput.fla if you need a bit of revision). However you do it, make sure that when you specify the enter text for your button, the text is set as static (in other words, it's not still set to Dynamic in the Properties panel):

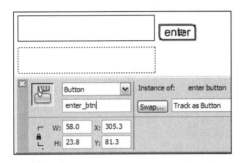

You now need to wire up the button with a little ActionScript. You'll do this by defining a callback for the button, just like you did in the last chapter.

Name the existing layer text and add a new layer called actions above it.

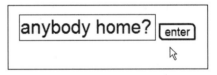

Lock the actions layer and select the first frame in this layer.

6. Select the first frame in the timeline and bring up the Actions panel. You'll start off by putting in the framework for an onRelease callback on the enter_btn button:

```
enter_btn.onRelease = function() {
};
```

Those of you who have come to this book from Foundation Flash or a similar beginner book might be thinking, "Wha . . .? Eh! You just told me to lock that layer . . . now I can't do anything with it, so why select it again?" Locking a layer locks only content related to the layer that's on the stage. You can still add scripts to a locked layer, and you can still edit the timeline (add or remove frames and keyframes). The only thing you can't do is add content to the stage on the locked layer. The actions layer is usually the layer you want to reserve for code only, and locking it permanently does just that.

7. The next step is to write some event handling code, so that something actually happens when the user releases the button and triggers the onRelease event. Add the following line:

```
enter_btn.onRelease = function() {
    output_str = input_str;
};
```

8. Now test the movie. This time when you enter any text, the bottom field doesn't echo your input . . .

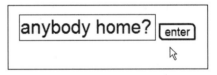

. . . until you click the enter button:

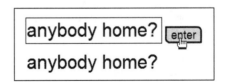

Make sure you hang on to this FLA because you'll use it several times later as a simple Flash UI. I've saved it with the filename `inputOutput.fla`.

Test the SWF again, but this time click the enter button *before* you type anything into the input text field.

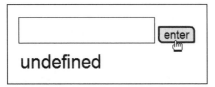

You haven't defined anything about your two variables `input_str` and `output_str`, so when you click the enter button, you get undefined back because that's exactly what's currently in the input field. You can prove that undefined and "nothing" aren't the same thing by running the SWF again and entering a character followed by the BACKSPACE key on your keyboard. Although there's nothing in the input text field, this time you have *defined* the contents of the text field (and therefore, `input_str`). More subtly, even though there's nothing in the text field, you've actually defined what **type** of nothing that nothing is—in this case, it's "" (a string of 0 length). This time if you click the enter button, you'll get back the contents of the top text field: rather than undefined, you'll see a blank.

If you think about it, such a case would very quickly become a problem if you wrote any code that read the value of the input text field. If your input text field was the bit where a buyer added the required car color, the buyer could end up ordering a car with color undefined. Better than mauve, I guess, but probably not what was intended—in fact, in most cases the unexpected appearance of undefined would be a bug in your code.

To fix this, you have to explicitly define all the variables in your code. Add the following new lines and test the SWF:

```
enter_btn.onRelease = function() {
  output_str = input_str;
};
var input_str:String;
var output_str:String;
```

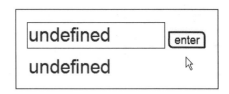

Hmm. Looks like a step backward, not forward! This time *both* text fields show undefined, and they do it before you click anything. Despite appearances, this is actually a *very* good thing because you know something is wrong immediately, as opposed to the last version of the FLA, which sat there hiding the bug until you performed some specific steps.

> *The new listing uses well-defined variables, and that's why the error appears quickly. This is a good thing because it tends to create workflows that result in better quality code, which is what I'll always aim for in this book in the techniques I teach, as opposed to the quicker ways through.*

So what's the problem? Well, last time around (i.e., using the FLA without the var lines) you didn't create `input_str` and `output_str` until the first time the line `output_str = input_str;` was run. This time around, you define the two variables straight away using var, and this reveals the problem immediately. The only remaining issue is that you've defined the variables, but not their contents. Add the following lines:

```
enter_btn.onRelease = function() {
  output_str = input_str;
};
var input_str:String;
var output_str:String;
input_str = "";
output_str = "";
```

This time, you create the variables and also define their contents. There's no chance of undefined appearing (although you can get it to show up "undefined" if you type it in, which is the text string undefined, not undefined).

You'll create a lot of variables in this book, so it would help if you could define them a bit quicker than this. The following code lines use var to both create variables and give them initial values:

```
enter_btn.onRelease = function() {
  output_str = input_str;
};
var input_str:String = "";
var output_str:String = "";
```

As you've learned here, creating variables is only part of being ready to use variables—you should also give them definite and well-defined values. If you don't, you'll probably come away with shorter code, but that code will also be more likely to have bugs hiding in it.

The process of creating variables and giving them starting values (also termed **initial values** by programmers) is called **initialization**. When you use Flash MX 2004's strict typing (as you will throughout this book), it's very important that you always properly define your variables by

- Giving them a name (e.g., input_str)
- Giving them a type (e.g., String)
- Giving them an initial value, even if this is just "" or 0 (number zero)

If you're working with your own files, save this FLA as inputOutput3.fla. You'll use this file as the starting point of another example later on in the chapter.

Using string expressions

Let's recap. To start putting together the first building blocks for inputting and outputting text within Flash, you've created simple text fields for obtaining and displaying the values of basic variables. Now that you know how to do this, your available lines of communication with the user (and levels of interactivity) have gone from basic mouse clicks to phrases and sentences.

Now that you have your text input and output working, you're going to look at how you can use string expressions to give Flash a more human face and communicate with users on a personal level. You'll create a string expression that combines the value of the variable input_str with some extra text to display more than users might expect.

1. Open the FLA that you've just been working on (or use the file inputOutput2.fla from the download file for this chapter).

2. Select the first frame of layer actions (if it isn't already selected) and open the Actions panel. Then select the line output_str = input_str; and alter it so that it matches this:

   ```
   output_str = "Hello " + input_str + "!";
   ```

   Make sure that you include the space after Hello, otherwise Flash will just crunch all the words together.

   When ActionScript encounters this, it takes the string literal "Hello ", adds the contents of the variable input_str, appends the second string literal "!", and stores the result in the variable output_str. This may sound confusing, but rest assured it will all make sense when you see it in action!

3. Test the movie and enter your name. Flash should greet you like a long lost friend:

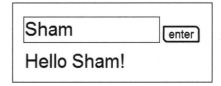

While I don't want to undersell what you've done here, I have to point out that there's a slight problem: you haven't been able to empower Flash with the grammatical knowledge to check whether what it's saying to you makes sense. Whatever you type in, Flash will give it back to you as part of the same answer:

```
Hi there!                    enter
Hello Hi there!!
```

I can't say that I have the solution to this for you here. I've shown you how to use string expressions to build in a degree of personalization, but be aware how quickly the illusion of intelligence falls apart. If you try this within a website project, be careful. Still, it's reassuring to know that computers still can't be more intelligent than we are!

Virtually all the variable examples you've looked at so far have dealt with storing strings. Of course, that's not the only type of data you can put into an ActionScript variable, so let's take a closer look at the other two types: **numbers** and **Booleans**.

Working with numbers

In everyday use, numbers can represent more than just raw values. Numbered seats in a cinema don't represent a chair's **value**, but its **position**. The ISBN for this book doesn't represent its value or its position, but is a **reference** or **index** to the book.

To a much greater extent than strings, numbers lend themselves to being operated upon: they can be added to, subtracted from, multiplied, divided, and so on. If you store numbers in variables, all kinds of possibilities are opened up.

Returning to those cinema seats, if you arrange to store the number booked so far in a variable called seatsTaken, then the number of the next seat available (assume you sell them in order) for booking is *always* going to be seatsTaken+1, regardless of the actual value stored in the variable. Look at this:

```
seatsTaken = seatsTaken +1;
```

This line says "Add 1 to the current value of seatsTaken and store the result back in seatsTaken." Each time ActionScript encounters it, the number

stored in the variable increases by 1. Remember, variables are all about giving ActionScript memory.

Let's try some of this out, using the interface FLA again. You can use inputOutput3.fla from the download file if you forgot to save it. In this exercise, you're going to get the user to input some numbers, and then Flash will perform some calculations on them.

Performing simple calculations

In the previous exercise, the values you saw going into input_str were actually string values, which is to say that they could include more than the numbers 0 to 9 and the decimal point that you would normally expect in numeric values. Before you start using input_str in numeric expressions, you need to take steps to prevent the user from entering characters that could spoil your work.

1. Select the input text box and turn your attention back to the Property inspector. Click the Character button next to the Var field to bring up the Character Options panel. Click the Specify Ranges radio button, and all options become available. Select Numerals [0..9] (11 glyphs). This allows you to enter the numbers 0 to 9 plus the decimal point.

You also need to change the variable names associated with the two text fields. Select each in turn and change input_str to inputNum, and output_str to outputNum.

4. If you now test the SWF, you'll start with zeros in the two fields. If you change the top zero to a number, the lower one will change to twice the entered value:

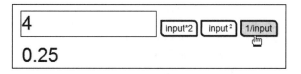

If you like, you can try changing the expression (or even adding buttons with new callbacks of their own) to give the following information:

- outputNum = inputNum^2; for the square of the amount entered
- outputNum = 1/inputNum; for the reciprocal of the amount entered

Here's a shot from one you can find in the download file saved as calculator.fla:

2. Now test the movie. You'll find that you're no longer able to enter anything other than decimal numbers, which is a step in the right direction.

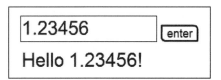

3. Close the SWF and select frame 1 on the actions timeline. Call up the Actions panel. Now that you know it's safe to treat input1 as a numeric value, you can perform a bit of simple arithmetic on it and assign the result to output1. Try this:

```
enter_btn.onRelease = function() {
  outputNum = inputNum * 2;
};
var inputNum:Number = 0;
var outputNum:Number = 0;
```

Computer programming languages use the asterisk (*) to represent multiplication in place of the traditional ×. The idea is to remove the chance of confusion with the letter "x".

Other uses for numeric expressions

Numeric expressions have a lot more to offer than making Flash do sums for you. For example, you could use the results of numeric expressions to control the position or orientation of an instance, allowing you to create some very complex movements. You could have an expression to tell your alien spaceship, Blarg, where to move after it makes its bombing run on a game player.

You can also use numeric expressions to jump to frames within a movie based on **dynamic** values, and not just to the fixed number values you've used so far. This allows you to control timeline flow to a much greater degree. For example, you could jump to an explosion if the player is hit by an alien.

the computer was having a bad day and I turned up at the bank wearing a lilac shirt. Computers base their decisions on statements of the yes/no or true/false variety. Their decisions have only two possible outcomes at a time, although they can apply lots of yes/no decisions in a row to tackle more complex outcomes.

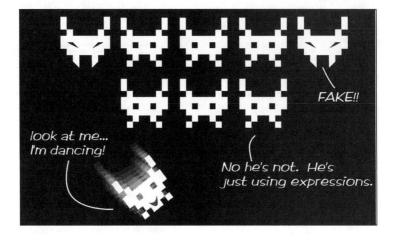

Some of the stuff you've looked at so far may have seemed a little removed from space invaders flitting about the screen and cool, ActionScript-heavy dynamic sites, but you're learning about the cogs that make these wheels turn. You'll continue to do that in the next section.

Working with Boolean values

If I buy a packet of cookies, I do so because they look tasty and I'm not on a diet. This is a very clear-cut decision: if two criteria are met, then I buy the cookies. In general, however, we don't tend to make such straightforward decisions; instead, we base our decisions at least partly on a comparison, our mood, or a predisposition. We might even base some decisions on inputs that have nothing to do with the choice at all: "I don't want to talk to him because I don't like the color of his shirt." Our decisions can have many more outcomes than simply "I will" or "I will not."

Computers, though, stick to decisions of the more clear-cut variety, which is a relief because a computer probably tracks my bank balance and transactions. I wouldn't like my balance to halve suddenly because

Suppose, for example, that you wanted to find out whether a number was higher or lower than 100. It could be the price of a share on the stock market. If the number is lower, you'll think about buying, and if it's higher, you'll think about selling. Depending on which side of 100 the price is, you'll perform one of two different sets of actions. Alternatively, it could be that you're writing a space invaders game in which the invaders move down the screen in an attempt to land on the player's planet. Once the distance of any invader from the top edge of the stage is greater than 100, you know it's at the bottom of the screen, and the player has lost.

Take the first case and assume that the share price you're interested in is stored in a variable called price. Now have a look at this:

```
buy = price < 100;
```

When you've seen code like this in the past, the expression on the right side of the equal sign has been evaluated, with the result being stored in the variable on the left side. But what *is* the value on the right side? Given the title of this section, you won't be surprised to discover that it's a **Boolean value**, which means that buy will be set to true if price is less than 100 or false if price has any other value. Flash's thinking goes like this:

- If the price is less than 100, then set buy to equal true.
- If the price isn't less than 100 (that is, it's greater than or equal to 100), then set buy to equal false.

true and false are the **only** Boolean values, and they're the only possible values on the right side.

> *Note that* true *and* false *here are neither strings nor variables. They're simply the two possible Boolean values.*

Testing whether statements are true

Until you start to look at conditional operators in the next chapter—which will indeed allow you to perform different actions depending on Boolean values—there's a limit to what you can do with them. However, you can at least check that what I've been saying is true and use them in some slightly more complex expressions.

1. Let's modify your movie again. Load inputOutput.fla (the file you saved earlier), making sure it's free of all the little tweaks you subsequently made to it. Alternatively, you can open greetings.fla again. Select the input text and change the selection in the Character Options panel again, so that you're only accepting numbers and a decimal point.

2. Now select the first frame in the actions layer and call up the Actions panel. Change the code it contains as follows:

```
enter_btn.onRelease = function() {
  outputBool = (inputNum < 100);
};
var inputNum:Number = 0;
var outputBool:Boolean = false;
```

3. You also need to change the variable names in the text fields, so select each text field in turn, changing the Var field in the top text field to inputNum and the lower one to outputBool.

4. Run the movie, and you'll see that Flash now looks at any number you enter and compares it with 100. If it's lower, input1<100 is a true statement, so you get true:

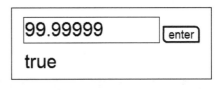

If it's greater than or equal to 100, input1<100 isn't true, so you get false:

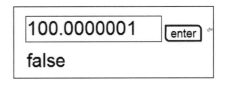

Logic operators

Think back to high school when you had lessons on electrical circuits. You may remember that there were logic gates that would open only if their conditions were made. These gates had crazy names like AND, OR, NOT, and NAND, and these **logic operators** also exist in ActionScript. Here's a list of the ones that it recognizes:

- &&: AND
- ||: OR
- !: NOT

If you need to, you can use these logic operators to make your test more selective. That's what you're about to do.

Take the earlier example about share prices. If you were prepared to buy shares if the price per share was below 100, then you might want to stop buying if the price went below 80, because such a sharp drop would indicate unfavorable market conditions. In plain text, you would need something like this:

If the price is less than 100 AND greater than 80 . . .

Bringing this closer to the expression in this example, you need this:

```
(input1<100) AND (input1>80)
```

Flash uses the && symbol to signify AND, so the ActionScript you actually want is this:

```
(input1<100) && (input1>80)
```

Testing for more than one thing at a time

Let's change the script to test for the double expression that you looked at earlier.

1. Alter your frame 1 script to read

```
enter_btn.onRelease = function() {
    outputBool = (input1 < 100) &&
➥ (input > 80);
};
var inputNum:Number = 0;
var outputBool:Boolean = false;
```

2. Now run the movie. You'll see that you get a true result only if the price is between 80 and 100.

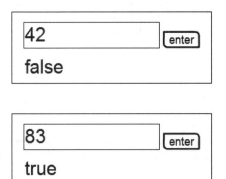

Using similar techniques, you can build up very complex conditions that involve a number of other operators and terms, and you'll start using them for real in the next chapter.

Before you do that, though, I'm going to demonstrate how you can get more out of your variables by using arrays.

Arrays

The easiest way to think of an **array** is as a container for a collection of variables, which you access using a single name. From the outside, it looks just like a single entity, but it can hold lots of different values at any one time.

In many ways, an array isn't dissimilar to a filing cabinet: the cabinet itself has a name, but it may contain several drawers, each of which can contain its own information. Each drawer is like a variable in its own right, but it's stored in a cabinet along with other drawers, because they all hold data that's related in some way.

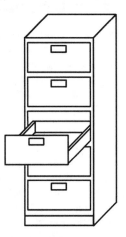

When you're looking at a variable array, you need to specify two things:

- The **name** of the array
- The **index** (or offset number) of the **element** (or "drawer") you want to use

Say you have an array called myColor that contains five pieces of information—that is, five elements. To refer to the first one (that's the bottom drawer in the cabinet), you use this:

myColor[0]

Note that the index (or offset) is surrounded by square brackets [ ], and yes, the first array location is 0, not 1 as you might have expected. If the fact that there is a 0th drawer confuses you, think of it this way: whenever you see an index value of n, you're referring to the drawer that's offset by n from the bottom. In theory, there's nothing stopping you from leaving it empty, but this isn't recommended, for practical reasons you'll learn about later on. It may seem a little odd to begin with, but you'll soon get used to it!

So, an index of 0 gives you the base element. The second element (the first drawer up from the base) would be

myColor[1]

The third element (offset by 2 from the base) is

myColor[2]

and so on. Likewise, say you want to get some information that you know is stored in the third drawer from the bottom of a filing cabinet called "contracts." In ActionScript terms, that filing cabinet is an array called contracts, and the third drawer can be accessed as the array element contracts[2].

Reasons for using arrays

There are several reasons why it can be useful to store variables in arrays, as described in the following sections.

Arrays let you store related information together

Say you're working with a list of birds, and you want to keep together information on all birds that live around water. You might put them into an array called wadingBirds, and element number 1 might contain the string "flamingo". You could have other arrays such as tropicalBirds (containing "parrot", "hummingbird", and so on) and another called tundraBirds (containing "ptarmigan" and "arctic owl"). As you can see, borrowing that *Birds of the World* book from the school library at nine years old has left its mark!

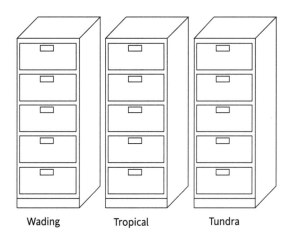

Wading   Tropical   Tundra

Arrays let you hold information in a specific order

Perhaps you want an array containing the names of pupils at a school, held in the order of exam rankings (best first, of course!). The variable pupils[3454] might well contain the name "Sham B"....

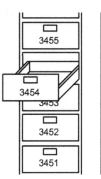

Arrays let you index information

For example, if you have an array to hold theater bookings, you could use the variable seatingPlan[45] to hold the name of the person who booked seat 45. In these circumstances, the numbering scheme is the most important thing, so you'd probably just ignore seatingPlan[0]—that is, unless the theater's seat numbering begins at 0 (a theater run by programmers, no doubt!).

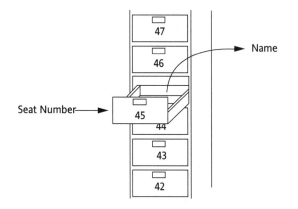

Arrays let you link information

Say you have a list of common plant names and another list that gives their Latin counterparts, and you store them in a pair of arrays called commonName and latinName. Assuming the lists have been arranged properly in the first place, you could cross-reference between the two. For example, say you look in CommonName[6] and find "common snowdrop." You can then look at the equivalent variable latinName[6] in the other array to find the Latin name *Galanthus nivalis*.

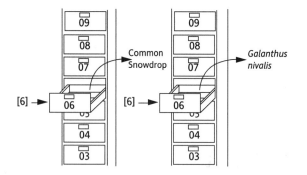

Creating a new array

Before you can do anything useful with arrays, you need to learn how to create them and pipe in information. Well, the first bit's simple enough. Say you want to create an array called my_array:

```
my_array = new Array();
```

The standard suffix for an array is (surprise, surprise) _array.

No problem! You now have an array, but it doesn't have any elements—it's like a filing cabinet without any drawers. It's easy enough to add them in, though:

```
my_array[0] = "Bill";
my_array[1] = "Pat";
my_array[2] = "Jon";
my_array[3] = "Tom";
```

Yes, you can assign values to the elements just as if they were plain old variables. Flash simply expands the array as you add new entries to it. You don't even need to use the same variable type for the different elements. Going forward from the previous example, you could easily write

```
my_array[4] = 1981;
my_array[5] = 1984;
my_array[6] = 1987;
```

This isn't the only way to define an array, though. You could write

```
myScores_array = new Array(1, 45, 34504,
➥ 31415);
```

or

```
myPets_array = new Array("cat", "dog",
➥ "pelican");
```

Note that if you set myArray[19], you're creating a *single* element. Flash *won't* create array entries [0] to [18] as well, so you have "missing drawers" that show up as undefined. This could be dangerous if subsequent code expects to see them filled with a sensible value (such as 0 or "").

It's much safer if you define each element right after you define the array. You would give each entry a default value. For example, the default value might be "" if you wanted an array of strings or 0 for an array of numbers.

In fact, there are various other ways to create arrays, but I recommend sticking to these for now—they should easily meet your demands.

Also worth noting is that the elements of an array can contain a mixture of the three different types of variables: number, string, and Boolean. The following is perfectly legal:

```
my_array = new Array();
my_array[0] = "Bill";
my_array[1] = 3;
my_array[41] = false;
```

Typing an array

An array has its own type, Array, which contains elements that can be numbers, strings, or Booleans. If you want to type your arrays when you define them, you should use the following syntax:

```
var my_array:Array = new Array()
```

The advantage of this is that Flash won't let you destroy your array by equating it to something else (number, string, or Boolean). If you did this:

```
my_array = 7;
```

all of the other definition lines apart from the preceding typed one would overwrite your entire array structure with the value 7—not something that you want to happen often! The typed version would raise an error:

As usual then, typed array definitions are much better than untyped ones, because they force Flash to give you more possible errors when you compile your SWF, and this leads to more robust code.

Using variable values as offsets

One particularly useful feature of arrays is that you can specify offsets in terms of other variables. So, you can use an existing variable (defined completely separately from the array) to specify which drawer you want to look in.

Let's take a look at a quick example:

```
var myColor_array:Array = new Array();
var offset:Number = 0;
myColor_array[offset] = "green";
```

Here, offset is a number variable set to 0, and you use it to specify which element in the array myColor_array should be given the value green. In this case, you've effectively said

```
myColor_array[0] = "green";
```

This approach can be *very* powerful. By simply changing the value of your variable, you can use one bit of code to work on as many different drawers as your array has to offer. This means that you can write generalized code for manipulating array elements and specify the offset quite separately.

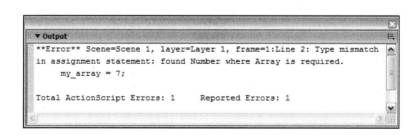

```
▼ Output
**Error** Scene=Scene 1, layer=Layer 1, frame=1:Line 2: Type mismatch
in assignment statement: found Number where Array is required.
    my_array = 7;


Total ActionScript Errors: 1     Reported Errors: 1
```

Using a number variable to select a text string from an array

Let's use our faithful interface inputOutput.fla to take a quick look at arrays in action.

1. Open the FLA and select the top (input) text field. Open the Property inspector, click the Characters button, and make sure the text field is configured to only accept numerals:

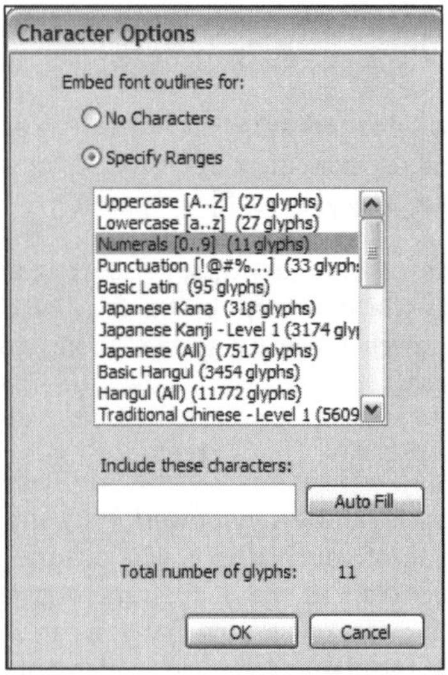

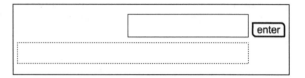

2. Now select frame 1 on the timeline and make the following changes to the code:

[handwritten: When button released]

```
enter_btn.onRelease = function() {
    output_str = bondMovies_array[inputNum];
};
var output_str:String = "";
var inputNum:Number = 0;
var bondMovies_array:Array = [];
bondMovies_array[0] = "Doctor No";
bondMovies_array[1] = "From Russia With
➡ Love";
bondMovies_array[2] = "Goldfinger";
```

[handwritten: Array Name set — leave output box empty — sets array]

[handwritten: listing array numbers]

3. Make the lower text field longer if it looks like it won't accept the length of "From Russia With Love".

4. Select the upper (input) text field and change its variable (the Property inspector's Var field) to inputNum.

5. Now when you enter a number in the first field and click the enter button, it's used as the offset for bondMovies_array. As long as the number entered is between 0 and 2, you'll be rewarded with the name of the relevant film:

> 1
>
> [enter]
>
> **From Russia With Love**

Well, if you happen to count the films from 0, that is.

Let's face it, most people would think your system was broken if they fed in the number 1 and got *From Russia With Love*. *Everyone* knows that was the second movie!

6. Well, let's fix this "broken" movie. Either you can change the array itself, leaving element 0 empty (or maybe hide *Casino Royale* away in there where nobody's likely to spot it), or you can tweak the offset. Between you and me, I have a soft spot for anything featuring Peter Sellers, so let's do the second:

```
enter_btn.onRelease = function() {
    output_str = bondMovies_array[inputNum-1];
};
```

7. Now you can run the movie, type a number, click enter, and see the title you expected:

```
3                        enter

        Goldfinger
```

Presto! Enter a number and get back a film title.

> *You'll see your old friend* undefined *if you enter* 0 *or anything greater than 3. Although that makes the code look unfinished, it's actually (again) a good thing you see* undefined *rather than a blank field or an incorrect value—it's a definite marker telling you this is something you have yet to address. Despite the code returning* undefined, *this doesn't represent a bug, but an expected value, and this is due in part to the fact that you're using* **well-defined variables** *throughout. Not only do you use meaningful* **variable names**, *complete with the appropriate naming style (camelCase and _suffixes), but also you define the* **value** *and* **type** *for each variable.*

Of course, I've barely touched on the power of arrays here, but hopefully you've seen enough to get a feel for what they are and what they do. Trust me, you'll be seeing a lot more of them!

In the next couple of chapters, you're going to look at decision making and looping, topics that really make the most of what you can do with both variables and arrays. You'll look at the decision-making functionality that you can build using Boolean values, use ActionScript loops to act on whole arrays in one fell swoop, and even build a fully functioning hangman game to tie all these threads together!

Book project: Starting the Futuremedia site design

In the last chapter, you looked at how the Futuremedia site works in principle. Now it's time to begin creating the basic graphics for the site. Although you won't be adding any scripts in this chapter, you'll start using the drawing tools in a manner that you may not be used to yet but that is critical for ActionScript. You'll place everything on the stage precisely by entering numbers in the Properties panel. You don't need to do this when creating more general sites, but in a Flash-heavy site the ActionScript needs to know where everything is to pixel accuracy, so you have to be precise.

The final file created in this chapter is included as `futuremedia_setup1.fla` if you get stuck.

> *The Futuremedia site uses a font called Century Gothic. If you try to open any of the prebuilt FLA files on a computer without this font installed, you may get a warning message from Flash. If you see this, you should select* _sans *as the substitution font for now.*

What you're going to do

In this section, you'll

- Learn about and set up the Flash stage and timeline for your ActionScript site.
- Create the text areas that are in the border area of the site. This includes the text at the top-left corner of the site and the black bar at the bottom.

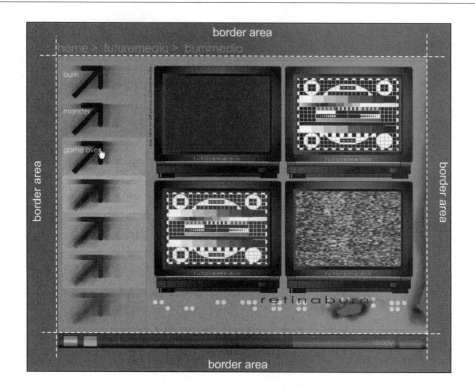

What you're going to learn

The concepts to take on board for this section of the book project are

- The level of accuracy and placement ActionScript sites require of the graphics, which is far more than you may be used to when creating sites that use much less ActionScript and loads of tweening. The easiest way to manage this is by adding lots of construction lines onto the stage early on in your development, so you have a framework into which you can place your design.

- The amount of preliminary sketching you have to go through to get it all right first time. This involves time spent away from the main task every now and again, and summarizing what you want via a sketch is time well spent. If you find your design changing, be sure to create a new set of sketches to maintain an overall design-eye view of where you're heading.

Choosing and setting the stage size

The Futuremedia site is designed for a screen size of 1280×1024 or more. This may seem a little high to some users, but bear the following in mind:

- I chose this size because it's easiest on the eye during development on a typical 1280×1024 development machine.

- Pixel sizes are pretty much meaningless in Flash in any case. If you want the site to be viewable on a (for example) 800×600 screen, you'll simply scale it during publishing.

As long as you create a stage size that's in the approximate ratio 4:3 (the standard monitor ratio), you can scale it to target it for any screen size you want by changing the stage size when you publish (File ➤ Publish ➤ HTML tab).

For those unsure of the minimum viewable stage size that will work on all common browsers at the standard screen resolutions, here's a quick table to help you (it takes into account both the Mac and PC):

Screen resolution	800×600	1024×768	1280×1024
Maximum Flash stage size	590×300	975×590	1230×845

Unless you're designing for portable devices, 800×600 is the minimum screen resolution you should assume. If a desktop can't show this size screen, it probably can't display Flash 7 content either!

Note that I haven't included sizes for 1600×1280 or above. This is because such screen sizes aren't widespread enough for you to safely design content for them.

You'll size your stage at 800×600, which is well within the 1230×845 stage limit for a 1280×1024 screen resolution.

> *Another, more subtle reason I chose 800×600 is related to performance issues. Flash really slows down if you create large-sized sites that contain a lot of motion, and 800×600 is around the maximum stage size for a responsive Flash site. By setting your stage to this size during development, you're able to more easily identify performance bottlenecks and sluggish animation.*

1. Open a new FLA with File ➤ New or select Flash Document from the Start New portion of the start page if you've just opened Flash.

2. Select Modify ➤ Document to access the Document Properties window (you can also get to this window by double-clicking the area under the timeline that displays the current frame, frame rate, and elapsed time).

3. Change Dimensions to 800×600 and Frame rate to 18. Click the Background color color brick and change it to the third gray selection down from the top, leftmost column (#666666).

Setting up the timeline

The next task is setting up the timeline for your proposed site. Although choosing layer names and setting up folders may seem trivial, remember that you're going to create a user interface that can handle a fairly large site and that will have lots of things whizzing around when it's up and running. A little thought and sensible planning at this stage works wonders!

1. Rename Layer 1 as actions and create two layer folders called frame and UI. The frame layer will contain all the symbols in the border area (or "the frame"), and the three strips (as discussed in the walk-through earlier) that form the main interface itself will be in the folder UI.

2. The actions layer is reserved for the code that will later animate your site. To make sure you don't inadvertently put graphics in this layer, lock the actions layer now.

On large site designs, I tend to change the layer color of the actions *layer to black, to signify code (some people use white for this purpose). To change the layer color, double-click the color square and select the new layer color by changing the* Outline *color in the Layer Properties window that will appear.*

As you can see from this sketch, the dotted construction lines are fundamental to the layout—they separate the main content area (which will eventually contain the sneaky tricolor/strip movie clip combo) from the border areas containing the position text and back strip areas. Although it isn't shown in the diagram, the border width in the final design is 30 pixels. Why 30 pixels? Well, I wanted the design to be flexible enough for you to customize it as required, and 30 pixels is a good size for any icons or other interface items you may want to add in the left and right borders. It's also more than enough for the position text and back strip to remain legible if you decide the scale the site design down if you need to customize it to work well in a screen resolution of less than 1280×1024.

Creating layout guides

Although you already know what the site design will look like, here's the first sketch that I created when I initially mapped out the site design:

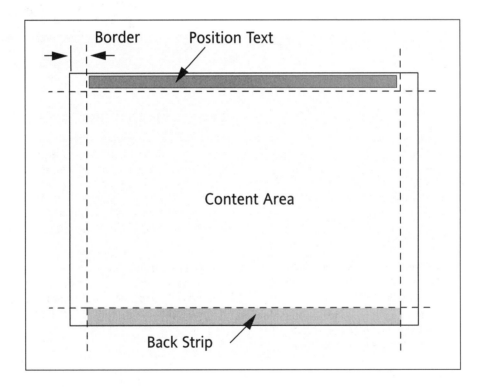

The sketch just presented (and others you'll see as you progress through the book) isn't a cleaned-up version of the initial sketch I made on a piece of paper—it's the actual sketch I created during the design process. The package of choice in creating such sketches isn't Auto Sketch or some other dedicated technical drawing application, but Flash itself. Using Flash, you can quickly mock up neat diagrams and sketches via a pen tablet, and you can allow Flash to straighten up your lines and curves as you go, so that you end up with a series of design documents that are fit to go straight into a book or show your client. In fact, many of the line diagrams for this book were created in Flash!

It would be a good idea if you could transpose these construction lines onto your actual stage, which is exactly what you'll do next.

1. Create two new layers in the layer folder frame and call them guideHoriz and guideVert. Hide the grid (View ➤ Grid ➤ Show Grid) if it's displayed.

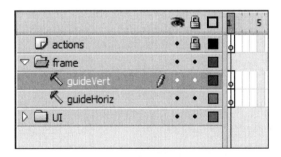

2. In layer guideHoriz, draw out two thin horizontal lines that span the width of the stage, plus a little more. Now, using the Properties panel, give one line a y value of 30.0 and the other one a value of 570.0. Lock this layer so you don't mess up the lines during the next step.

3. In layer guideVert, draw out two vertical lines in the same way as you did in the previous step, this time giving them x values of 30.0 and 770.0.

4. Make both of these layers guide layers (right-click/*CTRL*-click the layer title and check guide on the pop-up menu that appears). You now have your border clearly marked on your screen. Lock guideVert so that both of your guide layers are now locked.

Note that the reason you aren't using ruler guides is that you can't place them accurately with the Properties panel. You want a greater accuracy than just doing it by eye. It's not that I'm being overly fussy here—I know how particular ActionScript can be!

Adding the position and status text

At the top of your site is the position text, and this tells users where they are in the navigation (you'll get a better idea of what this does by looking at the final site design). Here's my second original design sketch, which now takes into account the status text:

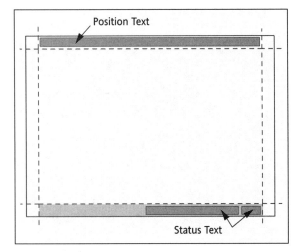

At the bottom right of the site, you'll notice some text that gives an indication of what Flash is doing. The leftmost bit of text gives a text message, and the rightmost one gives numeric feedback (such as the percent loaded when the site is online; at the moment it probably won't show anything if you're viewing the site from your local hard drive because load time will be instantaneous).

You'll be adding both of these text areas next.

Choosing a font

The Futuremedia site uses the font Century Gothic because

- Nobody else uses it (always a good reason for a designer!).
- Despite its lack of use within the web design community as a main font, it's actually a very common font, so you shouldn't have too much trouble finding it on the Web if it isn't already installed on your machine.
- Aesthetically, it's a very clean font with a modern feel to it, although it isn't so unsubtle to become another one of those techno font clichés.
- Its uncomplicated appearance has the advantage of making it bandwidth-light when you create a font symbol from it later in the book.

> Futuremedia uses the font Century Gothic although you can just as well use _sans

If you don't want to (or can't) use Century Gothic, you can use any sans font of your choice (or simply one that's installed on your machine). Typical choices will include the following:

- Trebuchet
- A font from the Humanist family (be warned that you're unlikely to get good versions of Humanist fonts from the Web without paying for them)
- Arial
- Helvetica

Failing any of these, you can simply use the default Flash sans font, _sans.

You can, of course, use a novel font of your choice. I've seen a good reworking of the Futuremedia site from a reader (of the Flash MX version of this book) that uses a handwriting font. The interface has been changed so that it looks like a piece of old parchment. For now, though, let's get the thing working first!

OK, the preamble is done. Time to get to work.

Adding the text

Still in the frame layer folder, add two new layers called status and mainTitle.

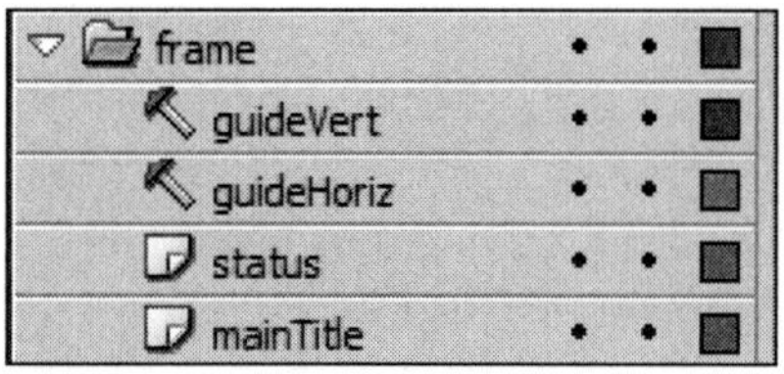

In the layer mainTitle, add a dynamic text field in the middle of the stage (size isn't important for now), and inside it enter the text title text. Using the Properties panel, change the text field's attributes and properties as shown in the following table and figure:

Text type	Dynamic Text
Instance name	main_txt
W	740.0
H	30.0
X	30.0
Y	0.0
Font	Century Gothic*
Font size	22
Font color	#999999
Lines	Single Line
Justification	Left

* Or your chosen font

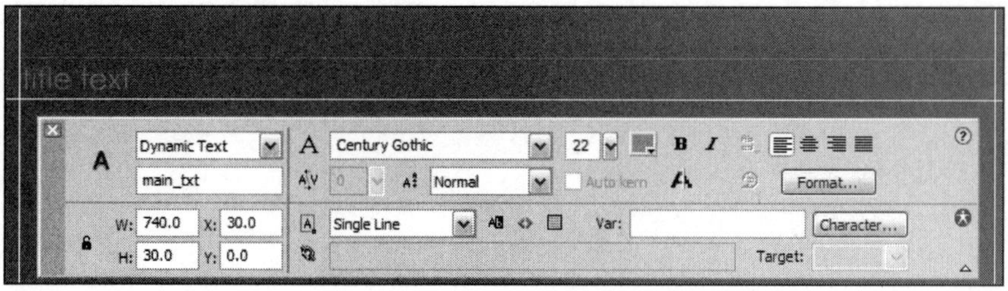

This will make your text field go to the top border and extend across it. Lock the mainTitle layer.

You may find that some of the values seem to have a life of their own. For example, 30.0 may become 29.9. If Flash starts adding or subtracting small amounts, subtract or add an equal amount. For example, if you see 29.0 instead of 30.0, change it to 30.1. This usually (but not always) fixes the problem.

Add another two text fields in the status layer, this time clicking the Show Border Around Text icon (in the Properties panel) before you place the text fields. In one text field enter the text ready, and leave the other field blank.

Using the Properties panel again, set the following properties and attributes for the text field with ready in it, as shown next:

Text type	Dynamic Text		Text type	Dynamic Text
Instance name	status_txt		Instance name	statusValue_txt
W	200.0		W	45.0
H	21.0		H	21.0
X	505.0		X	715.0
Y	575.0		Y	575.0
Font	Century Gothic*		Font	Century Gothic*
Font size	14		Font size	14
Font color	#999999		Font color	#999999
Lines	Single Line		Lines	Single Line
Justification	Right		Justification	Left

* Or your chosen font   * Or your chosen font

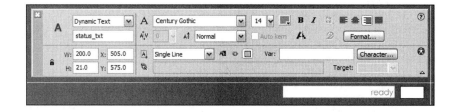

Select the remaining text field you haven't placed pre-cisely yet, and set it up as shown in the following figure and the table in the top-right:

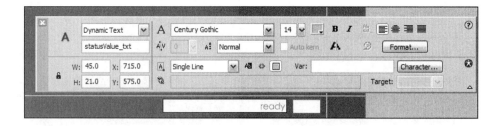

Note that the status text currently has a white background. In the final site, the background is a shade of gray that blends in better with the site design (see the following image). The reason you can't set the correct background color just yet is because you can only do it through ActionScript—the Properties panel doesn't allow you to set any background color other than white. Many properties are like this (and, in some cases, entire classes!).

You're simply not using Flash to its full potential and configurability until you start using ActionScript.

Embedding the font

Embedding a font (or parts of a font) forces Flash to save the font outline data, which allows Flash to treat text using the font as a vector graphic. The advantages of this are as follows:

- The text can be animated in just the same way a movie clip can—it can be scaled and rotated, for example. Text that isn't embedded will disappear if you do anything to it that changes its appearance drastically, because Flash simply doesn't have the information to work out how it should appear once you start altering it at the vector level, unless it has the vector outline data on hand.

- The text will appear with a vector edge. It will be antialiased, which means it will appear with a much less pixilated appearance. This is usually a good thing, except when you're using very small font sizes (you aren't in this case).

The Futuremedia site uses the same font throughout. This means you're best off embedding a major part of the font. To do this, follow these steps:

1. Select one of the text fields (it doesn't matter which). In the Properties panel, click the Character button. The Character Options window will appear.

2. Select the Specify Ranges radio button, and in the lower pane (which will become active) highlight the first four options. Depending on the font you're using, this should embed around 100 glyphs (individual characters). You also need the > character as part of your position text, so enter > in the Include these characters text entry box.

The final Futuremedia site uses an advanced technique in its font management. It uses a font symbol that's handled as a shared asset between the separately loaded movies (SWFs) that make up the site. The problem is that the FLA that defines your shared font symbol isn't the one you're currently working on (it's actually loaded in the preloader, which is loaded prior to the main site). You won't see the preloader if you view the site locally, but you can see it in action if you visit the Futuremedia site online (www.futuremedia.org.uk, or the friends of ED mirror site at the URL noted in the book introduction).

The font embedding you're doing at the moment is therefore a temporary measure to get you started.

Parting shots

The site at the moment looks like this:

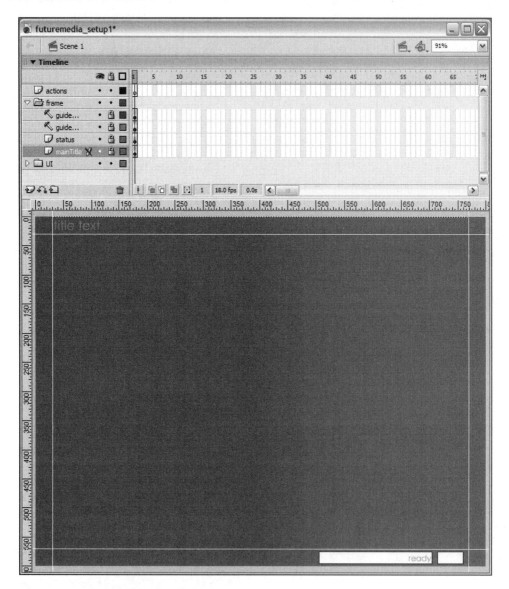

Not much to look at for sure, but its still early days. The ugly duckling will transform itself into that beautiful swan soon. Don't worry, it won't take all winter for this bird. . . .

More important than the appearance of this rather drab FLA, you'll by now have started to appreciate the major difference between working with Flash tweens (as you may have done in this book's sister work, *Foundation Flash*), where you can do everything to "by eye" and the much more precise world of ActionScript, which even seeps into the graphics associated with the scripts.

Summary

In this chapter you've looked at how ActionScript uses variables as containers for information you want to use in your movies. You've also covered the different types of values that a variable can store:

- Strings
- Numbers
- Booleans

You explored the differences between literal values and expressions, and you saw how to communicate with a user via string values and text fields. I then talked about rules for how you name your variables, so that they're acceptable to Flash and useful to you. You went on to look at working with numeric values (for performing calculations) and Boolean values (for storing the result of a true/false expression).

Rounding off the chapter, you looked at how arrays make it easy to store lots of related data together in a neatly structured way, which apart from anything else helps you find it easily!

You now have a good grounding in variables and values. Although you didn't build that many cool FLAs in this chapter, you have a solid foundation to move forward into Chapters 4 and 5, where every new thing you learn will allow you to do something cool and immediately useful. That's what you've built up to by slogging through this chapter!

As you work through the rest of this book, you'll see how variables lie at the heart of virtually all of the most exciting Flash effects you can create. Have a little break and get ready for Chapter 4.

Chapter 4

MOVIES THAT DECIDE
FOR THEMSELVES

What we'll cover in this chapter:

- Getting Flash to look at a situation and decide what to do based on what it sees
- Using sausage notation (or, "How I learned to stop worrying and love brackets")
- Giving Flash the intelligence to check passwords

So far, you've looked at a few simple ways to control Flash movies using actions, event handlers, and variables. The actions are like commands, telling Flash what to do. The event handlers are just sets of actions that get triggered by events from the movie so that Flash can respond in real time to things like button presses and entering a new frame. Variables give Flash memory so that you can store information away for when you need it later on.

Already, that gives you quite a lot to play with, but it's not without problems. Think about the last couple of examples from Chapter 3. When you made your "times by two" movie, you had to set up the input text field so that it would only accept numbers and dots. Otherwise, it might end up trying to double the value of "platypus," which wouldn't make sense at all!

That's cool, though—you dealt with it. But what about the array of movie titles? It works OK if you put in 1, 2, or 3, but it doesn't give you a bean if you try 4, 5, or 6. Who cares? Well, whoever's using your movie list will care if they're expecting to see something and they see nothing. At least you could put up a sign that says "Sorry, but this array doesn't list movies made after 1963."

This might not seem like much, but it's not something you can do with the tools you've seen so far. What you need is a way to **test** whether the input's good or not, and then **act on the result**. To put it in plain English, Flash needs to **make a decision** about what to do.

Decision making

Real-life decisions are rarely as simple as

I'll go to the open-air rock concert if it's not raining.

You're probably far more likely to think

If I have enough money, and it's not raining, I'll go to the open-air rock concert. But if I get home late from work, I won't be able to afford the time.

Your decision now is based not only on whether you'll get wet if you go to the concert, but also on whether you have enough money and can spare the time.

These sorts of issues are just as important when you're making decisions in ActionScript. You need to consider exactly what your conditions are, what should happen if they're met, and what should happen if they're not met.

OK, you may already know what you want to say, but that doesn't mean you know how to state your conditions in a way that Flash is going to understand. Say you write your concert dilemma out like this:

> *if (it's not raining) {go to the concert}*

Er . . . what's with all those brackety things? Well, you've already used the parentheses, (and), to pass arguments to actions—gotoAndStop(10), for example. They're information you give to an action to help it do its job. The curly braces, { and }, should look familiar too—when you learned to write callbacks back in Chapter 1, you used them around all the event handler actions. They represent a **code block**, which is simply a set of lines that are executed together.

> *I don't know about you, but I need silly ways to remember things. The way I think of this rather complicated syntax is as a string of sausages, with the contents of each set of brackets being a sausage. To make each sausage, you have to have a corresponding sausage start and end.*

As you saw, though, the real problem is a little more complex than that:

> *if (if I have enough money and it's not*
> ➥ *raining on the day and I can afford*
> ➥ *the time)*
> *{go to the concert}*

If you were programming this decision, you'd go through exactly this process. Writing a decision down on paper in the same way I've done here will help you to make sure you've considered all the conditions that need to be met.

Making decisions in ActionScript: The if action

So what about making this work for real? It's all very well having this **sausage notation** for working things out, but it's not much help if you can't use it in a movie.

Well, you're actually not so far off from using it in a movie. The **condition** (that is, the bit you place between the parentheses, (and)) can only ever be true or false. If it's true, you go to the concert. If it's false, you don't. Simple as that.

Now, if you can manage to stretch your mental faculties back to the previous chapter, you may recall looking briefly at Boolean variables. These can only ever hold two values: true and false. What's more, you looked at a couple of ways to generate true and false values, using > (greater than) and < (less than) to test whether one number was bigger or smaller than another.

> *Here's a tip for those not familiar with greater than and less than signs. The small end of the < and > characters always points to the smaller number and the big end always points to the bigger number when the statement is true. Thus, a > b is true if a is bigger than b, and a < b is true if a is smaller than b.*

So, once you've worked out an expression that gives you a true or false result, you can store it in a Boolean variable and use that Boolean (or even just the expression itself) as a condition. If the condition is met (i.e., the value is true), then Flash has to do something. If the condition isn't met (i.e., the value is false), then Flash doesn't have to do that something.

Let's add that information into the sausage notation. Assume you've already defined some Boolean variables like this:

```
var haveEnoughMoney:Boolean = true;
var notRaining:Boolean = true;
var affordTheTime:Boolean = true;
```

You know that && is something you can use to check whether one Boolean **AND** another are both true. Handily, you can even string several together to check whether one AND another AND another are all true, so this is what you could end up with:

```
if (haveEnoughMoney && notRaining &&
➡ affordTheTime)
  {go to the concert}
```

If any of the Booleans are set to false, you'll be staying in!

What about telling Flash to go to the concert? How does that shape up ActionScript-wise? That's going to depend on what your movie actually does. Maybe you're going to send a little stick man running up to a big stage, where he joins the screaming masses. Or maybe you're just going to make a little message appear that says "go to the concert". Well, the first one would look more impressive, but the second one would be quicker!

```
if (haveEnoughMoney && notRaining &&
➡ affordTheTime)
  {trace("go to the concert");}
```

If you want to make your own movie that shows a man running up to join the crowd, then you can write actions to make it do that. The important thing to remember is that you can put *any actions you like* in here, and Flash will perform them for you, but *only if the condition is true.*

So how do you make this into proper ActionScript that a movie's going to understand? You don't have to change a lot. In fact, if you type it in exactly as it stands, it should work just fine. However, to keep the syntax checker happy, you need to rearrange it ever so slightly:

```
var haveEnoughMoney:Boolean = true;
var notRaining:Boolean = true;
var affordTheTime:Boolean = true;
if (haveEnoughMoney && notRaining &&
affordTheTime) {
    trace("go to the concert");
};
```

91

Just put the opening brace { on the first line, indent the action (to remind you that it's **nested** inside the if statement), put the closing brace } on a line of its own, and add a semicolon ; on the end. Presto!

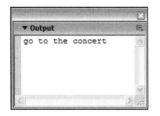

You can see the effects of changing your variables by making one or more of them false. Note that you *won't* get a "don't go to the concert" message; instead, you'll get no message at all.

So, in general, an if statement looks like this:

```
if (condition is true) {
    do this;
    do this;
    do this;
    ...
};
```

The code block (the lines of code within the { }) will run only if the condition is true.

The only structural difference between this and the sausage notation is that ActionScript prefers you to split the sausage itself over several lines.

The sausage notation will help you to write all your programming decision branches in terms that you can use to set things clearly in your mind before you start programming. You even have the bonus that it's written in correct ActionScript syntax, so you can convert it seamlessly into working code. Don't be put off by the silly "sausage" name—it really does help!

Now that you have the basic idea, let's apply this decision-making system to the kind of situation you might encounter when you're thinking out a Flash movie.

Defining a decision

You'll start by expressing your decision as simply and precisely as possible, in order to get a clear idea of what you want the code to do.

Say you're writing a game of space invaders in which the player controls a ship that can fire bullets up at the attacking alien hordes. In particular, you're considering the situation when the bullet has been fired (signified by bulletFired = true) and is moving up the screen (at a speed controlled by the numeric value of bulletSpeed). If it hasn't already reached the top of the screen (where the y-coordinate is 0), you want to move it further up. If it's *at* the top, you want to stop moving the bullet, remove it from the screen, and set bulletFired to false, indicating that the player is allowed to fire again. The value of variable bullet_y denotes the bullet's height at any point in time.

When you're faced with such a longwinded problem, there's only one way to simplify it: lose some of the words. The easiest way to do this is to draw a picture, which automatically drops your word count to zero:

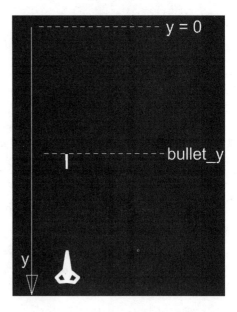

The player's ship is at the bottom of the screen, and the bullet is at some point above it, moving upward. The bullet will always move up in a vertical line, so only its y-coordinate will change, decreasing as it moves up the screen until it reaches the top and has a y-coordinate of 0.

You're now concerned with building a framework of decisions that will result in this behavior. You need to consider two questions:

1. How does the bullet behave when it's on the screen?

2. How does the bullet behave when it first goes off the top of the screen?

bulletSpeed is a variable that you'll use to hold a number that will tell Flash how many pixels to move the bullet up the screen. Each time the script runs, this value will be subtracted from the bullet's y-coordinate position, moving it to a new position. Making it large will make the bullet move quickly; making it small will make the bullet move slowly.

The y-coordinate of the bullet, bullet_y, starts off as a positive value and reaches 0 when it gets to the top of the screen. In other words, bullet_y will be positive before it hits the top and negative once it's gone off the screen.

- If bullet_y is positive, the bullet is on the screen and you should keep subtracting bulletSpeed so that the bullet moves upward.

- As soon as bullet_y is less than 0, you no longer need to animate the bullet, although you need it to disappear. You could make it disappear in a number of ways, but the easiest is to place it offscreen, say at bullet_y = -100. Also, once the bullet is off the screen, the player should be allowed to fire again, so you need to tell Flash this by making bulletFired = false.

So, your decision making breaks down into two branches. This is how they look in sausage notation:

> *if (the bullet is being fired and its*
> ➡ *y-coordinate is greater than 0)*
> *{move the bullet}*

and

> *if (the bullet is being fired and its*
> ➡ *y-coordinate is less than 0)*
> *{hide bullet and let user fire another}*

So what happens if the bullet isn't being fired? Well, neither of these branches will be relevant, and neither will do anything. In fact, that's just what you want: if bulletFired = false, the bullet should be safely hidden away above the top of the screen, and that's just where you want it to stay!

Let's put some variables into sausage notation:

> *if (bulletFired is true and bullet_y is*
> ➡ *greater than 0)*
> *{set bullet_y equal to bullet_y minus*
> ➡ *bulletSpeed}*

and

> *if (bulletFired is true and bullet_y is*
> ➡ *less than 0)*
> *{set bulletFired equal to false, set*
> ➡ *bullet_y to -100}*

Now you just need to convert this into proper ActionScript syntax. This is easy enough to do:

```
if (bulletFired && bullet_y > 0) {
    bullet_y = bullet_y - bulletSpeed;
};
```

and

```
if (bulletFired && bullet_y < 0) {
    bulletFired = false;
    bullet_y = -100;
};
```

There are several things to note about how I've written out the conditions here:

- Each condition is completely contained within the parentheses ( ).

This shouldn't come as a particular surprise, since that's how you did it before, but be warned! When you start using more complex conditions (with their own sub-terms in parentheses), it's all too easy to forget that *the condition as a whole* needs to be contained.

- I've replaced the subcondition bulletFired is true with bulletFired.

You may want to think about this for a moment. Just as you can use < and > to test whether one value is bigger or smaller, you can use == to test whether two values are the same. So why not do the obvious thing and replace `bulletFired is true` with `bulletFired == true`?

Well, `bulletFired == true` would only ever be true if `bulletFired` itself was true. Likewise, it would only ever be false if `bulletFired` itself were false. What this proves is that `bulletFired` will *always* have the same value as `bulletFired == true`, so one is just as good as the other. It should be fairly obvious which one looks neatest!

> *One more thing to consider is that the y-coordinate of –100 (which you use to put the bullet well clear of the visible screen) is a fairly arbitrary value. It's obvious what it does now, but 6 months from now you might find yourself asking, "What's that –100 doing in there?"*
>
> *The obvious way to make things clearer is to add a comment by this line. Another way to clarify is by using a descriptively named variable, such as HIDE. At the beginning of the game you could set HIDE to –100, and then in the main code you could make statements like `bullet_y = HIDE`, which makes what this value represents explicit. The fact that a variable name is in CAPITAL LETTERS also implies that it's a **constant** value—one that won't change.*

Password protection part 1: Setting up the stage

Let's walk through a simple example and put all this theory into practice. I've built a techno-gothic screen whose sole purpose is to extract a password from the user. If the user fails at this point, he or she won't be allowed to enter the rest of my site.

> *It's important to note here that this isn't a secure system. It's a good example of conditions, but don't think this will lock ne'er-do-well hackers out of your site for more than 10 seconds!*

1. Open `password_start.fla` from this chapter's download bundle. It consists of some basic graphics, a text field, and a button, and it uses the font OCR–Extended. What this movie *doesn't* have is the ActionScript required to make it run—that's where you come in!

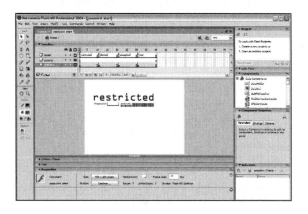

If you want to use the OCR–Extended font in your own movies, you should have no trouble picking it up from most free font sites. If you can't find it elsewhere, try the newsgroup `alt.binaries.fonts`. I've always found the folks on this newsgroup to be a pretty decent and helpful bunch, and someone there has always pointed me to exactly what I wanted whenever I've been looking for some fairly specific fonts.

> *For the download files, I've applied* Modify ➤ Break Apart *a couple of times (breaking all my type into shapes) and then grouped them together (for ease of use). You should therefore be able to see the screens just as I designed them, whether or not you have this specific font installed on your machine.*

2. Select frame 1 in the timeline, and you'll find the following screen (which is defined on the graphics layer):

There are two active items on this screen. The hollow rectangle is an input text field, where a user can enter his or her password. The text that reads _execute is actually a button, which the user will click after entering his or her password. Right now, neither one is configured, so that's the first thing you need to change.

3. Select the input text field and use the Properties panel to configure it like the following one. In particular, set the instance name to password_txt, set the line type drop-down to Password (so that Flash displays only asterisks in the text field when you type into it), and click the Show Border Around Text icon (so that the user knows where the text field is).

A	Input Text ⌄	A	Arial ⌄
	password_txt	A͟v 0 ⌄	A⥮ Normal ⌄
🔒	W: 63.0 X: 126.0	A	Password ⌄ AB̲ ⟷ ▤
	H: 17.4 Y: 119.7		

4. Now select the button and set its instance name to execute_btn:

👆	Button ⌄	Instance of: execute button
	execute_btn	Swap... Track as Button ⌄
🔒	W: 57.0 X: 194.3	
	H: 8.8 Y: 124.7	

The stage is all set up now, so you just need to wire it up to some ActionScript so that your active items can actually do something. Let's pause for a moment and consider what you're trying to achieve.

Once the user has entered a valid password, I want to take him or her to the next stage of the movie, which will start at frame 21. I've used the Properties panel to label this frame as accepted. This is the point where my site proper would begin, and this is what the user will see:

Before I let the user get this far, though, I want to check whether he or she has used the correct password. This needs to be checked just as soon as the user clicks the _execute button in frame 1, so that's where I need to attach the ActionScript that will make the system work. Let's work out that ActionScript now.

I need to make Flash look at what input the user gives me via the contents of password_txt, password_txt .text, and compare it with a predefined password. If they're the same, Flash will let the user into the site.

In recognition of one of my favorite films, I've decided that the password will be "I am the One". Also, to make life easier for the user, I'll make the password case-insensitive, so the user can enter I Am The One, or I am the one, or any combination of uppercase and lowercase letters.

Expressed in my shorthand, the decision I need to make here is as follows:

```
if (the lower case version of the text in
➡ myPass is "i am the one")
  {go to the "accepted" frame}
```

> Irrespective of what the user inputs, the text will be converted to lowercase before I make the comparison, so it doesn't matter if the user types I am the One or I AM THE ONE. The user will still be the One either way.

> This is a slightly different use of the gotoAndStop() action from what you've seen in the past, but the end result is the same: Flash jumps to the specified frame and stops there.

Note that I'm not considering what will happen if the password provided isn't a good match. In that event (for now, at least) I don't want to do anything. In ActionScript, I need to write

```
lowerCasePass = password_txt.text.
➥ toLowerCase();
if (lowerCasePass == "i am the one") {
  gotoAndStop("accepted");
};
```

The first line sets a variable called lowerCasePass to a lowercase version of the contents of password_txt (which is password_txt.text), which I get by sticking .toLowerCase() onto the end of it. At this stage, you don't really need to worry about *how* this works; just remember *what* it does and that the case of the letters the user enters for his or her password now doesn't matter.

The next three lines of code make up my decision-making system—that is, I have the structure I wanted:

```
if (something) {
  do this;
}
```

Note that my something expression uses the double equal sign == that I mentioned earlier. This is the **equality operator**, which tests whether the terms on either side have the same value. It will return true only if lowerCasePass has exactly the same value as the string "i am the one". If that *is* the case, the do this section will be executed, so the movie will jump to the frame I've labeled as accepted.

I don't want this script to be executed as soon as the movie starts—after all, I need to give the user a chance to enter his or her password first! Since I want it to run just after the execute_btn button has been clicked, it makes sense to put it into a function to be triggered by that button's onRelease event. Basically, I'm going to turn my code into an event handler and attach it to a callback for the execute_btn.onRelease event:

```
execute_btn.onRelease = function() {
  lowerCasePass = password_txt.text.
➥ toLowerCase();
  if (lowerCasePass == "i am the one") {
    gotoAndStop("accepted");
  }
};
var lowerCasePass:String = "";
stop();
```

Note that I've also had to tell the movie to stop, otherwise it would run straight on to the next page, whether or not the user entered a password, valid or not! I've also defined the variable lowerCasePass to be of type String. (Remember that although you can omit this line, it's a good idea to have it because it makes your code more robust in the long run.)

Password protection part 3: Wiring up the code

Now you're ready to plug this code into the movie and give it a test run.

1. Use the Timeline panel to select the first frame in the actions layer.

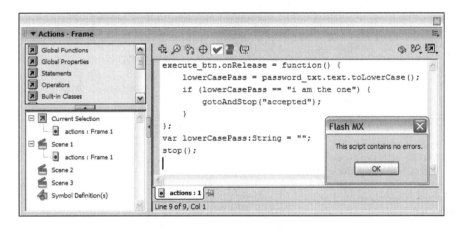

2. Now open the Actions panel, type in the code, and click the check syntax button to confirm that it's good to go.

3. You're now ready to test the movie. Choose Control ➤ Test Movie or press *CTRL/CMD+ENTER*. Type the password into the input text field. (You'll see each character represented by an asterisk, so that no one can see what you've typed. For the curious, this is achieved by selecting Password from the Properties panel for the text type, but the FLA has this set for you already).

4. Now click the _execute button. Assuming you typed in the password correctly, you'll now see the accepted message shown here:

Alternative actions

So what happens if you enter the wrong password? The answer: nothing at all. In fact, until you key in a valid password, it will look for all intents and purposes as though the _execute button is broken! If you've ever come across this kind of behavior, you know how frustrating it can be—you've typed in your password, but the movie/website/application still won't run properly and doesn't even hint at what's wrong.

Ideally, you should give the user some feedback when his or her password is invalid, and that means taking another look at your decision-making code. Here's the important bit as it stands, first in my sausage notation, and then in ActionScript:

```
if (the text in lowerCasePass is
➡ "i am the one")
  {go to the 'accepted' frame}

  if (lowerCasePass == "i am the one") {
    gotoAndStop("accepted");
  }
```

The most obvious way to deal with an invalid password is to add another if structure on the end, like this:

```
if (the text in lowerCasePass is
➡ "i am the one")
  {go to the 'accepted' frame}
if (the text in lowerCasePass is not
➡ "i am the one")
  {go to the 'denied' frame}

  if (lowerCasePass == "i am the one") {
    gotoAndStop("accepted");
  }
  if (lowerCasePass != "i am the one") {
    gotoAndStop("denied");
  }
```

That's another new symbol for you: just as == means "is equal to," != means "is not equal to." So, in the second if statement, the condition is true only if the text is **not** equal to your password. This works OK, but it's a bit of a waste of time—you're basically spelling out the same condition twice. It would be much easier just to write this:

```
if (the text in lowerCasePass is
➡ "i am the one")
  {go to the 'accepted' frame}
otherwise
  {go to the 'denied' frame}
```

Don't go looking for the otherwise action, though, because it doesn't exist. Flash uses else to do this:

```
if (lowerCasePass == "i am the one") {
  gotoAndStop("accepted");
} else {
  gotoAndStop("denied");
}
```

Acting on alternatives: The else action

The else action tells Flash to execute the attached commands whenever the if condition turns out to be false. The code you've just seen is a good example of the commonest sort of choice you'll find in programming. You have a condition with two possible outcomes (in this case, the password is either valid or it isn't), and you define an appropriate course of action for each one.

Access denied: Using the else action

Let's add this useful little nugget into the password movie.

1. Use the Timeline panel to select the first frame in the actions layer again.

2. Add the new lines of code into the Script pane of Actions panel, and click the check syntax button to check the syntax:

```
execute_btn.onRelease = function() {
  lowerCasePass = password_txt.text.
➡ toLowerCase();
  if (lowerCasePass == "i am the one") {
    gotoAndStop("accepted");
  } else {
    gotoAndStop("denied");
  }
};
var lowerCasePass:String = "";
stop();
```

3. You can now press *CTRL*/*CMD*+*ENTER* to test run the movie again.

4. Try clicking the _execute button when there's no text in the password box. You should now see the access denied message:

Great! That's just what you wanted. The only problem now is that you can't get back to the original screen to try again. Let's fix that right away.

5. Select frame 20 on the actions layer (see below). This is the last frame containing the access denied message. Press *F6* to create a keyframe here.

6. Now open the Actions panel and attach the following code to the new keyframe:

```
gotoAndStop("restricted");
```

As soon as the playhead reaches frame 20, this action will send you back to the original screen.

7. This is no good, though, unless frame 20 actually gets played, so you need to make a slight change to the original code. Specifically, gotoAndStop ("denied") needs to become gotoAndPlay ("denied"). Select frame 1 in the actions layer and make this change so that your Actions panel looks like the following (I've also closed the panes to the left of the Script pane by clicking the little left-facing arrow at the left side of the pane):

```
▼ Actions - Frame
execute_btn.onRelease = function() {
    lowerCasePass = password_txt.text.toLowerCase();
    if (lowerCasePass == "i am the one") {
        gotoAndStop("accepted");
    } else {
        gotoAndPlay("denied");
    }
};
var lowerCasePass:String = "";
stop();

  actions : 1
Line 11 of 11, Col 1
```

8. Press *CTRL/CMD+ENTER* again, and test the movie with no password again. This time, you should find that the access denied message is shown for less than a second before it returns you to the password entry screen. Problem solved!

More than one alternative: The else if action

Let's think about how you might improve this system even further. What if you wanted to create a special section of the site for executive users, to whom you've given a different password? If you take a look at

frames 31 through 40, you'll see that I've already made a screen (labeled neo) to welcome these VIPs:

You'll also need to pick a separate, executive password (I've chosen the word "Neo") and some more ActionScript to check whether it's been entered. You'll use some more sausage notation to confirm what you're doing:

```
if (lowerCasePass is "i am the one")
    {go to 'accepted' frame}
otherwise, if (lowerCasePass is "neo")
    {go to 'neo' frame}
otherwise
    {go to 'denied' frame}
```

You might have guessed from this that the ActionScript you need to make this happen looks like this:

```
if (lowerCasePass == "i am the one") {
    gotoAndStop("accepted");
} else if (lowerCasePass == "neo") {
    gotoAndStop("neo");
} else {
    gotoAndPlay("denied");
}
```

You effectively combine the else and if actions so that you can test for another condition if the first one isn't met. Of course, if neither one is met, you'll end up running the else command just like before. All it really means is "if the last condition tested was false, check if this one's true."

In fact, ActionScript treats else if as an action in its own right, and there are things you can do with an else if that you can't do with a plain else.

For example, you can put as many else if actions as you want after an initial if action, making Flash check if any number of conditions have been met (are true):

```
if (a) {
    do this;
} else if (b) {
    do this;
} else if (c) {
    do this;
} else if (d) {
    do this;
}
```

Breaking this down a little, consider the following:

```
if (a) {
    do this;
} else if (b) {
```

Flash will start by looking at the first condition, a. If it's true, Flash will carry out the associated {do this;} action (or series of actions) and then skip past the rest of the if...else if...else block. If a is false, though, Flash moves straight on to the next else if, which tells it to check if b is true.

Then, if b is true, Flash runs the associated {do this;} action and skips to the end of the block. It won't check c or d, and it won't run c or d's {do this;} action, **even if** c **or** d **is true**.

> This is an essential fact to understand, because it shows the importance of the order in which you enter your else if actions. If several conditions are satisfied, only the first one in the list will ever be acted on.

If, on the other hand, b is false, Flash moves on to c, and so on, and so on. You need to always remember that **only one** of your if/else if/else commands will run, and that it will be the first one in the list whose condition is true.

So, why not just use a string of separate if structures? Well, it's largely a matter of efficiency: once a condition within an else if command has been found to be true, Flash won't bother checking any of the subsequent else if conditions—it just follows the appropriate instruction. If you used separate if actions, you'd force Flash to check every single one, even after it had found a condition that had been met. If you want only one result, this is going to put a completely unnecessary strain on Flash and possibly slow down your movie.

Essentially, as you go down the ladder of else if actions, you're finding out what *isn't* true and then homing in on what *is* true by asking more and more precise questions based on what you know it *might be*.

Imagine that you're writing a piece of code that controls how a diving space invader attacks the player on its way down the screen, and you want to make your space invader do different things as it gets closer to the player's ship. You could write your decision like this:

```
if (distance is greater than 50)
    {make alien stay in formation}
else if (distance is greater than 25)
    {make alien start to fire on the ship
➥ and dive in a random downward direction}
else if (distance is greater than 10)
    {execute kamikaze tactics}
```

If the first condition in the if action is found to be false, you can deduce that on the first else if statement the distance is less than 50, because if it wasn't you wouldn't have gotten this far down the statement. If the condition in the first else if statement is found to be true, you know that the distance must be greater than 25 but less than 50.

> Note that the ordering of the if...else if decisions affects the order in which they're checked. If you put the "greater than 25" decision **after** the "greater than 10" decision, the "greater than 25" bit would never run!

101

So, to make your decision, you're using what you know the distance *isn't* as well as what it *is*.

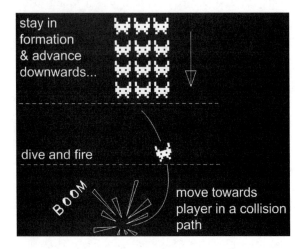

As the demarcation lines used to decide the kamikaze behavior move up the screen, the aliens' scope for attacking will increase as they acquire more room in which to perform their kamikaze maneuvers. So, if you gradually moved the lines upward as the game progressed, your aliens would appear to grow more aggressive over time. It's amazing how much an object's behavior can be modified by changing a single number.

As you can see from this explanation, else if has many more versatile uses than you're exploiting in this simple password exercise.

Speaking of that, let's get back to it now. You'll plug in your else if action so that Flash can distinguish between the two passwords and direct users to the appropriate part of the site.

Executive access: Using else if

Go back to your FLA. Your script should still be in the Actions panel.

1. Select the first frame in the actions layer and add the new lines of code (highlighted in the next listing) to what's already shown in the Script pane of the Actions panel. Remember that the second line converts all passwords to lowercase; this is why

Neo has become neo. Click the check syntax button to check the syntax.

```
execute_btn.onRelease = function() {
  lowerCasePass = password_txt.text.
➥ toLowerCase();
  if (lowerCasePass == "i am the one") {
    gotoAndStop("accepted");
  } else if (lowerCasePass == "neo") {
    gotoAndStop("neo");
  } else {
    gotoAndPlay("denied");
  }
};
var lowerCasePass:String = "";
stop();
```

2. Press *CTRL/CMD+ENTER* to test-run the movie again, and try the new password:

3. Click the _execute button and you should see the neo message:

You can find this complete version saved as `password_finished.fla` in the chapter download.

You've now looked at every stage of the if...else if...else cycle and considered the decisions that Flash makes at each point along the way. Hopefully, you're now starting to get an idea for just how much flexibility these decision-making structures can give your Flash movies. They don't just act and react—they can take a different course of action for each circumstance you plan for.

There's one more way to make decisions using ActionScript. While it doesn't actually do anything new, this method can be a lot tidier (not to mention shorter and more readable) than the `if...else if...else` cycle you've used so far.

Handling lots of alternatives: The switch action

When you last saw the password script, the meat of it looked like this:

```
lowerCasePass = password_txt.text.
➥ toLowerCase();
if (lowerCasePass == "i am the one") {
  gotoAndStop("accepted");
} else if (lowerCasePass == "neo") {
  gotoAndStop("neo");
} else {
  gotoAndPlay("denied");
}
```

It doesn't exactly take a degree in rocket science to guess what this does. Take out all the parentheses and braces, swap "is equal to" for the `==` symbols, swap "otherwise" for `else`, and stick it all on one line. Bingo! You've got something that's pretty close to plain English:

- If `lowerCasePass` is equal to "i am the one", go to accepted and stop there.

- Otherwise, if `lowerCasePass` is equal to "neo", go to neo and stop there.

- Otherwise, go to denied and play from there.

That's perfect for this situation: it's simple, concise, and easy to understand. Believe it or not, rule number one of good programming says that *all* code should aim to be these three things. Maybe someone should tell the programmers that!

In real life, though, you might want to add more users to the system, each with his or her own password, and each with his or her own set of actions to perform once he or she enters the password. In that case, you could end up with a great long string of `else if (lowerCasePass == "something")` terms. That's not so

bad in itself, but it does mean that you're testing the value of `lowerCasePass` over and over and over.

When that happens, it's worth considering using the switch action instead. Let's take a look at the `if...else if...else` password testing script when it's written out using switch:

```
switch (lowerCasePass) {
    case "i am the one":
            gotoAndStop("accepted");
            break;
    case "neo":
            gotoAndStop("neo");
            break;
    default:
            gotoAndPlay("denied");
}
```

Hmm. It's a bit further away from plain English than our ifs and elses. So what does it mean?

Let's take it one line at a time:

```
switch (lowerCasePass) {
```

The switch() action is very similar to if(), in that it uses a sausagelike arrangement of parentheses and curly braces. The big difference here is that you don't put a condition (something that will give you a true or false value) inside the parentheses. Instead, you put in a variable on its own (in this case, switch (lowerCasePass)).

So how does Flash know whether or not to run the actions inside the curly braces? The answer is that Flash doesn't need to: **it runs the actions in the curly braces anyway**.

OK, you're shaking your head now. Supper's ready, and this is all getting a bit strange. Just bear with me a moment longer, because this is the clever bit that will one day make your ActionScripting chores seem a hundred times easier!

When you take a look at what's inside the brackets, you'll see it doesn't look like anything you've seen before. There are a couple of new terms, case and break, plus colons : dotted around all over the place. What does it all mean?

Well, the first thing Flash sees when it starts running the actions is this line:

```
case "i am the one":
```

This line basically says "check whether the string "i am the one" is the same as what's being stored in the switch variable." In this case, the switch variable is lowerCasePass. If the string is the same as what's stored in the switch variable, then Flash runs the actions following the colon.

> This case *thing isn't actually an action, but a special* **keyword** *that helps the* switch *action to do its job. This might not seem like much of a distinction, but it's important to remember. If you try using* case *outside the curly braces of a* switch *statement, Flash won't understand what you mean.*

Let's look at what Flash sees when it starts going through those actions. First up:

```
gotoAndStop("accepted");
```

That's safe enough. We know what that does already. What about the next line, though?

```
break;
```

This action simply tells Flash to ignore the rest of the actions inside the curly braces. If the switch variable lowerCasePass *does* contain the string "i am the one", then you're all done now.

What if it doesn't then? Well, you continue through the contents of the curly braces.

No prizes for guessing what happens if the switch variable contains the string "neo"! The next line primes Flash for precisely that situation:

```
case "neo":
```

and then follows up with actions to run in that case:

```
gotoAndStop("neo");
break;
```

Finally, you set up a default case:

```
default:
    gotoAndPlay("denied");
```

Note that you don't need to use the case keyword here. You can think of default as being a bit like case's poverty-stricken cousin: they're both keywords that mean something only when they're used inside a switch statement. But while case is very fussy about the value of the switch variable, default sits at the bottom of the pile and grabs anything and everything that case lets through to it.

It's quite tempting to describe this default section as "what happens if none of the other cases work out." That's certainly what happens in this particular example; if either of the cases were good, you'd have hit a break by now and wouldn't even be considering the default case.

But what if you take the breaks out?

```
switch (lowerCasePass) {
    case "i am the one':
            gotoAndStop("accepted");
    case "neo":
            gotoAndStop("neo");
    default:
            gotoAndPlay("denied");
}
```

Zoinks! Even shorter than before, but is it actually what you want?

Say you have the value "i am the one" stored in lowerCasePass. You hit the first case statement, it sees a good match, and it gives you the thumbs up to run the subsequent actions. The playhead gets told to jump ahead to the accepted frame and stop there, but the ActionScript continues running.

When you hit the next case statement, Flash doesn't bother checking! You're already past security—and it really can't be bothered to throw you out now—so the fact that you're not "neo" doesn't stop you from seeing the playhead ordered to the neo frame.

That's pretty bad news, but there's worse to come! Flash is not content with letting you into the executive area of the site on the strength of a standard password. When you hit the default case, it will throw you out of the site regardless!

OK, I think you've established that's **not** what you want. But that's not to say you should never consider taking out the breaks—it's just that in this case you really do need them.

> *Before we move on from* switch, *it's worth mentioning that the* switch/case/default *structure is actually converted to* if *structures in the final SWF—the Flash player doesn't know anything about* switch *because it never sees it.*
>
> *The* switch *structure is more compact and easier to read than the same thing stated in* if, *especially if you have lots of nested decisions to be made (as you'll see in the next example). The downside to using* switch *is that the* if *structure is closer to the final compiled code that will live in the SWF, and it's easier to create optimized code if you only use* ifs—*something that you'll want to do if you're writing processor-intensive applications like Flash games.*

Before we finish off the chapter, let's look at another example of decision making in a Flash movie in which it *does* make sense to use a switch statement that doesn't have any breaks.

Switching without breaks

Just for a few pages, let's go back to school. Say you're creating a Flash movie that's going to let members of a college faculty access records. You can assume there are several different member types to allow for; for simplicity's sake, you'll just consider students, professors, and the head of the faculty.

- Students will want a link to timetables, lab allocations, and so on.
- Professors want a link to all the things students have access to, plus hall bookings, staff allocations, and so on.

- The faculty head wants all of the above, plus a detailed rundown of the faculty's financial status (and maybe links to stock prices for all the companies he or she has poured faculty money into over all the years . . .).

The important thing about this situation is that the information you give to each group isn't always **exclusive** to that group. In the password-handling movie, you always wanted to send the user to one frame *or* another, *or* another, but never to more than one.

In this example, you're dealing with basic faculty information about stuff like lecture timetables, and you want to make that information available to **everyone**. Then there's staff administration stuff that everyone *except* the students needs to know about. Finally, there's key financial information that the head of faculty wants to keep to him- or herself.

If you tried scripting this with an if...else if...else structure, it would look a bit of a mess:

```
if (user is a student)
  { show student info }
else if (user is a professor)
  { show staff info, show student info }
else if (user is the faculty head)
  { show accounts, show staff info, show
➥ student info }
else
  { tell user that this site is not for
➥ them }
```

It will work, but there's lots of pointless repetition in there. Just for a start, there are three lots of show student info, each one of which might consist of *loads* of separate actions.

The answer is to use a switch structure, just like the one you used before, but without any breaks:

```
switch (type of user) {
    case "head of faculty": show accounts
    case "professor": show staff info
    case "student": show student info
    default: tell user that this site is
➥ not for them
}
```

You start by finding out what type of user you're dealing with. For the sake of keeping the example simple and flexible, assume that this is something the user just types in.

> *Of course, in practice that's the **last thing** you'd want to do, since any old John Doe typing in* head of faculty *could then sneak a peek at privileged information! While security is an important issue to be aware of, it's a bit of a red herring while you're still on the learning slopes—that is, unless you're planning to try and base a real "secure" site on these very simple examples, which I wouldn't recommend for a millisecond!*

If the user claims to be the head of faculty, the first case statement shows the user a link to the faculty accounts page. If not, the user doesn't see the accounts.

Either way, you then move on to the second case statement. If you're dealing with a professor (or someone who's already been successfully cased, such as the head of faculty), Flash then shows a link to the staff info page.

Next, you move on to the third case statement, and if you're dealing with a student (or someone who's already been successfully cased, such as the head of faculty or one of the professors), then that person gets to see a link to the student info page.

Finally, the default action generates a message telling the user to go away. Anyone viewing the movie should see this.

Huh? Surely you don't want to tell bona fide members to go away! This highlights the difference between actions in an else clause within an if...else structure and actions in a default clause within a switch statement:

- An else action will run *only* if all the previous if tests fail.

- A default action will *always* run unless you break out before reaching it.

You don't want faculty members to see the default message, so you need to make sure there's a break somewhere before hitting the default keyword. No problem:

```
switch (type of user) {
    case "head of faculty": show accounts
    case "professor": show staff info
    case "student": show student info,
➡    break
    default: tell user that this site is
➡ not for them
}
```

Since all faculty members get to see the student info, they all get to break out before Flash has a chance to tell them to get lost.

The faculty links page

Now that you have a good idea of how your decision-making script should look, let's put it to work.

> *If you want to bypass all the graphics creation in this exercise and jump straight to the code, you can use the file* faculty_start.fla. *Using this file, you get to skip straight to step 7 in the following exercise.*

1. Open a new movie and click the stage to select it. Now use the Property inspector to set the background color to a pinkish-purple (I've used #CC66FF). Obviously, this isn't essential, but it does help make things look a little less drab!

2. Now rename Layer 1 as background, and add a white box like the one shown in the following image. Select frame 30 and press *F5* to insert a frame there.

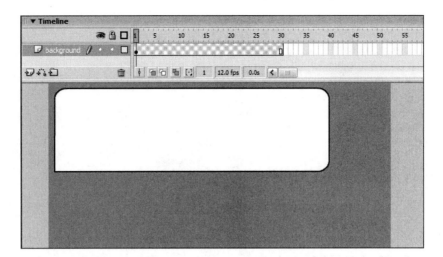

3. Now add a new layer called text. This layer will hold all your instructions for the user. On frame 1, you need to see the following:

Faculty records

What is your position within the faculty?

[   ] **Submit**

At the top of the white box, I've created a couple of static text fields. Underneath, there's an input text field, which I've set up like this:

At the top of the white box, I've created a couple of static text fields. Underneath, there's an input text field, which I've set up like this:

Note that I've selected the Show Border Around Text icon and named the instance input_txt. There's also a Submit button (which I've subtly recycled from Chapter 3's calculator movie) whose instance name is, predictably enough, submit_btn.

4. Still on layer text, select frame 10 and press *F6* to add a keyframe. You can delete the input field and the button from this frame, and change the text in the lower static field so that it looks like this:

Faculty records

Select the page you would like to view:

5. Add another keyframe at frame 20 and change the lower text again, so that it looks like this:

Faculty records

You're not permitted to view our records.

No prizes for guessing what this screen is for!

6. Now it's time to add some frame labels so that the gotoAndStop() actions you're going to use for navigation don't get too abstract. Create a new layer called labels and use the Properties panel to create and label keyframes at frame 1, 10 and 20 called start, select and denied as shown in the following timeline:

7. Now for another layer, called links. This is where the actual link buttons are going to sit. There are four of them, each based on its own button symbol in the Library. Again, I've based them on the calculator buttons from Chapter 3:

Because these buttons will have to go over the Submit button and text entry field, you may have to hide the text layer while you position your four new buttons:

8. Once you've positioned the buttons on the stage, give them the following instance names: student_btn, staff_btn, finance_btn, and back_btn. I'll leave you to work out which one's which!

If you run the movie at this point, you'll see some very strange behavior—not at all what you'd hope for. Apart from the fact that the movie is cycling through the entire timeline, the link buttons are visible and active all the way through, and they're covering up the input text field! What on earth have you done?

Don't panic. This is all quite intentional and part of the plan. You're going to make use of a nifty little trick that involves making buttons invisible. Now you see them, now you . . . where'd they go?

9. Create another new layer called actions (if you're using faculty_start.fla, this layer will already be there). Don't worry, I promise this will be the last new layer! Select frame 1, call up the Actions panel, and click the pushpin button, just to make sure you don't accidentally attach any script to the wrong place. Now add the script shown here:

```
// Hide the links
student_btn._visible = false;
staff_btn._visible = false;
finance_btn._visible = false;
back_btn._visible = false;
```

Just as you can use _x to control the x-coordinate of an instance on the stage (as you saw in the last chapter), you can use _visible to control its visibility. By setting _visible to false, you can make an instance invisible.

10. Test run the movie again, and you'll see immediately what a difference this makes! It's still looping, though, so add a stop() action to the end of the script before you go on:

```
// Hide the links
student_btn._visible = false;
staff_btn._visible = false;
finance_btn._visible = false;
back_btn._visible = false;
// Stop the movie
stop();
```

Apart from the actual links, your movie offers three ways for a user to interact: via the input text field (where the user states his or her position), the

Submit button (which the user clicks to submit the information he or she entered), and the Back button (which the user clicks to return to the original screen and try again). The input text is automatically stored in the variable userInput, so that's taken care of. You still have a couple of callbacks to write, though.

11. The Back button is the easiest, since all it ever needs to do is send you back to the frame labeled start and stop there. Add the following code above the existing lines:

```
// Callback for 'back' button release
back_btn.onRelease = function() {
    gotoAndStop("start");
};
// Hide the links
student_btn._visible = false;
staff_btn._visible = false;
finance_btn._visible = false;
back_btn._visible = false;
// Stop the movie
stop();
```

*As you may have gathered by now, it's normal to place callbacks before the main code. You might be thinking "Hey, wouldn't it be easier to organize the lines in the order in which they're actually supposed run, with the main code first?" The chosen order is the order in which things need to be **defined** by the code, which isn't exactly the order lines are run.*

*The callbacks are seen by Flash first of all and, although you don't see them run, they still do something: they define the button callbacks. The callbacks actually **run** every time you click the buttons. So, the code is written in the order in which code is actually **required** by Flash: define callbacks first (but don't run them yet), and then run the main code. In fact, the standard ordering of code is as follows:*

Define (callbacks and other similar structures)

Initialize (set initial values for all the variables via var)

Main code (run the main code—everything that's left)

12. The Submit button is more of a challenge. This is what you'll use to trigger your decision-making code (like the _execute button in the earlier examples). The action you want to take for each case is to **show** the relevant button (which will presumably link to some other part of the movie—I'll leave that part to you!). You can achieve this by resetting the button's visibility to true. Hold your breath and add the following code after the back_btn.onRelease callback:

```
// Callback for 'submit' button release
submit_btn.onRelease = function() {
    // Actions to perform in any case
    gotoAndStop("select");
    back_btn._visible = true;
    userType = userInput.toLowerCase();
    // Actions to perform depending on
➡ user type
    switch (userType) {
    case "head" :
        finance_btn._visible = true;
    case "professor" :
        staff_btn._visible = true;
    case "student" :
        student_btn._visible = true;
        break;
    default :
        gotoAndStop("denied");
    }
};
```

OK, you can breathe out now.

Let's go through this carefully—it's not nearly as hard as it looks!

When the user clicks and then releases the Submit button, they trigger off the preceding script, which starts off by shuttling the user on to the select frame. At this point, all the link buttons are still invisible, so the stage looks like this:

Faculty records

Select the page you would like to view:

Next, you make the Back button visible and store the contents of the text field (input_txt.text) in the variable userType. The stage now looks like this:

Faculty records << Back

Select the page you would like to view:

Now it's time to look at the real engine behind this movie. You have a switch action that tests for various different values of userType:

```
    // Actions to perform depending on
➡ user type
    switch (userType) {
    case "head" :
        finance_btn._visible = true;
    case "professor" :
        staff_btn._visible = true;
    case "student" :
        student_btn._visible = true;
        break;
    default :
        gotoAndStop("denied");
    }
```

If the value inputted is head (or any case-based versions of this, such as Head or HEAD), then the movie shows the Finance button and cascades through all the other cases (showing the Staff button and the Student button) before hitting a break.

Similarly, if the value is professor, it shows the Staff button, falls through to show the Student button too, and stops when it hits break.

If the value is student, it shows only the Student button before breaking out.

If the value of userType is none of the above, the default clause sends the user hurtling on to the denied frame, where the user is politely informed that he or she doesn't have permission to view faculty records. None of the link buttons is visible, apart from the Back button, which absentminded professors can use to return to the first screen and try to remember their job titles again.

Here's the full script listing for faculty.fla, which you can find in the download for this chapter:

```
// Callback for 'back' button release
back_btn.onRelease = function() {
  gotoAndStop("start");
};
// Callback for 'submit' button release
submit_btn.onRelease = function() {
  // Actions to perform in any case
  userType = input_txt.text.toLowerCase();
  gotoAndStop("select");
  back_btn._visible = true;
  // Actions to perform depending on
➥ user type
  switch (userType) {
  case "head" :
    finance_btn._visible = true;
  case "professor" :
    staff_btn._visible = true;
  case "student" :
    student_btn._visible = true;
    break;
  default :
    gotoAndStop("denied");
  }
};
// Initialize
var userType:String = "";
// Hide the links
student_btn._visible = false;
staff_btn._visible = false;
finance_btn._visible = false;
back_btn._visible = false;
// Stop the movie
stop();
```

Try the movie out one last time, and you'll find that each different type of user is presented with a different selection of link buttons to choose from:

Summary

This chapter covered a number of ways to make your Flash movies more intelligent by giving them the power to make decisions based on specific circumstances and user input:

- Using `if` and `else` actions, Booleans, and conditions to enable Flash to make decisions and act on them

- Adding `else if` actions to enable Flash to act on a variety of outcomes

- Using `switch` actions with breaks to allow one of a number of options to happen

- Using `switch` actions without breaks to allow several of a number of options to happen

You've designed some simple password systems to show this, although I would like to stress—just one last time—that these methods aren't very secure, so don't go using them commercially!

Once you have your head around these basic ActionScript building blocks, you'll be able to go on and create increasingly intelligent Flash movies with the power to implement intricate decision-making code.

In the next chapter, you'll look at how to write your code so that it works harder for you.

Chapter 5

MORE POWER, LESS SCRIPT

What we'll cover in this chapter:

- Using loops to make Flash repeat actions
- Examining several different kinds of loops
- Using loops with arrays to work on lots of information at once
- Building a hangman game with Flash and ActionScript

It's not exactly headline news, but computers are pretty dumb. Whatever far-fetched dreams we may have once had, the twenty-first century isn't buzzing with the conversation of HAL-9000 supercomputers—well, not yet at least! It's actually chock full of silicon number-crunchers, and (sorry to say) even your shiny new top-of-the-line Power Mac can't hold a candle to the raw intelligence of the simplest human being.

When it's a matter of crunching through commands and figures, though, the computer wins easily, both in terms of speed and accuracy. It's specifically designed to work on large, complicated jobs by breaking them down into gazillions of tiny instructions and getting them all done in the blink of an eye, so it's perfectly suited to repetitive jobs.

By and large, however, it's human programmers who have to tell a computer what to do and when, and they just don't have time to write out *every one* of those gazillions of instructions—especially when there are reruns of *Star Trek* to be watched on TV! And thus it was that **loops** came into being.

> *In Flash, a loop is a command (or a collection of commands) that makes your movie do something (or a collection of somethings) over and over again.*

Don't worry if this statement doesn't immediately make the whole world seem like a better place to live—it's just a definition of the word "loop." I'll spend the rest of the chapter persuading you that loops aren't just useful to Trekkies, but they can save *you* lots of time and effort, and open up some very cool possibilities.

Timeline loops

The simplest way to make a loop in Flash is by using gotoAndPlay() to repeat a section of the timeline. For example, to create a timeline loop, you could label frame 1 as loop and attach gotoAndPlay("loop") to one of the later frames:

When this timeline plays, it will play normally as far as frame 17, see the gotoAndPlay() action, and jump back to frame 1. Then it will play through frames 1 to 17 again before it runs the frame 17 actions again, jumps back to frame 1, and plays from there until it reaches frame 17. And so on, and so on, and so on . . .

So, this will set up a loop between frames 1 and 17, and Flash will quite happily let this repetition go on indefinitely. Of course you might be thinking, "Why bother with a gotoAndPlay() action? Flash normally repeats the timeline anyway." Well, there are lots of very subtle differences I could talk about, but there are a couple reasons that make the rest redundant:

- An automatic timeline loop is simple and dumb. It plays the whole timeline. It plays the whole timeline again. It plays the whole timeline yet again. And so on. What's more, any old user can tweak the player settings to turn it off, which is no good if your movie depends on it!

- A gotoAndPlay() timeline loop puts you, the author of the movie, in control of the looping. You can specify where the loop starts and where it stops, so it doesn't need to loop the entire timeline. You can even have several loops on the same timeline! You can use it within movie clips too. Even better, none of those pesky loop-stopping users can break it.

Timeline looping can be a very useful technique for getting the most out of what's already there on the stage (you can keep repeating a tween, for example), but it doesn't give you much of the value-added interactive power that ActionScript promises.

The real subject of this chapter involves another, quite different approach to looping. Instead of repeating a sequence of frames on the timeline, let's see how you can repeat a set of actions.

ActionScript loops

Loops really come into their own when you start using them to repeat scripts that you've already written. Maybe you have a long list of variables that all need to be tweaked in just the same way or lots of movie clip instances on the stage that all need to be shifted 1 pixel to the left. It's easy to write an action to change one of them and not so hard to write a couple more. By the time you've written 428, though, your energy might be starting to flag a little.

If, on the other hand, you write out your action once and stick it inside an ActionScript loop, you can tell the loop to repeat that action as many times as you like. Yes, it's time to capitalize on the fact that your computer will never get bored doing simple, repetitive jobs!

An ActionScript loop is a totally different beast from a timeline loop. A timeline loop involves playing through a sequence of frames, whereas an ActionScript loop exists entirely within a single frame. The ActionScript loop is defined in the lines of script you've attached to that frame, so Flash will stay on the same frame for as long as those lines are looping.

ActionScript has several looping actions specifically designed to help you out with this sort of thing. They all use the sausage notation you saw in the last chapter, so they hopefully won't look too alien to you.

while loops

A **while loop** is probably the simplest of all ActionScript loops to understand, since it's not much different from a simple if statement:

```
while (condition) {
  do these actions;
}
```

In fact, the only thing that *is* different from an if statement is the name of the action. Well, that and the end result, of course! You give the while loop a condition (something that will *always* turn up either true or false) and some actions to perform **while** the condition is true. Unlike in an if statement, Flash won't stop and move on once it has run the actions; it will perform them over and over and over for as long as the condition is true. It will move on to the next line of script (or the next frame) only when the condition turns out to be false.

That means that something like this:

```
while (false) {
  // actions
};
```

won't do a thing. The condition is always false, so any actions you put in the body will never run. On the other hand, something like this:

```
while (true) {
  // actions
};
```

will kill your movie stone dead! The condition is always true, so the loop goes on forever.

You can try making this happen if you like, but be warned: your computer may lock up for a while when Flash tries to compile the SWF. When Flash spots your mistake, it will show you the following message:

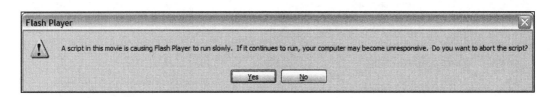

If you do ever see this dialog box, I strongly suggest clicking Yes. Although Flash can detect these "forever" loops, they can still **crash your computer** if you click No and let them run. I've seen the evidence for myself!

Any ActionScript loop that repeats indefinitely can be described as a **forever loop***. These will normally only ever happen if something has gone wrong.*

Useful things to do with while loops

So how can you do something useful with a while loop? Simple: base the condition on a variable, and put actions in the body of the loop that can change that variable. Here's an example:

```
var myCounter:Number = 0;
while (myCounter<10) {
  myCounter++;
}
```

You set up a variable called myCounter, giving it a value of 0. When you start the while loop, the condition you give it basically says "The value of variable myCounter is less than 10." Well, at this stage, that's most certainly true, so you run the actions inside the body of the loop.

There's only one action in the loop body, and while it may look a little odd, it's really nothing special. myCounter++ is just a shorthand way of saying "Add 1 to the number stored in myCounter." So that's what Flash does, just before it reaches the end of the loop.

Since you're still working through a while action, you loop back to the start. myCounter now has a value of 1, so myCounter < 10 is still true. You therefore run myCounter++ and loop back to the start again. And again. And again. This keeps happening until the value of myCounter reaches 9. At that point, you add 1 to the value, loop back to the start, and test whether the new value is less than 10. It's not! Now the condition is false, so Flash can stop looping and move on.

Of course, this just gives you the bare bones of a useful loop—it's not terribly exciting if it just adds lots of 1s to a boring old number variable. Let's flesh things out

so that this simple while loop actually does something practical in a movie.

Making actions run several times in a row

This quick example demonstrates a few of the things it's possible to do with a simple while loop.

1. Create a new Flash document and select frame 1 on the main timeline. Open the Actions panel and click the pushpin button to pin it to the current frame. Now add the following script:

```
var myCounter:Number = 0;
while (myCounter < 10) {
  // actions to loop go here
  myCounter++;
};
```

This is your basic loop, which will run a complete ten cycles.

2. The simplest thing you can do with this is to trace out the value of myCounter for each loop by adding the new line as shown:

```
var myCounter:Number = 0;
while (myCounter < 10) {
  // actions to loop go here
  trace(myCounter);
  myCounter++;
};
```

Run the movie, and sure enough this is what you get in the Output window:

This reminds you that `myCounter` takes values of 0, 1, 2, and so on up to 9, before the loop stops (when it hits 10). It's important to remember that you never actually *see* the value of `myCounter` traced as 10 because the loop stops as soon as it gets to that value.

This business of counting from 0 to 9 instead of counting from 1 to 10 should remind you of something you saw back in Chapter 2: arrays.

As you may recall, a single array can hold lots of different variables—the **elements** of that array. You can tell Flash which element you want to work with by specifying a particular offset number (or **index**). If you use a variable to specify the offset, the element you deal with depends on the variable's value. Then you can pick and choose from the array's elements by changing the value of that offset variable. You still with me?

Anyway, the upshot of this is that you can write generalized code for manipulating array element `i` (where `i` is a variable that contains a number value) and specify the value of `i` quite separately. If you happen to be looping through all possible values of `i`, this approach can be *very* powerful!

3. So let's try using `myCounter` as the offset value used to specify one particular element in an array:

```
var bondMovies:Array = new Array ("Doctor
➡ No","From Russia With Love",
➡ "Goldfinger", "Thunderball");
myCounter = 0;
while (myCounter<10) {
  // actions to loop go here
  trace(bondMovies[myCounter]);
  myCounter++;
}
```

Now you get something more like this:

Instead of just showing the counter value, you're using the counter value to show the first ten values from the bondMovies array. The only problem is that there are just four entries.

4. There's no point in looping ten times if there are only four entries in the array! In fact, you need your loop to loop only for as long as the array element you're looking at has a well-defined value. In other words, you should be looping "while bondMovies[myCounter] is **not undefined**." Sounds like you need to change your loop condition:

```
var bondMovies:Array = new Array("Doctor
➡ No", "From Russia With Love",
➡ "Goldfinger", "Thunderball");
myCounter = 0;
while (bondMovies[myCounter] !=
➡ undefined) {
  // actions to loop go here
  trace(bondMovies[myCounter]);
  myCounter++;
}
```

Run the movie once again, and you'll see that this has done the trick.

As soon as myCounter reaches 4, the while loop spots that bondMovies[myCounter] isn't defined, so the loop cuts out before it gets a chance to trace the word "undefined."

OK, this may seem like pretty cool stuff if you happen to enjoy making lists of movie titles. But what about doing some real Flash stuff?

Using loops to control what's on the stage

This time, you're going to use a similar loop to put a whole set of movie clips on the stage. Along the way, I'll introduce some useful tricks that you haven't seen before for controlling movie clips.

1. Create another new Flash document, make sure the stage is active, and use the Properties panel to give it a black background. In the Timeline panel, rename Layer 1 as particles and create a new layer above it called actions:

2. Select the particles layer and use Insert ➤ New Symbol (or press CTRL/CMD+F8) to create a new movie clip called particle. Now use the Color Mixer panel to set up a radial fill style that fades from opaque white at the center to transparent white at the perimeter:

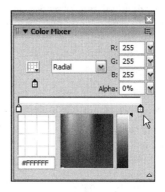

3. Add a circle with no stroke to the particle movie clip. Use the Properties panel to give it a diameter of 80 pixels (W: 80.0, H: 80.0) and place it smack in the center of the stage (X: −40.0, Y: −40.0):

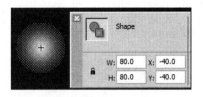

Now click the Scene 1 link to head back to the main timeline.

4. Press *CTRL/CMD+L* to call up the Library panel, and drag the particle item onto the stage to create an instance of the movie clip. Select the instance and use the Properties panel to place it at X: 250, Y: 150. While you're at it, don't forget to give it an instance name: particle_mc.

> *Remember, you always put _mc at the end of a movie clip instance name to remind you (and, more important, Flash) what sort of instance you're dealing with when you refer to it in the script.*

5. Now select frame 1 of the actions layer, open the Actions panel, and click the pushpin button to pin it to the current frame. Now add the following script:

```
var i:Number = 1;
while (i < 10) {
  // actions to loop go here
  i++;
};
```

This is just the same loop as you used before, except that you're using a variable called i as your counter instead of myCounter.

So what about all that stuff I said in Chapter 2 about naming your variables sensibly? OK, this is a bit of an exception. When you're writing actions inside loops, you often end up using the counter variable a lot, for array offsets and other such things. If you call it something like myCounter, these actions can get very long and complex-looking. It's therefore quite common to use a variable called i, j, or k instead. I won't bore you with an explanation of *why* these particular names are used; suffice it to say they hark back to the days of mainframe computers that had just 16KB of memory and needed to use short variable names to save memory. I promise it won't take you long to get used to this little quirk.

6. Now you're going to add an action into your loop that will duplicate the particle movie clip:

```
var i:Number = 1;
while (i < 10) {
  // actions to loop go here
  duplicateMovieClip(particle_mc,
➥ "particle"+i+"_mc", i);
  i++;
};
```

This is something totally new—and very useful! It doesn't take a genius to work out *what* an action called duplicateMovieClip does, but *how it works* is another matter.

This action takes a grand total of three arguments. The first is the instance name of the movie clip you want to duplicate—in this case, it's particle_mc—which doesn't need any quotes around it. The second argument is where you specify what the duplicate should be called. Each instance should have a unique name, so you build this up from two string literals and the counter variable. You're naming each duplicate instance as

```
"particle"+i+"_mc"
```

So when i has a value of 1, this works out as particle1_mc. Likewise, when i has a value of 2, it works out as particle2_mc. And so on up to 9. The third argument tells Flash which **level** to place the duplicate on. The only thing you really need to know about this (for now at least) is that you can have only one movie clip on each level. If you put two on the same level, the second will *replace* the first. You therefore need to change this argument for each new duplicate, so you use the counter variable i again.

The end result is that you wind up with ten duplicates of the particle_mc movie clip instance called particle0_mc, particle1_mc, particle2_mc, and so on. All this from one action inside a loop! Let's do something with them.

> The reason the first argument (the instance name particle_mc) didn't require quotes is that you don't mean the literal string 'particle_mc', *rather you mean the movie clip whose name is* particle_mc. *The former is a literal, and the latter is a* **reference**. *Think of a reference as the same thing as a variable name—it doesn't need quotes.*

7. Now that you have a grand total of 11 movie clip instances on the stage, you can start dragging them around in a variety of weird and wonderful ways. Say you recycle the mouse-following callback you brewed up at the end of Chapter 1:

```
particle_mc.onEnterFrame = function() {
  // move particle to mouse position
  this._x = _xmouse;
  this._y = _ymouse;
};
var i:Number = 0;
while (i<10) {
  // actions to loop go here
  duplicateMovieClip(particle_mc,
➥ "particle"+i+"_mc", i);
  i++;
}
```

> As usual, event handlers go before the main code.

Just pop this on the end of your script, run the movie, wiggle your mouse around, and watch that particle go!

8. Ahem. Well, you now have *one* particle following the mouse around—what about the other ten? Of course, you don't want to write separate actions to control every single one. That would be rather silly now that you have the power of loops to fall back on!

```
particle_mc.onEnterFrame = function() {
  j = 0;
  while (j<10) {
    // move particle to mouse position
    this._x = _xmouse;
    this._y = _ymouse;
    j++;
  }
};
var i:Number = 0;
var j:Number = 0;
while (i<10) {
  // actions to loop go here
  duplicateMovieClip(particle_mc,
➥ "particle"+i+"_mc", i);
  i++;
}
```

The only problem with this is that you're now updating the position of particle_mc ten times over, when you actually want to reposition a *different* instance each time.

9. Ideally, you want to build another string like "particle"+j+"_mc" and use *that* to specify which instance to reposition. Unfortunately, you can't just use this:

```
"particle"+j+"_mc"._x = _xmouse;
```

because Flash will think that you're trying to assign the value of _xmouse to something that isn't a variable or a property. It's not smart enough to spot that you're actually talking about the _x property of an instance called particle0_mc or whatever.

You need to give Flash a helping hand, and this leads straight into the second crafty trick for the day. Instead of writing this:

```
"particle"+j+"_mc"._x = _xmouse;
```

you can write this:

```
_root["particle"+j+"_mc"]._x = _xmouse;
```

The _root bit at the beginning tells Flash to look in the main (or **root**) timeline, and the stuff inside the square brackets [] tells Flash "The thing inside the square brackets [] isn't a literal but a *reference* (or, in plain English, a variable name or instance name)." It's as if _root is an array whose elements hold things like movie clips and use names instead of numbers. Once you've pulled out the element you want, you can use it as normal. Change the event handler as follows:

```
particle_mc.onEnterFrame = function() {
  j = 0;
  while (j < 10) {
    // move particle to mouse position
    _root["particle"+j+"_mc"]._x = _xmouse;
    _root["particle"+j+"_mc"]._y = _ymouse;
    j++;
  };
};
```

Now you'll find that all the duplicates follow your mouse pointer around, while the original sits still in the middle of the stage. Progress to be sure—but you're not done yet!

10. To finish things off, let's stagger the duplicate particles so that they form a blobby line between the original and the current mouse position. The original particle is centered on X:290, Y:190, so you start by working out the x and y differences between this point and the position of the mouse:

```
particle_mc.onEnterFrame = function() {
  // work out distances from
  // center to mouse
  xDist = _xmouse - 290;
  yDist = _ymouse - 190;
```

Now you're ready to move on to your loop, where you'll move each particle to X:290, Y:190 plus j tenths of the distance to the mouse. You also need to (rather, you should) initialize your new variables xDist and yDist:

```
  j = 0;
  while (j < 10) {
    // move particle to center plus
    // j tenths of the distance
    _root["particle"+j+"_mc"]._x = 290
➥ + (xDist * j/10);
    _root["particle"+j+"_mc"]._y = 190
➥ + (yDist * j/10);
    j++;
  };
};
var i:Number = 0;
var j:Number = 0;
var xDist:Number = 0;
var yDist:Number = 0;
while (i<10) {
  // actions to loop go here
  duplicateMovieClip(particle_mc,
➥ "particle"+i+"_mc", i);
  i++;
}
```

This means that particle0_mc will be at the same place as particle_mc. particle1_mc will be one-tenth of the way to the mouse pointer, particle2_mc will be two-tenths of the way there, and so on, until you reach particle9_mc at nine-tenths of the way to the pointer.

123

Test the movie again, and you'll see some fairly impressive results, even if you did need to do a little math to get them.

It's still not *quite* what you set out to achieve, though. There's a big fat blob at one end (where particle0_mc sits on top of the original) and a conspicuous gap at the pointer itself, where you have no particle at all. This all boils down to that old "counting from 0" business I mentioned before. This is one time when it would be much more useful if you could start counting from 1 (placing the first duplicate at one-tenth of the distance) and finish at 10 (placing the last duplicate at ten-tenths of the distance; smack-dab on top of the pointer).

11. In fact, it turns out that nothing could be simpler. Both of your loops currently use i++ (or j++) to bump up the loop counter at the end of each cycle. So what about changing the counter at the *start* of each loop instead? You'll need to change both loops, so here's the full script:

```
particle_mc.onEnterFrame = function() {
  // work out distances from
  // center to mouse
  xDist = _xmouse-290;
  yDist = _ymouse-190;
  j = 0;
  while (j<10) {
    // move particle to center plus
    // j tenths of the distance
    j++;
    _root["particle"+j+"_mc"]._x = 290
➥ +(xDist*j/10);
    _root["particle"+j+"_mc"]._y = 190
➥ +(yDist*j/10);
  }
};
var i:Number = 0;
var j:Number = 0;
```

```
var xDist:Number = 0;
var yDist:Number = 0;
while (i<10) {
  // actions to loop go here
  i++;
  duplicateMovieClip(particle_mc,
➥ "particle"+i+"_mc", i);
}
```

Now you start each loop with a counter value of 0. The first thing you do is bump it up to 1, use that value to do stuff with particle1_mc, and then loop back. The counter is less than 10, so you run the loop actions again: bump the counter up to 2, use it to do stuff with particle2_mc, and then loop back again.

You keep doing that until the counter is 9. That's still less than 10, so you run the loop actions, which bump the counter up to 10; use it to do stuff with particle10_mc; and loop back again. Only now does the while() action wise up to the fact that its counter<10 condition *isn't actually true anymore*.

Run the movie one last time, and you'll see a beautiful, homogenous line of particles stretching out from the middle of the stage to wherever your mouse pointer happens to be. Presto!

One final thing worth mentioning is that when you need to create lots of variables, Flash allows you to create more than one per var. You could have done this instead of your four separate var lines:

```
var i:Number = 0, j:Number = 0,
➥ xDist:Number = 0,
➥ yDist:Number = 0;
```

Because you also define the values of all your variables in the code after initialization, there's no need to set them all to 0, so this is also permissible (and used often by the . . . um . . . lazier programmers):

```
var i:Number, j:Number, xDist:Number,
➥ yDist:Number;
```

Be careful when you use this, though, because not defining variables as soon as you create them isn't good programming practice—you might start seeing your old friend undefined cropping up in your code unexpectedly. Quick shortcuts are fine, but as in real life, an easy life is hard work. There are usually no shortcuts, only unfinished jobs that come back to haunt you later!

OK, now that you've seen a little of what you can do with a while loop or two, let's take a quick look at the other sorts of loops available in ActionScript. "Other sorts of loops?" I hear you cry. "Surely there can't be *more* ways to send scripts running around in circles?" Well, no . . . and yes.

Most of the loops you've looked at so far use a pretty standard system: set up a counter variable, add 1 to the counter variable's value every cycle, and test each time whether the variable's value has gone above a certain value. This approach is *so* ubiquitous that there's a special action devoted to it.

for loops

Whenever you build a loop that uses some kind of counter variable to count how many cycles you've gone through, it's worth considering the humble for loop as an option. It doesn't actually add anything new to the possibilities offered by while(), but it lets you set things out in a way that brings all the counter-specific actions together on one line, neatens things up, and helps you keep things nice and clear.

Let's consider a loop you've already looked at:

```
var myCounter:Number = 0;
while (myCounter < 10) {
   trace(myCounter);
   myCounter++;
};
```

There are four important parts to this loop, one on each of the first four lines:

- Initialize the counter variable myCounter.
- Specify the loop condition myCounter<10.

- Perform the main loop action trace(myCounter).
- Bump up the value of the counter with myCounter++.

If you rewrite this loop as a for loop, you can cut it down to two lines:

```
for (myCounter = 0; myCounter < 10;
➥ myCounter++) {
   trace(myCounter);
};
```

You've now defined the whole range of the loop within the first line, so there's no need to set up a counter before the loop and no need to change its value as one of the looped actions. ActionScript takes care of all that for you.

You're probably not convinced yet. These for loops certainly don't lend themselves to useful explanations like "While the counter is less than 10, perform the following actions," and they *do* take a bit of getting used to.

> The crucial thing to register is the fact that every factor that could possibly influence how many cycles this loop goes through is **specified in the for() action itself**. Since these factors are all in one place, you'll find it a lot easier to keep track of what the loop is doing when you come across it buried in a mountain of other stuff.
>
> Since you can see how many loops a for loop needs to cycle through, it's less likely to give you a nasty surprise when you test your code. Also, you can easily modify a for loop so that it cycles only once, which can be tremendously useful while developing your code, since if you can see it working for a single loop, you can be confident that it will run for many cycles. In fact, the for loop is so useful that in most code it's the only loop structure you'll use.

Of course, you can still use the counter for all sorts of things other than simply counting how many times you've looped—for example, as the index for an array or variable, or for deriving a sequence of numbers (such as a multiplication table; 5, 10, 15, 20, 25, and so on).

Let's take a closer look at each of the three arguments you stick in the for() action.

init

The first argument is where you set up the counter variable. It's normal to set this to 0, though you're free to use any value you like. You can also name the counter as you wish. The total number of loops must always turn out to be a numeric variable, so valid start counter values are as follows:

- counter = 0: The counter starts at 0.
- i = startValue: The counter i starts at the value of numeric variable startValue.

condition

This is just like the condition in an if statement or a while loop: as long as the expression evaluates to true, the loop will continue cycling. Inside a for loop, though, the condition should always refer explicitly to the counter, normally in a form like "The counter is less than the stop value." Valid examples are as follows:

- i < 10: Loop as long as i is less than 10.
- counter >= 200: Loop as long as counter is greater than or equal to 200.
- x < xMax: Loop as long as x is less than xMax.

In the last case, it's important that you **don't let your loop actions change the value of** xMax—well, not unless you know what you're doing (in which case you'll probably be using another kind of loop anyway!). Flash won't stop you from doing this, but it will make your code very unpredictable, and it may even result in a forever loop.

One condition that beginners often get stuck with is this:

    counter == 10

Although this is OK as a condition, it's probably not what you want for a for loop—unless counter equals 10 on the first loop, it will stop the loop immediately and not do anything at all.

next

This is where you specify what should happen to the counter after every loop. Possible arguments you can add here are as follows:

- i++: Add 1 to i.
- counter--: Subtract 1 from counter.
- i = i+2: Add 2 to i.

You've already encountered the ++ trick for adding 1 to the value of a variable. Its partner in crime is --, which takes 1 *off* the value. Anything else you want to do to the counter needs to be written out in full.

Some useful examples of for loops

If you want to see the following for loops in action, simply use the Actions panel to attach them to frame 1 of a new movie and press *Ctrl/Cmd+Enter* to give the movie a test run. The Output window will then show you the counter value for each cycle (or iteration) of the loop.

Simple loop

This loop will count up from 0 to 12:

```
var counter:Number = 0;
for (counter=0; counter <= 12; counter++) {
  trace (counter);
}
```

Reverse loop

This loop will count down from 12 to 0:

```
var counter:Number = 0;
for (counter=12; counter >=0 ; counter-) {
  trace (counter);
}
```

Two at a time

This loop will count up from 0 to 12 in steps of two and show the value of counter once the loop has terminated:

```
var counter:Number = 0;
for (counter=0; counter<=12;
➡ counter=counter+2) {
```

```
        trace(counter);
}
trace("loop has finished");
trace(counter);
```

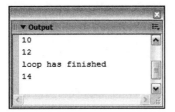

This demonstrates that the value of the counter just after the loop completes is the first value that doesn't satisfy your condition. In this case, that's two more than the maximum value of 12, namely 14.

Looping through elements in an array

As we've now established, loops are pretty darn useful for making a lot of actions run in a very short time. In particular, for loops give you a tidy way to cycle through lots of values with just a couple of lines of code. One particularly useful thing you can do with loops is use them to work with arrays.

Say you've written a set of actions that all act on element i of an array. By looping through all available values of i, you can quickly apply the actions to every element in the array. So a small piece of code can be made to work on large amounts of data.

You already saw a simple example of how you can use a while loop to look at all the elements in an array, and you even persuaded it to stop when the array ran out of defined elements. In fact, the combination of loops and arrays is so important that you're going to return to it now and look at a few more things they enable you to do.

Applying an operation to all the elements in an array

Consider an array of 200 values between 1 and 20 that you've stored in an array called rawData. You'd like to create a corresponding list of percentage values in a second array called percent. The nonloopy way to do this (or should that be "the *totally* loopy way"?) would be to write out 200 lines of script like this:

```
percent[0] = rawData[0]*5;
percent[1] = rawData[1]*5;
percent[2] = rawData[2]*5;
percent[3] = rawData[3]*5;
...
percent[198] = rawData[198]*5;
percent[199] = rawData[199]*5;
```

The sensible way to do it would be to use a loop, and since you know how many elements there are, it makes sense to use a for loop. First, you need to work out a generalized action for the "convert to percent" process.

That's not too hard: percent just means "out of 100," and 1 in 20 is just the same as 5 in 100. So you just need to multiply all your numbers by 5. Assuming you're using a counter variable called i, you can write this:

```
percent[i] = rawData[i]*5;
```

Now you loop through all values of i from 0 to 199, applying your line of code each time until you've converted the entire array:

```
var i:Number = 0;
var percent:Array = new Array();
var rawData:Array = new Array();
// code to set values of
// rawData goes here
// ...
// ...
for (i=0; i<200; i++) {
  percent[i] = rawData[i]*5;
}
```

What if you don't know how many elements there are in the array? You've already seen one way to deal with this issue using a while loop, which you could translate into for-style notation:

```
for (i=0; rawData[i]!=undefined; i++) {
    percent[i] = rawData[i]*5;
}
```

Hmm. Well, Flash won't actually *stop* you from doing this, but it goes against everything you've just learned about for loops. Sure, the loop condition still depends on i, but only loosely. It depends a lot more on the contents of the rawData array, and it's not at all obvious how many times you expect to loop. This is one situation in which things are best left to a while loop.

On the other hand, if you had some way to ask the array directly how many elements it had, then you could still get away with a condition like i<lengthOfArray. Of course, there's just such a way: every array has a property called length, which tells you how many elements it contains. So it looks like your best bet is to use i<rawData.length like this:

```
for (i=0; i<rawData.length; i++) {
    percent[i] = rawData[i]*5;
}
```

> *The length property is common to all arrays and tells you the number of elements an array contains. This technique gives you a very simple way to put limits on all your array loops.*

Searching an array for a specific value

Another thing you can do using a combination of loops and arrays is search through the elements in an array until you find a particular value. Say you have an array of book titles called myLibrary, and you use a variable called searchString to hold the name of a book you're looking for. There are two ways you could approach this.

You could write this:

```
searchString = "The Wasp Factory";
i = 0
while (library[i] != searchString &&
➡ i<library.length) {
    i++
}
if (library[i]==searchString) {
    trace("Match found: item number " + i);
} else {
    result = "No matches found.";
}
```

You don't know in advance how many loops you're going to need before you find a match, so you set up a while loop. You then keep adding 1 to the value of i until library[i] matches your search string or you run out of array elements. You then use an if...else to check whether the loop ended because a match had been found (in which case you trace out the relevant element number) or because it got to the end of the array without finding any matches at all (in which case you output the number of matches as zero).

On the other hand, you might want to do it like this:

```
searchString = "The Wasp Factory";
matchesFound = 0;
for (i = 0; i < library.length; i++) {
    if (library[i] == searchString) {
        trace("Match found: item number "
➡ + i);
        matchesFound++
    }
}
trace("Number of matches found: "
➡ + matchesFound);
```

This time, you assume that you're going to search the whole library, on the basis that there may be more than one copy of the book you're looking for. You therefore use a for loop, which cycles as many times as there are elements in the array (thanks go, once again, to the length property). Every time around, the if statement will check whether there's a match with the search string. If there is, you trace out details of the match and bump up the number of matchesFound. Once the whole array has been searched, you trace out the total matchesFound value.

Cross-indexing a pair of arrays

Once you've figured out how to search an array, you're only one step away from cross-indexing with another array. Let's consider two arrays, each containing a list of plant names. Each element in the first array contains the common name of a plant, while the corresponding element in the other array holds the Latin name of the same plant. They might look like this:

```
commonNames = new Array("foxglove",
➥ "palm tree", "rose",
➥ "California poppy",
➥ "witch hazel");
latinNames = new Array("digitalis",
➥ "trachycarpus", "rosa",
➥ "Eschscholzia californica",
➥ "hammamelis mollis");
```

What if you know the common name of a particular plant but want to find out what its Latin name is? You might ask the question, for example, "What is the Latin name for the California poppy?" You just need a loop that will cycle through elements in the commonNames array until it finds one that contains the string "California poppy". It could then use the successful index value (in this case 3) to call up the corresponding element from the latinNames array and find the answer: "Eschscholzia californica."

Here's how you might do it:

```
offset = 0;
search = "California poppy";
while (commonNames[offset] != search &&
➥ offset < commonNames.length) {
    offset++;
}
if (commonNames[offset] == search) {
    trace("Match found: " +
➥ latinNames[offset]);
} else {
    result = "No matches found.";
}
```

In this case, you don't necessarily want to search on every element—you'll stop just as soon as you've found a match. Since you can't know in advance how many

elements you'll need to search on, a for loop isn't suitable, so you use a while structure. As before, it loops around incrementing your offset variable for as long as the element commonNames[offset] doesn't match your search term and offset is less than the array length.

So, when the while loop finishes, it could be for one of two reasons: either you've found a match or you've reached the end of the array and found none. This method—finding an index and applying it to another related array—is known as **cross-indexing**.

Now that you've seen a few theoretical examples of combining loops with arrays, it's time to put your new-found skills to work. You're going to use Flash and ActionScript to create a game of hangman using arrays and loops together with more than a little string variable manipulation. As ever, a nice practical example should help lift the whole thing right off the page!

Hangman

It's an old game that's been around for centuries. Pick a word at random, write it out using a blank in place of each letter, and challenge a friend to guess what the word is by picking letters from the alphabet. If he chooses a letter that's in the word, you show him where it is in the word by filling in the blank. If he picks one that isn't in the word, you add pieces to a drawing of a scaffold. After five or six wrong guesses, the scaffold is complete, and you start adding a stick figure hanging from the gibbet. After about ten wrong guesses, the figure is complete—HANGMAN! The only way for your friend to win is to guess all the letters in the word before the stick figure is hanged.

Hangman is a brutal game when you think about it, and there's no hiding the fact that it's a game about someone getting hanged. All the fluffy bunnies in the world aren't going to soften the blow, but I've decided all the same to get my own version looking like it was drawn and painted by a child.

Let's start with a quick walk-through to give you an idea of how the gaming experience should pan out for your players.

1. When you start the movie, you'll see the following scene:

An empty field on a sunny day, with a title, a solitary flower, and play game button that you can click to start the game.

2. Once you click the play game button and the game starts, you're presented with a simple interface: a box for typing in your guesses, an enter button to submit your guesses, and a list of question marks indicating how many letters there are in the word you have to guess:

3. The next step is to type in a letter and click the enter button. Let's say the mystery word is "flash" and I've just tried the letter "a." This is what I should see:

There's one "a" in the word "flash," so Flash replaces the relevant question mark with the letter itself.

4. Say I now try a few more letters, such as "u," "x," "q," and "z." OK, let's just say I'm being deliberately dumb here. None of these letters occurs in the word "flash," so they're all bad guesses—now I have to pay the price:

I've guessed four wrong letters, so four sections of the gallows appear. If I don't start making some decent guesses soon, I'll be hung out to dry! As you can see from the preceding screenshot, I'm just about to guess the letter "g." I haven't clicked enter yet, so all is not lost. At least the game is intelligent enough not to let the player compound his stupidity by even forgetting what he's guessed so far—if I try entering "x" a second time, I'll find that I'm not able to enter it. The law in the world of hangman may be harsh, but at least it's fair!

5. Let's assume I now replace the "g" with an "f," click enter, and suddenly realize what the word is. I follow up with "l," "s," and "h," and the word is complete. This is what I should now see:

The gallows vanishes, and your would-be victim is now free to wander through the sunlit fields with a big red flower in his hand. How sweet.

6. However, there's an alternate reality in which I didn't recant my faith in the letter "f" . . . I left a "g" in the input box and clicked enter! With no clue as to what the word could be, I floundered around with such desperate guesses as "m," "n," "o," "p," and "q." There was no hope:

Our hero meets a grisly end, and the only solace to be found is in the little button that reappears behind the gallows, hinting that you can actually have another try.

Well, that's the game—and I did warn you things might get a little unpleasant! Now that you've got a good idea of how the game "hangs" together, let's start looking at how you can build it in Flash.

> *If you're in a rush and don't want to create all these graphics from scratch, you can find them all in this chapter's download, in the Library of a file called* hangman_start.fla.
>
> *If you want to concentrate on typing in the scripts only, you can start with* hangman_startScript.fla, *which has everything in place except the scripts. Using this file, you can get away with just reading the text up until the section that starts "Adding in the ActionScript."*
>
> *In case you're wondering, the font I've used throughout is called* kids. *If you don't have a similar font, don't worry—*_sans *will do just fine for now.*

You'll start by breaking down the game into symbols that you need in the Library. I've used four graphics (called flower, grass, sun, and title—no prizes for guessing what they all are) plus two buttons (enter and play), and I've put all the "hanging" material and interface stuff into a couple of movie clips (called hanging man and interface).

There's nothing terribly special about the buttons (one's a black box behind a bit of static text that says "enter," and the other's just a bit of text that says "play game." Select them and press *F8* to convert them to symbols and you're done), and the graphics should be self-explanatory (the sun is an orangey circle, the title says "hangman," and so on. Select them and press *F8* again . . . I'm sure you get the idea), so I'll skip to how you build the two movie clips.

The hanging man movie clip

This is where you pull together your scenery and animate the awful process of a hanging.

1. First, you need to create a total of four layers in a new movie clip, hanging man, which you should call labels, flower, hangman, and background:

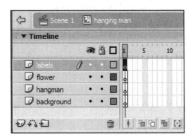

2. Select the background layer, and pull some sun and grass onto it from the Library:

Select frame 19 and press *F5* to insert a frame. You want this scenery on display throughout the clip.

3. Now select frame 1 on the labels layer and press *F6* to insert a keyframe. Press *F5* to insert a frame at 19, and press *F6* to add keyframes at 10 and 15. Use the Properties panel to label your three keyframes as play, lose, and win, respectively. Your timeline should now look like this:

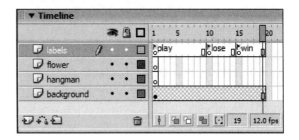

4. Now for the creative part. You're going to add the frame-by-frame animation of the gallows and hanging man. Select frame 19 of the hangman layer and press *F5* to insert a frame. Layer hangman should now look like an albino version of the background timeline.

Select frame 2, press *F6* to add a keyframe, and draw a horizontal brown line along the top of the grass. Select frame 3, press *F6* to add a keyframe, and add a vertical brown line at the right end. Select frame 4, press *F6* to add a keyframe, and add a diagonal brown line connecting the two lines you just drew.

Now keep going, building up the gallows a piece at a time and then adding your hapless victim (one piece at a time—no, I've never understood that bit either!) until you reach frame 10, which is where folks go when they've lost the game. Each keyframe represents one step closer to doom!

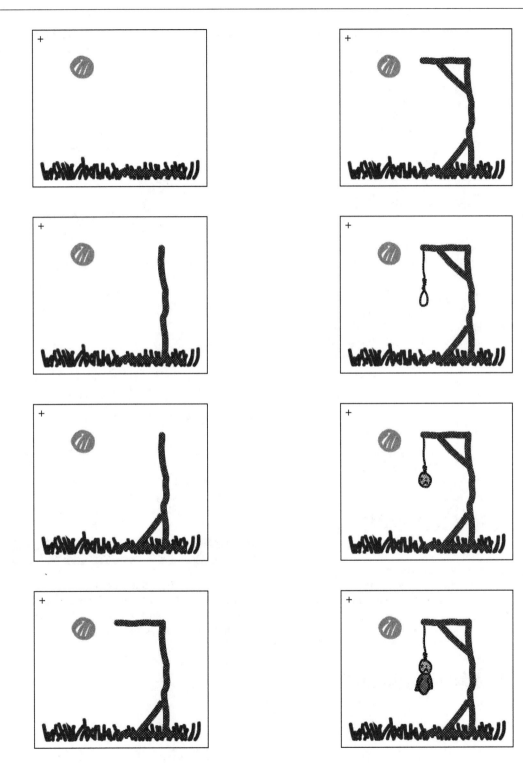

By frame 10, you should have something like this:

I've also added in some text here (still on the hangman layer), just to emphasize the fact that the player's tale is over.

5. Of course, if the player has won the game, you need to reward her efforts and give her a nice, uplifting image. Select frame 15 and press *F6* to add a keyframe. You can delete the gallows from this frame and replace it with something happier:

6. Now for a nice finishing touch. Select frame 1 of the flower layer, drag a copy of the flower symbol onto the stage, and nestle it down somewhere safe in the grass:

Now add a keyframe at frame 15 of layer flower and drag the flower across so that it looks as if it's being held in the hero's hand:

Select frame 19 and press *F5* to insert a frame.

Phew! After all that hard work, your "hanging man" timeline should look like this:

Aren't you glad I didn't show you that before you started? Now that you've dealt with the aesthetics of the game, let's take a look at the user interface.

The interface movie clip

You'll be glad to hear that this movie clip is a great deal simpler than the last one. There's one layer, one keyframe, and no fancy graphics to labor over. In fact, the following image sums it up quite well:

There are just four things on the stage:

- A dynamic text field called `display_txt` at the top.
- A static text field on the left that reads guess a letter:.
- An input text field called `input_txt`.
- An instance of the enter button, which I've called `enter_btn`.

You want the player to use only lowercase characters, so select the input text field and click the Character button on the Properties panel. In the Character Options dialog box, check the radio button for Specify Ranges, select Lowercase Letters [a...z] (27 glyphs), and click OK to confirm.

You also want the user to guess a letter at a time, so in the Maximum Characters box on the Properties panel (it's just below the character buttons) enter 1.

Once you've created each of these and set them up on the stage as described, you're all done. Now you're ready to take a look at the main timeline, arrange your movie clips, and wire them all up with a little ActionScript.

The main movie timeline

This timeline needs two layers, movie and actions, with just one keyframe on each:

- movie will contain the following:
    - An instance of the title graphic, which reads "hangman"
    - An instance of the hanging man movie clip called `hangman_mc`
    - An instance of the interface movie clip called `interface_mc`
    - An instance of the play button called `playGame_btn`
- actions will hold all your ActionScript.

135

Here's how the stage should look once everything's in place:

Well, you've got all the pictures in place—how about a little code? Now the code for this game might look a little hairy at times, but don't panic! Nothing you do here will be hideously complicated. If it all starts to look like a mess of brackets and semicolons swimming about in front of your eyes (yes, that sometimes happens to me too!), just take it one line at a time. Look for the structures you understand and think how they're being used to form the game I described earlier on.

Adding the ActionScript

Select frame 1 on the actions layer, open the Actions panel, click that pushpin button, and get ready to wire everything together. Although there are lots of actions to put in over the next couple of pages, they all need to be attached to the same frame. What's more, they break down into three neat pieces:

- **Initialization**: Actions to run when the movie starts
- **Game setup**: Actions to run when you click play game to start the game
- **Game play**: Actions to run when you click enter to submit a guessed letter

Let's get started!

1. The first chunk of code you need to add will set your movie up when it initializes. You begin by creating three arrays:

```
// MAIN INITIALIZING CODE...
// RUNS WHEN MOVIE STARTS
//
// initialize array of words
var wordList:Array = new Array("computer",
➥ "apple", "coffee", "flash",
➥ "animal", "america", "panel",
➥ "window", "import", "number",
➥ "string", "cake", "object",
➥ "movie", "aardvark", "kettle");
// initialize arrays for letters
var lettersNeeded:Array = new Array();
var lettersGuessed:Array = new Array();
```

The first of these arrays lists all the words you're going to choose from. If you want, you can add more by simply sticking them on the end of the list. Words must be in lowercase letters (since that's all you'll allow the user to enter).

You're going to be using the elements of lettersNeeded to store letters from your mystery word, while lettersGuessed array elements will hold a mixture of question marks and letters that the player has guessed correctly—these are the letters you'll show the player while he's playing the game. Why do you need two arrays? Well, there are two versions of the same word you want Flash to use: one that it keeps to itself and one that it shows you. For example, if the word to be guessed was "apple," lettersNeeded would contain the letters a, p, p, l, and e, whereas lettersGuessed would start off as ?, ?, ?, ?, ?, and become ?, p, p, ?, ? if the user guessed "p."

2. Next up, you need to initialize all the variables you use. Rather than explain each here, I'll explain them as you see them being used in anger once you get to the main code.

```
// initialize variables
var randomNumber:Number = 0;
var selectedWord:String = "";
var lettersLeftToGo:Number = 0;
var foundLetter:Boolean = false;
var notGuessed:Boolean = false;
var wrong:Boolean = false;
```

3. You then have to stop the main timeline, stop the hangman_mc timeline, and hide the game interface:

```
// hide the game interface
interface_mc._visible = false;
// stop the hangman and main timelines
hangman_mc.stop();
stop();
```

At this point in the game, all the basic data has been defined, and the game is all set up waiting for some user interaction. The screen will look like this after the main initialization code described in steps 1 and 2 has run:

Now that you've set up the movie with arrays and stopped timelines, it's time you laid down some actions that will get you ready for a game.

> *Remembering that event handlers go before the main code, the rest of the code goes in front of the lines you've just added.*

4. When the player clicks the play game button, there are several commands you need to give Flash before you can let the player start guessing letters. You can put these into an event handler for the onRelease event of the playGame_btn instance. It'll start out like this:

```
playGame_btn.onRelease = function() {
    // initialize graphics
    hangman_mc.gotoAndStop("play");
    playGame_btn._visible = false;
    interface_mc._visible = true;
```

First, you initialize the hangman movie clip, sending its playhead to the first frame. In fact, at this point in the game, it's probably there already, but you'll want to run these actions again when you set things up for a rematch, so this is an important thing to do.

You then make the play game button invisible (since you don't need it now) and make the game interface visible (you're certainly going to need that!).

5. Next up in the event handler, you select a word at random from the wordList array:

```
// select a word at random & count
// how many letters it has
randomNumber = Math.round(Math.random()*
➥ (wordList.length-1));
```

At first glance, you may think the first line looks pretty terrifying. All it actually does is pick a random whole number between 0 and wordList.length-1, and store it in a variable called randomNumber.

You then use that number to specify one of the elements in the wordList array, pull out the word it contains, and store this randomly selected word in selectedWord.

6. The next step is to set up a variable that's going to help you keep track of how many more letters the player still has to guess. At this stage, the player has guessed none, so this is just the number of letters in the word. Assuming the word you chose was "apple," lettersLeftToGo would be 5.

```
lettersLeftToGo = selectedWord.length;
```

7. Now it's time to break your word down into a list of letters. As I mentioned before, the lettersNeeded array is going to store all the letters your player has to guess. You set this up using a for loop and cycle through each letter in the word, putting it into the corresponding element in the array:

```
for (i=0; i<selectedWord.length; i++) {
    lettersNeeded[i] =
➥ selectedWord.charAt(i);
}
```

The charAt(i) bit at the end of the second line is new, but all it actually means is "Get the character at position i" of the selectedWord variable it's stuck on the end of. This loop would take your word "apple" and turn it into the letters "a," "p," "p," "l," and "e."

8. You do a similar thing for the lettersGuessed array but fill every slot with a question mark—this is only fair, since the player hasn't guessed any letters yet!

```
for (i=0; i<selectedWord.length; i++) {
    lettersGuessed[i] = "?";
    interface_mc.display_txt.text += "?";
}
};
```

Steps 3 and 4 describe the entire script that runs when you click the play game button and get to the following screen. The variable lettersGuessed is the one that's being displayed in interface_mc.display_txt, the top text field. Although Flash knows what the letters of the word to be guessed are (as held in the array lettersNeeded), it's showing a string of the same length but currently consisting of ?s.

Phew! Let's stop for a moment and take a breather. That's a lot of script and a fair number of new tricks along the way. Try running the movie now and click the play game button. Sure enough, the button vanishes, the interface appears, and a string of question marks appears just below the grass, exactly like in the previous image.

Now select Debug ➤ Show Variables, and you can check out the contents of all your arrays:

```
▼ Output                                                    ≡
        10: "string ,
        11: "cake",
        12: "object",
        13: "movie",
        14: "aardvark",
        15: "kettle"
    ]
Variable _level0.lettersNeeded = [object #2, class 'Array'] [
        0: "a",
        1: "p",
        2: "p",
        3: "l",
        4: "e"
    ]
Variable _level0.lettersGuessed = [object #3, class 'Array'] [
        0: "?",
        1: "?",
        2: "?",
        3: "?",
        4: "?"
    ]
Variable _level0.randomNumber = 1
Variable _level0.selectedWord = "apple"
Variable _level0.lettersLeftToGo = 5
Variable _level0.foundLetter = false
Variable _level0.notGuessed = false
```

As well as helping to reassure you that things are going according to plan, viewing your data in the Output window should also serve as a reminder that the information you store inside a Flash movie isn't that hard to pull out again. Sure, once you've compiled a SWF and set it loose in the outside world, it won't be quite this easy to peer inside at what's going on, but it's certainly not impossible. Anyone with a bit of tech-savvy and enough perseverance can figure out exactly what words you've got stored in wordList and cheat you out of a victory. You have been warned!

That aside, you've got a game to finish and an enter button to wire up. Let's get to it!

9. The enter button (instance name enter_btn) is actually *inside* the movie clip instance called interface_mc, so you need to set up your callback like this:

```
interface_mc.enter_btn.onRelease =
➡ function() {
```

Suffice it to say, interface_mc.enter_btn just means "the instance called enter_btn that's **inside** the instance called interface_mc." You'll learn a lot more about these dot-based shenanigans in the next few chapters, so don't let this oddity put you off just yet!

10. The first thing Flash has to do once the player clicks enter is assume that the player has guessed wrong and also clear the displayed text (because you need to redisplay the guess so far, replacing any ?s that have been guessed with the appropriate letters).

```
wrong = true;
interface_mc.display_txt.text = "";
```

Now you just loop through all the letters in the word (as stored in the lettersNeeded array) and change wrong to true as soon as you find a match with the input text field in interface_mc:

```
for (i=0; i<selectedWord.length; i++) {
  foundLetter = lettersNeeded[i] ==
➡ interface_mc.input_txt.text;
  if (foundLetter) {
    // guess matches a letter
    wrong = false;
    lettersLeftToGo--;
    lettersGuessed[i] =
➡ interface_mc.input_txt.text;
  }
  interface_mc.display_txt.text +=
➡ lettersGuessed[i];
}
```

The variable foundLetter gets its value from lettersNeeded[i] == interface_mc.input, which will always be a Boolean expression. It will be true only if the letter your player just entered is the same as the letter in element i of the lettersNeeded array.

You also bump down the number of letters left to guess, change the appropriate ? in the lettersGuessed array so that it shows the correct letter instead of a ?. At the end of each loop, you update the displayed text (display_txt) so that it reflects the fact that some of the ?s may now have been guessed correctly.

Hang on a minute, though! What if you picked the same letter more than once (such as guessing "p" in "apple")? If it matched the first time, it would match again and again; lettersLeftToGo would hit 0 before very long, suggesting that you'd won the game! It looks like you need to be a little more picky with the condition in your if statement.

11. Make the following highlighted additions to the for loop you just wrote:

```
for (i=0; i<selectedWord.length; i++) {
  foundLetter = lettersNeeded[i] ==
➡ interface_mc.input_txt.text;
  notGuessed = lettersGuessed[i] !=
➡ interface_mc.input_txt.text;
  if (foundLetter && notGuessed) {
    // guess matches a letter
    // we haven't already found
    wrong = false;
    lettersLeftToGo--;
    lettersGuessed[i] =
➡ interface_mc.input_txt.text;
  }
  interface_mc.display_txt.text +=
➡ lettersGuessed[i];
}
```

Now you check that your player's input is *not* the same as element number i in the array lettersGuessed. Now, if foundLetter and notGuessed are *both* true, you know you've got a brand-new correct guess!

12. Next, you empty out the input box, so that it's all ready for your player to try again:

```
// reset input text box
interface_mc.input_txt.text = "";
```

13. If the player's guess was no good (or the player was foolish enough to guess at a letter she had already gotten), the variable wrong will still have a Boolean value of true, in which case the next few lines kick in:

```
if (wrong) {
  hangman_mc.nextFrame();
  if (hangman_mc._currentFrame
➡ == 10) {
    // GAME OVER!!
    interface_mc._visible = false;
    playGame_btn._visible = true;
  }
}
```

First, you use nextFrame() to bump the hangman_mc playhead onto the next frame. You then check whether that happens to be frame 10, also known as HANGMAN!

If it is frame 10, you run the "Game Lost" actions. These just hide the interface (the text fields and the enter button) and show the play game button (so the player can play the game again if she feels the need). If it's not frame 10, you don't need to anything here.

14. Last bit now! You just need to test whether all the letters have been guessed correctly. If they have, the value of lettersLeftToGo should be down to 0. You use this fact to control whether or not the "Game Won" actions should be run:

```
if (lettersLeftToGo == 0) {
    // GAME WON!!
    hangman_mc.gotoAndStop("win");
    interface_mc._visible = false;
    playGame_btn._visible = true;
}
};
```

These simply send hangman_mc to the win frame (where you get to see your hero holding a flower and smiling in gratitude), hide the interface, and show the play game button.

Now that you're all done, you can sit back and relax—and maybe have a quick game! Of course, the tension won't be quite so high now that you've seen the full list of words your movie gets to choose from. All the same, though, it's nice to see that all this script will actually do something.

> *Also worth looking at is* hangman_advanced.fla. *This FLA prevents you from entering the same letter twice (using the rather handy* restrict *property of a text field) or a blank space as your guess.*

Book project: Creating the static graphics

You're not yet at the point of writing any ActionScript in the book project, and you're still in the process of creating the graphics.

In this section, you'll create the graphics in the border area. Not only do the graphics you're about to create have no ActionScript associated with them right now, but also they *never* will because they're **static**—they just sit there looking pretty.

I know what you're thinking: "Wha . . .? I thought this was a book on ActionScript!" It is. It's just that coding up a Flash site—even one that's heavily ActionScript oriented like Futuremedia—isn't just a straight programming exercise. There's a strong graphical aspect to it. A bit of a code respite will probably also soothe some jangled nerves after that hangman game!

> *There will be some readers coming into this book who have JavaScript or other web programming experience, and some who have spent some time already with Flash and just not "gotten it." If this is you, don't worry. I was the same.*
>
> *The thing that makes Flash so different from other programming languages is the closeness of the relationship between the code and graphics. Unlike what you may be used to, a significant portion of your setting up in Flash has to do with graphics and layout rather than code. This is to be expected. Despite recent advances in the ActionScript language, Flash is still predominantly a visual environment. Unlike JavaScript, whose most common use is browser control or client-side validation, the main use of ActionScript is animation. For that to take place, you first have to have some graphics.*

As always, I'll first review what you'll be doing this chapter section through the use of a trusty rough sketch. You'll create the back strip at the bottom of the site plus another hidden graphic that you didn't notice when you looked at the finished site: a frame that sits around the border of the site.

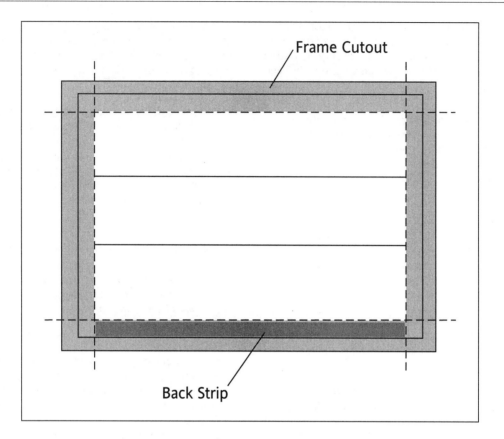

The function of the back strip is obvious when you look at the final site: it's a design widget that pulls together all the parts of the interface that sit at the bottom of the screen.

What does the frame cutout do? Well, rather like a puppet-show booth shows the puppets but hides the puppet master, you want the user to see what's going on during the zoom transition, but you want to hide all the tricky stuff you're doing behind the scenes, and this is what the cutout does. It hides what's *really happening* by hiding the portions of the screen that you don't want the user to see. As the three-color stripes scale up, they would start to fill the border area, but you stop this from happening by placing the frame cutout in front of them.

In short, the frame cutout prevents the viewable site from changing size as the zoom trick takes place. And yes, you can't see the frame cutout in the final site, and that's because it's the same color as the stage and HTML background. Despite being hidden, it's crucial to the final effect and helps give the impression that the navigation is more complicated than it actually is (a designer trying to deconstruct the effect using code only would fail without the frame cutout).

Some of the trick that makes most Flash ActionScript sites cool is code, but some of it comes down to graphic design. As noted at the beginning of this section, not all the clever stuff that happens in Flash is related to the code!

The starting point of this section is the work in progress from Chapter 3. If you don't want to use your own file (or you get stuck and want something to compare notes with), you can use the file `futuremedia_setup2 .fla`.

OK, that's the all-important preamble out of the way. Let's get down to some Flash authoring!

Setting up the timeline layers for your graphics

In the frame layer folder, add two new layers called graphics and frame. Lock all layers except graphics.

Creating the back strip

Follow these steps to create the back strip.

1. Although the back strip looks black, it actually has a subtle gradient on it to stop it from looking flat. The first step is to create this gradient. Using the Color Mixer (Window ➤ Design Panels ➤ Color Mixer), create a linear gradient for the fill color as shown. The gradient has three control colors.

   The two edge colors are almost black: R: 34, G: 34, B: 34, Alpha: 100% (or #222222 for the HTML heads).

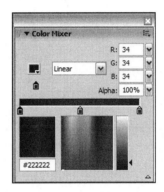

   The center color is a slightly lighter shade of almost-black: R: 68, G: 68, B: 68, Alpha: 100% (or #444444).

2. Select layer graphics. On the stage, draw out a long black oblong with no stroke. Don't worry about the size or position too much, or the fact that the gradient doesn't look right. You will fix all that almost immediately.

3. Bring up the Info panel (Window ➤ Design Panels ➤ Info). Select the oblong and set the registration point on the Info panel (via the little matrix in the following screenshot) to the top left. Set the width to 740.0 and the height to 30.0. Set the position of the oblong to X: 30.0, Y: 570.0. This will move and scale the oblong so that it fills the lower edge of the border as shown:

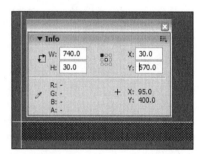

4. The gradient runs vertically, but you want it to run horizontally. To fix this, you need to use the Fill Transform tool. You'll do some close scaling in a moment, and although Flash will want to lend a helping hand, you don't need it, so make sure all snapping options in the View ➤ Snapping submenu are unchecked.

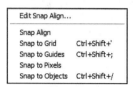

5. Deselect the back strip by clicking any other area of the stage, and then reselect it with the Fill Transform tool. Rotate the fill by 90 degrees (it doesn't matter in which direction; either clockwise or counterclockwise is fine). Scale the envelope until it's about the same height as the back strip. Finally, move it up slightly so that you end up with an envelope whose lines run parallel with the long edges of the strip and whose center point is about one-fifth of the way down from the top edge of the back strip, as shown:

Adding structure to the Library

OK, so now you have a primitive (that is, it isn't yet a Flash symbol) rectangle on the screen. You should really make it into a symbol, but before doing that, let's create some structure for the (many) symbols that you'll be adding later on. This includes two things:

- A well-defined library folder structure
- A well-defined naming structure for your symbols

1. In the Library pane (Window ➤ Library or *C_{TRL}+L*/*C_{MD}+L*, but you knew that already, didn't you?), create a new folder called User interface. Inside that folder, create another folder called non active UI stuff.

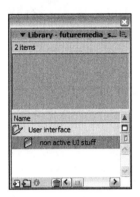

2. Now with the back strip selected, press *F8* and make the back strip a graphic symbol with the name sy.backStrip.

So why do you call your symbol something with sy at the front? Well, the Flash Library sorts by alphabetical order by default. Adding your own prefixes forces Flash to sort by some criteria you set. You can see this in a typical shot of the final site.

Name	Kind	Use Count	Linkage
mc.icon	Movie Clip	0	Export: icon
mc.page	Movie Clip	1	
mc.pageStrip	Movie Clip	6	
mc.placeholder	Movie Clip	0	
non active UI stuff	Folder		
mc.stripShine	Movie Clip	0	Export: stripShin
sy.backStrip	Graphic	1	
sy.registration	Graphic	0	
sounds	Folder		
snd.blip1	Sound	0	Export: blip1
snd.blip2	Sound	0	Export: blip2
snd.uiblip1	Sound	0	Export: uiblip1
snd.uiblip2	Sound	0	Export: uiblip2
content for future work>print>...	Folder		
assets	Folder		
mc.personalWork	Movie Clip	0	Export: draconis

Library - main, 168 items

As you can see, things are going to get complicated around your currently solitary sy.backStrip! The way I use prefixes forces Flash to sort my symbols so related groups are listed next to each other.

Flash allows you to do something very similar without using the prefixes. If you click the kind *column, the Library will sort on symbol type. That's great, but sometimes you want to subdivide further, such as between* mc *(standard movie clip),* ma *(movie clip containing only ActionScript), and* mp *(movie clip placeholder).*

Getting in the habit of using meaningful prefixes helps immensely when you're building very large Flash sites, but you'll find that it works even in smaller sites. It's amazing how many symbols even a modest site creates. The web version of Futuremedia contains a few hundred symbols, but you couldn't count that many just by looking at the finished site!

That's the first of your graphics done—one more to go.

Creating the frame cutout

Follow these steps to create the frame cutout.

1. Lock layer graphics and unlock frame. Hide all layers except the two guide layers and layer frame. Select layer frame.

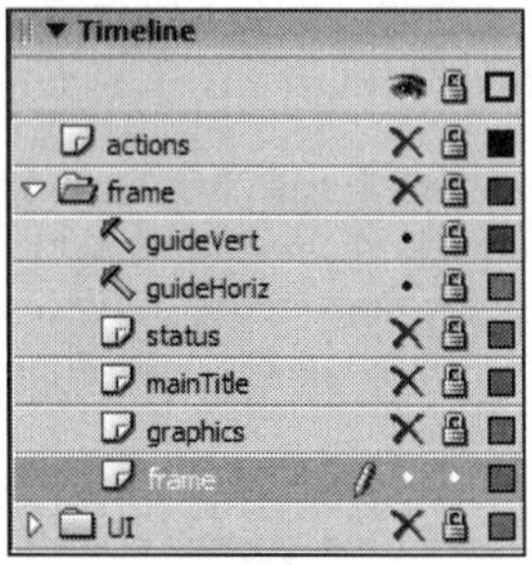

2. Select the Rectangle tool with no stroke and a fill color that contrasts with the background (such as bright green).

3. Select View ➤ Snapping ➤ Snap to Objects, and draw out a rectangle starting from the top-right corner and going off stage, down toward the bottom right, making sure that it covers the border gutter and some of the area off the stage (see the following diagrams). As you get close to the guide lines you added, the cursor will snap to them. You want the rectangle to go up to (but not beyond) the guide lines, so that the rectangle covers only the border.

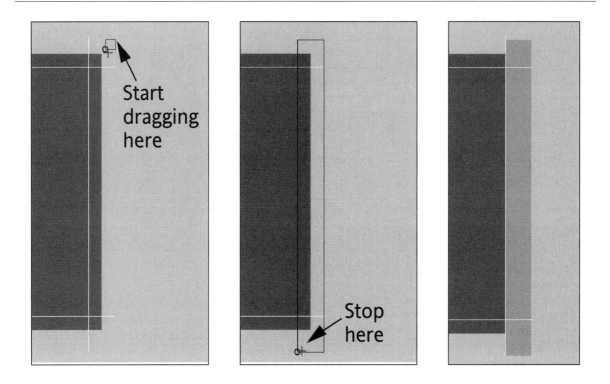

Start dragging here

Stop here

4. Repeat until you have a hollow frame shape (rather like a picture frame) that covers all the border areas and extends a little beyond the stage edges on all four sides.

5. Use the Fill tool with the fill color set to the background color (#666666, or use the Eyedropper tool to sample the background color), and then change the frame cutout color to this color.

6. Group the frame with itself (select it and press *CTRL/CMD+G* or select Modify ➤ Group). That may seem a little strange—why group a graphic when there's only one? Well, if you were to later inadvertently draw over the frame with other graphics, they would tend to split your frame or cut shapes out of it, unless you group the graphic or make it into a symbol. There's no need to make the graphic into a symbol because there will only ever be one (and making symbols when you don't need to only clutters up the Library). So instead, you just group it with itself.

Revealing the frame cutout and finishing the FLA

The frame is now well hidden, given that it's the same color as the stage. It now looks like part of the stage (which is exactly what it does in the final site). That's great, but it will only confuse you in the authoring environment as you develop your site further. The way around this is to make your shape appear in a different way while you're editing the FLA.

1. Make the frame layer show outlines only by clicking the colored brick for this layer.

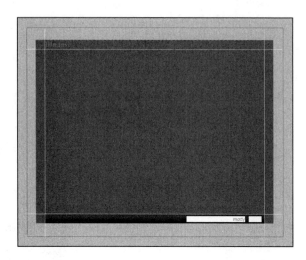

2. To finish up, show and lock all layers, and then save your file.

Parting shots

So, you now have a FLA that looks only marginally less boring than the one at the end of Chapter 3.

Well, that's certainly one way of looking at it, but you've started off slowly because you're following a *design process*. You already know how the final site will work in principle. You know which parts you've done so far (and you can probably guess at what's outstanding).

More important, you've learned that code alone doesn't make an ActionScript site. You have to set up the graphics first or at least give them some thought before you plow into code:

- That little dumb back strip may have only taken a few minutes to create, but it's something that has a large effect on your final site's look and feel.

- The frame cutout didn't take long to create either, but the thought process I had to go through to create it was significantly longer. I had to consider alternative implementations such as using masking (too processor intensive) or doing away with the border altogether (which would prevent adding any icons or other controls around the edges later on, making the design less flexible).

These thoughts, tests, and design decisions were worked out without using any code. I used the "animate or draw it manually in Flash and see what the issues are as you move the whole interface by hand" trick for the code-centric problems, and I designed the back strip outside Flash (I mocked it up in PhotoShop, which is where I designed the initial colors for the final UI also).

Although these tests and issues aren't included in the book, you're still at the nonprogramming stage and currently working it all out using standard Flash drawing tools, sketches, and basic graphic design.

> To put all this into some sort of perspective for the beginner who is possibly still thinking "Where did he get all these ideas from? I would never have come up with any of this!" it took almost **3 days** to get to the point where I knew what I was doing would work and had a good idea how to do it in principle, and I had completed the final FLA to the stage you've just reached. You'll see the amount of time you spend go down rather than up as you start adding major portions of code to the site, because you thought through the design at this initial stage.

Now that you've completed the static parts of the UI, you'll look at the moving parts—the **dynamic graphics**—in the next chapter. After that, you'll get down to some *serious* scripting. By the end of the book, you will have a 400-odd-line script to control this currently rather bleak-looking FLA. So don't get complacent by this slow initial pace. It's going to get busy around here real soon.

Summary

In the course of this chapter, you've looked at three different ways to make something loop in Flash:

- Timeline loops using the gotoAndPlay() action
- ActionScript loops using the while() action
- ActionScript loops using the for() action

That's not to say there are no other looping actions—there's do...while, which is almost exactly the same as while, except that it tests its condition *after* running the loop actions each time. There's also for...in, which you can use to loop through all the elements in an array or all the instances in a timeline. When all's said and done, though, they don't offer much beyond what you've already achieved. As you've seen, even for loops are really just a specialized version of your basic

while loop—just a particularly useful one! I haven't set out to try and be comprehensive here, since the three loops covered in this chapter should do for most of your needs. The only question is when you should use each one.

Here are some simple rules of thumb for deciding when (and when not) to use an ActionScript loop or a timeline loop:

- If you want Flash to perform an action (or set of actions) many times over in the shortest possible period of time, you should use an ActionScript loop. Every cycle of the loop is attached to one frame, so (unless you run over 200,000 cycles, when Flash starts getting a little nervous and decides your code has a forever loop in it) they'll always complete before you move on to the next frame.

- If you want to make something move gradually across the stage, you're best off using a timeline loop to nudge it by a few pixels each frame. An ActionScript loop will work its magic much, much faster, so all you're likely to see are the start and end points.

If you've settled on an ActionScript loop, picking between the while and for loops is fairly simple:

- If the values you use to define the looping behavior are all known in advance, then it's best to use a for loop. Otherwise, a while loop will almost always do the trick.

This chapter has had the biggest variety of examples so far, because the full range of the ActionScript skills you've been learning is really starting to come together. You've learned some important new techniques, and even more important, you've seen large sections of ActionScript working together in a finished application.

Don't worry if you've only skimmed though this chapter. The important thing is that a standard has been set in your mind, and you've probably picked up a lot of useful little snippets without even realizing it. That's what coding is all about. You're probably looking at all the long pieces of code and thinking, "Why has he done that? Why didn't he do it this way?" The proof is when you start doing your own programs and recognize things you're trying to do in terms of the programs I've listed here.

Each of the last three chapters has been an important step forward, building up the range of things you can do once you start throwing information around behind the scenes of your movies. Now that you've seen how to work with variables, arrays, decision making, and looping, you should be getting a very good idea of just how much a few lines of ActionScript can add to your Flash movies.

You're not even halfway through the book yet, and you're already moving away from the level of novice ActionScripter. In the next few chapters, you're going to look at more ways of bundling together actions and information, and you'll start thinking about how your scripts are structured. You may already feel confidant enough to wire the odd snippet of ActionScript into your own projects—if so, that's great! Soon enough, though, you'll be all set to start taking on some full-sized challenges.

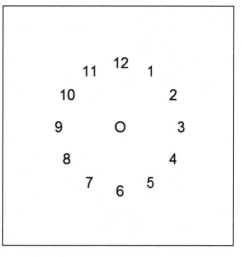

Chapter 6

MOVIES THAT REMEMBER HOW TO DO THINGS

What we'll cover in this chapter:

- Introducing functions as containers for storing actions
- Breaking down tasks into subtasks and using functions to structure your code
- Using callbacks to set up functions
- Using functions to recycle blocks of script
- Using arguments and returning results

As you've seen, the ability to handle information in your movies opens up a lot of possibilities. A few chapters back, I introduced variables as containers for data, whether that data is in the form of a string, a number, or a true or false Boolean value. I also covered arrays, which let you store lots of variables under a single name.

Variables and arrays help you to store and organize your data, but data is only half of the deal when it comes to writing scripts. What about actions? Literally anything you do with ActionScript is going to involve at least one action (or command) giving Flash an explicit instruction to do something or other. That's the whole point of ActionScript—of course, that's why it's called *Action*Script in the first place!

This is where functions come in. Say you have a sequence of actions you need to use at several different points in a movie. Rather than writing them out in full each time, you can write a **function declaration** that contains these actions, and then call out for that function whenever you want the actions to run. You just need to give Flash the name of the function, and it will track down the function definition for you and make sure it runs everything inside.

> *In many ways, a function does for actions what a variable does for data: it acts as a container for things you want to reuse later in the movie.*

This turns out to be very useful for organizing your scripts too. Functions let you wrap whole blocks of script into easy-to-handle sections, and if you pick those script blocks wisely, you'll ensure that each one focuses on a specific subtask.

Breaking down a task

Think about the whole business of writing a script in everyday terms. Whatever you happen to be working on, you're essentially trying to break down one complex task into several simpler ones.

When you go shopping, there are lots of actions you'll perform as part of the overall task: walk to the store, find the items you want to buy, take them to the checkout counter, find out the total cost, hand over a sum of money, receive change (hopefully!), leave the store, and walk home with your items.

This is all so obvious that you barely need to think about it. If someone asks you to fetch something from the store, you already know what that's likely to entail. Of course, the person will need to tell you what he or she wants, and possibly which store he or she wants it from, but the basics of "go shopping" are already there.

Most of the examples you've looked at so far have involved taking an overall task and breaking it straight down to the level of individual actions. This works well for the small programs you've been dealing with so far, but once your programs start to grow in size, things can quickly turn nasty. As I'm about to demonstrate, functions give you an opportunity to break down your overall movie mission into tasks and subtasks just as quickly or slowly as you want to.

There are two very good reasons for using functions to wrap up your code into blocks:

- **Reusability**: You can use each block over and over again with the minimum of fuss.
- **Structure**: You can break up huge reams of code into easily identifiable sections.

Now that you know why functions are a good thing, let's look at how you can actually use them.

Bundling actions and running them afterward

Working with functions isn't hard at all, especially in light of what you've already done since the beginning of this book. There are really only two steps involved:

- **Declare** the function by giving it a name and telling it what actions to perform.
- **Call** the function by telling Flash to summon it and run those actions.

Say you were writing a monster-attack game and wanted a function called hideAllMonsters that would make all the monsters invisible in one fell swoop. It will probably contain a loop that cycles through all relevant values of counter variable i, making monster number i invisible each time around. Here's what the function definition might look like:

```
hideAllMonsters = function() {
  for(i=0 ; i<numberOfMonsters ; i++) {
    _root["monster"+i+"_mc"]._visible =
➥ false;
  }
};
```

When it comes to picking a good name for a function, the issues are similar to those you looked at for naming variables. You should make the name relevant and recognizable, and take care not to use one of Flash's reserved words.

Of course, this should look very familiar: you're defining your function by writing a callback, just as you've done in the past for all your event handlers. In fact, this isn't the only way to define a function, but it's easily the most flexible approach, and what's more, it's one you've already seen! Let's take a quick look at the other way, though, just so you can see how the methods differ:

```
function hideAllMonsters() {
  // actions here
};
```

This is the way that Flash 5 ActionScripters (and users from other languages) will most often write a function. It's just using an action called function, followed by the name of the function being declared and the usual sausagelike arrangement of braces, where you write out the actions that make up the function body.

You're doing largely the same thing when you write a callback. The big difference in using the *something = function(){* syntax is that you're actually defining your function as an instance or object. A cool side effect of

this is that you can define your function to exist somewhere other than the current timeline (that is, you can attach it to something else via dot notation). That might sound a bit complex, but you've been doing this all the time when you've defined event handlers. The following onEnterFrame function may be defined on the main timeline, but it's actually an event handler for the timeline monster1_mc:

```
monster1_mc.onEnterFrame = function() {
    // actions for attacking Tokyo
};
```

The other thing that stops an event handler from looking like the first version of a function earlier is that it has no name. In the preceding script, the function is simply assigned to the onEnterFrame function of monster1_mc. This is called an **anonymous function**.

So what about *using* these function-thingies, then? Simple. Use them just as if they were actions. Here's how you might call your monster-hiding function from elsewhere in the script:

```
if (mutantInvisibilityRayIsActive) {
    hideAllMonsters();
};
```

Note that you can't do this with an anonymous function because it has no name.

You can even think of a function as being like your own custom action—one that's totally exclusive to your movie!

Using functions to hide evil math

Let's start with a very simple example. Say you're writing some ActionScript within a Flash movie that has to perform an evil bit of math on a variable called myVariable. It's not nice, but it's sometimes necessary to get the jaw-dropping effects you're after. OK, you'll hold back on the *really* evil math for now and just do something like "add 5 and double." That seems simple.

You're probably already thinking of something along the lines of this:

```
// input number
var myVariable:Number = 4;
// add five
myVariable += 5;
// double it
myVariable *= 2;
// show the result on the screen
trace(myVariable);
```

That's easy enough, but what if you need to do exactly the same thing another 20 times in various places throughout your movie? Of course, you could just type out the same code over and over again, but this will quickly get to be a real drag, especially if your calculation runs to more than a couple of simple expressions and you wind up having to type out seven or eight lines every time.

This is the perfect time to use a function, so let's fix one up. First, you need to write a declaration:

```
notSoEvilMath = function() {
    myVariable += 5;
    myVariable *= 2;
};
```

There you are—you've created a simple function to take myVariable, add 5, and double it. Now you can use a notSoEvilMath() function call in place of your original math:

```
notSoEvilMath = function() {
    myVariable += 5;
    myVariable *= 2;
};
myVariable = 4;
notSoEvilMath();
trace(myVariable);
```

Create a new Flash movie and attach this script to the first frame.

> It's very important to always write a function declaration before you call it; otherwise, Flash won't understand the function call and will just ignore it. You should declare all your functions near the beginning of the first frame, before you write any script that needs to call them.

Run the movie, and you should see the Output window pop up with the answer:

There you are: a simple function declaration and function call.

OK, you may be thinking it looked easier to do it the old way. Don't forget, though, that your functions will often be much more complicated than one simple expression!

There's another benefit to using functions here. Say you suddenly find you need to alter the code so that it triples the input instead of doubling it. If you had done it ten times the longhand way, you would need to change ten different lines of script. With the function, you need to change only one character on one line:

```
notSoEvilMath = function() {
    myVariable += 5;
    myVariable *= 3;
};
```

Every time it's called now, notSoEvilMath() will add 5 and *triple* the value of myVariable, just as if that was what it had always done:

Once you've used functions a few times, you can't imagine how you ever managed without them! Of course, their usefulness becomes more obvious when you're using them for something practical and when you're using them several times in one movie. Let's look at another situation where functions can help you out.

Using functions to take care of repetitive jobs

Think back to the hangman game you put together at the end of Chapter 5 and the faculty records movie you made in Chapter 4. In both cases, you used _visible to make buttons appear and disappear when you wanted. This is a very powerful way to control what's shown on the stage in Flash, and you'll often find it being used to substitute one button (or movie clip) for another.

For example, the hangman movie had a play game button and an interface movie clip. You only ever wanted one of them on the screen at any particular time: you needed the interface while you were playing the game, and you needed the button when you weren't playing the game. That meant writing this at one point in the script:

```
playGame_btn._visible = false;
interface_mc._visible = true;
```

and this a little later on:

```
playGame_btn._visible = true;
interface_mc._visible = false;
```

Eagle-eyed readers will have already spotted that these two bits of script are almost identical. The difference boils down to which instance gets shown and which one gets hidden. In fact, even this isn't much of a difference: in both cases, the visible one gets hidden,

while the invisible one gets unhidden. You can write this out in script as follows:

```
playGame_btn._visible =
➥ !playGame_btn._visible;
interface_mc._visible =
➥ !interface_mc._visible;
```

The ! sign is called a **NOT operator**, and it shows you the opposite Boolean value of whatever comes straight after it. If playGame_btn._visible is false, !playGame_btn._visible must be true, and vice versa. In effect, both lines of code now say

if it's hidden, show it -
➥ *if it's showing, hide it*

with one line of code doing that for each instance. You now have a script that you can reuse whenever you need to swap these two instances, so let's make it into a function:

```
swap = function() {
    playGame_btn._visible =
➥ !playGame_btn._visible;
    interface_mc._visible =
➥ !interface_mc._visible;
};
```

Once you've added this declaration to your hangman script, you can replace each of the true/false pairs with a quick and simple call to the new swap() function:

```
playGame_btn.onRelease = function() {
// initialize graphics
    hangman_mc.gotoAndStop("play");
    swap();
    ...
};
interface_mc.enter_btn.onRelease =
➥ function() {
  wrong = true;
  ...
  if (wrong && notGuessed) {
    hangman_mc.nextFrame();
    if (hangman_mc._currentFrame == 10) {
      // GAME OVER!!
      swap();
    }
  }
};
```

You've used swap() only twice, but it's already making the script shorter and easier to follow. Think how much more of a difference it would make if you had 10 or 20 swaps to do!

Note that in this case, you can get away with declaring the swap() function at the end of your script. This is because the only sections of script that ever call it are tucked away inside event handlers, so they won't be run until the user clicks one of the buttons on the stage. By that time, all the script on frame 1 should have run, so Flash will know all about your function and what to do about lines that just say swap().

Choosing which actions to bundle and where

Say you want a script that tells your movie to go shopping ten times in a row. In the past, you'd write a loop (probably a for loop, since you know it needs to cycle ten times) containing all the actions involved in "going shopping." If there are only two or three of these actions, that's probably fine as is, but what if there are two or three *hundred*? Don't laugh—it's quite possible!

Sure, you can still pop them all inside the for loop, but it will make your script a real pain to follow. Another option is to define a function called goShopping that contains all the actions to go shopping once. The loop that calls goShopping() ten times over will then look like this:

```
for(i=0; i<10; i++) {
    goShopping();
};
```

That simplifies things here, but what about in the function declaration? Oh, no . . . now *that's* going to go on for six or seven pages, and you have the same problem of readability you had before!

Actually, you've already worked out a way around this particular problem. A "go shopping" task is too big and complex, so you break it down into subtasks. What about this:

```
for(i=0; i<10; i++) {
    walkToStore();
    findItems();
    walkToCheckout();
    findCost();
    payForGoods();
    checkChange();
    walkHome();
};
```

Of course, you'd have to work out how all these other functions work and declare them as well, but each one will be *much* smaller than the goShopping() declaration would have been.

What you can do at this point, even though you haven't worked out what will go into each function, is use **empty functions** (also called **stubs**) to build up some skeleton code:

```
walkToStore = function () {
  trace("I am going to the store...");
};
findItems = function () {
  trace("I am finding the items...");
};
walkToCheckout = function () {
  trace("I am walking to the checkout...");
};
findCost = function () {
  trace("I am being told the bill...");
};
payForGoods = function () {
  trace("I am paying for the goods...");
};
checkChange = function () {
  trace("I am checking my change...");
};
walkHome = function () {
  trace("I am walking home.\n\n");
};
for (i=0; i<10; i++) {
  walkToStore();
  findItems();
  walkToCheckout();
  findCost();
  payForGoods();
  checkChange();
  walkHome();
}
```

The `trace()` actions give you a rough indication of which functions will run when, and in what order. The preceding listing gives the following output:

```
▼ Output                                    ⬚  ≡
I am walking to the checkout...         ▲
I am being told the bill...
I am paying for the goods...
I am checking my change...
I am walking home.


I am going to the store...
I am finding the items...
I am walking to the checkout...
I am being told the bill...
I am paying for the goods...
I am checking my change...
I am walking home.                      ▼
```

Already you can see the shopping trip coming together.

A listing consisting of empty function stubs is sometimes called a **skeleton**. You write a skeleton consisting of empty function stubs, and then test it with `trace()` messages to make sure it does roughly what you expect. When you're happy with the skeleton, you start adding the flesh by adding code to the functions to get it to do what you really want: move graphics around, act on variables to create an effect, or solve a problem.

> *The beauty of using functions in this way is that you can make high-level changes early on when your code is still easy to change—at the skeleton stage. This is preferable to making changes at the end when more of your code is written, simply because then there's more that could go wrong.*
>
> *Also, using a skeleton allows you to avoid using another form of planning that most computer classes seem to teach (but that is actually all but useless in event-driven code): flowcharts.*

Arguments and redundancy

Another thing you can spot here is **redundancy**—that is, three of these functions are doing almost exactly the same thing. The only difference between `walkToStore()`, `walkToCheckout()`, and `walkHome()` is the destination they send your imaginary customer walking off to. So is there anything you can do about this? Of course there is!

You've already seen that some actions (`gotoAndPlay()`, for example) will let you feed in arguments between the parentheses that influence how they're carried out by Flash. Well, you can do exactly the same thing with functions.

Say you set up a general function called `walkTo()` that lets you feed in a string argument that tells it where you want to walk to. Still sticking with basic stubs, you might declare it like this:

```
walk = function(destination) {
  trace("I am now walking to
➥ "+destination);
};
```

The main difference between this and the other functions you've declared is the fact that you've stuck a variable called `destination` between the parentheses following function. This variable is called a **function parameter**, and you use it to store the value of the argument with which the function was called.

Confused yet? Let's take a step or two back and think about what happens when you call the `walk()` function. Say you write a line of script like this, which calls the `walkTo()` function using the argument `"the store..."`:

```
walkTo("the store...");
```

Flash sees this, and since it doesn't recognize `walkTo()` as an ActionScript action, it hunts around for a function called walkTo. It finds the declaration you wrote and spots that there's one parameter in there, which is called destination. Currently, destination has no value, but that doesn't last long—Flash now takes the argument value `"the store..."` and stores it in destination, ready for the actions within the function (in this case, the `trace()`) to make use of it.

> As you're probably already beginning to realize, you've already used arguments. When you write gotoAndStop(5), the 5 is an argument to the gotoAndStop() action. There's not much difference between actions and functions, except Macromedia has already written the actions for you, and functions are something you write yourself. Fundamentally, though, they're the same thing.

Here's the full script using arguments:

```
walkTo = function (destination) {
  trace("I am now walking to
➥ "+destination);
};
findItems = function () {
  trace("I am finding the items...");
};
walkToCheckout = function () {
  trace("I am walking to the checkout...");
};
findCost = function () {
  trace("I am being told the bill...");
};
payForGoods = function () {
  trace("I am paying for the goods...");
};
checkChange = function () {
  trace("I am checking my change...");
};
walkHome = function () {
  trace("I am walking home.");
};
for (i=0; i<10; i++) {
  walkTo("the store...");
  findItems();
  walkTo("the checkout...");
  findCost();
  payForGoods();
  checkChange();
  walkTo("my home.\n\n");
}
```

Later on, if you want to make the "walking" part of this movie any more complex, you'll just need to change the declaration. You don't need to do anything to the

three calls inside goShopping(), since they just tell Flash to use this string to do whatever actions are in the walk() function.

Local variables and modular code

The process of fleshing out each stub into final code is best done using something programmers call a **modular process**. This means that you should be able to write each function as if it was a separate little program (or **module**) in its own right.

For this to happen, each function block should ideally have its own set of variables that are *local* to the function. For example, if two variables have a variable called myVariable, the two versions of myVariable will be different and separate variables—they just happen to have the same name. The advantages of doing this are massive:

- You can use the same function in different SWFs because each function defines its own variables within itself and keeps all its internal calculations to itself. It's unaffected by other code around it.

- Because each function is effectively a self-contained mini-script, a lot of other things also stay contained within the function, the most important being *bugs*. A bug that occurs within your function will tend to make the function behave incorrectly, but it's less able to cross over into other functions and make them go wrong as well. If you use no functions at all, it's difficult to constrain errors in this way.

- You can test each function separately, which also means that you can usually design each function separately (or, at least, you can once you define your skeleton). The great thing about this is it makes it easier for a team to work on a single application. By splitting up your problem into self-contained functions, you can assign the writing of each function to a different team member. You can equally tackle each function as a separate problem yourself.

So what is a **local variable**? A local variable is one defined within a function. It will exist only for as long as the function is running. As soon as the function ends, the variable is deleted.

Let's see how this would be useful. Suppose you want to expand the checkChange() function to check the amount of money you'll receive. Change the checkChange() function so that it looks like this:

```
checkChange = function (cost,
➡ moneyTendered, moneyReturned) {
  var money:Number = 0;
  trace("I am checking my change...");
  money = moneyTendered-cost;
  if (money == moneyReturned) {
    trace("  Correct change given");
  } else {
    trace("  Incorrect amount!");
  }
};
```

The variable money is the local variable: it exists only within your function block and is discarded when you exit the function. It's used to give you moneyTendered-cost, and this is the value of money you expect back (the money you tender to the cashier minus the cost of your purchases). If the money you get back from the cashier, moneyReturned, is the same as the money you expect, money, all is well and good. If it isn't, you have received the incorrect amount. What you do in this case will probably depend on the level of the difference, in whose favor it is, and how indignant/honest you are, but let's leave that issue alone for now.

To see the code in action for a correct amount, change the main code to the following (note that you now remove the loop, which makes the output easier to handle):

```
walkTo("the store...");
findItems();
walkTo("the checkout...");
findCost();
payForGoods();
checkChange(12.50, 15.00, 2.50);
walkTo("my home.\n\n");
```

Also, to check for an incorrect change value, try using this:

```
checkChange(12.50, 15.00, 2.55);
```

That's cool, but it doesn't really tell you the advantage of your local variable money. Well, suppose you have

an amount of money to spend at a restaurant later on in the day, and you also store this in a variable called money but on the main timeline. How would this affect your money local variable in the function checkChange()? Let's find out! Change the main code as shown:

```
var money:Number = 30;
walkTo("the store...");
findItems();
walkTo("the checkout...");
findCost();
payForGoods();
checkChange(12.50, 15.00, 2.50);
walkTo("my home.\n\n");
trace("My restaurant money is $"+money);
```

```
▼ Output                                    ≡
I am now walking to the store...
I am finding the items...
I am now walking to the checkout...
I am being told the bill...
I am paying for the goods...
I am checking my change...
  Incorrect amount!
I am now walking to my home.


My restaurant money is $30
```

See that? The variable money on the main timeline is unaffected by the local variable money in the function checkChange(). Here's the sequence of events that makes this possible:

1. At the start of the main code, you define a variable called money.

2. You run through the functions. One of them, checkChange(), creates a different variable also called money within its code block. This version of money is constrained to the function block in which it was created, so it doesn't affect the version on the main timeline.

3. When you check the money value on the main timeline, it's still $30.00, so you can go and have that meal after all.

Now try it again, but this time remove the line that starts with var in checkChange(). This time, the variable money *is* changed. Why?

Well, when within a function, Flash will assume a local variable *only if there's one defined*. If there isn't a local variable called money defined, the function will be able to see the one outside the function and will use that.

> *This is a consequence of scope and the* **scope chain**. *A variable defined within a function will "mask out" a same-named variable defined outside the function. If there's no local variable, the version used will be the one outside the function, but on the same timeline. If there's no variable on the current timeline with the same name, then Flash will look in* _global. *If Flash still can't find a variable of the required name, it will either return* undefined *(if you're trying to read the variable value) or create a variable on the current timeline (if you're trying to write a variable value).*

Returning values from a function

Let's look at another function stub and refine it a little. Looking at the train of events in the shopping trip, you could reasonably expect that the findCost() function would be required to calculate the bill by adding up the prices of every item you bought. There are two problems here.

- You don't know how many items you've bought. As well as the prices for the items being different, the number of items is different every time, so you don't know how many arguments to add. The way around this is easy: use an array. An array is essentially a list of values, which is just what you need here.

- You haven't defined what you've bought anywhere yet. That's no problem either—you can simply make up some data for now. Making up some variables (or code) so that your functions under development can be tested properly (even though your skeleton isn't yet developed enough to work with the functions) is called adding a **test harness**. A test harness is a bit of code you add so that you

can develop a module (function) further without having to wait for other code (which is required to provide the real data) to be written.

OK, test harness first. Add the following to the main program:

```
var money:Number = 30;
var priceTags:Array = new Array();
walkTo("the store...");
findItems();
priceTags = [0.50, 1.40, 3.60, 7.00];
walkTo("the checkout...");
findCost();
payForGoods();
checkChange(12.50, 15.00, 2.50);
walkTo("my home.\n\n");
trace("My restaurant money is $"+money);
```

You've defined an array of price tags called priceTags. This array contains a set of numbers to represent the goods bought: $0.50, $1.40, $3.60, and $7.00. These values should really be generated by findItems(), but since that isn't yet written (and neither is a database of stuff the store sells, which you would also need), you just insert priceTags into the code where you would expect it to be available.

Next up, you need to write the findCost() function code. Change the findCost() function as shown here: .

```
findCost = function (prices) {
  var i:Number = 0;
  var money:Number = 0;
  for (i=0; i<prices.length; i++) {
    money = money+prices[i];
  }
  trace("I am being told the bill...");
  return money;
};
```

The function takes in an array, prices, and adds all the array element values to create a local variable, money (so now you have *three* versions of the same variable!). The last line of this function is something you haven't seen before: a return. A returned value is just that—a value that's returned to the main program. You can read this returned value by equating the function call to something:

```
myVariable = findCost(prices);
```

This will return the value of money (the version in findCost() that is equal to the sum of all the prices) into myVariable. Try it by changing the main code to start using this new function:

```
var money:Number = 30;
var priceTags:Array = new Array();
var total:Number = 0;
walkTo("the store...");
findItems();
walkTo("the checkout...");
priceTags = [0.50, 1.40, 3.60, 7.00];
total = findCost(priceTags);
trace(total);
payForGoods();
checkChange(12.50, 15.00, 2.50);
walkTo("my home.\n\n");
trace("My restaurant money is $"+money);
```

When you trace the value total, you see that it has taken on the value of the sum of your prices, courtesy of the code in findCost().

Typing functions

So far, you've been making lots of small changes to the code, and looking at it now you can see already something is beginning to emerge that's starting to look seriously complicated. Luckily, this complexity is being managed by your use of functions. You look at only one thing at a time by working on one function at a time. In short, the problem is split into distinct bits of manageable code via functions.

The next thing you'll examine will make your functions look like that geeky hard-core stuff you see in big, thick books you'd rather not read, but trust me, it's really not that bad.

In the same way you can type variables, you can also type functions. There are two things you can type: the arguments and the returned value. The returned value can be either nothing or something. If it's something, it has to be one of the following types: number, string, array, or Boolean. If it's nothing, Flash returns void, which is computer-speak for nothing.

The difference between zero, void, and undefined is worth mentioning. Zero is a number that represents "none." It has no value, but it does have a type: number, as in "number zero." Not only is void a nonvalue, but also it has no type—it is really nothing! undefined is when you get nothing, but for a slightly different reason: it represents missing information that stops you from defining something. A variable can be undefined or only partially undefined. For example, a variable could have an undefined value but a defined type (or even vice versa).

> *Looking at this in a non-programming-centric way, consider the number of CDs a person owns by the band Curve. If I'm a fan of the band, but I don't have any Curve CDs because I can't get hold of them, I have zero records. If I don't have any Curve CDs because I've never heard of the band, then the whole question is a void—I have no Curve CDs and they aren't something I would have anyway. If I have some Curve CDs, but they're a band I used to be into in the early 1990s, and I don't listen to Curve much nowadays so I'm not sure how many CDs I have, I have an undefined number of Curve CDs.*

A function can have a type defined for each argument, plus one for the returned value:

```
myFunction = function (argument:type,
➥ argument:type):type {
  // do stuff
};
```

For each argument, you can define a type in much the same way as you do a variable. For the return value, you place the type between) and { at the end of the first line of the function definition. If the function doesn't return any value, then the return type is Void.

The listing so far with fully typed functions looks something like this:

```
walkTo = function (destination:String):
➡ Void {
  trace("I am now walking to
➡ "+destination);
};
findItems = function ():Void {
  trace("I am finding the items...");
};
walkToCheckout = function ():Void {
  trace("I am walking to the checkout...");
};
findCost = function (prices:Array):Number {
  var i:Number = 0;
  var money:Number = 0;
  for (i=0; i<prices.length; i++) {
    money = money+prices[i];
  }
  trace("I am being told the bill...");
  return money;
};
payForGoods = function ():Void {
  trace("I am paying for the goods...");
};
checkChange = function (cost:Number,
➡ moneyTendered:Number,
➡ moneyReturned:Number):Void {
  var money:Number = 0;
  trace("I am checking my change...");
  money = moneyTendered-cost;
  if (money == moneyReturned) {
    trace("  Correct change given");
  } else {
    trace("  Incorrect amount!");
  }
};
```

```
walkHome = function ():Void {
  trace("I am walking home.");
};
var money:Number = 30;
var priceTags:Array = new Array();
var total:Number = 0;
walkTo("the store...");
findItems();
walkTo("the checkout...");
priceTags = [0.50, 1.40, 3.60, 7.00];
total = findCost(priceTags);
trace(total);
payForGoods();
checkChange(12.50, 15.00, 2.50);
walkTo("my home.\n\n");
trace("My restaurant money is $"+money);
```

The advantage of using typing in this way is that it tightens up your skeleton. If you put a void in where you actually return a value, Flash will raise an error (the return value isn't actually void because you create a return value). If you set an argument as a string but then make that argument a number, Flash will raise an error. There are a number of errors Flash will raise because typing makes it become very fussy about what it will allow to run. For a beginner that may seem like a really bad thing, but it's actually very good. Although it takes more effort to make code run, when it does, *the code is more likely to run correctly.* Typing tends to create more robust and structured code than untyped styles.

Typing functions makes your skeleton much more precise in the way it defines the flow of data between the main code and functions (and, in more complex code, between functions). It prevents you from making big mistakes later on in the development cycle by imposing some well-defined skeleton code early in the planning stage.

Typing is very useful, but it really only comes into its own in longer scripts. You'll use typing extensively in the Futuremedia site code later on in the book.

Running in circles

Say I wanted to give you a real scare. I could put a sheet over my head and jump out at you shouting "Boo!" On the other hand, I could stay where I am and whisper the word "trigonometry" in your ear. Similar effect, I should imagine (it's certainly been my reaction in the past!).

Don't panic—I'm not about to try to give you a boring lesson in pure math. I'm just going to show you two very cool little functions that you and your movies might find rather useful.

```
circleX = function(distance, angle) {
    var distance, angle;
    return distance *
➡ Math.sin(Math.PI * angle/6);
};
circleY = function(distance, angle) {
    var distance, angle;
    return -distance *
➡ Math.cos(Math.PI * angle/6);
};
```

Now, if you can look at these lines without breaking out in a cold sweat, that's great. If not, it doesn't matter, because I'm not going to talk about *how* these functions work, and you don't need to understand any of what's going on inside them. All that's really important is *what* they do.

So far in this book, all the ActionScript animation you've looked at has dealt with things moving about the stage in straight lines. Even the moving blobs you created in Chapter 4 were basically just an animated straight line connecting the pointer to a fixed point on the stage.

That's pretty cool as far as it goes, but what about making circles instead of straight lines? Sounds hard, but with these two functions, it's not a problem. You can use the functions to turn circle-based values like "distance from center" and "angle" (that is, how far around the circle you are) into x- and y-coordinates that you can use to position things on the stage.

Let's start off by drawing a clock face—well, the numbers on a clock face anyway.

1. Create a new Flash document, change the frame rate to 18 fps, and create a dynamic text field on the stage. Make sure the field is big enough to hold the text 12 in whichever type you decide to use. Enter number_txt in the instance name field of the Properties panel:

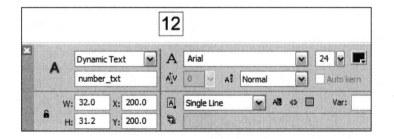

2. Use the Properties panel to place the text field at X: 200, Y: 200; replace 12 with the uppercase letter O; and click the Align Center Text button (at the top right of the Properties panel) to center-justify the text.

```
O
```

3. Now add a new layer called actions, open the Actions panel, and click the pushpin button to make sure you don't accidentally lose focus. Let's start by putting in the two functions I showed you just a few moments ago. Just key them in exactly as shown:

```
circleX = function(distance, angle) {
    var distance, angle;
    return distance *
➥ Math.sin(Math.PI * angle/6);
};
circleY = function(distance, angle) {
    var distance, angle;
    return -distance *
➥ Math.cos(Math.PI * angle/6);
};
```

4. Now for the main script. It's very simple—you'll just loop through values 1 to 12 and make a duplicate of the number_txt text field each time:

```
for (i=1; i<13; i++) {
    duplicateMovieClip(number_txt,
➥ "number"+i+"_txt", i);
    // position text field
    // change text in text field
};
```

As you can see, I've added comments to mark where you need to add a couple more things. Let's start with the second of these, since it's the simpler of the two:

```
for (i=1; i<13; i++) {
    duplicateMovieClip(number_txt,
➥ "number"+i+"_txt", i);
    // position text field
    // change text in text field
    _root["number"+i+"_txt"].text = i;
};
```

This is a new way of setting the text in a text field, but hopefully it shouldn't worry you too much. In the past, you used the Var field in the Properties panel to give Flash the name of a variable to store the text in. You don't do that this time. Since you're making 12 copies of the text field, they'd all end up using the *same* variable! Instead, you hack straight into the dynamic text field's text property—just as you've done in the past with other properties such as _x, _y, and visible—and change it to the current value of i.

This gives you 12 new text fields, showing numbers 1 through 12. Note that the for loop starts at i=1 and stops as soon as i hits 13. Run the movie now, and you'll see all the text fields sitting on top of each other:

Ugh! Let's move them, quick!

The plan is to put the 12 new text fields in a circle around the original one, which still has its top-left corner sitting at X:200, Y:200. This is where your functions come in. You give them two arguments: a distance from the center and the number of a position around the edge of the circle. Here's the script you need to add:

```
for (i=1; i<13; i++) {
    duplicateMovieClip(number_txt,
➥ "number"+i+"_txt", i);
    // position text field
    _root["number"+i+"_txt"]._x =
➥ 200+circleX(100, i);
    _root["number"+i+"_txt"]._y =
➥ 200+circleY(100, i);
    // change text in text field
    _root["number"+i+"_txt"].text = i;
};
```

For each text field, you set the x-coordinate to 200 plus the return value of circleX() and the y-coordinate to 200 plus the return value of circleY(). You'll look at how you call these functions in a moment. First, though, reassure yourself that this does actually work by testing the movie now. This is what you should see:

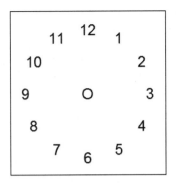

Cool! You've made a circle without resorting to any evil mathematical equations. Well, actually you have, but they're hidden away inside the functions, so you don't need to worry about them. All that really matters is this pair of lines:

```
_root["number"+i+"_txt"]._x =
➥ 200+circleX(100, i);
_root["number"+i+"_txt"]._y =
➥ 200+circleY(100, i);
```

and the fact that circleX() gives you the x-coordinate for each number, while circleY() gives you the y-coordinate for each number. What about all those numbers you used on the right side, though? They do look a bit confusing, so let's figure out what they do.

Changing how the circle appears

All the values in the first line determine x-coordinates for the text fields, while all those in the second line control y-coordinates for the text fields. There are three different things to look at in each line, and each controls a different aspect of how the overall circle appears.

1. First up, you have the 200s that go on the beginning of each line's right side. These tell Flash what point on the stage to draw the circle around. Try changing them to see how they affect things:

```
_root["number"+i+"_txt"]._x =
➥ 250+circleX(100, i);
_root["number"+i+"_txt"]._y =
➥ 250+circleY(100, i);
```

Now you should see something like this:

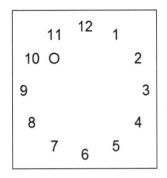

The central O is still where it was, but all the numbers have moved down and across to the right because you've added 50 to the center coordinates.

2. OK, so the first pair of values controls the position of the circle. What about the first of the arguments in each of the functions? At the moment, they're both set to 100, so let's try changing them and see what happens. Don't forget to put the 200s back first:

```
_root["number"+i+"_txt"]._x =
➥ 200+circleX(200, i);
_root["number"+i+"_txt"]._y =
➥ 200+circleY(50, i);
```

You doubled the top value and halved the bottom one, so you should now see something like this:

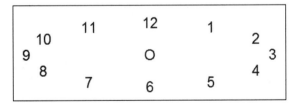

Yes, you can use the first argument in circleX() to control how wide the "circle" is and the first argument in circleY() to control how tall it is. In fact, the values you give tell Flash the horizontal and vertical distances from center to edge, so this "circle" is all of 400 pixels wide and 100 pixels high.

167

Now for the second of the arguments. Right now this is simply i for both of them, and you can probably guess that this is what controls the angle (or rotation) of each position—that is, where on the circle each number will appear. If the second argument has a value of 6, you'll get a position at the bottom of the circle. Likewise, a value of 9 gives a position on the far left of the circle. To see this in effect, let's play with the values again:

```
_root["number"+i+"_txt"]._x =
➡ 200+circleX(200, i+2);
_root["number"+i+"_txt"]._y =
➡ 200+circleY(50, i+2);
```

This will give you the following:

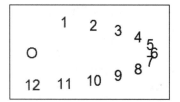

All the numbers have shifted around the clock face by two places. Even better, you don't need to stick to using whole numbers—for example, a value of 1.5 will give you a position halfway between the 1 and 2 positions. So what about halving the value of i?

```
_root["number"+i+"_txt"]._x =
➡ 200+circleX(200, i/2);
_root["number"+i+"_txt"]._y =
➡ 200+circleY(50, i/2);
```

Now the numbers will run from clock positions 0.5 to 6, so they're all on the right side of the circle, and none remain on the left:

As you can see, with these two circle functions, you can do some pretty impressive stuff. What's more, you don't need to know anything about what goes on inside them—you can just plug in a few numbers and draw circles, ovals, and arcs to your heart's content!

Before you get too carried away with this, there's another important lesson to learn about functions and what you can do with them.

Nesting functions

It may seem like an obvious point to make, but there's no reason you can't call one function from inside another. Say you have a simple function, double(), declared like this:

```
function double(x) {
    var x;
    x = x * 2;
    return x;
}
```

Now, if you want to create a new function quadruple() that multiplies a specified value by 4, you can set it up so that it calls the double() function twice over:

```
function quadruple(y) {
    var y;
    y = double(y);
    y = double(y);
    return y;
}
```

In fact, you could make this even shorter by actually passing the first double() function call as an argument in the second:

```
function quadruple(y) {
    var y;
    y = double(double(y));
    return y;
}
```

Here, Flash first calculates the result of the second function call, and then it uses this value as the argument for the first function call. Now, if you follow it up with something like this:

```
x = 4;
x = quadruple(x);
trace(x);
```

you'll get the value 16 in the Output window. First Flash doubles 4 to get 8, and then it doubles 8 to get 16. Easy. But what does this mean for scriptwriting in general?

It means that you can have as many layers of functions as you want between your overall problem and the separate actions that make up a scripted solution. Not only can you break down the task into various subtasks, but also you can break down each of the subtasks into its own sub-subtasks, and so on, for as long as you find it useful.

Using nested functions

The most obvious benefit of nesting functions is that you can call your own functions from inside an event handler. For instance, if you put your clock face script inside the onEnterFrame event handler for the root timeline, you can update it in real time.

Let's have some fun with this right away and make the number circle follow your mouse pointer around the stage.

1. Put the main script in an onEnterFrame event handler (so it updates all the text field positions once every frame) and change the 200s to _xmouse and _ymouse, respectively:

```
circleX = function (distance, angle) {
    var distance, angle;
    return distance*Math.sin(Math.
➡ PI*angle/6);
};
circleY = function (distance, angle) {
    var distance, angle;
    return -distance*Math.cos(Math.
➡ PI*angle/6);
};
onEnterFrame = function() {
    for (i=1; i<13; i++) {
        duplicateMovieClip(number_txt,
➡ "number"+i+"_txt", i);
        // position text field
        _root["number"+i+"_txt"]._x =
➡ _xmouse+circleX(100, i);
        _root["number"+i+"_txt"]._y =
➡ _ymouse+circleY(100, i);
        // change text in text field
        _root["number"+i+"_txt"].text = i;
    };
};
```

Run the movie again, and sure enough, the circle of numbers goes where the mouse pointer leads it. Wherever the pointer is, it's always in the middle of the circle.

2. Now let's see what happens if you use the mouse pointer to control the circle's width and height. Don't forget to put the positioning 200s back in, or you'll see some very strange things going on!

```
    _root["number"+i+"_txt"]._x =
➡ 200+circleX(_xmouse-200, i);
    _root["number"+i+"_txt"]._y =
➡ 200+circleY(_ymouse-200, i);
```

Now, as you move the mouse pointer across the stage, the circle's width changes accordingly. Likewise, the circle's height changes as you move the mouse pointer up and down the stage:

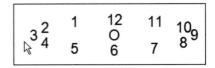

I've used _xmouse-200 and _ymouse-200 here, so that the circle collapses down on itself when the pointer's directly over the center (that is, when both have values of 200).

3. No, it isn't looking much like a circle any more, is it? Let's use the same value to control both the width *and* the height. You'll get the value from the x-coordinate of the mouse pointer and store it in a variable called size:

```
size = _xmouse-200;
_root["number"+i+"_txt"]._x =
➥ 200+circleX(size, i);
_root["number"+i+"_txt"]._y =
➥ 200+circleY(size, i);
```

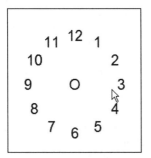

4. OK, you've figured out how to tweak the position of the circle, and you've just been fiddling with the width and height. What else is there? Well, there's still another function argument to play with.

Let's use _ymouse to control the rotation of the number circle. Since _ymouse can take values up to 500 or so, you'll divide it by 100 first, which will give you lots of fine control but with a rotation range of about 5. That's almost halfway around the clock, which should be enough for you to see that it's working OK.

```
size = _xmouse-200;
rotation = i + _ymouse/100;
_root["number"+i+"_txt"]._x =
➥ 200+circleX(size, rotation);
_root["number"+i+"_txt"]._y =
➥ 200+circleY(size, rotation);
```

Of course, you still need to add i to the _ymouse-based value; otherwise, all the text fields will end up in the same place. Now the circle turns around as you move the mouse up and down.

5. Let's quickly recap the full script listing:

```
circleX = function(distance, angle) {
    var distance, angle;
    return distance *
➥ Math.sin(Math.PI * angle/6);
};
circleY = function(distance, angle) {
    var distance, angle;
    return -distance *
➥ Math.cos(Math.PI * angle/6);
};
onEnterFrame = function() {
  for (i=1; i<13; i++) {
    duplicateMovieClip(number_txt,
➥ "number"+i+"_txt", i);
    // position text field
    size = _xmouse-200;
    rotation = i + _ymouse/100;
    _root["number"+i+"_txt"]._x =
➥ 200+circleX(size, rotation);
    _root["number"+i+"_txt"]._y =
➥ 200+circleY(size, rotation);
    // change text in text field
    _root["number"+i+"_txt"].text = i;
  };
};
```

Not bad, considering what you've achieved!

Using more function nesting to tidy up your script

Before we wrap up this chapter, let's see if you can't tighten up the script a little. Not everything in the onEnterFrame event handler actually needs to be there, and it makes sense to put the lines of code that position the text fields into their own function (so you can turn variables like size and rotation into function parameters and make the code easier to customize in future).

Let's leave the opening pair of functions alone (unless you're feeling very adventurous) and brew up a couple of brand-new ones just underneath.

1. The first of these new functions is called createTextFields(). It creates all the text fields for you when the movie starts.

```
createTextFields = function () {
    for (i=1; i<13; i++) {
        duplicateMovieClip(number_txt,
➥ "number"+i+"_txt", i);
        // change text in text field
        _root["number"+i+"_txt"].text = i;
    };
};
```

You're assuming that the actual text you put into each of the fields isn't going to change while the movie's running, so you set that up here as well.

2. You'll put all the other stuff into a function called positionTextFields().

```
positionTextFields =
➥ function (centerX, centerY,
➥ size, rotation){
  var centerX, centerY, size, rotation;
  for (i=1; i<13; i++) {
    field = "number"+i+"_txt";
    _root[field]._x = centerX +
➥ circleX(size, i+rotation);
    _root[field]._y = centerY +
➥ circleY(size, i+rotation);
  };
};
```

This function has four parameters that control exactly where the circle appears, how large the circle is, and the angle at which the numbers start around the circle.

3. Now that all the positioning script is tidily wrapped inside a function, the onEnterFrame event handler gets a lot simpler:

```
onEnterFrame = function () {
    positionTextFields(200, 200,
➥ _xmouse-200, _ymouse/100);
};
```

4. Finally, you need to run the createTextFields() action, so that the fields actually get set up:

```
createTextFields();
```

You can leave everything else to the onEnterFrame handler function.

5. Here's the finished script:

```
// DECLARE FUNCTIONS FIRST
circleX = function (distance, angle) {
    var distance, angle;
    return distance*
➥ Math.sin(Math.PI*angle/6);
};
circleY = function (distance, angle) {
    var distance, angle;
    return -distance*
➥ Math.cos(Math.PI*angle/6);
};
createTextFields = function () {
    for (i=1; i<13; i++) {
        duplicateMovieClip(number_txt,
➥ "number"+i+"_txt", i);
        // change text in text field
        _root["number"+i+"_txt"].text = i;
    };
};
positionTextFields = function (centerX,
➥ centerY, size, rotation){
    var centerX, centerY, size, rotation;
    for (i=1; i<13; i++) {
        _root["number"+i+"_txt"]._x =
➥ centerX + circleX(size, i+rotation);
        _root["number"+i+"_txt"]._y =
➥ centerY + circleY(size, i+rotation);
    };
};
// DECLARE onEnterFrame EVENT HANDLER
onEnterFrame = function () {
    positionTextFields(200, 200,
➥ _xmouse-200, _ymouse/100);
};
// ACTIONS TO RUN WHEN MOVIE STARTS
createTextFields();
```

Hmm. The code is actually a bit *longer* than it was before. So why is it worth making all those changes? Well, apart from the slight improvement in speed (now that you're not making a whole set of duplicate text fields every frame), you've pulled out the main circle variables as parameters in the positionTextFields() function. This makes it loads easier to change how you control the appearance of the circle. Of course, you've hard-wired certain features into the function—for example, the width and height will always be the same, the numbers will always be evenly spaced around the whole circle, and so on. There's nothing stopping you from changing that, though.

Now that you've seen how easy it is to use functions like circleX() and circleY() to make a funky little circle of text fields, you might like to start experimenting with them yourself. What you've done here is only the tip of the iceberg, and there are plenty of other possibilities left for you to explore. What about changing the value of rotation steadily from one frame to the next? Or using different values of size for the different text fields, so they spiral into the center? Or even changing the text fields for something completely different, like an animated movie clip? Now you have the basics down, the sky is the limit!

The important thing to realize in all this playing around is that you've taken a general feature (that is, being able to define points around a circle) and written it as a function. You have then largely forgotten about the circleX and circleY functions, and played around with the script that uses the functions—you've been able to forget the code inside the functions.

This modular "build a function, make it work, then forget about how it works and just use it" process is a hallmark of modular design in general. Not only does it prevent you from constantly reinventing the wheel, but also it allows you to repurpose code to do several things or simply to experiment.

Summary

Functions give you a way to bundle useful sets of actions so that you can define them once and reuse them as many times as you like. Not only can this help cut down on repetition and keep your scripts shorter, but also it can help you make your scripts more structured.

By breaking each task in your movie into several well-defined subtasks, you can keep your blocks of script relatively short and focused on specific goals. This makes it much easier to build your movie script in nice, easy-to-digest chunks. What's more, by nesting functions inside other functions, you can put as many levels of functions as you need between the overall goal of the movie and the individual actions that actually get the job done.

Let's recap the benefits of using functions:

- **Conciseness**: You define the function once, and you can call it as many times as you like.

- **Maintainability**: You change the function definition once, and you update its functionality throughout the movie.

- **Versatility**: You use arguments to apply the same function to different things.

Because functions are so crucial in the use of ActionScript, here's a summary of the different guises you will find functions in:

- The classic form of a function is as follows, and although it's the most common form in other languages, it suffers in the multitimeline world of Flash from the fact that it can exist only on the current timeline.

```
function someFunction(){
    // do stuff
};
```

- The basic "function as object" form of the function is as follows:

```
someFunction = function(){
    // do stuff
};
```

The cool thing about this form is that you can attach the function on a timeline other than the current one:

```
someMovieClip.someFunction = function(){
    // do stuff
};
```

- Finally, event handlers are simply functions in disguise. They have no name and are called **anonymous functions**. They are also referred to as **callbacks** because of the way they work. The event handler is associated with the function such that when the event occurs, the handler is invoked, and this in turn calls back along the association to the function.

```
someMovie.onEnterFrame - function(){
    // do stuff
};
```

Now that you've started to look at how you can structure to the actions behind your scripts, you're ready to go a step further and bring data back into the frame. In the next chapter, you'll see how you can bundle functions *and* variables, helping you make scripts that are even more self-contained and reusable.

The practical benefits of all this stuff may not seem particularly obvious at this stage, since even the largest scripts you've written so far have been pretty small (by professional standards, anyway). All the same, it's obvious that you'll want to move on to larger projects, so keep at it and you'll soon be in a position to reap the rewards! Buckle up, now—Base Camp 1 is well behind you, and the slopes are starting to kick in. Take a break and prepare to unlock the ancient secrets of Mount ActionScript.

Chapter 7

OBJECTS AND CLASSES

What we'll cover in this chapter:

- Using objects to describe things with state and behavior
- Storing related collections of variables and functions
- Creating custom object classes
- Working with ActionScript's core built-in objects

I spent much of the last chapter discussing how functions can help give your scripts a nice, clear structure—especially when you choose them wisely and name them sensibly! One of the techniques you looked at dealt with nesting functions. That way, you can break down any complex task into a few slightly simpler sub-tasks, break each of those down into even simpler sub-subtasks, and so on, until each one reaches a level at which it needs just a few simple actions to do its job. You end up with lots of short, tightly focused functions, each playing its own special part in the overall movie script.

On their own, functions can be fairly useful, but they also have one or two drawbacks:

- A function can't remember anything for itself. Any variables you use set up inside the declaration will be created when the function starts to run and destroyed as soon as the function is done. If you call a function three times in a row, it will do exactly the same thing every time, because the third call doesn't know anything about the first two.

- If a function does make a lasting change to the movie, it's because it contains script that acts on things that are defined somewhere else in the movie. For example, the swap() function you considered for the hangman game refers specifically to a named button instance *and* a named movie clip. Neither of these things is part of the function, but the function itself is no use to anyone unless both the button and movie clip exist in the movie.

OK, but so what? You've used functions, and they worked fine. What's the problem?

The problem is this: as your movies get bigger and bigger, it gets harder to keep track of what's where. This makes it much more difficult to get away with writing functions like swap(), because they rely on things that may or may not exist somewhere out there in the murky depths of your Flash magnum opus. To help avoid this sort of thing, you have to make your code more *general*. You need to learn how to work with **objects** and **classes**.

Introducing objects and classes

Suppose you were having one of those deep, meaningful conversations concerning what reality is all about. (I sometimes get into this sort of conversation after a good night out and too much beer to shut up but not enough to sleep.) Just what is stuff all about? What are the material objects all around us, and what is their relationship to each other? Well, this probably isn't the answer, but it's a good preamble and link into what I want to talk about, so here goes:

Objects are individual things such as

- My car, which has a unique license plate to differentiate it from others on the road

- The keyboard that I'm writing this book with, serial number KY24000BXXXA

- The weird latex frog toy that Karen gave me, which sits on top of my monitor and I've named Flash the frog

The individual objects around us are unique things that conform to a set of broader groups that defines them, for example:

- My car is a particular model and make, and this defines its basic features and function.

- My keyboard is an Apple Pro keyboard, and it looks and works like all other Apple Pro keyboards.

- There is a factory somewhere that makes loads of latex frogs according to a basic design. This design specifies all of them as being equally weird as Flash the frog, and they'll have the same trickery involved in them that makes Flash feel permanently wet when you touch him, but your hand is always dry.

These groups that objects are defined by can be called a number of things depending on what you're describing—species, model, or blueprint. However, they all broadly mean the same thing: **class**, which you can define as "a template that defines all objects within it."

You don't just have lots of different classes, though—you have **hierarchies** of them. For example, my keyboard is an Apple Pro, but it's also part of a larger class of electronic things called **input devices**, and **input devices** are part of another class you could define called **computer peripherals**.

So now you might be thinking, "Hey, you should be on talk shows that specialize in personal-relationship dilemmas for spouting the obvious like that! C'mon, Sham, what does any of this have to do with coding?" Well, quite a lot. The concept of individual objects and a hierarchy of classes that defines them underpins a set of modern coding techniques that many computer languages, including ActionScript 2.0, conform to, and these techniques go by the grand name of **object-oriented programming** (**OOP**).

> There are several flavors of OOP. The OOP flavor Flash MX used (the previous version of the one you're using) is a stripped-down one, with only predefined classes. It's referred to as **prototype based**, and you won't consider it in this book. The OOP flavor Flash MX 2004 uses concentrates on building classes and their interrelationships to define objects, and it's sometimes called **class based**.

In fact, it's precisely *because* objects and classes of objects are familiar things from the real world that they're useful to us. Say you have a car. It could *be* a red Ferrari with a 2400cc engine. Lovely. Common sense tells you there are certain things it can *do*: start, stop, change gears, reverse, and so on. It's nice to imagine actually doing those things, but there's no great mental strain involved.

On the other hand, say you have a brick. It could *be* 2 pounds in weight, brown, made of clay, and part of the top of a wall. But it can't *do* much; it just sort of . . . sits there.

These two examples highlight the important characteristics of real objects: they're things that have **state** (all the things they *are*—where they are, what they look like, what they're made of, and so on) and **behavior** (all the things they can possibly *do* to change that state in some way). Because they're examples of objects that

you've encountered in the real world, you already have a good idea of what these things can and can't be. Common sense tells you that you can't change gears on a brick (unless, perhaps, it's one of those lovely new LEGO blocks), so you're not likely to try!

Based on this idea, ActionScript objects give you another sort of descriptive container (like variables are for data and functions are for actions) that can *be* and *do* lots of different things, just like the objects you see around you in the real world. The *being* is taken care of by **properties** (for values that can vary, such as position), while the *doing* is defined in terms of functions, which are now called **methods** in the OOP system.

Once you start digging around behind the scenes, you'll find that objects and classes are fundamental to everything that goes on in Flash and ActionScript. You don't need to create them all from scratch, as you've done in the past with variables and functions, because Flash already has plenty of built-in classes for you to work with. You can, however, create new classes if you need (for example) to model weird latex frogs via ActionScript. Commonly in web design you don't need that many frogs, but you do need a class of objects that you can click and create web navigations with. Such a class might be called Button. You might also want a class that represents timelines full of tweens and graphics, and call it MovieClip. Sounding familiar yet?

Objects are very much fundamental to programming, and people call them different things. Another common name is **instance**. Ah! Now we're back on track!

There are two final things you need to fit into your linkage between Flash OOP, the things I've discussed so far in the book, and the real world, and you'll have cracked it: **type** and **abstraction**.

Type and object-oriented programming

Typing is simply the process of differentiating between classes and not allowing different classes to mix. For example, if you were running a zoo, you would try to treat the birds differently from the fish. You wouldn't get far if you put all the fish in a big cage with perches and plenty of unobstructed space to fly around in, and fed them seed plus a little fat in winter.

In the same way, objects need to be treated differently depending on what they are, and this is what type is all about. You use type to tell Flash what each object is, so that if you try to keep your hummingbirds in a 6-foot-deep tank containing saltwater, gravel, and a faux underwater cave, it can tell you there's a mismatch between the type (bird) and the context you're using it in (glug glug).

In Flash, type doesn't give you faster or neater code, and you don't have to use it if you don't want to. Although in the real world you know birds and underwater grottos don't mix, in the world of Flash objects, what does and doesn't go together can get a little technical and may have no real-world analogy you can use to sort it out in your own mind. Typing your code allows Flash to keep track of your data zoo and keeps all your information in its own cage, fed by the appropriate functions and watered by the correct interfaces.

> **Strict typing** *is all about maintaining the integrity of your data so that the different sorts of information (or, more specifically, the different classes of information) are kept separate.*

Classes, generalization, and abstraction

So what use is this class thing? This object-class philosophy-of-stuff seems very neat and sensible, but what is it good for? What if I instead defined a code model based on the sayings of Forrest Gump's mom? Some of that was sensible as well. Well, the thing about thinking in terms of classes is that you can generalize and abstract. Let me explain.

There's a cool thing about my Apple Pro keyboard, and that is that my computer *isn't a Mac*. It's a PC. Because I know from experience that an Apple Pro keyboard is the best keyboard for the sort of constant typing that a full-time author has to do, I use it in place of the decidedly variable keyboards PCs come with. The reason that

the Apple Pro keyboard works on my PC is that although it has basic classes (model, Apple-specific keyboard layouts and keys, and so on) that are different from PC keyboard models, if you go back far enough, PC keyboards and Mac keyboards have the same master class: they're all in the same **computer input devices** class. Among other things, input devices in this master class have the same connection: **universal serial bus (USB)**. So I can plug my Apple Pro keyboard into my PC, and the PC won't say, "Uh oh, that's a Mac object—I can't use it. Sorry, I think I feel a blue screen coming on." Instead, it will say, "Oh, OK, that's a standard USB keyboard object. Let me get the general interfaces to identify and run that from the Windows CD-ROM, and you can get going on your next opus almost immediately."

I guess a programming philosophy based on Forrest Gump sayings would be cool because the rules would be funny in a wry, "idiot talks rubbish but there's a deeper postmodern meaning in what he says" kind of way, but they wouldn't give us Apple Pro keyboards that work anywhere or general ActionScript that can be used for many different purposes, because the underlying code philosophy is about generalization.

Seeing arrays in a new light

Back in Chapter 3 you started playing with arrays. As you've seen since then, arrays can be terribly useful for storing lots of variables in one place, and with the power of loops added in, they're clearly a force to be reckoned with.

Well, you ain't seen nothing yet!

The humble array happens to be one marvelous example of an ActionScript class. You already know it as a container that holds lots of variables (rather like a real-world numbered list). It also has a few tricks up its sleeve (as you may have guessed after seeing that join() business I used during the hangman game). You can see what's on offer by taking a look in the Actions toolbox (on the left side of the Actions panel), where you'll find Array listed under Objects ➤ Core, with three entries beneath it in the hierarchy:

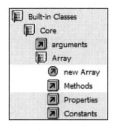

> In the simplest possible terms, you can think of an object as a bunch of related values, constants, and functions, wrapped together to make a neat, self-contained building block that you can use in your movie script. When you're dealing with classes, there are special technical names you give to the three parts of an object: the values are called **properties**, the **constants** retain the same name, and the functions are referred to as **methods**.

> As well as preventing you from mixing data, using strict typing has another advantage: Flash knows you're talking about an array without having to run the code to find out. This means that it will use code hinting to show you all possible properties, methods, and constants as soon as you type letters. It will do this without your needing to use the _array suffix that nontyped versions of ActionScript (those before ActionScript 2.0) require.

> Also worth noting is that when programmers use the term "an array," they mean an instance that is an array. When programmers say "Array," they mean the class that defines what an array is. When referring to the Array class, you always use an uppercase letter "A" in the term, both in the code and in written text.

The Array constructor method

The first of the Array methods is new Array, and this is a special sort of action known as a **constructor**. Why? Because it's what you use to *construct* an Array instance (or, to use the alternative term, an object) in the first place. You've seen this used quite a few times already, for example:

```
letters = new Array("f","l","a","s","h");
```

This line tells Flash to construct a new object of type Array, give it five string elements (with values as shown), and store it in the container letters. Of course, that's pretty much as you understood it before—or at least, I hope it is!

If you want to create a typed variable to avoid the "kestrel found dead in tropical fish aquarium," zoo-shocker type errors, you would use something like this to do the same thing:

```
var letters:Array = new Array("f", "l",
➥ "a", "s", "h");
```

If you use the typed version of your constructor, you'll see that hints will work straight out. If you use the seemingly quicker nontyped version, you'll have to change the array name to letters_array before Flash knows you're talking about the Array class, so you'll probably get more mileage on the "save typing" front by using strict typing.

For example, if you type the code shown in the following image, Flash will know letters is an array by the fact that you've defined its type as Array. This means that as soon as you key the text letters. (letters followed by a dot) into the Script pane, Flash will know the next thing you need to add is a method or property of the Array class, and it will show you a drop-down menu with the possible choices.

```
var letters:Array = new Array("f", "l", "a", "s", "h");
letters.
        concat
        join
        length
        pop
        push
        reverse
        shift
        slice
```

If you don't use strict typing (that is, you don't include the first line of the preceding code), the only way you can tell Flash that letters is an array is by calling it letters_array.

Other Array methods

Now take a look in the Methods book, and you'll see a list of all those tricks I mentioned earlier:

You should recognize at least one of these—you used join() in Chapter 5 to join together all the elements in a long string. It took one argument, which specified a string for it to place between each element and the next:

```
// returns "f,l,a,s,h" (default)
letters.join();
// returns "flash"
letters.join("");
// returns "f l a s h"
letters.join(" ");
// returns "f+l+a+s+h"
letters.join("+");
```

Just like the functions you saw toward the end of the previous chapter, the join() method simply returns a value—a string, in this case—and has no effect on the array on which it operates. That's not always the case, though:

```
// reverses the order of elements
letters.reverse();
// now returns "hsalf"
letters.join("")
// sorts elements alphabetically
lettersGuessed.sort();
// now returns "afhls"
lettersGuessed.join("");
// adds new final element "MX"
letters.push("MX");
// now returns "hsalfMX"
letters.join("")
```

I won't go through the rest of the Array methods, or we'll be here all day! Besides, the ActionScript Dictionary (under the Help menu) does a pretty good job of describing what the rest of the methods do if you feel the need to find out more. The important thing is that you know how to use the methods: simply write the name of the array you want to work on, add a dot, and write the name of the method you want to apply, followed by a pair of parentheses. Sometimes you'll want to add an argument or two between the parentheses, but more often than not, you'll just leave them empty for the simpler methods you'll be using as a beginner.

Array properties

Look in the Properties book, and you'll find a single entry called length. Of course, this is just the property you used in Chapter 5 to tell you how many array elements to loop through:

    elementsInLettersArray = letters.length

No parentheses here, because it's a property, not a method. OK, been there, done that. But is that *it* for the array properties? What about all the elements? Surely there are array properties too? Yes, there are. But think about it for a moment, and you'll see why they aren't among the built-in properties listed in the Actions toolbox. It's because they're *not* built in! All the elements you add to an array are **custom properties**. In other words, they don't need to exist until your script specifically defines them, so they aren't part of ActionScript's general definition of what an array is.

Eagle-eyed readers will notice that they've used exactly the same dot notation to run actions, functions, and now methods. Very spooky!

Unfortunately, the ActionScript Dictionary doesn't make much of a distinction between classes and instances—for example, Array is always described as an object. OK, this isn't wrong, but using one word to talk about two different things can confuse matters. Since I'm all for keeping things clear, I'm not going to make any shorthand approximations.

Creating classes and objects (instances) in Flash

As discussed so far, a class is really just a template for a particular type of object (whereas "type" actually means the same thing as when you "strictly type" a variable) that defines how the object should be constructed, what the object should be able to do, and so on. In the same way as a physical building always starts off as a blueprint on an architect's drawing board (or on an AutoCAD-enabled desktop), an object always begins life as a class.

The class contains a list of the common characteristics that all objects constructed from it should have. For example, imagine you have a class called Plant. It might have a template that includes the following:

- Name of the plant
- Height of the plant
- Color of the plant's flower
- Flowering month
- Recommended soil type

This might not seem particularly useful in a Flash movie, unless that is, you suddenly landed a big contract with a international chain of garden centers, found yourself commissioned to design an interface for the "create a garden" page on the company's website,

and needed a way to keep track of all the different plants the company sells. You never know when this sort of thing might come in handy!

Take a quick browse through the Actions toolbox, and you'll notice that all the built-in ActionScript class names (Array, Boolean, Date, Function, and so on) begin with an uppercase letter. This helpful convention reminds you that you're dealing with a class or an instance in your script.

Instances

Just as a single set of blueprints can be used as the basis for lots of physical buildings, one class can be used to produce lots of distinct instances of Array class objects. Any object instance based on the Plant class would feature a corresponding list of values (or properties). So, you might have an object instance called myFirstFlower (of class Plant) that includes the following properties:

- daffodil
- 20cm
- yellow
- March
- normal

Now you could use this information to cover a virtual garden with daffodils and show them flowering in March (or dying if the soil turned out to be too acidic). Another instance might store information about sunflowers, another one might contain information about lilies, and so on.

The Object object

All the classes you've looked at so far have been fairly specific, such as Array and MovieClip. A more general class is the slightly confusingly named Object class.

Wha . . .? A class called Object? What's an object of this class called? Um . . . an Object instance or, if you really like it silly, it's called an Object object (note the "O" and "o").

Right. Well, there is method to this madness, as you'll see. Suppose you want to create a single object that defines a plant. To define an object to hold some information (properties) about daffodils, you would use something like this:

```
myFirstFlower = new Object();
myFirstFlower.name = "daffodil";
myFirstFlower.height = 20;
myFirstFlower.flowerColor = "yellow";
myFirstFlower.flowerMonth = "March";
myFirstFlower.soilType = "normal";
```

Here you create another object from the built-in Object class, just like you did with the Array class before. You then step through each of the properties you want and tell Flash what values to put in which slots, just like when you define variables, except all the value containers are properties inside the myFirstFlower object.

Viewing an object in Flash

You can view the structure of the object myFirstFlower if you *debug* your movie.

1. Assuming you've entered the code in the preceding section (attach it to the first frame of a new FLA), select Control ➤ Debug Movie to enter test mode with the Debugger panel active.

As your code starts handling more and more complex data, you'll begin to realize that the content the user sees on the stage is less important to you as a programmer than the unseen stuff that's going on. It's the data created and manipulated by your ActionScript that's the major thing in your SWF. The Debugger panel is a window into this data and an important tool for the ActionScript developer.

2. The movie will appear paused. Click the ▷ icon (it's the one the cursor is near in the next image). Your movie will start. You'll see nothing on the stage when you do this. Your code defines myFirstFlower but does nothing with it or the stage.

3. You can look at the definition of myFirstFlower via the Debugger panel. You first need to get the left side of the Debugger panel to show the three panes shown in the following image. If you've never used the Debugger panel before, the middle (tabbed) pane will be hidden. To reveal it, click-drag the top of the Call Stack (lower panel) downward.

4. To find your object, you need to specify where it is (that is, the *scope* of myFirstFlower). In the top panel, click _level0. This is another name for the root timeline and is the scope of your object.

The Variables tab name is a little misleading, because this view also shows objects. Your object is the second one down (the first one, $version, is a number containing the version of the Flash player currently being used to display your SWF).

5. Click the plus sign (+) next to myFirstFlower to see the hierarchy of properties you've created in your script. The Value column tells you the value of each property.

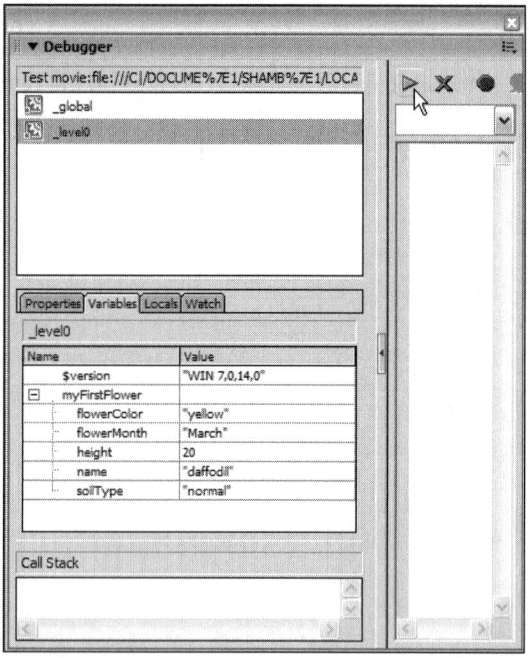

As you can see from the preceding image, the object is a tree diagram, with the properties branching from the object itself. The usefulness of an object is tied into this tree: it defines a **structure** *for your object, and this structure makes it easy for code to read the many property values. You may hear objects called* **structured data**, *and it's this tree that the term "structured" refers to.*

You could have defined the data associated with myFirstFlower *as a set of separate variables, but that would result in* **unstructured data**, *something that is easy to do if you want only one flower, but if you want 50,000 different flowers, you'll find it difficult to manage your code.*

You'll see the advantages of structured data when you start to use methods shortly.

Constructors

Object is a totally stripped-down class that has the bare minimum of properties and methods (none of which you really need to know about at this level) to let you add in properties like those in the preceding section. It therefore gives you a clean slate on which to build your own objects.

The only trouble with the code as it stands is that you've only made an instance of the Object class. There's no way to create a second instance (called mySecondFlower, perhaps) with the same set of properties without going through all of these lines setting up properties—and doing it again, and again, and again, for every new flower you decide to add in.

Instead, you need to define a Plant constructor function, like this:

```
function Plant(name, height, color,
➥ month, soil) {
  this.name = name;
   this.height = height;
  this.flowerColor = color;
  this.flowerMonth = month;
  this.soilType = soil;
};
```

You're probably wondering what all that business with this is all about. this is a keyword that refers to whichever object happens to have called your function. At this point it has no meaning, but as soon as you try plan A again . . .

```
myFirstFlower = new Plant("daffodil",
➥ "10cm",yellow", "March", "normal");
```

This time, Flash uses the Plant function to construct an object called myFirstFlower, with the properties name, height, and so on. The arguments you use make sure they're all given values to hold: "daffodil", "10cm", and so on. The advantage of doing it this way is that if you want to create another object instance of Plant (say, mySecondFlower, a 15 cm red tulip that grows in normal soil and flowers in June), you'd just need one more line to define it.

```
mySecondFlower = new Plant ("tulip",
➥ "15cm", "red", "June", "normal");
```

In fact, Object *is an extremely important class for ActionScript, as it's the class that* all *others are based on. It defines the basic rules for all ActionScript objects, and one of these is that it lets you add in properties as you go along. The great thing about working with* Object *is that it won't bog down your* Plant *objects with features that they don't need. It would be foolish to use the* Array *class as the basis for an object like this. There would be no point in having* sort() *and* reverse() *methods for an object whose sole purpose is to describe a plant—what on earth would those methods do? No, the* Object *class gives you a lean, mean instance that stores several pieces of associated data, ready for you to use further down the line.*

183

You can now read and write property values in myFirstFlower just as if it were any other object:

```
// traces "daffodil"
trace(myFirstFlower.name);
// traces "10cm"
trace(myFirstFlower.height);
//
myFirstFlower.height = "15cm";
// now traces "15cm"
trace(myFirstFlower.height);
```

Usually, though, you don't want to be messing about with properties—that would just make them like overly complicated variables. This is where methods come in. They do all the work of manipulating the properties for you. Let's see how that would work. Change the listing as shown:

```
function Plant(plantName:String,
➥ plantHeight:Number, plantColor:String,
➥ month:String, soil:String):Void {
  this.plantName = plantName;
  this.plantHeight = plantHeight;
  this.plantColor = plantColor;
  this.month = month;
  this.soil = soil;
  this.listPlant = function() {
    trace("name: "+this.plantName);
    trace("height: "+this.plantHeight);
```

```
    trace("color: "+this.plantColor);
    trace("month: "+this.month);
    trace("soil type: "+this.soil);
  };
  this.plantInSummer = function() {
    if ((this.month.toLowerCase() ==
➥ "june") || (this.month.toLowerCase()
➥ == "july") || (this.month ==
➥ "august")) {
      return true;
    } else {
      return false;
    }
  };
}
```

This time, you also type your constructor to make your code more able to detect errors, and you add two functions, listPlant() and plantInSummer(), inside the constructor.

The best way to see how this code works is to try it out. Add the following definition:

```
myFirstFlower = new Plant("daffodil",
➥ "10cm", "yellow", "March",
➥ "normal");
```

Whoops—you've done something wrong!

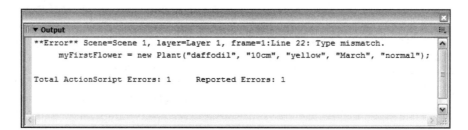

The plant length for `firstFlower` is given as `"10cm"`, which is a string. The constructor expects a number at the head of the constructor:

```
function Plant(plantName:String,
➥ plantHeight:Number,
➥ plantColor:String, month:String,
➥ soil:String):Void {
```

Change the line as follows:

```
myFirstFlower = new Plant("daffodil", 0.1,
➥ "yellow", "March", "normal");
```

Better—ah . . . except that it does nothing! Well, you've actually done something: you've created an object that defines `firstFlower`. What you aren't doing is using it. Now add the following:

```
myFirstFlower = new Plant("daffodil", 0.1,
➥ "yellow", "March", "normal");
myFirstFlower.listPlant();
```

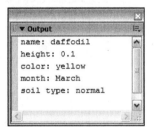

The method `listPlant()` lists all the properties of your object. Add the following lines to try it with another object, `mySecondFlower`:

```
mySecondFlower = new Plant("tulip", 0.15,
➥ "red", "June", "normal");
mySecondFlower.listPlant();
```

Finally, try the other method, `plantInSummer()`. This will look at the object properties to see whether it can be planted in the early-to-mid summer months. It will return `true` if it can and `false` if it can't. Add the following lines at the end of the current script:

```
trace(myFirstFlower.plantInSummer());
trace(mySecondFlower.plantInSummer());
```

You'll see `false` for the daffodil and `true` for the tulip.

So what can objects do that variables can't?

- They allow you to create data with custom structures. Your plant data is a far more complex set of data than simple, single-value numbers or strings, and it's a little more advanced than Array lists. In real-world solutions, data is always complex in the same way, and objects are one very good way of managing this.

- The plant objects can handle their own information via methods. Rather than write custom code to look at whether you can plant in summer, you simply ask the object itself. The object uses its methods to act on its properties, and it gives you the answer you want via stuff (properties and methods) that's part of the object itself. In short, the data and the means to handle it are both encapsulated in one "thing": the object.

A word of warning: the form of object you've just looked at is an example of an object that uses the pre-defined Object class. You don't create a class here; rather, you create a constructor function. The problem with it is that each object gains its *own* template rather than all your objects having the same template (which is what happens with class and true OOP).

Later on in the book, you'll look at the Flash MX 2004 class-based way of handling complex data, but for now, you need to take away the fact that objects consist of methods and properties, arranged in such a way that they become extremely useful for representing (and manipulating) data.

Objects, objects, everywhere . . .

So far, you've seen how the new constructor coupled with the class name Array will make an instance of the Array class. Likewise, you can pair new with the class name Object to create an instance of the Object class, and you can even write constructor functions that new can use as templates (but not quite full Flash MX 2004 classes), from which to create custom objects. So is this new business the only way to create object instances?

Actually, no it isn't. Most of the time, ActionScript does lots of work behind the scenes so that you can use objects without even realizing it. For example, it's pretty easy to create a variable:

```
myName = "Ben";
```

You probably never realized it before (but you've probably picked up a few hints!), but variables themselves are based on classes. When you create a string variable, it inherits various properties and methods from a class called String, which you can find listed under Built-in Classes ➤ Core ➤ String.

As you might be coming to expect, the String class has a constructor method new String and a length property just like the one you saw for the Array class. It also has a bunch of methods that can be (and have been) used to manipulate the characters in the string. You may remember using the toLowerCase() method as part of your password-protected movie back in

Chapter 4. Well, this is where it started life—as part of the String class.

All the methods of the String class (as found in Built-in Classes ➤ Core ➤ String ➤ Methods) are things that you might want to apply to the letters in a string. Many of them are similar (if not the same) as the Array methods you saw earlier, letting you mess around with letters in a string in the same way as you messed around with elements in your array.

Lurking objects

There are certain ActionScript classes that, for one reason or another, you don't need to construct for yourself before you put them to use.

*The technical term for these classes is **static**. A static class doesn't need to be defined, usually because there's only one. For example, there's only one stage in Flash, and your computer will have one mouse pointer on the screen and one active keyboard. In each case, you have no reason to create more than one object to work with any of these. To keep things simple, Flash defines the one instance that you'll need.*

One of these classes is called Math, and it's designed to work a bit like a simple calculator. It has methods that let you do complex mathematical operations (pow, sqr, sin, and cos) and generate random numbers, and properties that store "useful" mathematical constants. No, don't laugh! I assure you, when you start wanting to put 3D effects into your movies, you *will* find them invaluable.

Unlike most calculators, though, Math doesn't have a memory, so in many ways, it acts like a library of math commands that you can use whenever and wherever you need them. Since all the properties are constants (that is, they all have values that can't be altered), it doesn't make much sense to construct instances of Math. They'd all be exactly the same, and you wouldn't be able to change any of their properties, so what on earth would you do with more than one instance of the

Math class? The answer is, you don't need more than one. You access the single Math class directly like this:

```
output1 = Math.sqrt(input1);
```

Notice that you don't have to define new Math() before you start using it.

You can wire this up by using the file inputOutput.fla you created back in Chapter 3. Open this FLA and change the script to the following:

```
enter_btn.onRelease = function() {
    output_str = Math.sqrt(input_str);
};
```

This takes input1 as an argument in the sqrt() method, which works out the square root of its value (that is, it figures out the number you have to square to get input1).

Text fields always assume a string value, unless you tell them otherwise, so (although in this case your code works because the Math class is clever enough to figure it out) you should really use this:

```
enter_btn.onRelease = function() {
    output_str = Math.sqrt(Number
    (input_str));
};
```

Number() makes sure the input value is taken to be a number. Of course, that doesn't stop you from seeing NaN (not a number) as an answer if you click the enter button without entering a number, or if you enter a string such as "cat:", but you already know that from Chapter 3, and the fact that you can limit the inputs to what you want (such as numerals only) . . . see Chapter 3 for a refresher if you need reminding.

Another object you access directly via its class name is Stage. As mentioned earlier, the reason this is a static class is because there's only one stage, so you go ahead

and start using Stage as if it was always there, because, um . . . it was.

So what use is this Stage object? Well, say you want to know the current dimensions of the stage. You can call up the width and height properties like this:

```
xDimension = Stage.width;
yDimension = Stage.height;
```

Big deal! You knew that from the Properties panel. But say, for example, you want to make a movie that shows a ball bouncing around on the stage, within the *confines* of the stage. Sure, you could set up a couple of variables (xLimit=550 and yLimit=400) telling it where the far edges of the stage were.

So what then if you *changed* the size of the stage, but *forgot* to update the variables? Bingo—busted movie! It's much safer if you use Stage.width and Stage.height to set your limits, because then they're both updated for you automatically.

You can find the Stage class listed in the Actions toolbox under Built-in Classes ➤ Movie. Listed with the Stage class, you'll see one or two familiar names. Yes, these objects really are *everywhere*, including the stage itself!

Now that you've learned how to work with purely ActionScript-based objects, you're all set to discover what objects have to offer you in the graphical realm.

Making a show reel

Lots of sites out there use dynamic animation in a *functional* way. That is to say, the animation serves a purpose rather than just acting as eye candy. Navigation systems are perhaps one of the most useful things you can do with ActionScript. In this example, you're going to build an image gallery using a sideways scrolling motion to navigate through a show reel. You could use it for anything you want, whether that's showing off your holiday pictures or presenting an online portfolio.

In the process, you're going to use objects as a means of passing information to functions. You can find the finished show reel, saved as showreel.fla, in the download for this chapter. Copy it to a directory on your machine and put copies of the three accompanying JPG files (cobblestones.jpg, planet.jpg, and water.jpg) in the same directory. Load the FLA and give it a test run to see what it does.

> *It looks like these objects aren't content with meddling about behind the scenes! They're making a bid for freedom and starting to take over the stage itself. Is nothing sacred?*
>
> *OK, I confess these aren't all my own work. Credit and thanks must go to Photoshop masters Scott Hamlin and Scott Balay (of Eyeland Studio, www.eyeland.com) from whose book 40 Photoshop Power Effects (friends of Ed, 2002) came the spiffing techniques whose end results you see here.*

It's very simple to use: just move the pointer toward the left, and the show reel will scroll over to the left. Move the pointer toward the right, and the show reel will scroll back to the right. The scrolling increases in speed as you move the cursor farther from the centerline.

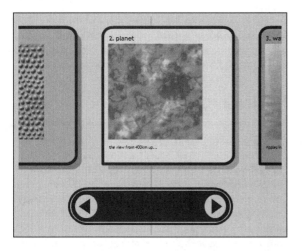

Remember the movies you made back in Chapter 1, when you looked at a tiny script that could make various objects (including a car, a bat, and a Starfleet SpaceCruiser) follow the x-coordinate of the cursor? Well, this is essentially the same thing—just a little

more elaborate. The original ball scroll was done with just two lines of ActionScript, and this effect doesn't take many more. This is the type of site navigation that just isn't possible with timelines; you have to start making use of ActionScript as a major part of your site.

Let's start building the show reel movie. First off, you need to prepare a few movie clips and give yourself something to work with on the stage.

1. Create a new Flash document and give it a total of four layers in the root timeline. You should call the layers actions, pictures, control bar, and center line. I've also made my stage a little smaller than the default (500×400 pixels), given it a frame rate of 18 fps, and given it a pale blue background (#CECFFF), so that it doesn't look quite so stark.

2. Next, you'll add the graphics that will help guide your users about the stage. I've used a vertical line to mark the middle of the stage (250 pixels across, on layer center line) and a chunky black bar to show in which direction the show reel will scroll (on layer control bar).

> *Note that the images themselves aren't built into the movie. As long as you have the files cobblestones.jpg, planet.jpg, and water.jpg in the same directory as the movie, Flash can pull them in when it needs them. It doesn't even matter what the images are—as long as you use the same filenames, you can replace the chapter's images with your own pictures and the movie won't miss a beat.*

Neither graphic actually *does* anything, so you won't have any more to do with them and you can lock their layers if you wish. Now for the important part: you're going to start building the show reel. It will consist of a long string of individual cells, with each one holding a single picture and information about the picture.

3. Use Insert ➤ New Symbol to define a new movie clip called `cell`, and give it four layers called content, border, background, and shadow.

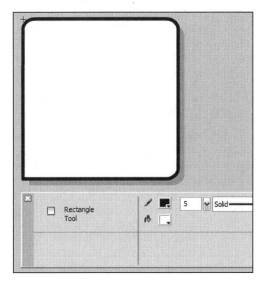

4. Select the background layer and add a white square with a 5 pt black border using the Rectangle tool. You can use the Round Rectangle Radius button to give it curved corners if you like that sort of thing. It should be 250 pixels wide, 250 pixels high, and positioned with its top-left corner at X:0, Y:0.

> *You can create a square by holding down the SHIFT key when you drag out with the Rectangle tool.*

5. Select the border, and use Edit ➤ Cut *and* Edit ➤ Paste in Place to move it into the layer called border.

6. Select the background layer again and copy the white fill you left there to the clipboard using *CTRL+C/CMD+C*. Paste it in place into the shadow layer using *CTRL+SHIFT+V/CMD+SHIFT+V*, and then move it slightly down and to the right of the original. Use the Color Mixer panel to change its color to black, and set Alpha to 20% so that it's almost transparent.

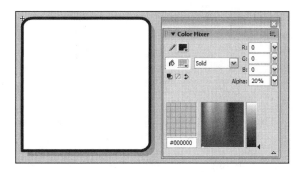

7. Select the background layer one more time, and press *F8* to convert this layer's contents to a movie clip. You'll use this movie clip to give your show reel cells some color. Go straight back to the cell timeline, and you'll find an instance ready and waiting. Use the Properties panel to give it the instance name bgnd_mc.

8. Now select the content layer and add a pair of dynamic text fields, one at the top and one at the bottom.

10. This part is a lot simpler than the cell was. You just need to create a new movie clip called reel in the Library, and inside your new, blank movie clip, put in a single instance of the cell movie clip. You should call the instance of cell cell_mc.

Use the Properties panel to name the text fields name_txt and description_txt. The lower one should also be set to Multiline, so that you can put in lots of nice descriptive text about your images.

9. Still on the content layer, add a black box in the space between the two text fields. Set its transparency (or Alpha) to 50% and press *F8* to convert it to a movie clip. Head straight back to the cell timeline and set its instance name to placeholder_mc. Now that you've set up the individual cell as a movie clip, you'll do the same for the complete show reel.

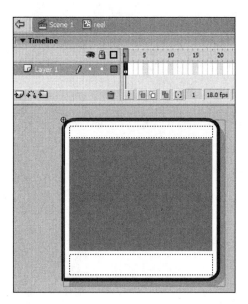

So now I imagine you're screwing up your face and saying, "What—just one instance? The FLA we looked at the start had *three* images in it. . . ."

Yes, just the one instance. You obviously don't want to run out of cells, but there's no point in making more than you need. So that your show reel movie stays as flexible as possible, plan on using duplicateMovieClip to add more cells as and when they're needed. All the decision making then goes on within the ActionScript, giving you a much more versatile movie.

Neat, huh? OK, you'll believe it when you see it—it's a trick, obviously.

11. There's just one more thing you need to do before the stage is all set: add an instance of the reel movie clip to the main timeline, on the pictures layer. Use the Properties panel to name it reel_mc and position it at X: 20, Y: 20:

All done!

Now that the stage is ready, it's time to add some ActionScript wiring behind the scenes and make all your movie clips perform some magic. Just like the hangman example you saw in Chapter 5, there's quite a lot of script to get through here, but don't let that put you off! It all breaks down into simple chunks, and you'll take them quite slowly.

> *The code here is fairly involved, so I've created an untyped version because it's easy for beginners to follow. You'll also find a typed version (one that defines all its data types fully) at the end of this exercise.*

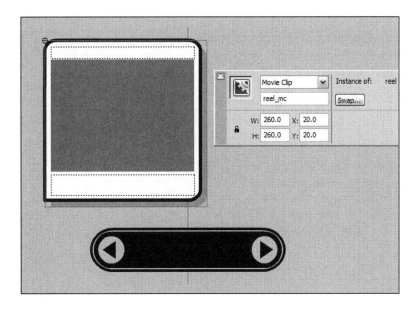

Even if you don't understand every single line, you should be able to get an idea of how the movie hangs together (and see how to tweak the important bits so that you can create your own variations). The first of these chunks controls the scrolling. It looks at where the mouse x-coordinate is in relation to a centerline and moves the reel_mc movie clip instance based on that distance. The direction (left or right) takes care of itself as long as you also consider the *sign* of this distance—whether it's positive or negative. You're not interested in the y-coordinate of the reel, because you're only moving the movie clip from left to right. You're not moving it up and down at all, so it will always stay at the same y-coordinate.

Before you start working on the code for the scroll, you need to make sure that you're very clear on what you need to do. Remember, if it won't work on paper, it won't work when you code it. You need a diagram, so here's a cleaned-up version of the sketch I drew to figure out how this scroll movement should work:

1. Here's the basic script, which you need to attach to frame 1of the actions layer:

```
_root.onEnterFrame = function() {
  reelSpeed = (_xmouse-center)/10;
  reel_mc._x += reelSpeed;
};
center = Stage.width/2;
```

Like I said before, it's not dissimilar to the stuff you did back in Chapter 1.

According to this diagram, you need to relate the distance between the mouse and the centerline to the speed at which the reel scrolls. In other words, you want the reel to scroll faster the farther away from the centerline the mouse gets. You've already defined center as the "halfway across the stage" value (the x = 275 line in the diagram, which assumes a default stage size of 550×400).

```
reelSpeed = (_xmouse-center);
```

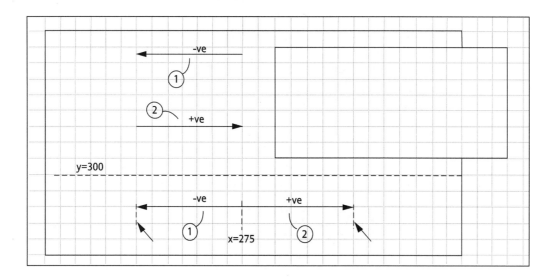

You use reelSpeed to tell Flash how many pixels to move reel_mc across the screen every frame. Except, in the finished FLA, it's actually this:

```
reelSpeed = (_xmouse-center)/10;
```

The original line made it scroll too fast, so I just divided it by 10 (after trying a few values to see what gave a good movement) to make it scroll at a more sensible speed. Try running the movie now, and you'll see an instant result: the one-cell show reel moves from left to right under mouse control, just as you want it to.

When the mouse pointer is to the left of the centerline (case 1 in the sketch), _xmouse-center will be negative, giving you a negative speed and reel_mc moving farther to the left with every new frame. If the mouse pointer is to the right of the centerline (as in case 2 *in the sketch*), you'll get a positive speed and the reel scrolls to the right.

2. There's still a problem, though. The reel doesn't stop when it gets to the edge, so it's quite easy to lose it off the side of the stage! To fix this, you need to put some limits on where reel_mc can move. Let's set up a stop value at either end. You can stop changing reel_mc._x if it ever tries going beyond these values:

```
// Handler to move show reel left and
// right across the stage
_root.onEnterFrame = function() {
  reelSpeed = (_xmouse-center)/10;
  reel_mc._x += reelSpeed;
  // Apply limits to reel position
  if (reel_mc._x<LEFTSTOP) {
    reel_mc._x = LEFTSTOP;
  } else if (reel_mc._x>RIGHTSTOP) {
    reel_mc._x = RIGHTSTOP;
  }
};
cellWidth = reel_mc.cell_mc._width;
center = Stage.width/2;
LEFTSTOP = 0-cellWidth/2;
RIGHTSTOP = Stage.width-cellWidth/2;
```

Now, if the reel moves too far in one direction or the other, you stop it dead in its tracks.

The LEFTSTOP and RIGHTSTOP values are set up so that the registration point of reel_mc will go past them when half of reel_mc is offscreen in either direction. The half of a width comes from cellWidth, which contains the width value of the cell. The new if statement detects either of these conditions and stops the clip from moving any farther in the same direction.

The maximum that you can now go in either direction is shown in the following images, which show the SWF as viewed in a browser.

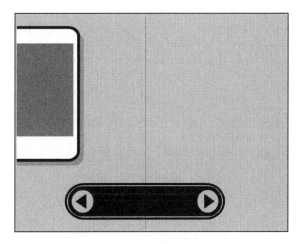

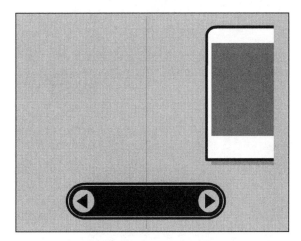

Note that some of the variables are in uppercase letters. It's customary to denote constants in this way, which is what the left and right stops are. Once they're defined, you never change them.

That's fine as long as you have only one cell in the show reel, but what about when you add some more? With the stops as they are, you can't scroll anything off the left side of the stage, so you're never going to see a third or fourth cell, let alone a fifth, a sixth, or a seventh.

3. It looks like you need to rethink the stops. Ideally, you should be able to scroll far enough to see *any* one of the cells in the middle of the stage, no matter how many you have. The following should do the trick (change the last two lines in the listing so far):

```
...
...
cellWidth = reel_mc.cell_mc._width;
center = Stage.width/2;
LEFTSTOP = center - reel_mc._width +
➡ cellWidth/2;
RIGHTSTOP = center - cellWidth/2;
```

The stops now ensure that the middle of the cell at either end of the show reel doesn't go past the centerline. In the following screenshot from the finished application, you can see this. The cell is at the farthest right it can go, halfway across the centerline.

If you run the movie now, you'll see that you've killed the scrolling movement! The single cell is trapped in the middle of the stage; the new stops mean that it can't move either left *or* right. You can prove that this is the case (and not that you get no movement because you've somehow broken the animation) by changing either LEFTSTOP or RIGHTSTOP to what it was previously.

Believe it or not, this is a *good* thing. The same cell occupies the left *and* right ends of your show reel, so the fact that it's confined to the center of the stage proves that your stops have worked. Of course, they'll be a lot more useful when you've added in a few more cells!

At this stage, you have a perfectly good scroller. You just need to add in some pictures and text, and take it away. You could add some more cell instances, import some graphics, add some static text fields, and so on. Great.

However, you're aiming a bit higher than that. Now that you have some ActionScript power, you'll make it really work for you. Rather than hard-wiring cells and images into your movie, you're going to get ActionScript to figure out what you want and do it for you.

Next chunk, then: you'll write an ActionScript function that adds new cells.

4. You know how to write functions, and you know how to make duplicate clips, so let's put the two together. The function will define two arguments: num (telling it *which* cell you want to set up) and details (telling it *how* you want the cell set up). Here's the basic function declaration:

```
newCell = function(num, details) {
  originalClip = _root.reel_mc.cell_mc;
  newClip = originalClip.
➡ duplicateMovieClip("cell"+num,
➡ num);
  newClip._x = num*300;
};
```

You start off by using `originalClip` to store a reference to the original cell instance, which is tucked away inside `reel_mc` in the root timeline. This just means you can now use the `originalClip` container in your script in place of the bulky `_root.reel_mc.cell_mc`, which is a bit of a mouthful in anyone's book!

Next, you use `duplicateMovieClip` to make a copy of the original cell. The new movie clip is called `cell1`, `cell2`, or whatever (depending on what value `num` has), and you store a reference to *that* in a container called `newClip`.

Now you tell Flash to set the `_x` property of `newClip` to `num*300`. `newClip` doesn't actually have an `_x` property, but it's pointing to something that does: the new movie clip. The end result is that your first cell (num=0) gets placed at X:0, while the second cell (num=1) goes to X:300, the third (num=2) goes to X:600, and so on.

I chose the number 300 here because for the container clips (260 pixels wide), this leaves a space between containers of 40 pixels, which seems to look about right. You'll find that many of the numbers you end up using in a Flash movie are based on what looks right or moves the way you want, rather than the result of some long-winded calculation.

5. Now just add a couple of function calls to the end of the script:

```
newCell(0, "");
newCell(1, "");
newCell(2, "");
```

Run the movie and you'll see you now have a grand total of three cells that scroll back and forth across the screen (shown below). All your new movie clips are created *inside* `reel_mc`, so the coordinates are relative to that. Your original script moves `reel_mc`, so all the cells move with it.

6. So you've got lots of nice blank cells on the stage. They scroll OK, but they aren't much to look at. You need to pass your `newCell` function some more information—a name, for example. There's a new line in the function that sets value of the name text field. You use the `details` argument to pull strings out of the function calls:

```
newCell = function (num, details) {
originalClip = _root.reel_mc.cell_mc;
newClip = originalClip.
➡ duplicateMovieClip("cell"+num,
➡ num);
newClip._x = num*300;
newClip.name_txt.text = num+1 +
➡ ". " + details;
};
newCell(0, "Ben");
newCell(1, "Sham");
newCell(2, "Matt");
```

7. Alternatively, you could use details to pass information about what color you want to make the new cell's background. Here's how you might do that:

```
newCell = function (num, details) {
originalClip = _root.reel_mc.cell_mc;
newClip = originalClip.
➡ duplicateMovieClip("cell"+num,
➡ num);
newClip._x = num*300;
// Set color of cell background
myColor = new Color(newClip.bgnd_mc);
myColor.setRGB(details);
};
newCell(0, 0xFF9999);
newCell(1, 0x99FF99);
newCell(2, 0x9999FF);
```

This time, you use the `Color` object to set the color of bgnd_mc inside each new clip.

8. Most important of all, you want to tell Flash which images to use in each cell. There's a useful action called `loadMovie()` that you can use to call up image files, but it still needs to know which file you want!

```
newCell = function (num, details) {
originalClip = _root.reel_mc.cell_mc;
newClip = originalClip.
➡ duplicateMovieClip("cell"+num,
➡ num);
newClip._x = num*300;
// Set cell content
content = newClip.placeholder_mc;
content.loadMovie(details);
};
newCell(0, "cobblestones.jpg");
newCell(1, "planet.jpg");
newCell(2, "water.jpg");
```

This time, the new lines load the image specified by details and use it to replace the placeholder_mc movie clip instance in each new cell:

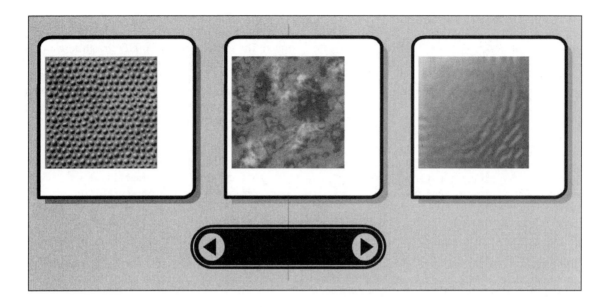

Of course, you actually want all three of these—and perhaps more! You could give the newCell function a few more arguments, passing picName in one, picColor in the next, and link (to the filename of the image to display) in the next.

However, there's another option: you could send the details argument an object. So far, you've always used simple variables as function parameters, passing strings and numbers to help the function do its job. But there's no reason you can't feed it objects as well—then the function can pull out various property values as and when it needs them. You don't have to deal with lots of parameters, and you can define your object properties wherever you like.

1. Let's start by declaring a constructor function for a Picture class of object. Every Picture object will have four properties, name, link, color, and description, so it will look like this:

```
picture = function (picName, link,
➥ picColor, description) {
  this.picName = picName;
  this.picLink = link;
  this.picColor = picColor;
  this.description = description;
};
```

2. Assuming you pass your newClip function one of these Picture objects via its details argument, you can use its properties like this:

```
// Define function for creating
// cells in the show reel
newCell = function (num, details) {
  originalClip = _root.reel_mc.cell_mc;
  newClip = originalClip.
➥ duplicateMovieClip("cell"+num,
➥ num);
  newClip._x = num*300;
  newClip.name_txt.text = num+1+". "+
➥ details.picName;
  newClip.description_txt.text =
➥ details.description;
  content = newClip.placeholder_mc;
  content.loadMovie(details.picLink);
  myColor = new Color(newClip.bgnd_mc);
  myColor.setRGB(details.picColor);
};
```

Here you combine all the earlier cell customizations (plus a new one that sets the description text) into one version, which uses the four properties of the Picture object referred to by details. Of course, this relies on you calling NewCell with proper parameters.

3. Here's the last piece in the puzzle:

```
// Set up picture objects
// Set up picture objects
pics[0] = new picture("cobblestones",
➥ "cobblestones.jpg", 0xFF9999,
➥ "from an English country
➥ lane...");
pics[1] = new picture("planet",
➥ "planet.jpg", 0x99FF99, "the view
➥ from 400km up...");
pics[2] = new picture("water", "water.jpg",
➥ 0x9999FF, "ripples in a pond...");
newCell(0, pic0);
newCell(1, pic1);
newCell(2, pic2);
```

You create three objects, specifying properties as you go, and you create the three cells quite separately. In fact, this would be even tidier if each Picture object was one element in an array. Then you can simply loop through all the elements and create a new cell for each:

```
pics = new Array();
// Set up picture objects
pics[0] = new picture("cobblestones",
➥ "cobblestones.jpg", 0xFF9999,
➥ "from an English country
➥ lane...");
pics[1] = new picture("planet",
➥ "planet.jpg", 0x99FF99,
➥ "the view from 400km up...");
pics[2] = new picture("water", "water.jpg",
➥ 0x9999FF, "ripples in a pond...");
// Loop through array of picture objects,
// creating a new cell for each
for (var i = 0; i<pics.length; i++) {
  newCell(i, pics[i]);
}
```

Phew! I'm sure you'll be very pleased to hear that the script is done! Try the movie out again, and you should get the full effect of a scrolling picture gallery.

So, was all that hard work *really* worth it? You seem to have spent quite a lot of effort getting nowhere very much. The scrolling effect is pretty straightforward, and most of the script seems to just be mucking about with data behind the scenes. That's as it may be, but thanks to all that mucking about, you have a show reel whose contents are completely defined by four lines of script. Here's that script in full:

```
// Handler to move show reel left and
// right across the stage
_root.onEnterFrame = function() {
  reelSpeed = (_xmouse-center)/10;
  reel_mc._x += reelSpeed;
  // Apply limits to reel position
  if (reel_mc._x<LEFTSTOP) {
    reel_mc._x = LEFTSTOP;
  } else if (reel_mc._x>RIGHTSTOP) {
    reel_mc._x = RIGHTSTOP;
  }
};
// Define constructor function for
// Picture objects
picture = function (picName, link,
➥ picColor, description) {
  this.picName = picName;
  this.picLink = link;
  this.picColor = picColor;
  this.description = description;
};
// Define function for creating cells in
//  the show reel
newCell = function (num, details) {
  // Create a new cell
  originalClip = _root.reel_mc.cell_mc;
  newClip = originalClip.
➥ duplicateMovieClip("cell"+num,
➥ num);
  // Set cell position and text fields
  newClip._x = num*300;
  newClip.name_txt.text = num+1+". "+
➥ details.picName;
  newClip.description_txt.text =
➥ details.description;
```

```
// Set cell content
content = newClip.placeholder_mc;
content.loadMovie(details.picLink);
// Set color of cell background
myColor = new Color(newClip.bgnd_mc);
myColor.setRGB(details.picColor);
};
// Initialize useful variables and
// picture array
cellWidth = reel_mc.cell_mc._width;
center = Stage.width/2;
pics = new Array();
//
// Set up picture objects
pics[0] = new picture("cobblestones",
➥ "cobblestones.jpg", 0xFF9999,
➥ "from an English country
➥ lane...");
pics[1] = new picture("planet",
➥ "planet.jpg", 0x99FF99,
➥ "the view from 400km up...");
pics[2] = new picture("water", "water.jpg",
➥ 0x9999FF, "ripples in a pond...");
// Loop through array of picture objects,
// creating a new cell for each
for (var i = 0; i<pics.length; i++) {
  newCell(i, pics[i]);
}
// Define constants (these cannot be
// defined until the pictures have been
// placed onscreen)
LEFTSTOP = center-reel_mc._width+
➥ cellWidth/2;
RIGHTSTOP = center-cellWidth/2;
```

Anytime you want to change the content or appearance of one of your cells (or even add a completely new one), you can simply change (or add) an element in the pics array.

As I said before, don't panic if you don't understand every line in here—that's not the point. What you should be starting to appreciate is that it pays to *structure* your scripts. Break them down into task-focused chunks, and the ease with which you can modify them later on should more than make up for the extra effort involved in writing them in the first place.

You should also add as many comments as you need (and more than you need, because you'll most likely forget what's going on in your code 6 months down the road!). I haven't added that many comments because I'm explaining what's happening in the text of this book (plus the fact that you have to type all the code in, so fewer lines are better), but for your own code, go to town with comments.

Oh, and one final thing for the fast-trackers: the same script, this time with strict typing. You'll see it's essentially the same, but it looks a lot longer and more complicated (and I didn't want to scare anyone off!):

```
// Handler to move show reel left and
// right across the stage
_root.onEnterFrame = function() {
  var reelSpeed:Number =
➥ (_xmouse-center)/10;
  reel_mc._x += reelSpeed;
  // Apply limits to reel position
  if (reel_mc._x<LEFTSTOP) {
    reel_mc._x = LEFTSTOP;
  } else if (reel_mc._x>RIGHTSTOP) {
    reel_mc._x = RIGHTSTOP;
  }
};
// Define constructor function for
// Picture objects
function picture(picName:String,
➥ link:String, picColor:Number,
➥ description:String):Void {
```

```
  this.picName = picName;
  this.picLink = link;
  this.picColor = picColor;
  this.description = description;
}
// Define function for creating cells in
// the show reel
function newCell(num:Number,
➥ details:Object):Void {
  var originalClip:MovieClip;
  var newClip:MovieClip;
  var picContent:MovieClip;
  var myColor:Color;
  // Create a new cell
  originalClip = _root.reel_mc.cell_mc;
  newClip = originalClip.
➥ duplicateMovieClip("cell"+num,
➥ num);
  // Set cell position and text fields
  newClip._x = num*300;
  newClip.name_txt.text = num+1+". "+
➥ details.picName;
  newClip.description_txt.text =
➥ details.description;
  // Set cell content
  content = newClip.placeholder_mc;
  content.loadMovie(details.picLink);
  // Set color of cell background
  myColor = new Color(newClip.bgnd_mc);
  myColor.setRGB(details.picColor);
}
// Initialize useful variables and
// picture array
var cellWidth:Number =
➥ reel_mc.cell_mc._width;
var center:Number = Stage.width/2;
var pics:Array = new Array();
//
```

```
// Set up picture objects
pics[0] = new picture("cobblestones",
➥ "cobblestones.jpg", 0xFF9999,
➥ "from an English country
➥ lane...");
pics[1] = new picture("planet",
➥ "planet.jpg", 0x99FF99,
➥ "the view from 400km up...");
pics[2] = new picture("water", "water.jpg",
➥ 0x9999FF, "ripples in a pond...");
// Loop through array of picture objects,
// creating a new cell for each
for (var i = 0; i<pics.length; i++) {
  newCell(i, pics[i]);
}
// Define constants (these cannot be
// defined until the pictures have been
// placed onscreen)
var LEFTSTOP:Number =
➥ center-reel_mc._width+cellWidth/2;
var RIGHTSTOP:Number =
➥ center-cellWidth/2;
```

Here are some notes for the typed version:

- The reason you use the *function something()* { form of functions is that the *something = function()* { form doesn't like to have its return value typed in Flash.

- You could have also had Function as the type for details in the function definition for details in newCell. This is because although details is an object, it's actually defined via a constructor function, and you're passing the function as an argument (yeah, that's an obscure one!).

```
  function newCell(num:Number,
➥ details:Function):Void {
```

Summary

So, what have you learned in this chapter? You've been introduced to objects, which are merely ways of grouping related variables, constants, and functions so that they more closely resemble actual things that you might want to represent in your Flash movies.

As they represent real-life things, objects have state and behavior (they not only *are* things, but they *do* things as well). In ActionScript, objects are described by their **properties** with their actions described by **methods**.

ActionScript has some built-in objects, which represent the sorts of standard elements that you'd want to include in your movies (such as numbers, strings, and math symbols), but you can also create your own objects to represent anything you wish. You've learned the difference between **classes** (which are general definitions of an object, such as *Car* or *Tree*) and **instances** (which are specific objects, such as *Ferrari* or *Oak*).

In the next chapter, you're going to tie the general concept of objects within code to something you've been using in Flash since before you'd heard of ActionScript—the movie clip—and you're going to see that you've been using objects all along, without even realizing it.

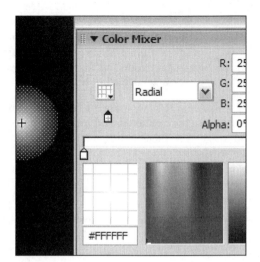

Chapter 8

OBJECTS ON THE STAGE

In this chapter we'll cover:

- Understanding how items on the stage correspond to objects in scripts
- Structuring scripts to take advantage of nested movie-clip timelines
- Using the properties of graphical objects to build advanced interactivity

OK, let's not waste any time here. There's one main idea to wrap your brain around in this chapter: the movie clips, buttons, and text fields you've been using since way back when **are all objects**.

Not only does this fact make it a lot easier to explain a whole variety of ActionScript syntax, but it also opens up a lot of possibilities for what you can do to the things you see on the stage in the course of a movie.

> *The clues were all there, but kudos to you if you spotted this fact already! If not, don't worry, because you're about to take a fresh look at these old friends.*

You already know that objects are useful for grouping methods and properties that have some sort of common theme. But what do the pure ActionScript objects (like Array and String) have to do with movie clips and things? Nothing at all, except that they have the same basic internal structure. They're all objects (or instances, which means the same thing), and they all contain properties and methods.

Words like "instance" and "property" have cropped up a few times when I've discussed items on the stage and, although movie clips have a visual appearance and a timeline, they're really just the same as data-only objects such as numbers and strings.

> *The reason you can see a movie clip is that Flash represents some of the properties of the movie clip class visually in the Flash authoring environment. This appearance, however, is still fundamentally tied to the same things: methods and properties.*

Movie clips and buttons as objects

As you know, to control an item on the stage, you need to give it an instance name, and you can do this via the Properties panel. For example, say you have a movie

clip called bat in the Library. When you drag an instance of bat onto the stage and select it, the Properties panel will look like this:

From here, you can set the instance name of this particular bat symbol and also tweak its position, width, height, and even color. Any changes you make will affect only this particular instance (which you'll call bat_mc), and any other bat instances you decide to put on the stage will have their own quite separate properties.

Once you've assigned an instance name to your movie clip instance, you can control these properties (and many more) from ActionScript. What's more, you do it in the same way as you controlled object properties in the last chapter. For example, you can set the x-coordinate like this:

```
bat_mc._x = 200;
```

So to control the bat's x-coordinate, you set a property called _x for the bat_mc movie clip instance. You did something similar when you used the _visible property to hide instances and used the text property of a dynamic text field to control what text appeared in it.

> *The reason some properties start with an underscore (_) and others don't is due to a historical oddity. In older versions of Flash, all properties started with _, but more recent additions to the language don't.*

You know that there are plenty of things a movie clip can *do*, so you expect to find at least one or two methods. For example, you can stop the bat_mc timeline like this:

```
bat_mc.stop();
```

But surely that's just the good old stop() action being applied to bat_mc? Yes, it is. But think for a moment about *what* an action really is. It's just an instruction to your movie (or to a movie clip) to *do* something. As far as ActionScript is concerned, there's no difference between applying the stop() action to a movie clip and calling a movie clip's stop() method. They both mean the same thing: stop that movie clip!

> *When you're just starting out with Flash, you can talk about actions or commands and nobody will notice, but using their proper name,* **methods**, *will never fail to impress. Knowing how to apply methods in Flash is crucial if you want to make it as a top-class ActionScripter.*

You've already seen a few other movie clip methods, such as duplicateMovieClip(), which you can use to make copies of a movie clip instance.

So, each instance (whether it's an input text field, a dynamic text field, a button, or a movie clip) has a set of **properties** that relate to its physical appearance. This is a movie clip, so the properties correspond to things like the clip's position, size, visibility, and total number of frames, while the methods do things like play, stop, load, and duplicate it. A button instance has its own particular properties and methods, which (among other things) let you control whether or not it can be clicked. Text fields also have their own properties and methods, the majority of which determine how the text will appear on the screen.

> *If you look in the Actions toolbox, you'll see that the classes (MovieClip, Button, and TextField) behind each of these instances also contain lists of events. Yes, the events are part of the objects too—is anything safe? I won't talk about how they fit into the world of objects, since that's pretty advanced stuff, which you can safely get along without at this stage. It's useful to know they're there, though, if only as a reminder of what events are available and as a place from which to start your own investigations.*

Using object (instance) properties

Let's have a quick reminder of movie clip properties in action.

1. Draw a circle on the stage, and with the circle still selected, press *F8* to make it a movie clip called ball. Give the instance on the stage the instance name ball01_mc.

2. Copy the ball01_mc instance and paste another instance onto the stage called ball02_mc.

3. Create a new layer called actions in the root timeline, and add the following script:

```
ball01_mc.onEnterFrame = function() {
  _x += 1;
};
```

Run the movie, and you'll see both balls move across the screen. Surely you've defined a callback only for the first ball, so why are both moving? Simple: when you specify _x in the event handler, you're actually working with _root._x, the x-coordinate of the root timeline, which controls the *whole stage*. Both balls are on _root, so both balls move. This occurs because if you don't tell Flash which movie clip you're talking about when you state a property, Flash will search for the nearest timeline, and this is always the one the code is actually attached to. Put in technical terms, Flash will use the **code scope**—in other words, where the code is.

4. Change the code like this:

```
ball01_mc.onEnterFrame = function() {
  ball01_mc._x += 1;
};
```

Now ball01_mc moves on its own. This is what you want: the onEnterFrame event handler for ball01_mc controls ball01_mc and nothing else.

5. Of course, that's not to say you can't make it control something else:

```
ball01_mc.onEnterFrame = function() {
  ball02_mc._x = ball02_mc._x+1;
};
```

Now the ball01_mc event script controls the _x property of ball02_mc.

It's quite easy to get a feel for a movie clip object, because its properties and methods relate to its physical appearance. As you've seen, not all objects are so intuitive. In general, they can be collections of any number of properties and methods that may or may not have an obvious visual representation.

Symbol behavior

When I mention symbol behavior in this book, I'm not talking about drag-and-drop behaviors that appear in the Behaviors panel (Window ➤ Development Panels ➤ Behaviors)—that's the stuff Macromedia put in for beginners, and you're already past all that! I'm referring to the behavior that you see when you press *CTRL+F8/CMD+F8* to create a new symbol:

Symbol behaviors are slightly different from methods and properties, and they aren't so fundamental to how you *define* objects on the stage. However, they're very useful when you come to use Library items, as they allow you to create instances of one symbol type from Library items of another type.

All symbols of a given type have a certain set of behaviors. A movie clip will behave like a movie clip (with frames, a playhead, and a stop() method), while a graphic symbol has a distinct visual appearance and not much else—certainly nothing that allows you to control it via ActionScript. There's really not a great deal more to know about symbol behavior than common sense tells you. One exception here is when you want to give graphic symbols properties that allow you to animate them, like those the MovieClip class has. To control a graphic symbol from ActionScript, you simply need to use the Properties panel to change its symbol *behavior* to that of a movie clip by changing the Behavior radio button from Graphic to Movie clip.

Hang on, though! From the earlier discussion, it sounded like bat_mc was an instance of a class called bat (as defined in the Library). But now you've seen a MovieClip class in the Actions toolbox and discovered it's possible to change the instance behavior without changing the Library item. So what's going on?

Two sides of the same object

The first thing to get clear is this: the Library doesn't *define* object classes. Actually, it just serves as a place where you can collect resources for dropping into your movies. A Library item won't normally have anything to do with the compiled movie unless you put an instance on the stage. If the Library item is set up as a button symbol, it will store resources that you'd expect to find useful in a button, such as four frames labeled Up, Down, Over, and Hit, which will be shown when the appropriate mouse events trigger them. On the other hand, if the Library item is set up as a graphic symbol, it needs only one frame.

So, if you drag a button symbol onto the stage and tell it to behave like a graphic, Flash will create a graphic based on resources from the first frame of the button symbol. Likewise (as you saw just now), if you drag a one-framed graphic symbol onto the stage and tell it to behave like a movie, it won't suddenly acquire more frames—the resources simply aren't there—but it will take on the ability to *behave* like a movie clip. You're basically telling Flash to create a movie clip and use the (limited) resources of the graphic symbol to give it some kind of visual presence on the stage.

This "behaving like a movie clip" business is all part of the MovieClip class. Likewise, a button's behavior is defined by the Button class. The behavior of a graphic is notable by its absence—it just sits tight and (hopefully) looks good—so you have no need for a class to define what it can do.

As you can probably see, the Library is a bit of an anomaly when it comes to ActionScript. Symbols in the Library seem to be there for a good reason when you aren't thinking of code (that is, the Library is your asset storehouse), but when you think about classes and instances, the status of symbols in the Library has no real meaning. They aren't yet fully instances, but they aren't classes either. The best way to describe them is as "partly populated instances." They're graphic shells ready to be populated by a class, and this occurs when you move them to the stage.

So, is there any way to tap into these Library resources from your ActionScript? After all, you're trying to find out how to control as many things as possible from ActionScript, and you could save a lot of time and effort if you could make the script drop all your instances onto the stage.

Working with Library items

The good news is that this isn't very hard at all. The main stumbling block is that when Flash generates a SWF, it normally ignores any Library symbols that aren't already being used to help define instances on the stage. This isn't a great problem if you're happy to add an instance of every symbol before you start scripting. Of course, you'd also need to name them all. And hide them all. And be prepared to take a bit of a performance hit if there are lots of them. But, if you have lots of time on your hands and you're not fussy about making your movie efficient, that's just fine. *(Silence.)* Hmm. That's a no, then.

If you've never scripted before (and possibly if you have), this may be the first time you realized this was possible, let alone seen it done. With nonscripted movies, you *always* have to put stuff on stage manually.

What I'm talking about here is quite different: you'll use ActionScript to take a movie clip *directly* from the Library and put it onto the stage. At first this may seem like a minor thing, but you can make some really cool features with this technique. For example, you can let users pick what symbols are used to control a movie—even while it's running. You'll certainly find it lurking behind stacks of the awesome effects produced by famous Flash designers. Let's cut to the chase and see how you can use placing movie clips directly on the stage to create a cool effect.

Making a swarm of particles

In this example, you're going to create a small cluster of particles, each of which will move about in tiny, random steps, giving the appearance of a swarming mass of . . . well, who knows what! I hope you'll agree that the end result is sufficiently eye-catching to make the effort worthwhile.

1. Create a new movie (*Ctrl/Cmd+N*). Make sure the stage is active and use the Properties panel to give it a black background and a frame rate of 18 fps. In the Timeline panel, rename Layer 1 as actions.

The default frame rate of 12 fps is a little dated now, and most computers capable of showing Flash in circulation will handle 18 fps to create significantly smoother graphics.

2. Use Insert ➤ New Symbol to create a new movie clip called particle. Use the Color Mixer to set up a radial fill style fading from opaque white at the center to transparent white at the perimeter. Now add a circle to the particle movie clip (mine's about 70 pixels in diameter).

207

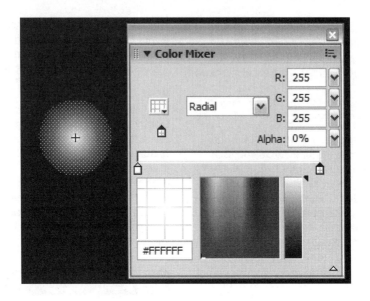

Now click the Scene 1 link to head back to the main timeline. In a moment, you're going to write some ActionScript that will put several copies of the particle movie clip onto the stage. First, though, you must tell Flash to include it in the final SWF and how to identify it. When you create a symbol (graphic, button, or movie clip) in Flash, the name you give it in the Library is really just for your benefit—it's a descriptive name to help remind you what the symbol is for and so that you can refer to it easily in text and speech. As far as ActionScript is concerned, that name doesn't exist. So, to call up a Library symbol from ActionScript, you need to give that symbol a special code-centric name that ActionScript can see. This is called a **linkage identifier**.

As you've learned, if there aren't initially any instances of a symbol on the stage (and this will certainly be the case for the particle movie clip), Flash won't normally bother including it in the SWF it generates. If this happened, your ActionScript would end up asking for something that wasn't there. Let's do something about that.

3. Call up the Library panel (press *CTRL+L*) and *CTRL*-click (right-click on a PC) the entry for your particle movie clip. Select Linkage from the context menu that appears, and you'll find yourself presented with the Linkage Properties dialog box. This is where you link your movie clip to the ActionScript environment.

Enter particle in the Identifier text box, select the Export for ActionScript check box (so the movie gets exported to the SWF, ready for ActionScript to play with it), and click OK. In this case, you use a linkage identifier that's the same as your descriptive Library name, which saves you from any possibility of a mix-up. Remember, though, that they're quite separate names (one for you, one for ActionScript) and could just as well be completely different if that was what you wanted.

208

The Export in first frame *check box will automatically be checked when you select the* Export for ActionScript *box. Do not uncheck the* Export in first frame *box!*

4. Select frame 1 of the actions layer (in the root timeline), and with this frame still selected, open the Actions panel. This is where you're going to attach all your ActionScript.

5. Begin by putting a single instance of the particle movie clip onto the stage, using the attachMovie() method:

```
_root.attachMovie("particle", "particle1",
➡ 1);
```

This will leave you with an instance of the particle movie clip (called particle1) on level 1 of the root movie timeline. If you test run the movie now, you'll see the movie clip sitting there, lifeless and still at the top-left corner (because the particle, particle1, has _x and _y properties of 0). Let's do something about that and bring it to life.

6. Change the script to the following:

```
myParticle = _root.attachMovie("particle",
➡ "particle1", 1);
myParticle.onEnterFrame = function() {
  this._x += (Math.random()*4)-2;
  this._y += (Math.random()*4)-2;
};
```

The first line creates the particle1 movie clip as before, but it also creates a *reference* to it called myParticle. You can use this reference to attach an onEnterFrame to the just-created clip.

Those two lines are fairly involved, and there are actually a few ways you could write them. Here are the alternative code snippets for those who want to delve further:

```
_root.attachMovie("particle", "particle1",
➡ 1);
_root["particle1"].onEnterFrame =
➡ function() {
```

```
this.attachMovie("particle", "particle1",
➡ 1);
this["particle1"].onEnterFrame =
➡ function() {
```

```
var myParticle:MovieClip = this.
➡ attachMovie("particle", "particle1",
➡ 1);
myParticle.onEnterFrame = function() {
```

The third code snippet is the one you'll write when you fully understand ActionScript 2.0 (it uses fully typed code and general paths). The others are a little old-fashioned. They create a pointer by changing a value (in this case, particle1) *into a reference (that is, a dot path),* _root.particle1 *or* this.particle1.

OK, on to the next line. Math.random() generates a random decimal number between 0 and 1, such as 0.56478903454. By using Math.random()*4, you get a random number between 0 and 4, and then subtract 2, giving you a value between –2 and 2.

If you want to be sure you get a whole number (that is, 78 rather than 78.456734324), you can use Math.round(myVal) to round the value up or down to the nearest whole number, or you can use Math.floor(myVal) to simply chop off the decimals and round down.

7. Note that you're using a timeline loop to animate the particles. It's only because the movie will, by default, repeat indefinitely that the particles move at all. So what about the ActionScript loop? Well, you actually want to put a whole lot of particles onto the screen. You could just cut and paste the previous code (creating lots of different clips with several attachMovies), but that would be a waste of time when you have the power of loops to fall back on. Add/change the following highlighted lines in your ActionScript:

```
var myParticle:MovieClip;
for (var i = 0; i<10; i++) {
  myParticle = this.attachMovie("particle",
➡ "particle", 1);
```

```
myParticle.onEnterFrame = function() {
  this._x += (Math.random()*4)-2;
  this._y += (Math.random()*4)-2;
 };
}
```

Here, you set up a for loop, using the variable i to keep track of how many loops you've been through and using "i is less than 10" as its condition. Everything inside the brackets will be repeated until the expression counter<10 turns out to be false. Fortunately, counter++ will add 1 to the value of counter every cycle, so after ten cycles counter will reach 10 and the loop will stop looping.

As you can see, the braces also contain the code you used to create the particle1 instance of your particle movie clip (on level 1 of the root timeline). Now that you're executing that code ten times, it will make ten separate particles, won't it? No, it won't, unless you make a few changes.

First, you need to give each instance a different name, so that ActionScript can tell them apart. Second, you can attach only one instance to each depth level. At the moment, they're all being attached to level 1, so each one gets wiped out when the next is attached. You also need to change the depth number every time you call attachMovie().

You already know about one way to do all this, because back in Chapter 5 you did something similar using the function duplicateMovieClip() and a counter variable called i:

```
duplicateMovieClip(particle_mc, "particle"+
➥ i+"_mc", i);
```

In fact, duplicateMovieClip is a MovieClip object method, so you could write this as follows:

```
particle_mc.duplicateMovieClip("particle"+
➥ i+"_mc", i);
```

This time, you don't have an instance on the stage to begin with, so you call attachMovie() from the root movie timeline. Apart from that, though, the same basic principles apply.

So here's how you can attach a brand-new particle movie clip instance to the stage for each new value of counter:

```
myParticle = this.attachMovie("particle",
➥ "particle"+i, i);
```

You use + to add (or concatenate) the current value of i to the end of the string literal "particle" to create a new, unique string for each loop.

You may have already noticed that _root shares many similarities with the movie clips you put into it. In fact, you can almost think of it as a movie clip in its own right: it has a timeline, as well as properties and methods you'd expect from any movie clip. The main difference is that it's always there, so you don't need to create it yourself. If you run the movie now, you'll see the gently pulsating cluster of particles you've been working toward.

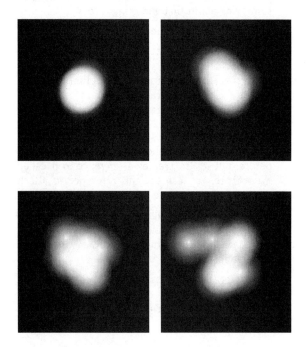

Wow—it's a genie!

Navigating the timelines

Whenever you use ActionScript to define a variable, a function, or even an object, you're always defining it in the context of a particular timeline. If your script is attached to the root timeline (which it probably will be most of the time), a variable called myVar will have the full name _root.myVar (or _level0.myVar if you look in the debug variables; unless you're into heavy stuff like loading multiple movies, you can assume that _level0 is always equivalent to _root).

The _root bit at the beginning is called a **dot path**, and it tells Flash what route it needs to take to get to the correct timeline. As soon as you have several instances of a movie clip in your movie, this becomes very important.

Different place, different variable

Say you define a variable called igor in the timeline of a movie clip called castle. If you then add an instance of castle called glamis_mc to the main (_root) timeline, the full name of the igor variable inside would be _root.glamis_mc.igor.

So why go to this trouble? What's wrong with just calling it igor? Well, if you add another instance of castle (called cawdor_mc) to the root timeline, then you'll have another variable called igor sitting in there too. Its full name would be _root.cawdor_mc.igor, and the two igor variables would be quite separate.

> *Remember, since you address variables in the same way as you address movie clips in a path, it's always handy to include the _mc suffix on the end of the clips' instance names so you can easily tell them apart, unless you're using strict typing and references. (It will probably take some time to get used to this, so suffixes may be the only option for a while.)*

Most variables are **scoped** to a particular timeline. Identically named variables in different paths are quite distinct entities and can hold different values or types. Flash would recognize your two igors as being different, no problem, but you would have to be very careful to ensure that *you* remember the difference!

Locating variables from inside a callback function

This seems obvious enough when you're placing your scripts within your movie clips and buttons, but I've already expressed a preference for centralizing code. Ideally, you should keep as much of the code as possible on the first frame of your root timeline. So, how do you locate a variable when you're using it as part of a callback function?

The normal place to define a callback is on the root timeline of the movie. Flash will assume that any variables you use inside the function are to be found on that timeline and *not* in the button your callback references. Say you want to model the changing bat population in each of your castles, and you put the following code in the root timeline:

```
glamis_mc.onEnterFrame = function() {
   batCounter = batCounter + 1;
};
cawdor_mc.onEnterFrame =function() {
   batCounter = batCounter - 1;
};
```

From this, you might expect to find Glamis's bat count going through the roof (no pun intended), with Cawdor's quickly plummeting to zero. Actually, both callbacks are changing the same variable, _root.batCounter (to give it its full name), and because one bumps it up while the other bumps it down every frame, its value never changes. You need to make it explicit that you want each event handler to work on a different variable batCounter, with one defined for each castle, so their full names are glamis_mc.batCounter and cawdor_mc.batCounter:

> *A variable has a value and a name, but like streets with identical names in two different cities, a pair of like-named variables can be quite different beasts. If you pick the wrong one, you can get hopelessly confused. For example, say you were in Ealing, London, and you asked a cab driver to take you to Broadway. You might be a little worried if he whisked you off to Manhattan for an audience with Liza Minnelli!*

```
glamis_mc.onEnterFrame = function() {
  glamis_mc.batCounter =
➥ glamis_mc.batCounter + 1;
};
cawdor_mc.onEnterFrame =function() {
  cawdor_mc.batCounter =
➥ cawdor_mc.batCounter - 1;
};
```

You now have two variables of the same name but in different places, so they can have different values and not interfere with each other.

Reusing callbacks

Suppose you introduce a third castle into your scenario. This castle is called rosslyn_mc, and it has a bat infestation problem similar to that of glamis_mc. You might simulate it like this:

```
glamis_mc.onEnterFrame = function() {
  glamis_mc.batCounter =
➥ glamis_mc.batCounter + 1;
};
cawdor_mc.onEnterFrame =function() {
  cawdor_mc.batCounter =
➥ cawdor_mc.batCounter - 1;
};
rosslyn_mc.onEnterFrame = function() {
  rosslyn_mc.batCounter =
➥ rosslyn_mc.batCounter + 1;
};
```

Of course, that will work fine, but between you and me, there's a simpler way to do it. The event handler code you just added is almost exactly the same as what you wrote before for glamis_mc; the only difference is

that one works on glamis_mc, while the other works on rosslyn_mc.

The folks at Macromedia have thought of all this, and they've made it nice and easy to recycle callbacks. There are two steps involved:

1. **Multiple assignments**: Write one event handler to deal with several events.
2. **Relative paths**: Use this to refer to the scoped timeline.

> *"So what?" you may ask. "It's just a couple of lines!" Sure, it's no big deal in this case, but if you're writing full-blown movies with event handlers that go on for pages, it's a real pain if you have to duplicate everything and change all the names. As the environmentally conscious among you will appreciate, extra keystrokes make the keys on your keyboard wear out quicker, which means more plastic key production and a swifter onset of global warming. Oh, yeah, plus it makes your movie bigger and generates extra opportunities for code errors—both Very Bad Things as well!*

The first step may sound a bit intimidating, but (as usual) it really isn't! When you write out a callback, the equal sign does the same thing as it does when you use it to set a variable: it takes whatever's on the right side and assigns it to whatever's on the left side. You may hear programmers refer to the equal sign as the **assignment operator** for precisely this reason ("equal sign" will do fine for us, though). The handy thing is that you can do this more than once. If you write this:

```
myVar1 = myVar2 = "Sham";
```

you're setting the values of two different variables (myVar1 and myVar2) to the string literal "Sham". Likewise, if you write this:

```
glamis_mc.onEnterFrame =
➥ rosslyn_mc.onEnterFrame = function() {
  glamis_mc.batCounter =
➥ glamis_mc.batCounter + 1;
};
```

you're setting the same callback for the onEnterFrame events of both glamis_mc and rosslyn_mc, and you have to write it out only once.

Hang on, though! If you do this, you're in trouble, since the batCounter variable specified here is the one for glamis_mc. What about rosslyn_mc.batCounter? This is where the second step comes in. You've already used the this keyword. As you may recall, it always refers to the **source** of the event that's being handled—that is, the timeline that generated it. If you're handling the glamis_mc.onEnterFrame event, this points to glamis_mc. Likewise, if you're handling the rosslyn_mc.onEnterFrame event, this points to rosslyn_mc.

So, to make your callback recycling work properly, you just need to generalize the event handler like this:

```
glamis_mc.onEnterFrame =
➥ rosslyn_mc.onEnterFrame = function() {
  this.batCounter = this.batCounter + 1;
};
```

Now you have two callbacks for the price of one!

Even better, you could make the event handler a general function and then use it on any line you want:

```
batController = function() {
  this.batCounter = this.batCounter + 1;
};
glamis_mc.onEnterFrame = batController;
rosslyn_mc.onEnterFrame = batController;
```

Notice that you don't refer to the function with batController(), but with batController. This is because you're creating an *association* in this version, rather than asking Flash to *call* the function.

> *Inside a callback,* this *in front of a variable name changes its scope from the timeline the code is attached to, to the timeline where the triggering event came from.*

You now have a neat way to keep your code centralized but still have it behave in the logical way that you want it to. Let's see how you can put this to work.

Same Name, Different Variables

Let's start off with our faithful friend, the inputOutput.fla movie that you saved back in Chapter 3. Since you want to look at the effects of nesting variables inside a movie clip, you'll change the enter button to a movie clip.

1. Change the symbol behavior of the enter button instance to Movie Clip via the Properties panel. As a reminder that you're now dealing with a movie clip, give it the instance name enter_mc:

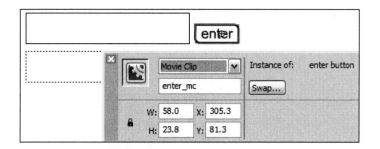

2. Select the first frame of the timeline and use the Script pane of the Actions panel to change the script attached to this frame as follows:

```
enter_mc.onRelease = function() {
  input_str = "root";
  output_str = input_str;
};
enter_mc.stop();
```

Test the movie and click the button without typing anything. You'll see that both of the boxes display the word root.

> To write an all-purpose handler, just scope your variables to the **controlling** timeline (by putting this in front of their names) rather than to the timeline to which they're **attached**. This is a fundamental concept to come to grips with. Once you have, you've taken a major step forward in mastering Flash ActionScript!

This is because you just told the button's onRelease event handler to do that! It sets the input box to display root and then sets the output box to mimic the input box. The extra line you added simply sets the value of input1. Remember that, unless you specify otherwise, a variable exists in the timeline it was created in. At this point, there are no explicit paths in your code, so input1 is interpreted as _root.input1, and it's set to hold the string literal "root".

You also have to treat the movie clip slightly differently from the button. A movie clip will start playing as soon as it appears on the timeline, so you have to stop enter_mc.

3. Since you define output_str for use by the dynamic text field (which is also sitting in the root timeline), its full name is likewise _root.output_str. You can therefore make this whole callback more explicit by rewriting it as follows:

```
enter_mc.onRelease = function() {
  _root.input_str = "root";
  _root.output_str = _root.input_str;
};
```

Since your script is attached to the root timeline, you don't actually *need* to do this. But what if you want to access variables or properties that *aren't* defined in the root timeline?

4. Add the following lines to the top of your script:

```
enter_mc.onPress = function() {
  this.input_str = "movie";
};
```

This sets up an event to trigger as soon as the movie clip is clicked, which creates a variable called input1 *inside the movie clip*. It contains the value "movie".

5. Now you can really see what's going on. At the moment, if you test the code you'll still get the root timeline showing in both boxes. Go back to the onRelease handler and change it like this:

```
enter_mc.onRelease = function() {
  _root.input_str = "root";
  _root.output_str = this.input_str;
};
```

All you've done is added a this path in front of the second variable, but if you test the movie, you'll see what a big difference this makes. The input text box is still being set on the root, so it still displays root, but the output text box is now being set to display the variable you defined inside the movie clip (enter_mc.input_str), so it reads movie.

Now that you've told your enter button to behave as a movie clip, there's no built-in rollover behavior, because that's something a button does, not something a movie clip does.

Well, not unless you tell it to! Let's write some event handlers that will make your movie clip behave like it's a button.

1. First, you can add some actions to your existing handlers. When you click the button, it should go to the down position at frame 2:

```
enter_mc.onPress = function() {
  this.gotoAndStop(2);
  this.input_str = "movie";
};
```

2. Likewise, when you release the button, it should go back to the up state at frame 1:

```
enter_mc.onRelease = function() {
  this.gotoAndStop(1);
  input_str = "root";
  output_str = this.input_str;
};
```

Once again, you've used this to tell Flash what path to use. In both cases, you want to gotoAndStop() on the instance called enter_mc. Since that's the object on which you've defined the callback, you can refer to it using this.

3. You can finish this off by adding mouseOver and mouseOut event handlers, and making the movie clip stop at frame 1 automatically:

```
enter_mc.onRollOut = function() {
  this.gotoAndStop(1);
};
enter_mc.onRollOver = function() {
  this.gotoAndStop(2);
};
```

Run the movie one more time, and you'll see the movie clip behave just as if it were a button. So, a few lines of extra code to get the same effect you had to begin with—what's the big deal? Well, apart from the fact that you've seen how this helps you make sure you're running actions on the right timeline, you now have the framework for a totally customizable button behavior, all written in ActionScript.

Using this script as a starting point, you can make up your own button rules from scratch. What's more, you can have as many complex transitions as you like on this movie clip button—not just the three frames and click zone you have with the normal button.

At this point, you might well be thinking one (or both) of the following: "I want to be good and include clear paths in my callbacks, but I really don't want to write this out 100 times in my code. Can't I just define a variable that *any* movie clip or button in my entire movie can talk to without having to mess around with remembering a path?" Luckily, there are simple solutions to both problems.

Changing the scope

Instead of writing this in front of every variable in a callback, you can nest the handler code inside a with() action. Here's an example:

```
enter_mc.onRelease = function() {
  with (this) {
    input_str = "root";
    output_str = input_str;
  }
};
```

> Normally, if you use a variable without specifying which timeline it's on, Flash assumes it's on the current timeline. Inside a with() statement, though, Flash will assume the variable is on the timeline specified in the with() action.

You use the with() action to specify a timeline when you start, and any variables you use in the with() body that aren't specified with an absolute path (in this case, just input1) are assumed to be on that timeline. You have to prefix the other variables with _root because you're now looking inside the enter_mc movie clip, but the text boxes are still on the root timeline. You don't need anything extra for the final input1 variable because its path is already set as the enter_mc movie clip, thanks to the with() action. The usefulness of this approach is more obvious if you have lots of this variables to consider:

```
glamis_mc.onEnterFrame = function() {
  this.batCounter = this.batCounter + 1;
  this.visitors = this.visitors - 1;
};
```

becomes

```
glamis_mc.onEnterFrame = function() {
  with (this) {
    batCounter = batCounter + 1;
    visitors = visitors - 1;
  }
};
```

You can also use this technique to define functions in other timelines. Say you have a movie clip on the root timeline with the instance name mathClip_mc. If you want this clip to contain a simple doubleIt function, you need to use code like this:

```
doubleIt = function(result) {
  var result;
  result = result*2;
  return result;
};
```

Let's run through a quick example to see this technique in action. Here, you'll use it to make a movie clip accelerate off the screen.

1. Create a new FLA document and create a simple shape on the far-left side of the stage. Convert this shape into a movie clip and give it the instance name mathClip_mc.

2. Attach the following code to the first frame of the root timeline:

```
with (mathClip_mc) {
  doubleIt = function (result) {
    var result;
    result = result*2;
    return result;
  };
  _x = 1;
}
mathClip_mc.onEnterFrame = function() {
  this._x = doubleIt(this._x);
};
```

You can see here that you use a with() command to tie the two pieces of code (defining the function and setting the _x property) to the mathClip_mc timeline. You then use a callback to run the function every frame. If you test the movie, you should see the shape zoom off the screen.

> *Although* with() *is a useful way of shortening your code, it doesn't always suit Flash. When the FLA is compiled to a SWF, using* with() *doesn't produce the most optimized compiled code. If you want your code to run as fast as possible, don't use* with()*, although it's fine if you aren't that bothered about speed and just want to save some typing.*

There's another way to add functions to a movie clip (or any object, for that matter). Just as all string variables are automatically able to use the methods defined in the String class, all functions have automatic access to methods in the class called Function. You can find the Function class among the Core objects in the Actions toolbox:

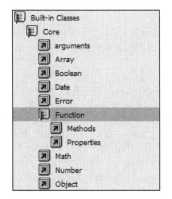

The method you're going to look at here is called apply. This method enables you to take a generic function and apply that to any movie clip you like.

1. Start a new movie and draw a shape on the stage in the top-left corner. Convert your shape into a movie clip called ball. Give the instance on the stage the instance name ball_mc.

2. Create a new layer called actions above the current layer. Open the Actions panel and select frame 1 of layer actions. Type the following into the Script pane of the Actions panel:

```
mover = function () {
  this.onEnterFrame = function() {
    this._x +=
➥ (_xMouse - this._x)/this._width;
    this._y +=
➥ (_yMouse - this._y)/this._height;
  };
};
```

Here, you embed an event within your main function and just refer to the movie clip as this. One of the most powerful things about the Function.apply method is that it defines this as the object that you're applying the function to, which makes it totally generic. Now to call the function . . .

3. Add this line after the previous piece of code:

```
mover.apply(ball_mc);
```

As you can see, you're addressing your function as you would any other object, using dot notation to specify the method and then passing the argument (the name of the movie clip that you want to apply the function to) inside the parentheses.

That's it! Run the movie and you should see your shape follow the mouse pointer around the screen. For practice, create another couple of shapes on the stage and use the apply method to apply the function to them too. Depending on the instance names you used, your final code should look something like this:

```
mover = function () {
  this.onEnterFrame = function() {
    this._x +=
➥ (_xMouse - this._x)/this._width;
    this._y +=
➥ (_yMouse - this._y)/this._height;
  };
};
mover.apply(ball_mc);
mover.apply(shape1_mc);
mover.apply(shape2_mc);
```

Now that you've written the function, you can apply it to any object at all. Use it to move a ball, a tree, a dog—anything you like, really. You can see how powerful this feature is in creating concise and reusable code, and what a benefit it can be to your toolbox. It can initially feel a bit strange thinking of a function as an object, but as with many of these things, the less deeply you think about it, the more sense it makes, and one day you'll be innocently using it when the concept will suddenly click into place and you'll wonder why you ever found it confusing. Flash is often like that, and ActionScript even more so. The secret is to keep at it, and continue making the most inane Flash movies, trying strange and different things, until they no longer seem strange and different, just normal.

Global variables

To fully answer the second of the two questions from earlier on (I know—you thought I'd forgotten!), I need to introduce a new concept: the **scope** of a variable is the part of the movie in which it can be referenced. There are three different types of variable scope, the first two of which are familiar to you:

- **Local**: Variables are available only within the script block braces {} in which they're defined.
- **Timeline**: Variables are available to any timeline (provided you use a target path).
- **Global**: Variables are available to any timeline (and you don't have to use a target path).

You've already seen how you can use var to declare **local variables** inside a block of script. You'll most commonly do this when working with loops, which often recycle their counter variables. You don't want counter from one loop to interfere with counter from another loop, so you make each variable local to its own loop. They're both destroyed as soon as the loop is finished, and neither has any idea of the other's existence.

As for timeline variables, you've already learned that their path is part of what makes them unique; their position in the movie is part of what defines them. Whenever you define a plain old variable, you have to ask *where* you've defined it. Say you define a variable in some ActionScript that you've attached to a movie clip. The variable's **location** will be the timeline of that movie clip. As long as you know where to look path-wise, you can access the variable from anywhere you like.

That's fine, but sometimes it would be nice not to use paths at all. What you really want to do is define a variable that has the entire movie as its scope, so it doesn't need you to specify a target path. Such a variable is called **global**. It has a scope of "everywhere."

Creating a truly global variable in Flash is as simple as this:

```
_global.myVar = "This is available anywhere
➥ in the movie!";
```

If you were then to trace this variable from anywhere else in the movie, you could simply write this:

```
trace(myVar);
```

and the correct value would be displayed in the Output window. Try it if you like and see. It's worth noting that you can use the short name only to *access* the variable, not to *set* it. Say you now add the following code in the root timeline:

```
myVar = "Ben";
```

This would *not* change the global variable myVar to "Ben"; instead, it would create a new variable. Assuming your code is attached to the main timeline, this new variable would be _root.myVar.

If you really wanted to set the global variable to something else later on in the movie, then you'd have to go back to the way you initially did it, by prefacing it with _global:

```
_global.myVar = "Ben";
```

Summary

This chapter covered a wide range of concepts and skills having to do with objects, including the following:

- Using movie clips and buttons as objects, object properties, behaviors, and classes
- Using the Library contents directly through ActionScript
- Navigating timelines and using paths
- Using functions as objects
- Creating and using global variables

Congratulations! You're well on your way to mastering the scripting skills that will take your Flash work to new heights. You've learned the basic ActionScript structures that underpin everything else, and you're now ready to explore the amazing stuff that's possible when you put those structures to work. Time for a well-deserved rest! In the next half of the book, you're going to look at building whole projects and adding in cool new features like sound and sprites. The visibility on this mountain is improving with every passing minute, and now it's time to start focusing on the summit.

Chapter 9

MODULAR ACTIONSCRIPT

What we'll cover in this chapter:

- Realizing the advantages of creating reusable ActionScript
- Building components that you can reuse in any FLA
- Creating self-contained movie clips

If you're like me, you want to learn anything and everything to help make your Flash skills commercially valuable, so you can get something back for all the hard work you've put in. You want to perform coding tasks in the minimum amount of time, using the simplest and easiest methods available. What's more, you don't want to get bogged down with irrelevant stuff that you'll never use in the real world.

I wrote this book to help you achieve these aims, and this is where you start getting really serious about those good returns. This chapter holds out the tantalizing prospect of being paid many times over for a single piece of code.

Instead of bolting everything together from scratch every time you start work on a new project, you want to keep a bag full of standard bits and pieces that just need a little tweaking to fit right in with what you're doing. This is what modular ActionScript is all about: writing efficient, reusable code. It's efficient, so you need less of it. It's reusable, so you have to write it less often.

Yes, you've guessed it. I *like* being paid twice for the same piece of coding! You can have lots of identical little movie clips following the same short, simple bit of code, but when taken together, the overall behavior is *complex*. This is a good concept to explore because the code you actually need to write to create this apparent complexity is *short* and *simple*.

This chapter will show you how to create reusable blocks of ActionScript that will enable you to make graphic effects you can use over and over again.

Modular ActionScript

Many functions and effects require Flash to be doing a number of things at the same time. To do this, you need to work with several timelines, with each one handling a bit of the problem and all of them working at the same time.

Suppose you have a big problem and need to solve it in code. One way is to have an equally big slab of code (the task block in the following diagram) sprawling all

over the place in the process. You may end up with an enormous number of lines of code, making it difficult to properly structure or document your project—and heaven help you when you want to add new functionality!

The next diagram shows the **modular** approach. Here you split the monolithic task into three subtasks: A, B, and C.

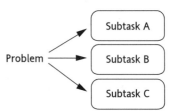

This way, you have separate sections of code that handle different parts of your problem. Each subtask is compact, with a well-defined problem to solve, which makes it easy to read and code. Furthermore, since you've broken down the specific task at hand into smaller (and probably more generic) subtasks, you're likely to find these subtasks come in handy elsewhere.

If a similar problem arises in future, you can either reuse your existing subtasks in a slightly different context or tweak them a bit to fit the bill. Either way, you'll wind up spending much less time on development than if you were to write the whole project from the ground up.

Black-box programming

In programming, a **black box** is a piece of code that you can reuse without necessarily knowing all the details of how it works. You can't see inside the box because it's "black" (in other words, its contents are unavailable to you, or **encapsulated** inside the box), but you don't need to. The black-box approach stipulates that all code must be *self-contained* and *distinct* from any other code.

You're interested in only two things here:

- What the code *does* to the outside world (its function *or* method of working)
- What the code *needs* from you and *gives* back to you (its interfaces)

One example of a black box that should be very familiar is the remote control for your TV. While you may not have the faintest idea of how it works or what goes on inside it, you can still use it to change the channel. You provide it with input (by pressing buttons), it does some processing and talks to the TV, and you get a nice, predictable response: the channel changes.

*The black-box concept promotes **portability**. I'm not talking about how easy it is to hold the remote control here; rather, I'm referring to the ease with which you can carry the remote control's usefulness from one situation to another. If you've used one remote control, you should have a good idea of how all remote controls tend to work. In programming, there are similar advantages that make programming in this way beneficial. If you've cracked one problem with modular code, you've most likely created code that will solve similar problems. You can handle the differences between specific problems by changing one or two modules, but you'll be able to leave a significant part of your code the same.*

Additionally, if you're working as part of a team of programmers for a given overall programming project, each programmer on the team doesn't need to know how the others are implementing their allocated parts of the project, so long as the interface specification (that is, the inputs and outputs of the black box) is observed. The TV development team members don't need to know how the remote control unit works; they just need to know about the interfaces (in this case, which signals the remote control will zap at the TV and what the TV needs to do when it senses each one).

So how does this black box relate to what you're doing? The first rule is that, to make code self-contained, it really should be within something that separates itself from other code. There are three main ways to do this in Flash:

- **You can use functions within the same overall listing**. You've already done this for other reasons. Creating event handler code and splitting code into separate functions to create modular code entail much the same process.
- **You can "hide" or encapsulate your code in Flash's own black boxes: movie clips**. There are several ways you can do this, but the most modular is via a special kind of black box called a **component**.
- **You can create separate text files containing code only**. Each file is created to perform a specific set of tasks, and you can have a number of such files. You then refer to these files from the FLA at compile time (that is, when you create the SWF).

I'll discuss the first two ways of creating modular code in this chapter. The third way is usually used for more advanced code modules than you know how to work with at the moment, so I'll defer using separate text files, or (to use the proper terminology) external AS (ActionScript) files and class libraries.

Creating components

A component is a Flash-specific black box. It contains code within itself, and sometimes it also talks to other component black boxes to perform its tasks. The beauty of components is that you don't have to look inside them and know how they work to be able to work with them. All you have to know is what the components do and what their interfaces are.

Flash comes complete with a number of precreated components, which you can see in the Components panel (Window ➤ Development Panels ➤ Components). The Macromedia components that ship with Flash are underpinned with class-based (and rather long) code structures, but you don't want to go down that road at this point. You will instead start the ball rolling with something much simpler.

But, for your component (which is fundamentally just a movie clip) to be useful as a black box, it must be able to control something *other* than itself. In other words, the code inside the movie clip must be able to reach out of the box and control something outside the movie clip. You have to tell your component what it needs to control as well.

There are several ways to do this, but one of the easiest is to make what the movie clip needs to control (the **target**) something general. Rather than name a particular movie clip, you define the target as "whichever movie clip you see at this particular place."

This solution uses a special path called _parent, which refers to whichever timeline the movie clip has been attached to. You can think of the hierarchy of movie clips inside a movie as being like a big matriarchal family tree. The movie itself is the head of the family, which has several daughters. Each daughter may (or may not) have daughters of her own, and so on, and so on. If you ask anyone in the family who her parent is, she'll point to whichever woman is one up the tree from her—assuming none of the men in the family are about!

_parent always refers to a movie clip relative to itself, so you describe it as giving a **relative path**. You've already seen one relative path: when this is used inside a function definition, it points to whatever it was that called the function. Now that you're attaching script directly to movie clips, it's useful to know that this can also refer to the movie clip your script is attached to. Just as _parent is like a path to "my mother," this is like a path to "me."

> It almost goes without saying that you should document black-box code well so you know what interactions to expect when you use it. Good documentation is important at all times, but when you're writing code for later reuse, it's vital. You'll rarely remember the intricacies of something you wrote when you come to reuse it while chasing a deadline 6 months later. Even if it seems like a waste of time now, document it!

Creating a modular set of playback controls

There are many cartoons and other full-length features on the Web at the moment. If you're creating such features, it's a good idea to design them with the sort of control you get with a normal video. In this section, you'll create a modular set of video controls that you can drop onto any stage containing tween-type animations.

If you get stuck at any point, you can get the finished version, videoControl.fla, from this chapter's download file.

Creating the buttons and black box

Follow these steps to create the buttons and black box.

1. Create a new FLA document. You'll first need the video control buttons. I selected Window ➤ Other Panels Common Libraries ➤ Buttons and then chose the Playback folder, where I found a set of buttons complete with all the play and rewind symbols (shown next).

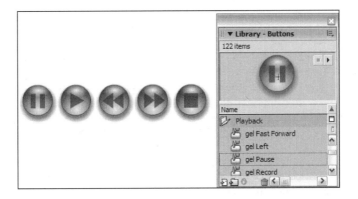

Drag your buttons from the common Library onto the stage and arrange them in a strip as shown, giving them the instance names (from left to right) pause_btn, play_btn, rewind_btn, fastForward _btn, and stop_btn.

> *Remember to use* fastForward, *not* fastforward— *ActionScript is case sensitive!*

This strip consists of five buttons. The Pause button should freeze the target timeline at the current frame. Then, every time it's clicked, it should advance to the next frame. The Play button should undo any other button and start to play the movie from the current frame. The Rewind and Fast Forward buttons should work like standard video fast-search buttons and thus cause the movie to play at a faster rate (say ×4), either backward or forward. The Stop button should stop the movie at its current frame.

2. Select all of the buttons (either drag a selection box around them or hold down the SHIFT key and click each in turn until you've selected them all). Press *F8* to convert them to a movie clip called videocontrols. Now double-click the movie clip to enter edit in place mode. Rename the layer containing your buttons as buttons, and create a brand-new layer called actions:

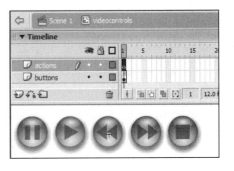

Let's start defining actions for these buttons. The Play and Stop buttons should be relatively painless, so you'll look at them first.

Adding the play and stop code

In this exercise, you'll add the play and stop code.

1. The Play button simply has to make the timeline on which your video controls sit (which will be their _parent timeline) start to play. All you need to make this happen is an onRelease event handler containing a _parent.play() command.

   Pin the Actions panel to frame 1 of layer actions and add the following script. You'll add all further scripts as a continuation of this script, so there's no need to unpin for a while yet.

```
play_btn.onRelease = function() {
  _parent.play();
};
```

2. The Stop button isn't much different from the Play button, except that it needs a _parent.stop():

```
stop_btn.onRelease = function() {
  _parent.stop();
};
```

Testing the SWF so far

Now that you have a little functionality to play with, you'll try out the controls. You're going to add a simple motion tween so that you can see when the timeline is running and when it isn't.

1. Go back to the main timeline, rename the existing layer as controller, and add a new layer called tween. Select frame 20 in both layers and press *F5* to insert frames.

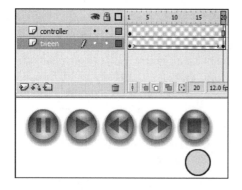

2. Select frame 1 on the tween layer and draw a circle just below the Pause button. With the circle still selected, press *F8* and make the circle a graphic symbol called circle. Select frame 20 in the same layer, choose Insert ➤ Create Motion Tween, and press *F6* to insert a keyframe.

With this frame still selected, *SHIFT*-drag the circle over to the right until it's directly below the Stop button.

3. Run the movie to see the tween in action, and try clicking the Stop and Play buttons to check that they work. The Play button will do nothing if the animation is already playing, but it will restart the animation if it's stopped. The Stop button will do nothing if the animation is already stopped, but it will stop a playing animation.

Now you'll move on to some slightly trickier code.

Adding the Pause button code

The Pause button needs to do one of two things. If the movie is playing, clicking the Pause button should bring the movie to a halt, just as clicking the Stop button does. However, if the Pause button is clicked when the movie is *already* paused, it should do what many video recorders do, something called **single stepping**. Every time you click the Pause button after the initial pause, the movie moves forward by a single frame and then stops again.

Let's say you're sneaky about this, and you enter the single step mode right away (that is, you go to the next frame and pause for *all* Pause button clicks). How many people will actually notice? How many people have ever noticed that video recorders do two different things on the first and second press of the Pause button? That's right: none, because the frame rates are too fast for anybody to realize what's happening.

The onPress action for the Pause button is actually the same as that for the Stop button: a simple _parent.stop(). The onRelease action is a little harder. You want the _parent timeline to gotoAndStop on its next frame. There is an action to do this, nextFrame(), but you haven't seen it yet. The code _parent.nextFrame() will send the timeline videocontrols is on to the next frame.

Add the following code to the listing:

```
pause_btn.onPress = function() {
  _parent.stop();
};
pause_btn.onRelease = function() {
  _parent.nextFrame();
};
```

Adding the fast forward and rewind code

The Fast Forward and Rewind buttons are also a little tricky because you want them to change the speed of the movie for as long as they're held down. The trouble is, Flash doesn't give you any controls to change the frames per second. If you want to play the movie at three times the normal speed, you must do this by playing just one frame out of every three.

You can achieve this by writing event handlers for the onEnterFrame event in the videocontrols timeline. Every time the playhead enters a frame, it should kick the parent's timeline on to the next frame but two (if you're fast forwarding) or the last frame but two (if you're rewinding). These behaviors should kick in when the relevant button is clicked, and they should switch off as soon as that button is released.

This gives you three possible tasks for the onEnterFrame event handler:

- **Normal mode**: Do nothing.
- **Fast forward mode**: Go to the current frame plus 3.
- **Rewind mode**: Go to the current frame minus 3.

As you know, you can't define multiple event handlers for a single event, so how do you make onEnterFrame behave properly in each circumstance? Well, you could define a variable to specify which mode you're in, use your button events to set it, and write an all-purpose handler (perhaps using a switch...case structure) that picks appropriate actions based on its value.

Then again, why not cut out the middleman? You want to use button events to modify what the handler does, and there's no overlap between the different modes and what they do. Let's just get your button event handlers to completely *redefine* the onEnterFrame handler as required.

There's an important distinction to note here: onPress and onRelease are both user-generated, "one-shot" events, whereas onEnterFrame is generated by the timeline and fired for every frame. You can think of onPress and onRelease as manual and automatic (or internally generated by Flash events). By using one to control the other, you're producing some pretty complex behavior. When the user causes a button event (such as onPress and onRelease), Flash will run the associated button event handlers, but these handlers can themselves set up *other* events such as onEnterFrame.

This relationship between user-generated and Flash-generated events is one of the core tricks in advanced motion-graphics programming. Clicking a button doesn't necessarily just have to cause navigation by jumping around the timeline. It can also cause new events to become active, and these new events cause the real responses to the initial button event to take place. The reason for doing this is that the initiating event (button event) may not be the best event handler for your response to the button click. The Futuremedia site contains a good example of this, where clicking a colored strip causes several things to happen in sequence. You'll see the code associated with this start to take shape at the end of this chapter. The simple video controls you're developing here are a precursor to it.

1. You'll define each of the onPress button event handlers so that they set up a handler for onEnterFrame that will fast forward or rewind the parent timeline. The buttons' onRelease handlers then delete the timeline's onEnterFrame handler by making it undefined. Add the following code in the Actions panel:

```
fastForward_btn.onPress = function() {
  onEnterFrame = function () {
    _parent.gotoAndStop
➡ (_parent._currentFrame+3);
  };
};
```

Remember: fastForward, *not* fastforward!

This script defines an onEnterFrame handler for the current timeline within the button event handler, making the parent timeline advance at three times the normal speed. This will continue indefinitely until you redefine or remove the onEnterFrame handler.

The script works by examining at which point the parent timeline is by looking at the property _currentFrame. This property contains the current frame number. As well as reading it, you can also *change* it, and that's what the code does to give you the "skip frames so that the animation runs faster" effect.

I mentioned earlier that ×4 would be a good approximation of a faster rate for a fast forward or rewind function. When you're calculating this, you need to bear in mind that Flash advances one frame in the time it takes for the script to run anyway, so for a Fast Forward button, you want Flash to advance by three frames to make up the four frames for a fast forward.

Notice that this states the _parent path for both the method *and* the property:

```
_parent.gotoAndStop(_parent._currentframe
➡ +3);
```

As an aside, the onEnterFrame *handler is attached to the timeline of* videocontrols, *not the* _parent *timeline. You do this because in the black-box approach you keep all your code in the back box (that is, the* videocontrols *movie clip) and try not to affect the* _parent *timeline via anything other than the video-controlling features.*

2. To stop fast forwarding, you need to delete the onEnterFrame script. The instant you do this, the Fast Forward button is released.

```
fastForward_btn.onRelease = function() {
  onEnterFrame = undefined;
};
```

3. You need to do the same for the Rewind button.

```
rewind_btn.onPress = function() {
  onEnterFrame = function () {
    _parent.gotoAndStop
➡ (_parent._currentFrame-5);
  };
};
rewind_btn.onRelease = function() {
  onEnterFrame = undefined;
};
```

This does exactly the same for the Rewind button as the Fast Forward button, except that you move backward. You want to move backward by four frames at a time, but because the timeline may actually be moving forward one frame per second, you subtract 5.

Now that you've defined actions for all your buttons, you can use the videocontrols movie clip to control any timeline it's thrown at. Test this by placing the movie clip on *any* timeline that contains just tween animations, and it will work in the same way. Here's the full code listing before you do this, shown in both plain text and as a screenshot:

```
play_btn.onRelease = function() {
  _parent.play();
};
stop_btn.onRelease = function() {
  _parent.stop();
};
pause_btn.onPress = function() {
  _parent.stop();
};
pause_btn.onRelease = function() {
  _parent.nextFrame();
};
```

```
fastForward_btn.onPress = function() {
  onEnterFrame = function () {
    _parent.gotoAndStop
➡    (_parent._currentFrame+3);
  };
};
fastForward_btn.onRelease = function() {
  onEnterFrame = undefined;
};
rewind_btn.onPress = function() {
  onEnterFrame = function () {
    _parent.gotoAndStop
➡    (_parent._currentFrame-5);
  };
};
rewind_btn.onRelease = function() {
  onEnterFrame = undefined;
};
```

```
1  play_btn.onRelease = function() {
2      _parent.play();
3  };
4  stop_btn.onRelease = function() {
5      _parent.stop();
6  };
7  pause_btn.onPress = function() {
8      _parent.stop();
9  };
10 pause_btn.onRelease = function() {
11     _parent.nextFrame();
12 };
13 fastForward_btn.onPress = function() {
14     onEnterFrame = function () {
15         _parent.gotoAndStop(_parent._currentFrame+3);
16     };
17 };
18 fastForward_btn.onRelease = function() {
19     onEnterFrame = undefined;
20 };
21 rewind_btn.onPress = function() {
22     onEnterFrame = function () {
23         _parent.gotoAndStop(_parent._currentFrame-5);
24     };
25 };
26 rewind_btn.onRelease = function() {
27     onEnterFrame = undefined;
28 };
```

There's one more thing you need to do: make your movie clip into a component.

4. Open the Library panel (*CTRL+L* or Window ➤ Library), click the Create Folder icon to add a new folder, and name it videocontrols assets. Drag all the gel buttons into it. Now right-click (or *CTRL*-click) the videocontrols movie clip in the Library and select Component Definition. This will bring up the Component Definition dialog box.

5. Tick the Display in Components panel check box and give it the tooltip text video controls:

Click OK, and the movie clip should now appear in the Library as a component.

You can now use this set of controls on *any* timeline that consists of tween animations, anywhere, in any FLA. All you have to do is drop it into the target timeline! So how have you achieved this feat of coding?

Well, your video controls don't refer to any *specific* timeline, but to _parent (that is, whatever timeline videocontrols finds itself placed on). The controls don't need to know anything about this timeline—not even how many frames it has. Since the controls are completely self-contained, you can drag them onto *any* timeline and they'll work.

> As well as being self-contained (or inside a black box), well-written modular code has to be general. In this exercise, you achieve this by using the _parent *path to define the target timeline.*

The fact that you've wrapped the whole thing up as a component means that you can drag videocontrols from its place in the Library and onto any other timeline, whether it's in the same movie or not. All its assets (that is, the bits and pieces it needs; in this case, the gel buttons) are automatically copied across with it.

6. Save your file as videoControl.fla and close the FLA.

You now have a completely self-contained building block, so you should be able to reuse it elsewhere. Let's try this out.

Dark Valentine

A couple of years ago, I started a little side project of creating a deck of playing cards based around photography and Photoshop manipulation. I came across a photographer called Martinus Versfeld and collaborated with him for one of the images called "Dark Valentine." This was my initial set of interpretations for the queen of hearts:

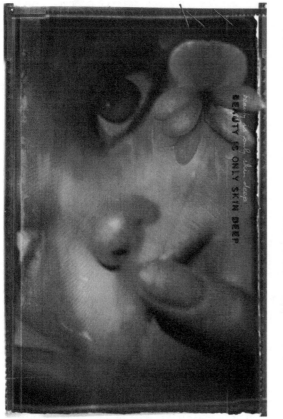

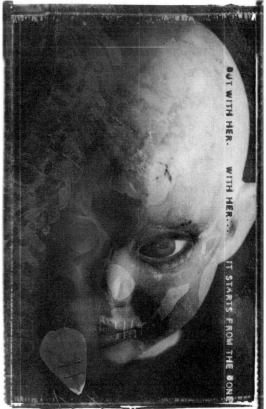

At around the same time, people were beginning to use Flash (Flash 4) for e-greeting cards. Most of the cards were pretty saccharine, and I thought images like Dark Valentine would make a nice antidote, so I set about creating a simple Flash animation using my Photoshop images as a base. You can find the results in the download for this chapter as dark.fla.

> *Because the Dark Valentine work uses some rather hard-to-find fonts, I've converted them to vectors so all readers will see the same animation irrespective of whether they have the fonts installed. This has the side effect of increasing the file size of the animation, but the actual version (with the fonts correctly embedded and "real text" used throughout) was designed to stream correctly on a 56K connection.*

Using your component with Dark Valentine

This exercise will show you how easy it is to drop video controls onto another timeline, by using them to control the Dark Valentine animation.

1. Open dark.fla and create a new layer called control on the main timeline. This is where you're going to put your controls. Make sure that it's the topmost layer because you want your video controls to appear over the Dark Valentine animation.

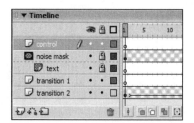

2. Now use File ➤ Import ➤ Open External Library to open the Library of videoControl.fla to give you access to the videocontrols component. Make sure the control layer is selected and drag the component onto the stage.

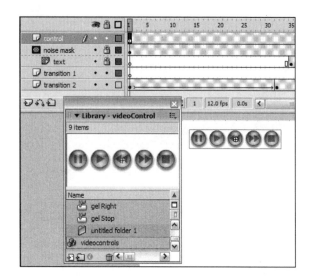

3. If you now look at the Library for dark.fla, you'll see the videocontrols component listed along with its assets folder (which contains definitions for all the gel buttons).

Yes, a tidy Library is a happy Library. It's always a good idea to keep things neat in a document as complicated as this, and you don't need me to tell you why! If you run the movie now, the video controls will operate as expected. You can even use the controls in pause mode to see that scary bit where the skull X-ray appears suddenly.

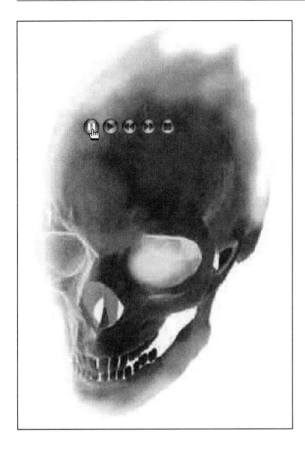

Eek!

Of course, this set of controls will act only on a single timeline. If your animation consists of other movie clips as well as the timeline that holds videocontrols, it won't control them, just the timeline that it's placed on. You could modify the controls so that they can be hidden. You could even add a drag bar or use the _alpha property to make the controls semitransparent when they're not in use. You could build up a whole site navigation system using a little TV remote control unit for your navigation—click the channel buttons to move about, and use the video controls to control the movies. Enough of my ideas, though. I'll leave you to experiment.

You've now seen how to build a reusable component, which gives you a convenient timeline controller that you can use in all sorts of different situations. This has lots of consequences for how you write your Flash movies in the future, but so far you've seen only the tip of the iceberg.

Modular control of movie clips

Imagine you have a movie clip called blob and an instance of it called blob_mc on the stage. Say you want to make it do several things at the same time. Perhaps you want it to move around the screen in a particular way (based on one set of criteria), but you also want to change its appearance (based on a completely separate set of criteria) as it moves. The simplest solution would be to write a couple of functions that refer specifically to blob_mc and trigger them whenever the relevant criteria are met. The better way is to write a set of general functions that can refer to *any* movie clip. But for now, you'll limber up by sticking to a more graphical, component/movie clip–based way of looking at modularity and general code.

> *You'll look at an even more general way of arranging code into modules using inheritance and code-based hierarchies (as well as timeline-based daughter/parent hierarchies) when you continue work on the Futuremedia book project later in this chapter. In the last chapter of the book, you'll explore using high-end code to achieve modularity with class-based or prototype-based scripting. You certainly won't be a beginner anymore when you get to that point!*

Which brings me to the other way of creating modular code: using components again. Supposing, though, you have a number of blobs, all of which you want to move in a slightly different way. You *could* use a different component per blob, but a better way is to use components that allow configuration via *arguments*. You'll develop this feature in the following section.

> Of course, the other "other way" Flash implements modular code in a drag-and-drop fashion is via behaviors. The behaviors that ship with Flash are aimed at raw beginners and aren't designed for people with any coding experience. For this reason, I won't address them in this book.

> Objects have mass, so they can't start (or stop) moving immediately. When they start to move, it takes time for them to build up speed. When they stop moving, it takes time for them to come to a halt. This is called **inertia**.

How to simulate realistic movement

Before you look at coding, you're going to take a quick detour. You're well on your way to the top of the ActionScript mountain, so you won't settle for just *any* functionality here—you'll go for the big one: **real movement**. This is motion based on real physics, and it takes into account the fact that objects in the real world have mass and therefore move in a fairly complicated way. Let's work out what number-crunching code needs to go into your component before you start building it.

Don't panic, though! There's very little math involved here; there's just a lot of common sense, along with some precise observations (and, because Flash isn't a graphics speed-demon, there's a lot of approximation) that you may need to think about carefully. If you find it hard going, just take it slowly. It's not difficult—just a bit different—and it's well worth knowing about if you want to go on to build the kind of sites and effects that have everyone gaping in awe.

Creating realistic motion isn't that different from what you've already done in Flash, but it can seem quite challenging, simply because you have to account for little things like the laws of physics. OK, come out from behind the couch. It may sound scary, but it's not. Really.

Real objects have **mass**. This is what makes them feel heavy, and it's also what makes it hard to start and stop them moving. Just think about how much less effective your accelerator and brake pedals are when your car is full of people. For a more dramatic example, just think about pushing a massive oil tanker along a flat stretch of road with your bare hands—or worse still, trying to stop it!

You'll be pleased to know that this is all the physics you really need for this simulation. Of course, if you let it, this could start getting all mathematical and tricky. You don't really want that, so let's break down the process into some commonsense steps. Common sense is well known as an ancient and powerful approach to problem solving, and it's usually less scary than physics.

Let's look at the blob movie clip again and slowly develop some motion code as you go along.

Linear motion

Say you place an instance of the blob movie clip (called blob_mc) on the stage at coordinates X:100, Y:100. You want it to move across to X:200, Y:100 in a smooth movement.

1. Open a new Flash movie and select Modify ➤ Document (alternatively, just double-click the area at the bottom of the timeline, where the frame rate is listed). In the Document Properties window that appears, set the frame rate to 18 fps. This is a normal frame rate for smooth animation.

2. Draw a small (around 30×30 pixels in size) filled circle, then select it and press *F8*, making the circle into a movie clip called blob. Give the version on the stage an instance name of blob_mc, and use the Properties panel to give it an X position of 10.0. This should place your blob at the left edge of the stage.

3. Rename the current layer as graphics, and add another layer above it named actions.

4. Select frame 1 of layer actions, and in the Script pane of the Actions panel enter the following code:

```
blob_mc.onEnterFrame = function() {
  if (this._x<200) {
    this._x += 4;
  }
};
```

Every time you enter a new frame, the event-handler code checks whether blob_mc's x-coordinate is less than 200, and it adds 4 if it is. When the movie starts playing, the x-coordinate is 10 (where you originally put the blob). After one frame blob_mc is at x-coordinate 14, after two it's at 18, and so on. Eventually it's at x-coordinate 200 and it stops moving.

Well, that was easy! If you try it out, though (and you can if you run blob1.fla from the download), you'll see that it moves quite unnaturally—it moves at the same speed throughout and stops abruptly. This makes it look a little fake.

Motion with acceleration

So how can you fix this? Let's pause for a moment and think about what you're trying to do. You'll keep it simple for now: make the blob slow down before it reaches the target. At the moment, it moves at the same speed throughout. The line that does this is

```
this._x += 4;
```

which moves the blob by 4 pixels for every frame. What if you change 4 to something else? Well, changing it to 1 will slow the whole thing down, and changing it to 20 will speed the whole thing up, but neither would actually do what you want and give the blob different speeds at different times. What you want is something that can vary—a variable!

Let's say you use a variable called speed to tell you how fast to change the position:

```
this._x += speed;
```

Now you just need to figure out what value to give speed. You know where to start looking: the blob begins at X:10 with a speed of 0 and ends up at X:200 with a speed of 0. Of course, you can also guess that it needs some more speed in between; otherwise, it won't ever get to X:200!

You need to find a value that starts positive (when the movie starts) and then drops away to 0 as the blob approaches its destination. That's easy: you use the distance between the blob and the target. You can work this out by finding the difference between blob_mc._x (the blob's current x-coordinate) and target (the x-coordinate of the destination). When you do the sums, you find it starts off at 190 (200 − 10 = 190) and finishes as 0 (200 − 200 = 0), which is just what you need.

You know where the blob is heading, so the last bit should be easy. You have the following equations and values:

```
target = 200
speed = target - _x
this._x += speed
```

So, if x is less than 200, the speed is positive and the blob moves to the right. If x is 200, the speed is 0. Just what you wanted, isn't it? Not quite. You see, the first time your movie works out the value of speed, it will be 190. Add that to x, and it will take you straight to the end, before you have time to blink. Try it if you don't believe me by rewriting the code as follows:

```
blob_mc.onEnterFrame = function() {
  if (this._x<target) {
    speed = target-this._x;
    this._x += speed;
  }
};
//
var speed:Number = 0;
var target:Number = 200;
```

OK, then, let's scale down the speed a little by making it one-tenth of the distance. Change the line that sets speed as shown:

```
blob_mc.onEnterFrame = function() {
  if (this._x<target) {
    speed = (target-this._x)/10;
    this._x += speed;
  }
};
//
var speed:Number = 0;
var target:Number = 200;
```

Now the speed value will start out as 10 and get smaller as the blob closes in on its target. This approach gives great results—check out blob2.fla to see this simple example in action (if you aren't following along by creating your own FLAs).

Let's consider what you've done here. As the blob gets closer to its destination, you want it to slow down. Or, to put it in terms you can describe in ActionScript, you want it to travel less and less every frame. You use speed to control how far the blob moves for each frame, by making it a specific fraction of the distance remaining. That figure of 10 I used to scale down the speed was actually very important. If you're adventurous, you may already have tried plugging in some different values here; it's not like I gave you any good reason to use 10 after all! Say you used 2 instead and traveled half the remaining distance in each frame. It would work just as well, only quicker.

In fact, this value directly controls how quickly the blob slows down (or **decelerates**, for the more technically minded among you. Engineers would say it controls the **stiffness** or **feedback** of the system). If it's a large number, the blob will take ages to reach its destination because the speed starts off low and falls off too quickly. If it's a very small number (between 0 and 1), the blob will overshoot the target because the speed doesn't fall off quickly enough.

How do I know all this? Well, it comes down to a bit of math beyond the scope of this book, but interested readers can do some research on **control theory***.*

In fact, you can generate very specific behavior by carefully picking your value and testing the code. Change the code as shown first (you remove the if):

```
blob_mc.onEnterFrame = function() {
  speed = (target-this._x)/10;
  this._x += speed;
};
//
var speed:Number = 0;
var target:Number = 200;
```

Now try plugging in different values for 10:

- If it's less than 0.5, the blob accelerates past the target and never stops.

- If it's equal to 0.5, the blob will overshoot by exactly the original distance, overshoot back again, and so on, **oscillating** around the target forever.

- If it's greater than 0.5 but less than 1, the blob will overshoot slightly but come back and stop on the target after a few "bounces."

- If it's exactly 1 (or you simply leave it out), the blob goes straight to the target, as you saw earlier.

- If it's between 1 and 2, the blob slows down and stops at the target without overshooting.

- If it's over 2, the blob will never *quite* reach the target in theory, but because of computer rounding errors, the blob will get to the target after a second or so.

Of course, the easiest way to find a value you like is to play around with the numbers and see what happens, but I hope these pointers will help give you some idea of what to expect. I personally find a value between 1.8 and 2 gives the most aesthetically pleasing result. It's fast enough without being so fast you see a jerky movement.

We can sum it up like this. For each frame, you work out the blob's new position as follows:

```
New position = current position + ((target
➥ position - current position) ÷ constant)
```

Why is this important? Well, it's the simplest, most processor-friendly equation you can use to add realism to movement in your Flash movies. This is because it simulates acceleration, which suggests the blob has a whole host of real physical properties and processes acting on it (such as weight, viscosity, friction, inertia, and more).

Although this equation is about motion changes with time, it has no explicit reference to time. That's because the movie is based on frames, and it's the frame interval that creates the time-based motion. The frame rate defines how often this equation is run, and this rate defines the time taken for the journey.

You may be thinking, "Um, that still doesn't answer my question! Why is this important to Flash web design?" Good question.

Well, compare your smooth decelerating motion with the linear motion you had at the start. Not only does the nonlinear motion appear *smoother* but, almost paradoxically, it's *faster* as well!

When you're designing anything that moves in Flash, from a space invader to moving parts in a cool Flash UI, you should use movement with inertia.

For a practical Flash web design application of inertia, you don't need to look very far. Take a look at the finished Futuremedia site and you'll see that when you click one of the strips, the UI zooms and fades with an inertia effect. This makes the effect both smooth and pleasing to the eye, and it's also faster than boring old linear motion.

This is, of course, why I chose inertial or "real" motion to illustrate modular programming. Both subject areas are vital in Flash web design.

You've now spent a little time looking at some fairly heavy concepts behind simulating real movement, but you haven't really tied it in with modular programming. It's surely about time you did—after all, that's what the chapter is all about! Let's make some movies to practice what you've learned so far.

Trailing the pointer (a mouse follower)

In this example, you're going to create a component that will control a movie clip and make it chase the mouse cursor. Remember the following equation:

```
New position = current position + ((target
➥ position - current position) ÷ constant)
```

In this case, your target will be the mouse pointer, whose position coordinates are stored in _xmouse and _ymouse. The movie clip instance will be called trail_mc, and you'll use its properties _x and _y to maneuver trail_mc about the screen. You therefore need to use the equation twice: once for the x-coordinates and once for the y-coordinates.

```
_x = _x + ((_xmouse - _x) / n)
_y = _y + ((_ymouse - _y) / n)
```

Note that you use a variable called n to denote the constant. You'll also need to remember to define that somewhere in your code.

Just in case you get stuck at any point, you can find a complete version of this exercise saved as inertia.fla in the download file for this chapter.

Creating the movie clips for the mouse follower

Follow these steps to create the movie clips for the mouse follower.

1. In a brand-new Flash document with the frame rate set to 24 fps, open the Library and create two movie clips called trail and inertiaFollower. The first will be the "blob" you use to follow the pointer, and the second will define the component that will contain your code.

2. Open trail (double-click its entry in the Library) and draw a black circle about 50 pixels across in the center of the stage. You don't need to do anything else to this movie clip—all your code will sit in the self-contained "black box," inertiaFollower.

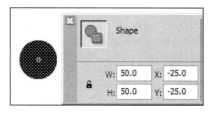

3. Now open inertiaFollower. Add a new layer, and rename your two layers as actions and icon.

4. In the icon layer, draw a small red square. This is purely so you can see that inertiaFollower is there. The inertiaFollower component will consist of only code, which would otherwise make it have no graphical appearance.

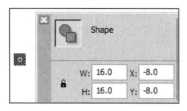

Now you want to make inertiaFollower a component that you can drag and drop onto objects on the stage, such as instances of blob_mc. To do this, you have to make it a component and define a special component parameter called _targetInstanceName.

Why do you need to do this, and what was wrong with the videocontrols component you created (which didn't require a _targetInstanceName parameter)? Well, the last component wasn't completely general—it has to be placed in such a way in the timeline hierarchy that it's the daughter clip to the clip it will be controlling. It always has to be on the timeline of the target it will be controlling so that the _parent path is valid and points to the correct movie clip. As you'll see, _targetInstanceName is more general because it becomes equal to the name of whatever you drop the movie clip onto. You don't have to worry about ActionScript hierarchies or anything else—just find the movie clip you want to control, and drop the component onto it!

It has to be said that the components you're creating here aren't structured like the ones that ship with Flash. The version 2.0 components that come with Flash MX 2004 are class based and horrendously complicated, and they aren't normally the sort of thing you would create yourself, unless you've spent a serious amount of time understanding their structure (something that you'll begin to do in Chapter 13). The components you're creating are simple, self-contained, black-box containers used to separate code from content. They're quick to create, develop, and understand.

5. Right-click (or *CMD*-click) the inertiaFollower movie clip in the Library, and select Component Definition (shown below). Now click the plus sign (+) at the top of the Component Definition window that appears. This adds a parameter in the pane below it, currently populated with default values, that you need to change. In the Name field, enter myTarget, and set Variable to _targetInstanceName. Be sure to type this word correctly, complete with an underscore at the beginning, or the feature won't work. You can leave the other fields (Value and Type) as they are. While you're at it, you can check the Display in Components panel check box (at the bottom of the window to the right of Options) and enter mouse follower with inertia in the Tool tip text field. Finally, in the lower-left corner, you'll see a little icon (it's below the Description title and above Options). This defines the icon that appears in the Library panel against the component. Click it to reveal a drop-down list of alternate icons, and select ActionScript Component icon.

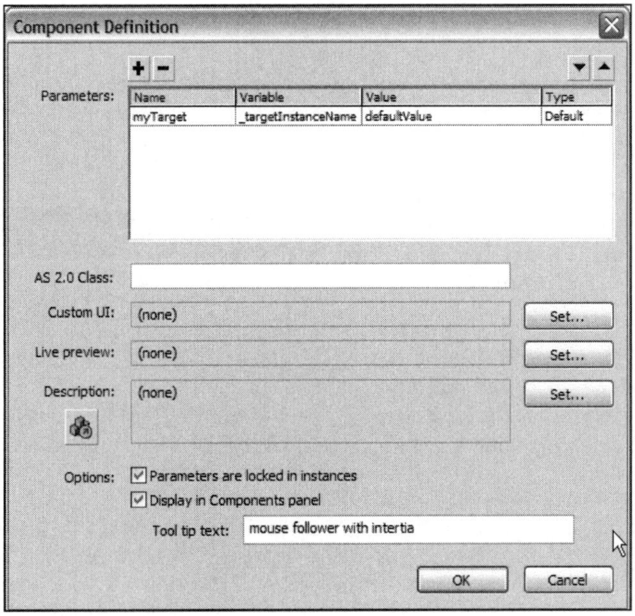

What have you done? Well, you turned your inertiaFollower movie clip into a component for a start! You'll now see inertiaFollower change its appearance in the Library to reflect that it's now a component. Its icon will change from the standard movie clip icon to the ActionScript component icon.

The property _targetInstanceName is a special component property that changes to reflect the name of the movie clip you drop it onto during author time—you'll make use of this in a moment. You'll also make your component appear in the Components panel, and this is what the tooltip text and the two check boxes are all about.

Testing drag-and-drop functionality

Let's test the drag-and-drop feature. For this to work, you need to enable the Snap to Objects mode. You can do this by either clicking the magnet icon in the main toolbar (at the top of screen, above the timeline) or selecting View ➤ Snapping ➤ Snap to Objects. The magnet icon also appears in the Tools window (or "toolbox," as most non-Macromedia people call it) for certain tools. It appears in the Options area.

1. Place an instance of the trail movie clip on the stage and give it the instance name trail_mc. Now drag a copy of inertiaFollower from the Library and onto trail_mc.

2. Take a look in the Properties panel, and you should see the following:

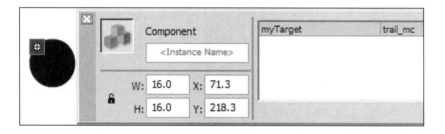

This means your component has read the name of the instance you dropped it on. "Um . . . so what?" you may be thinking. Well, since you know the name of the instance, *you can control it.*

> *If you don't see this, make sure you have the* inertiaFollower *component selected on the stage and that you're looking at the* Properties *tab in the* Properties *pane (you'll see two tabs at the right of the Properties panel when you select the component).*

You can perhaps see that drag and drop is much more versatile than the previous videocontrols component, which used _parent. The video controls require you to know enough about ActionScript to know what _parent is, but inertiaFollower doesn't require you to know what _targetInstanceName is—you just have to drop the component on what you want it to control and you're off and running.

> *In short, the black box for* inertiaFollower *is general, and this makes it a better modular package.*

Adding the inertial code

It's time for some scripting. Remember, though, that you can't edit a component in place. The only way you can get inside it is via the version in the Library.

Open the inertiaFollower component from the Library and select frame 1 of layer actions. Add the following code:

```
inertia = function () {
    // Capture mouse positions...
    targetX = _root._xmouse;
    targetY = _root._ymouse;
    distX = targetX-myTarget._x;
    distY = targetY-myTarget._y;
    // Apply inertia equation...
```

```
  myTarget._x =
➥ Math.round(myTarget._x+(distX/5));
  myTarget._y =
➥ Math.round(myTarget._y+(distY/5));
};
// Initialize...
var myTarget:MovieClip =
➥ _parent[_targetInstanceName];
var targetX:Number = 0;
var targetY:Number = 0;
var distX:Number = 0;
var distY:Number = 0;
// set animation event...
this.onEnterFrame = inertia;
```

Although this is a fairly short bit of code, there are *lots* of little tricks here for the unwary to potentially miss, so let's spend some time looking it over. You'll see what it does first, then you'll look at how everything is set up behind the scenes, and finally you'll examine the code itself.

If you test this FLA (Control ➤ Test Movie), you'll see the little red icon (that is, of course, your component instance) stays where it is, whereas the ball follows the mouse. That's odd for a start, because all the code is in the square, not the circle, but you've already come to expect that.

The more significant thing to do is run the movie in debug mode (Control ➤ Debug Movie). When you view what's happening in the debugger, you'll see the modularity at work.

- If you click the Variables tab and look inside the trail_mc instance, you'll see that there's nothing there. No variables, no attached event handlers—nothing.

- If you click the Variables tab and then look inside the component (it's called instance1) you'll see that everything is there. So that's where the party is! The event handler is attached to the red square, and all your variables are there as well. Even the code is in there (because, of course, this is the timeline you attached it to).

What are the advantages of this? Well, although the trail_mc movie clip is animated by the component, *it isn't affected by the component in any other way*. This has several advantages:

- The component doesn't care what it's controlling, and the clip under the control of the component is oblivious to the component. This means that when you create either (component *or* movie clip), you don't have to worry about the other. This is the black-box concept again—you can forget about the finer details.

- A consequence of the preceding point is that your component will be oblivious to *other components* dropped onto the same movie clip. This means that you can add as many components as you want to each clip. Not only does this allow you to create very complex animations by using several components, but also it allows you to create lots of individually simple components, rather than one big complicated component.

> *In modular design, not only are the final modules separate when you use them, but also the development of the software that forms each module can be separate. This is a major advantage of modular coding techniques.*

Let's now turn our attention to how this modularity is actually implemented.

Understanding the inertial code

Let's look at the initialization first. The code sets up a reference (or path) to the target movie clip, which is _parent followed by the name of the target, _targetInstanceName. You then set up the variables you need for the inertial effect, defining the name, type, and initial value for each. Finally, you assign the onEnterFrame event handler for the animation. This event handler is *not* attached to the movie clip being animated, but to the component.

```
// Initialize...
var myTarget:MovieClip =
➡ _parent[_targetInstanceName];
var targetX:Number = 0;
var targetY:Number = 0;
var distX:Number = 0;
var distY:Number = 0;
// set animation event...
this.onEnterFrame = inertia;
```

> *Note the use of square brackets to enclose the variable (or dynamic) part of the path. Without it, Flash would assume that the path was the literal string* "parent.myTarget" *and go looking for a movie clip called* myTarget. *In reality, you want it to look for the movie clip instance* trail_mc, *whose name was stored in the property* _targetInstanceName *(and copied to the variable* myTarget*). The brackets are how Flash knows that this is what you want to do.*

The function inertia() sets up your inertia equations and uses them to control the target movie clip. The thing to note is that you never use this. The code is actually attached to the same timeline that the event this function will define (onEnterFrame for the component) will be attached to, so adding or not adding this makes no difference—the path remains the same. You're already effectively at "this": the component.

The only time you need a path is when you come to animate the target movie clip (the last two lines of the function). You need to move the target, not the component, so you need to refer to myTarget._x and myTarget._y.

```
inertia = function () {
  // Capture mouse positions...
  targetX = _root._xmouse;
  targetY = _root._ymouse;
  distX = targetX-myTarget._x;
  distY = targetY-myTarget._y;
  // Apply inertia equation...
  myTarget._x =
➡ Math.round(myTarget._x+(distX/5));
  myTarget._y =
➡ Math.round(myTarget._y+(distY/5));
};
```

There are a couple of problems with the code as it stands. One problem is that you can still see the red square that represents the component. Although it's useful when you're editing the FLA, it isn't something you want to show up in the final FLA. The other problem is that you can simply drag and drop the component, which is cool, but you can't really configure it. You can't change the inertia constant to the different values that would create a fast-moving, slow-moving, or oscillating ball, for example.

Let's look at these issues now.

Fine-tuning the component

Making the component disappear is easy. You just set the _visible property of the component to false.

1. Add the following line to the code so far. When you now test the FLA, you'll see that the red square is no longer visible. The _visible property is a flag that tells Flash "Don't draw this."

   this._visible = false;

Setting the _visible property is the preferred way to make something disappear. Setting _alpha to a very low value isn't recommended to do the same thing. In the latter case, Flash may still be drawing your "hidden" graphics, and this can slow down your movie considerably.

2. Next stop: adding some configurability. If you think about it, the only thing that defines your motion is the variables that are used to control it. So the way to configure the inertia effect is to allow the setting of one or more variables on a per-instance basis. Here's how this is done.

Come out of editing inertiaFollower and back onto the main timeline. Right-click (CTRL-click) the inertiaFollower component in the Library to bring up the Component Definition window again.

3. Add a new parameter via the + button. Give this new parameter the name inertia value and the variable name n. Change the Type field from Default to Number, and change the default value to 5:

In the same way that _targetInstanceName was passed to the code within the component, a new variable called n is created every time you drag and drop an instance of inertiaFollower onto the stage. This variable is created inside (or with a scope of) the instance you just dragged and dropped.

4. You now need to use your new parameter in your script. Go back into inertiaFollower (remembering that you have to double-click the version in the Library to do this with a component). Change the lines highlighted in the following code in frame 1 of the actions layer (n now appears where 5 was previously).

```
inertia = function () {
  // Capture mouse positions...
  targetX = _root._xmouse;
  targetY = _root._ymouse;
  distX = targetX-myTarget._x;
  distY = targetY-myTarget._y;
  // Apply inertia equation...
  myTarget._x =
➡ Math.round(myTarget._x+(distX/n));
```

Parameters:	Name	Variable	Value	Type
	myTarget	_targetInstance...	defaultValue	Default
	inertia value	n	5	Number

The Name field is just a bit of descriptive text that describes the parameter, and it doesn't have to follow the rules of variable naming (specifically, the rule stating that there should be no spaces in a variable name). The Variable field defines the variable name, which can be a little counterintuitive, because it may seem more logical that this is what the Name column should do. In any case, the Variable field is the actual variable name, and this entry should follow the rules of variable naming.

```
  myTarget._y =
➡ Math.round(myTarget._y+(distY/n));
};
```

5. Now delete everything from the stage and add four instances of trail. You don't need to give them instance names, as you've done previously when controlling movie clips with ActionScript. Flash assigns them instance names if you don't, because all objects must be named.

6. Drop an `inertiaFollower` component on each circle, and use the Properties panel to give them inertia values of 2, 4, 6, and 8:

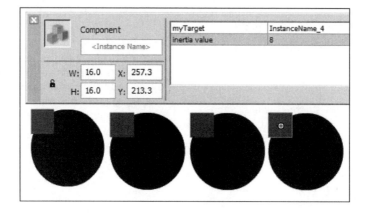

7. Now test the FLA. You'll see all four circles follow the mouse. Each is controlled by a separate instance of the `inertiaFollower` component, each of which is configured with its own value of inertia.

Finally, have a look at the download version of the FLA (if you haven't already), `inertia.fla`. You've replaced the component square with a more descriptive icon that gives a pictorial clue as to what the component does.

By giving each instance a slightly different value, you've built an altogether more complex animation. This is all happening through modular clips and code reuse.

The techniques I've discussed here have to do with timeline modularity. The advantage of such structures is that you have a graphical black box in which the code is placed and modularized. The component defines all the interfaces (component parameters) via graphical interfaces—things such as drag and drop and the Properties panel. This makes using modular movie clips and components a cool way to introduce Flash modular code to designers who, as I noted earlier, tend to think graphically.

There are two big disadvantages of using modular movie clips:

- **It places code all over the place**. Drag and drop is fine when you're thinking about ease of use, but when you have 20 of these cool components scattered all over a timeline, it can get difficult to think in terms of code. The code is all over the place and, although your code is still modular and well defined, there's no real overall code structure (although there is a well-defined graphic structure; the components are always on top of the thing they control).

■ **The way the code is modularized isn't recognizable as modular code to non-Flash programmers.** Anyone from a JavaScript background reading the preceding sections will have had a heck of a time. This "timelines as code containers" stuff is easy for nonprogrammers to grasp, but it's tough for programmers from other fields who are new to Flash—they just don't have anything like it!

As Flash moves further toward true programming, using timelines and components in the way you've done so far is being replaced by another kind of code modularity. It is this type of modularity that you'll look at next: function-based modular code.

> *You need to know about function-based modular code before you can start to look at other, more advanced coding styles commonly used with ActionScript. I've already briefly mentioned these advanced styles: prototype based (object-based programming) and class based (object-oriented programming, or OOP).*

Modular code and functions

The next example may look daunting from a distance, but it's based quite closely on `inertiaFollower`, and it took me only half an hour to put together. Of course, I've had a bit of practice with Flash, but I guarantee

that you'll be doing the same within 6 months if you stick with it! All I've done with the end file, `swarm.fla`, is start off with a simple set of premises and build it up from there. The story doesn't end here, either—there's much more I could do with this code, and I'll discuss that in a moment.

> *If you go away with one thing from this section, remember that Flash allows you to quickly visualize modular code–based changes under the control of ActionScript. Once you have the basic ingredients, it's easy to build up to a stunning, dynamic, reusable effect. This idea isn't easy to grasp, but bear with me because it's important, and once you see it, it's easy to do.*

Swarming behavior

You're going to look at modeling a swarm of flies. The swarm as a whole will follow the mouse around (like in the last example), but individual swarm members have slightly different destinations. Why? Because in real life it's difficult to occupy the same place as something else! So a swarming fly will land slightly to one side of its neighbor. That's the nature of **swarming**. The individual members of a swarm are actually all trying to go to the same place, but they can't, and they're always trying to maintain a position in an area with limited space.

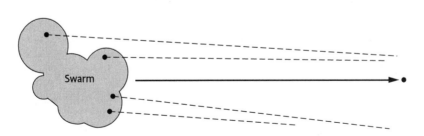

There's also the *type* of motion. A swarm in motion will tend to be spread out when it's traveling because each member needs space to fly. When it's at rest, the swarm can become tightly packed, because speeds are now much lower, and some of the members may be just stationary and hovering rather than actually moving. There's something here about the *density* of a swarm.

Where did I get all that information? Nowhere. No books on flies or queuing theory, chaotic motion, or fluid dynamics. I just used my observations of two inertiaFollower balls moving around and following my cursor, and I combined that with a memory of walking down a country path with my partner a few summers ago and having to dodge past the odd congregation of swarming bees.

The file swarm.fla is exactly the same as inertiaFollower except for a few things:

■ I've added two new terms, flockX and flockY, which denote random positions around the target destination (which is again the cursor) where the movie clip heads for. Since the positions are random, they're different for each member of the swarm.

■ This "flock" position changes according to whether the cursor is moving or not. If it's moving, the swarm is traveling, so the spread gets bigger. If it isn't moving, the swarm is stationary and won't be so spread out.

■ I've used the variable oldTargetX to determine whether or not the cursor is moving. If the current target is the same as the old target, then it's safe to assume the cursor is stationary.

■ Every now and again, there's a chance that a swarm member will change where it wants to go, due to its neighbors getting in the way. You therefore want to simulate this.

> *Note that you only need to check either the x-coordinate or the y-coordinate to work out oldTarget. If the cursor moves, then it's likely that both will change. This is why there's no oldTargetY.*

Although the code looks quite a lot longer, these really are the only changes I've made. If you want to kickstart the swarm, increase the frame rate from 12 fps to 18 fps or 24 fps (Modify ➤ Document). The more you increase the frame rate, the more it looks like an angry swarm. I can almost hear the buzzing!

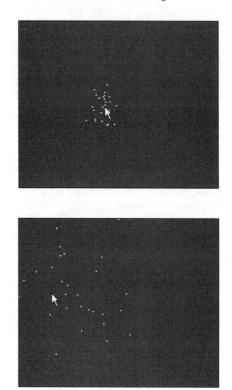

The final FLA is called swarm.fla. Test the movie. If you leave the mouse still, you'll see the swarm bunch up and flit around it as a dense swarm. If you move the mouse, the swarm gets less dense as its members move apart. Here's a happy bonus: leave the cursor still for a bit and then move it slightly. It's almost as if the swarm has been disturbed and is getting angry! It's funny how when you model simplicity, complex behaviors seem to just emerge.

If you look at swarm.fla, you'll see that it's a one-frame timeline that contains a single script attached to frame 1. The script is also modular; it's split into sections within the single listing via functions. These functions are treated in much the same way as the black boxes, although this time the boxes have no graphical appearance.

There are many advantages to creating code-heavy FLAs in this way rather than using code-containing movie clip black-boxes or components:

- All your code is in one place: the first frame of the timeline.
- Drag and drop is cool, but it has limitations. Just consider the difficulty in placing a component over every fly in your swarm! In the swarm code, the black boxes are attached to their targets using *code* rather than manually, which saves your eyesight.

I won't go too far into this code (given that the Futuremedia site is a better example and is more specific to real web design using Flash), but the swarm FLA shows how Flash can simply be **fun**. Think of a problem you want to visualize, and Flash has the power to allow you to write the code and see stuff whizzing around the stage.

> The book Flash Math Creativity *(friends of ED, 2003) showcases the use of Flash explorations via ActionScript experiments. Many of the FLAs in this book are just exploration for exploration's sake, but many clever UI ideas spring from such tomfoolery!*

Open swarm.fla and select the only frame in the FLA. You'll see the script appear in the Script pane of the Actions panel. The main code is at the bottom of the listing (line 45 onward):

```
var i:Number = 0;
var bugClip:MovieClip;
for (i=0; i<30; i++) {
  bugClip =
➥ this.attachMovie("bug", "bug"+i, i);
  fly.apply(bugClip);
}
```

The loop creates 30 movie clips, bug0 to bug29. The last line of the script applies a function fly to the currently created movie clip, whose name is stored in the movie clip reference (or "path to the movie clip"),

bugClip. The function.apply(target) method of the Function class creates a copy of the function function on the timeline of the movie clip target.

Hang on a minute. That's just the same as the drag-and-drop FLA earlier! When you used components, you physically placed code on a target timeline by putting the component "code container" on the actual movie clip you were interested in. When the SWF runs, this component sets up code structures that animate the target.

This time, you use a function as the code container: the function fly. You have generalized the black-box concept as far as you can. There's no longer a physical (rather, *visual*) box for the code, and you instead use ActionScript directly to define your black boxes using code only.

So what does fly do? Well, look at line 1 and you'll see the start of it. Ignoring the actual code and concentrating on just the functions, you have this:

```
fly = function () {
  this.animate = function() {
    // code
  };
  this.initialize = function() {
    // code
  };
  this.initialize();
  this.onEnterFrame = this.animate;
};
```

The function fly contains *other* functions—black boxes within black boxes! You have modularized the code into a problem-solving *hierarchy*. The function fly is the "this is what a fly does" box, and this is split into two functions that tell Flash "This is the initialize part of the what a fly does" code and "This is the animate part of the what a fly does" code. Although you could do this via embedded timelines and components, you'll tend to find that your code ends up very fragmented—split across all sorts of timelines. This way, you see the full "Russian-doll" hierarchy in a single script.

I won't go through the ins and outs of the full code because you've learned as much as you need from this and you'll see a better example in the Futuremedia project. Feel free to pick at the code, though.

The way you've used Function.apply() here isn't the most efficient way of doing this. Because you apply the set of functions to each fly, you end up with a large number of identical functions—as many sets of the fly function as there are fly movie clips.

Using a prototype-based approach, you can tap into the functions that define the movie clip itself and insert your fly function there. You effectively change *all* movie clips by changing what a movie clip actually is, and make it more like a fly. This is cool because you need only one set of functions to do this. Another way is to create a *new* type of movie clip that's exactly like a standard movie clip but is called something else (flyClip, say). You can do this with either prototypes and classes or just classes.

Either way, the *principle* of creating function-based black boxes instead of doing so visually is common to all ways of performing the task via code only. Let's review the more advanced advantages of the new, function-based code before moving on:

- It makes code **target independent** (that is, you don't need to know what the thing you're controlling is called when you write your code; you simply use the general path "this," as in "this bug movie clip").

- **It makes code position independent** (so you don't need to know where your code will end up). Nested timelines that use the _parent trick are only target independent. They still rely on position because they have to be the daughter of the clip they're controlling. The code in swarm.fla is *totally* independent of the application you wind up using it for, and that makes it more reusable. You could take the script and just place it into another FLA, change the main loop at the end slightly to refer to some other movie clips, and the whole thing would work.

- You have more control over the final effect. For example, change the i<20 part of the for loop at the end of the script to 200, and rerun the script. Now think how long it would take you to do the same thing manually. The way you've written the code makes it easier to tweak because all the controls are software parameters rather than manual "put 50 of these on the stage" deals.

- You can define event handlers *before* the movie clip you're applying them to exists. If you think about it, you've defined an onEnterFrame handler without having anything to attach it to. That makes for flexibility. You can choose to *not* attach the swarm event, or you can allow the user to control the effect and select from different events at runtime. For a good example of this, change the for loop at the end of the script as follows:

```
this.onMouseDown = function() {
  var i:Number = 0;
  var bugClip:MovieClip;
  for (i=0; i<200; i++) {
    bugClip =
➥ this.attachMovie("bug", "bug"+i, i);
      fly.apply(bugClip);
  }
  this.onMouseDown = undefined;
};
```

This won't attach all the script to the instances (in fact, it won't even create the instances) until you click the mouse. You've taken the generation of script away from a linear path and made it **conditional**. This not only leads to increased flexibility, but also allows more complex structures to be built that support cool things like adaptive behavior.

Taking the swarming effect forward

Let's say I want to develop the code further. Instead of swarms chasing the cursor, I want them chasing food. The food would be a plant called "Spore" growing on a distant planet. The user could cause Spore to grow or die by changing the climate.

The functions that control the swarm members aren't fixed. They can mutate in response to the changing conditions. The members can be grazers instead of flies that eat Spore; or they could evolve to be stronger and eat other grazers; or they could become scavengers, eating Spore but keeping an eye on the weaker grazers.

There are all sorts of other possible code-based stuff you could add via additional modules like pollution (a function that causes swarm elements to die if they come too near a new kind of movie clip called a pollutant), growth (the attributes of a grazer change over time to represent a born-live-die cycle), and aggression (variables define how tenaciously a swarm member tries to get to its target). I might well call this game "Ecology," and it stops being a trick FLA and starts to become something useful and fun to kick around.

OK, that's enough to whet the appetite for future days. Let's look at something else for today and *now*.

Book project: Starting to code

You'll begin adding the final code for the Futuremedia site in this chapter. You need to start with the file from last time, futuremedia_initialize.fla. The finished FLA for this chapter is called futuremedia_code01.fla. Feel free to refer to it if you get stuck or need something to compare with yours.

The Futuremedia code style

The code you're developing in the Futuremedia site is in a general, beginner-level (but fairly advanced) style called **modular programming**. It's the precursor of all other styles you'll come across in Flash as you develop further in ActionScript, including prototype-based and class-based code.

Although there are differences in intent, the way that all three styles of programming just mentioned use functions to split up code into related but separate and well-defined sections is a common concept.

Making it modular

So, after going through the earlier parts of the chapter, you know that modular code in all its various forms is good, but what do you need to modularize for Futuremedia? Well, this can sometimes be a difficult question for the designer learning how to program, but Flash helps you out here because it's arguably the easiest application for design/visual-based people to use when learning advanced code. Why? Because, as you've seen, Flash is a visual environment.

Your graphics are already arranged in a visual hierarchy, and that is your clue to how you need to modularize your code. You have a single clip containing three smaller clips (that is, the tricolor and three strips shown below), and you'll need to reflect this hierarchy in the code. The easiest way to do this is to use the same hierarchy.

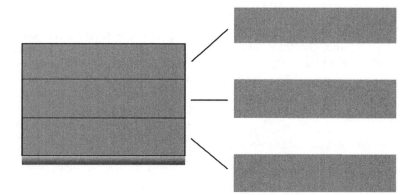

The three strips within the instance tricolor are still the dull-looking slabs of gray they have been for some time. I think that has gone on for long enough. Itís time to add some color into their lives. You also need to start adding some code to get them moving.

The code associated with the strip and tricolor functionality will get quite involved, so it's better to separate it out into functions that you can write separately. You'll call the function that sets the tricolor page up (unsurprisingly) stripPage.

Now, here's the problem. Your code will be on the main timeline, _root. You actually want to control the movie clip tricolor with your soon-to-be-written function stripPage, though. There are two ways to do this in ActionScript:

- Make stripPage an event handler of tricolor. This enables you to scope tricolor via this.
- Change the scope of stripPage so that it scopes tricolor instead of the main timeline of the current FLA, _root (or _level0), using Function .apply().

Let's go for the second option. Why? Because you want to use stripPage to simply initialize tricolor. You don't want it to do anything interactive or animation-specific, which is what the first option (events) is for.

Continue working with the file you created last time, futuremedia_initialize.fla from Chapter 8. Type in the following code below the definition of the existing navStrip variables:

```
// Initialize UI...
stripPage.apply(tricolor);
```

You now need to write this function. Where do you write it? Well, the temptation is to write it *after* the code you have so far, but the convention is to define all functions at the top of your code. You'll therefore add the functions *before* the main code you've written so far.

There are two main things the function stripPage needs to do:

- Define the code that *sets up* the ability to change color, and also include the *ability* to change the colors. You have to *initialize* this ability as well as *include* this ability.
- Define the event handler scripts that change position. As you'll see later in the case study, there isn't just one event handler to perform the animation, but a sequence of them, each handling a particular part of the animation before handing over control to the next event handler in the sequence. You'll start the ball rolling by adding the first one in this sequence, navigate.

Writing the code to set up the events and function hierarchy

You could make stripPage a massive piece of code that does all your code setup, but there's a much easier way to keep all your code manageable: make stripPage refer to two other functions in a modular fashion.

- One function defines the color-changing abilities.
- One function defines the movement (animation) abilities.

The problem with calling two new functions is *speed*. It's a bit like me trying to talk to you through a third person because we don't speak the same language. I say "Hi!" to Frank, and then Frank says "Hi!" to you. Then you say "Hi, Sham!" to Frank, and Frank says it to me. Not good. It would be far better if I learned your language, and then I could just say "Hi!" directly. The function-based version of this is **inheritance**. Rather than *call* another function, you can make stripPage *assimilate* these other functions into itself. That's cool because you can still write the functions separately, but at runtime you just call stripPage, and stripPage contains all the other functions you need without having to go and ask.

Here's the code. You need to add it above the code so far as shown:

```
// DEFINE MAIN SETUP SCRIPTS
stripPage = function () {
  // note use of Function inheritance
  this.inheritEvents = stripEvents;
  this.inheritCols = stripCols;
  this.inheritEvents();
  this.inheritCols();
};
```

This calls out two new functions, stripEvents and stripCols.

Sanity check #1

Although this is a deceptively short bit of code, there are a few things to notice here. Some of them are revisions to general modular code techniques you've already looked at in the book so far, but some of them are a new slant on old ideas and concepts. Let's go through them all, given that you need to know them to really understand the Futuremedia site, and some are easy to miss.

- Inheriting a function is written differently from calling it. This line of code means "Make me the same as another function called myFunction":

  myInheritedFunction = myFunction;

  The following code is saying, "Run myFunction and make me equal to the result it returns (if any)":

  myReturnedValue = myFunction();

- The implied target of this is important. What does this mean in stripPage? Well, you've applied stripPage to the movie clip tricolor, so this means the instance tricolor.

- Inheriting a function doesn't mean that it's executed. When you cause a function to inherit another, it doesn't mean that you also run the function. So, as well as inheriting the functions stripEvents and stripCols as inheritEvents and inheritCols, you have to run the newly inherited functions at some point. This is something you don't have to do for functions that act as event handler callbacks, as you'll see soon.

> *Inheritance only defines where functions will end up (that is, what their scope is). It gives them position, but it doesn't actually run the functions themselves, in the same way that putting dinner on the table means it's dinner time, but not that you've eaten anything yet.*

OK, so you've written the stripPage function. Now you have two other functions to write. Here they are. You need to write them above stripPage but below the DEFINE MAIN SCRIPTS comment.

```
// DEFINE MAIN SETUP SCRIPTS
stripEvents = function () {
  // attach button events to the 3 pages...
  this.strip0_mc.onRelease = navigate;
  this.strip1_mc.onRelease = navigate;
  this.strip2_mc.onRelease = navigate;
};
stripCols = function () {
  this.colStrip0 =
➥ new Color(this.strip0_mc);
  this.colStrip1 =
➥ new Color(this.strip1_mc);
  this.colStrip2 =
➥ new Color(this.strip2_mc);
  this.setCol =
➥ function(col0, col1, col2) {
    var col0, col1, col2;
    this.colStrip0.setRGB(col0);
    this.colStrip1.setRGB(col1);
    this.colStrip2.setRGB(col2);
  };
};
```

Let's look at these functions in turn.

The stripEvents script attaches the onRelease button events to your three strip instances inside the bigger tricolor instance. Notice the way you do this. Rather than using an anonymous function

```
MyClip.onRelease = function() {
// do this
};
```

you're this time actually using a *named* script called navigate. To do this, you again omit the () at the end of the function (in much the same way as you did with inheritance earlier).

So why did you then have to go through the extra step of executing the inherited functions, but this time you don't? Well, when you're attaching to an event, Flash knows that the function has to be run each time the event occurs. When it isn't an event, there's nothing to actually run the script, so you have to do it yourself.

The second thing to notice about the stripEvents function is how it's referring to the individual instances inside the tricolor movie clip. The stripEvents function takes tricolor as its subject because the function that called stripEvents, stripPage, also had tricolor as its subject. That's quite powerful if you think about it. Functions can *pass on the memory of the movie clip (or more correctly, the timeline) that called them to other functions through their scope*.

Although the this of stripEvents is tricolor, look what happens next: you have three lines that refer to the embedded instances this.strip0_mc to this.strip2_mc. Eh? Well, what you're saying here (through the code) is that inside this (tricolor) you'll find another movie clip called strip0_mc (or one of the other two).

That's OK, but the *really* cool thing is when you look at the full line:

```
this.strip0_mc.onRelease = navigate;
```

You're no longer calling navigate with the subject this as tricolor—you've *changed it* to the three movie clips *inside* tricolor! The function navigate won't take this as tricolor, but each of the movie clips strip0_mc, strip1_mc, and strip2_mc.

As your functions work back from the first function, stripPage, they're fanning out to cover more and more of the stuff that needs defining, *and they're doing this on their own*. All you do is say "Set up tricolor," and you've written the function modules further down to know that stripPage consists of three new movie clips, and those need defining as well. You're following

the exact same hierarchy as the movie clips, with the strips inside the tricolor, but instead of relying on the graphics, you're creating this structure via code, through things like inheritance and scope.

The stripCols function is also something new. If you look carefully, it does something strange: it defines a function *within itself* called setCol. It's rather like those nested Russian dolls, where you open the big one to find a smaller one inside, and another smaller one inside that, and so on. This is another structure in your code that's following the tendrils of your problem up through the trunk and out to the branches. Your initial function has to apply itself only to the single trunk, and the code will split and redefine itself as it encounters the problem branching out.

So why do you do this? Well, in the case of the color functionality, you don't need to just define the function, you also need to define some other stuff, and the function stripCols does just that.

So now that you have some insight into the structure of this bit of code, how about what it actually does? The first thing you need to do is set up a color object in each stripn_mc clip. This is an object with methods that allow you to change the color of a movie clip. Only after you've done that once for each strip can you actually use the line that does the color change. Let's take a look at the embedded function:

```
this.setCol = function(col0, col1, col2) {
  var col0, col1, col2;
  this.colStrip0.setRGB(col0);
  this.colStrip1.setRGB(col1);
  this.colStrip2.setRGB(col2);
};
```

This function takes some arguments: the three colors you want the three strips to be, col0... col2. You then use the setRGB() method of the color object to apply the color transition.

There's one final subtlety here, and you need to be aware of it. The lines that are actually executed when you call stripCols and setCol are different. When you call stripCols from stripPage, the following lines are executed:

```
this.colStrip0 = new Color(this.strip0_mc);
this.colStrip1 = new Color(this.strip1_mc);
this.colStrip2 = new Color(this.strip2_mc);
```

setCol is then *defined* but not *executed*.

If you make a call to setCol (as you will in the main code at the end), only the function setCol is run. The rationale for this is obvious if you step back and think about it. The stripPage function is setting everything up, and to do that it has to set up the color objects and define setCol, but not execute setCol. When you actually use the interface, you will be changing colors and want setCol to set colors to create your transitions. In that case, you'll call the *embedded* function setCol.

If you're having trouble with this, think of stripCols as a two-stage rocket. stripCols is the first and second stages that together make the complete rocket. When you launch (initialize) the rocket, you want only the lower first stage to burn (execute). Once the rocket is up in orbit, you want the smaller, second stage to actually do stuff, and that part is called setCol. At this point, you don't need the first stage to run (the part that initializes the color objects), and to achieve this you have split your rocket (stripCols) into two stages (stripPage and setCol).

OK, what have you done so far? You've set up the part of the code that creates the event handlers, but you haven't yet written the event callback function that you refer to, navigate. Your color functionality is complete, though, because there are no more outstanding functions to consider.

Setting up the event handler callbacks

You won't finish the navigate code sections yet. They require some decision-making capabilities that you won't put in yet, but you can set up something called a **stub**. A stub is an incomplete program section that acts as the placeholder for some code that you'll write later. It will prove that you're on the right track, but it won't yet animate anything. You need to put it above the code so far, at the top of the Script pane of the Actions panel. Here it is:

```
// DEFINE EVENT SCRIPTS
navigate = function () {
    // initialize navigation
    // event handler here
    trace("");
    trace("you pressed me and I am"),
➥   trace(this._name);
    trace("but you need to fully define me");
    trace("before I start doing anything
➥ else!");
};
// DEFINE MAIN SETUP SCRIPTS
stripEvents = function () {
    // attach button events to
    // the 3 strips…
…
```

The function navigate will output some text when you click a strip, but you're almost ready to run the FLA, so I'll leave what it actually does for you to find out in a moment.

Invoking the color change

So far, you've only set up the color-changing code, setCol. You'll now add the code to run it. This code is part of the main script (the stuff at the very bottom of the listing):

```
// Initialize UI...
stripPage.apply(tricolor);
// Set UI colors...
tricolor.setCol(color0, color1, color2);
// now sit back and let the
// event scripts handle everything!
stop();
```

The active part here is the following line:

```
tricolor.setCol(color0, color1, color2);
```

This line calls the setCol function that you placed within tricolor to allow you to make color changes to the individual pages. You are passing the three color values you defined earlier.

OK, you're ready to test the FLA. Did it work?

Sanity check #2

With a script as long as this, there are bound to be errors, so if it doesn't work as expected, here's a quick run-through of potential problems:

- Check that all your instance names are correct on the movie clips tricolor and strip0_mc, strip1_mc, and strip2_mc. If you used futuremedia_initialize.fla as your starting point, you don't have to worry about this.

- Check that all the variable and function names are correct. A good way to do this is to use the Find icon, which is the second icon from the left at the top of the Actions panel. If searching for a variable doesn't stop at every line you expect it to, then the missing line has a typo.

Finally, here's the code listing you should have so far:

```
// DEFINE EVENT SCRIPTS
navigate = function () {
  // initialize navigation
  // event handler here
  trace("");
  trace("you pressed me and I am"),
➥ trace(this._name);
  trace("but you need to fully define me");
  trace("before I start doing anything
➥ else!");
};
// DEFINE MAIN SETUP SCRIPTS
stripEvents = function () {
  // attach button events to the 3 pages...
  this.strip0_mc.onRelease = navigate;
  this.strip1_mc.onRelease = navigate;
  this.strip2_mc.onRelease = navigate;
};
stripCols = function () {
  this.colStrip0 =
➥ new Color(this.strip0_mc);
  this.colStrip1 =
➥ new Color(this.strip1_mc);
  this.colStrip2 =
➥ new Color(this.strip2_mc);
```

```
  this.setCol =
➥ function(col0, col1, col2) {
    var col0, col1, col2;
    this.colStrip0.setRGB(col0);
    this.colStrip1.setRGB(col1);
    this.colStrip2.setRGB(col2);
  };
};
stripPage = function () {
  // note use of Function inheritance
  this.inheritEvents = stripEvents;
  this.inheritCols = stripCols;
  this.inheritEvents();
  this.inheritCols();
};
// Define screen extents for later use...
Stage.scaleMode = "exactFit";
var BORDER:Number = 30;
var BOTTOM:Number = Stage.height-BORDER;
var TOP:Number = BORDER;
var RIGHT:Number = Stage.width-BORDER;
var LEFT:Number = BORDER;
Stage.scaleMode = "noScale";
// Define initial screen colors
// (further colors will use these
// colors as their seed)
var color0:Number = 0xDD8000;
var color1:Number = 0xAACC00;
var color2:Number = 0x0080CC;
// Define navigation strip variables...
var NAVSTRIP_X:Number = BORDER;
var NAVSTRIP_Y:Number = BOTTOM;
// Initialize UI...
stripPage.apply(tricolor);
// Set UI colors...
tricolor.setCol(color0, color1, color2);
// now sit back and let the event
// scripts handle everything!
stop();
```

Running the FLA: The results

Here's what you'll see if all has gone according to plan:

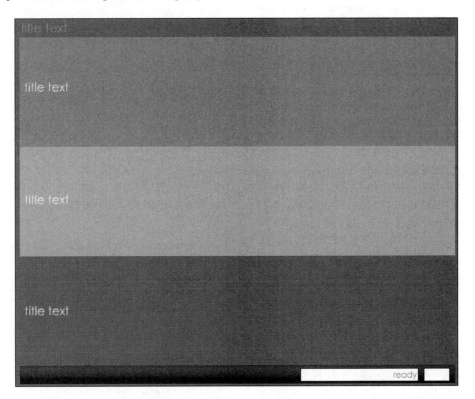

First off, you have color! The three color variables color0 to color2 have been applied to the three strips strip0_mc to strip2_mc. You can play around with the values you've equated with the color0, color1, and color2 variables if you wish. For example, you can design alternative colors in the Color Mixer and replace one or more of the values used in the code here:

```
// Define initial screen colors
// (further colors will use these
// colors as their seed)
color0 = 0xDD8000;
color1 = 0xAACC00;
color2 = 0x0080CC;
```

For example, try changing color2 as follows:

```
color2 = 0xAAAA22;
```

This will give you yellow instead of blue. Change color2 back to its original value when you're finished, so you're building the same site. Next, mouse over any of the three strips, and the mouse will turn to a hand icon. This means that the strips are now acting as buttons. If you click any of them, you'll see the following text appear in the Output window:

```
you pressed me and I am
strip1_mc
but you need to fully define me
before I start doing anything else!
```

The name will change depending on whether you click strip 0, 1, or 2. This shows that the site is aware of where you're asking to go, because each strip returns its own name.

255

Parting shots

You may not think you're very close to a fully working site here, but you have a lot of important features covered in the code so far.

- You've set up the variables that tell Flash what the UI looks like and where all the important points are on the screen. If you ever need to change the stage size or position of any of the major parts (something you'll have to do when it's time to customize the site for your own purposes), you know that these will be the only variables you'll have to redefine. This makes your design *flexible*.

- You've defined a structured code hierarchy early on in the project. This makes your code easy to *modify*.

- You've initialized the main functions that define your UI and attached all the main events.

You'll complete the site in later chapters, but for now, it's a good idea to play around with the code for a while using the debugger to see where everything actually ends up. As you move forward, the basic structure of the code will start to get a little difficult to see as you add more lines, so now is a good time to familiarize yourself with it.

Another point worth mentioning at this stage is that this is *not* a beginner site. Neither is it a super-advanced code-fetish site that uses all sorts of highbrow code for the sake of it.

You're more than halfway through the book, and you're no longer a beginner. On the other hand, you don't want to go off creating more code than you have to. I'm assuming that all readers of this book want to make some money out of Flash design at some point, and code for code's sake is a bad bet for profitability!

The Futuremedia site you're developing is the sort of thing you would be expected to come up with if you set your mind to creating an ActionScript site that someone else was paying you to create. In short, it's a real site that will stand up to commercial scrutiny.

Summary

In this chapter you've taken a look at some seriously professional ActionScript techniques. You've learned

- Best practices for modular, black-box programming using a few different techniques

- How to create modular movie clips

- How to build ActionScript to create real movement

- How to create a swarming effect and how to improve it using functions as objects

More important, you finished the chapter by looking at how you can use modular code to break up the problems associated with a real and moderately complex website design, Futuremedia.

In the next chapter you'll cover sprites, and how to create and work with sprite functionality.

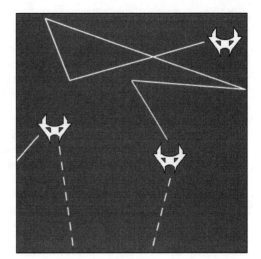

Chapter 10

SPRITES

What we'll cover in this chapter:

- Investigating what a sprite is
- Creating sprites, and assigning movement and collision behaviors
- Detecting a collision
- Creating the zapper game

This chapter covers sprites and ties them into the related building blocks that you learned about in the last two chapters. You'll look at basic sprite functionality and how to create it, before deconstructing an entire game so that you'll know enough about sprites to start making your own games.

In this chapter you'll create a Flash video game. This isn't the steep cliff-face at the top of the mountain it may seem at first; rather, it's the integration of the concepts you've examined in isolation in earlier chapters. You're going to take the separate areas of ActionScripting and put them together to create something that's much bigger than the sum of the parts. The glue that holds advanced ActionScripting together is your ability to see through problems with forward planning and your familiarity with the separate building blocks.

What is a sprite?

A **sprite** is a screen-based object whose motion and actions are controlled by dedicated code that's integral within itself. This means that the main code can let the sprite get on with whatever it's doing in terms of movement, collision, appearance, and so on, secure in the knowledge that the sprite can look after itself.

The sprite can be a space invader or a happy little spider that follows you around a website, helping you when you run into trouble. The sprite should be able to do three things without you having to keep an eye on it, none of which should be new to you:

- Move
- Detect collision
- Act independently

The first point is that a sprite should be able to move around the screen in an intelligent way. It should know if it's moving into areas where it shouldn't be (such as off the visible screen area), and it should take its own remedial action.

The second point involves collision detection. A sprite should be able to detect when it has hit another sprite and take the appropriate action—for example, move away, explode, or cause what it hit to explode.

The third point involves the programming techniques you learned earlier when I talked about modular programming. The sprite should keep the main program informed of what it's doing and what its status is. This strongly implies that sprite routines should be designed using a **black box** or **modular** approach. The main program shouldn't have to bother with taking care of the sprite's movement or collision detection; it needs to know only what's necessary. The sprite is really just a self-contained movie clip that has methods that it applies to itself to control itself.

You've already covered the principles of something that goes beyond animation and moves into the realm of **simulation**. *When you looked at inertial motion, you were simulating real motion, complete with acceleration, but that's only the start.*

Simulation is the cornerstone for all that's related to advanced animation and specifically the way sprites interact with each other. To create a believable game world, you define rules for it, and everything in the game world has to conform to those rules. The interaction of the game sprites with each other is the difference between creating real-time games and creating separate advanced animated effects for websites.

> *For example, a ball that hits a wall has to know that it has hit a wall, and then it has to respond to this event. Similarly, a ball sprite that has hit a wall has to know that a collision has happened, and then it has to run code to react to this (that is, it has to bounce away).*

You've learned the principles that underpin the basic elements of sprite construction—it's just that you never knew you were a games programmer.

There are three basic factors you need to consider for sprite construction:

- Control
- Movement
- Collisions

Let's take them one at a time.

Control

Control is all about simulating intelligence and giving the impression that the sprite is aware of what's going on around it. Control is just a *way of changing the properties of a movie clip (or anything else) so that the movie clip seems to act in an appropriate way.* For the game you create in this chapter, you'll steal the swarm effect you created earlier and reuse it for a swarm of aliens.

Now that you're giving the sprite some independence, you need to remember that it has to be aware of its own surroundings and their rules. It's not talking to the main program anymore, so it needs to know this itself. It's moved out into the real world now, and it has to do its own laundry. As well as knowing about what's going on around it, the sprite needs to be aware of its own internal status. These are two separate *levels* of influence: external and local.

External and local data

Think of sprites as people. As people, we have internal influences, such as our own thoughts and emotions. We also have information coming to us to say what's going on in the immediate environment or television news about what's going on in another country. Our internal influences are the most important to us, but we need to be aware that we may have to adapt them in reaction to what's going on around us.

Similarly, a sprite's internally generated processes control it in the way our thoughts control us. At the same time, though, the sprite must also check whether its actions are beginning to break the external rules by looking at the immediate environment. The sprite doesn't have the same level of complexity we do. Its repertoire of interaction is as follows:

1. Set my next movement as per my controlling code.

2. Check whether I'm breaking any rules.

3. If I'm not breaking any rules, modify my external environment. Otherwise, move me as per step 1 (and keep repeating the three steps).

That might sound a bit vague, but consider your bouncing ball. It will keep moving forward, checking if it has hit something. If nothing is hit, the ball will move in its current direction. If something gets in the way, the ball can't continue forward. To do so would break a rule—the ball can't occupy the same space as something else. Instead, the ball will have to move away. It will have to *bounce*.

> *Note the subtle way the code version is different from real life. In real life, a ball is dumb. The ball bounces because there are physical laws that prevent it from going through anything it hits without changing direction. In the digital world, you have no laws, and impossible things can happen unless you force more sensible things to happen. The problem is that for a ball to be aware of physical laws and how they affect it, it has to know about them. It's no longer a dumb and passive ball, even if it looks this way on the screen. The digital ball has to know what the rules are before it can follow them, whereas a real ball simply follows them.*

Yeah, I know, it's been a long time without a friendly sketch to help you! Let's fix that by looking at the steps graphically. The simplest way to illustrate these steps is to look at **boundary violation**.

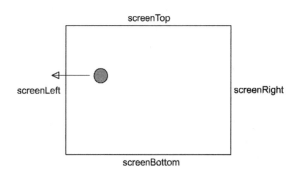

The ball sprite in the diagram has a set of rules driven by code that causes it to move off the visible screen boundary. How do you tell it not to do that? One option would be to put some information about the size of the screen into the sprite itself, but that's not true to life. In real life, you know when you're about to hit a wall when you see the wall, rather than because you know that the coordinates of a wall are (234309, 324322) and you are at (234308, 324323) and about to hit it! Putting the size of the screen in the sprite also makes its responses less adaptable. In the future, you might want the sprite to change depending on a different external factor such as a differently positioned wall. Having to build everything again doesn't really fit in with the modular lessons that you've been learning.

In real life, you don't carry around information about your environment with you; you perceive the *environment itself*. An easier and more consistent way to tell the sprite not to move off the visible screen is to realize that the screen boundary positions are a **worldwide** or **external** set of attributes, or something that everything in the sprite's world should know about.

The contrast to this is **local** information that's contained within the sprite's immediate environment and not in the wider world. As an example, once the sprite moves, it assesses where its environment ends by looking outside of itself (or the _parent timeline). The sprite checks variables on this external timeline that tell it that it's violating an external rule, and it would modify its motion. In the same way, the internal thoughts of the sprite (I'm getting rather close to this other sprite) are only required by the sprite itself, and if anything else wants to know this information, it should have to ask the sprite. You can see that information in your game world is also in two *levels*. The external information about the world is the lowest level, and as you get more and more specific, it gets less centralized and more concerned with individuals within the world. One alien sprite on one side of the screen doesn't really need to know that two alien sprites on the other side of the screen have just collided. It might put the former off trying to kill the evil human at the bottom of the screen!

The key word here is "levels," because it's something that Flash has already and something that you've been learning about throughout this book. You've seen that _root is the highest level and that the individual movie clips have their own timeline on which you can place (scope) information as variables. So, to know external information about the "world," a movie clip needs to look at the timeline outside itself, which could be _root but is more generally _parent. If the sprite needs to talk to or know anything from another inhabitant (sprite) within the world, it looks at the movie clip timeline owned by that inhabitant's movie clip. The world data is therefore structured around levels, and these levels are based on timelines.

There are actually three definite levels that a sprite can access:

- _global
- _root
- this (the timeline of the sprite itself)

So what do you use each for? I've made global constants (such as the screen boundaries or physical constants such as gravity) live in _global, with the shared data (which I define as global data that's also dynamic or open to change) living in the main timeline the simulation is running on (which is invariably _root). Finally, local data lives on the local timelines, or this.

It's important when reading the scripts in this chapter to recognize which level each piece of information is on. The way to do this is as follows:

- Global data is preceded by g. This isn't something that Flash requires; it's a naming strategy I've used to avoid confusion.
- Shared data has no path (and will be therefore placed on _root, because it's where the scripts are).
- Local data is preceded by this (which means that it will be placed on the timeline scoped by the current function, and this will usually be the timeline of the sprite itself).

If you want to see this in action, check out boundary.fla. It consists of two balls, one called slowBall_mc and the other called fastBall_mc. They live in a world that consists of the Flash stage area, denoted by a dotted set of lines.

The rules of this world are very simple:

- The boundaries of the world are defined by a set of global variables: gTOP, gBOTTOM, gLEFT, and gRIGHT.

- The two balls both have two variables on their timeline, xSpeed and ySpeed, and these variables define the speed at which the balls travel.

- The two balls use an external function, mover(), that controls their motion. This function looks at the timeline of each clip to see the value of the current ball's speed, and it also checks for collisions between each ball and the four boundary values, making the ball bounce back into the stage if a collision occurs.

The code for this world looks like this:

```
mover = function () {
  this._x += this.xSpeed;
  this._y += this.ySpeed;
  if (this._x<gLEFT) {
    this._x = gLEFT;
    this.xSpeed = -this.xSpeed;
  }
  if (this._x>gRIGHT) {
    this._x = gRIGHT;
    this.xSpeed = -this.xSpeed;
  }
  if (this._y<gTOP) {
    this._y = gTOP;
    this.ySpeed = -this.ySpeed;
  }
  if (this._y>gBOTTOM) {
```

```
    this._y = gBOTTOM;
    this.ySpeed = -this.ySpeed;
  }
};
// set up global constants
// (globally available)
_global.gLEFT = 5;
_global.gRIGHT = 545;
_global.gTOP = 5;
_global.gBOTTOM = 395;
// set up local values
// (inside slowBall_mc)
slowBall_mc.xSpeed = 4;
slowBall_mc.ySpeed = 4;
slowBall_mc.onEnterFrame = mover;
// set up local variables
// (inside fastBall_mc)
fastBall_mc.xSpeed = 12;
fastBall_mc.ySpeed = 12;
fastBall_mc.onEnterFrame = mover;
```

As you'll see when you run the FLA, the two balls move at different speeds. This is because they use their own *individual speeds*, as stored within themselves and denoted in the code by the two ball instance names. For example, fastBall_mc.xSpeed is a variable local to fastBall_mc.

The two balls live in the same world, however, and to simulate this they check against the *same* boundary limits. So you have two balls that

- Have different speed values, because this is localized

- Move around in the same world area, because they check the same world limits via the global variables

- Move in the same general way, because they pick up the same external movement function

Notice the way this hierarchy (which you've known about all along—it's just timelines, after all!) is becoming very powerful here. By changing the global values, you can *change what both balls do*. You can try this by changing the line

```
_global.gBOTTOM = 395;
```

to

```
_global.gBOTTOM = 295;
```

By changing the local variables per ball, you can change *what an individual ball does*. Change

```
fastBall_mc.xSpeed = 12;
fastBall_mc.ySpeed = 12;
```

to

```
fastBall_mc.xSpeed = 24;
fastBall_mc.ySpeed = 24;
```

and you'll see `fastBall_mc` get faster, but `slowBall_mc` is unaffected by the change. This hierarchy of black boxes within black boxes (or, in practical terms, movie clips within movie clips) is what makes advanced motion graphics in Flash tick.

The next issue surrounding sprite construction is a vital one: movement.

Movement

Movement is the most important attribute to the gamer, but to the programmer it's merely a consequence of control. You've already seen this in things such as the swarm code, which wasn't a movement so much as a section of code that controlled properties of a number of movie clips. The fact that these properties were actually associated with position is how the movement occurred, but you could just as easily have applied it to size, color, and so on.

I don't need to say much more about movement. Movement is a visual property that we think is important in real-time applications, but to us as programmers, it's really just a consequence of all the control and relationships that we've set up in our simulated world. Talking about movement in isolation isn't meaningful. Instead, you'll concentrate on the control you define that creates this movement in the first place.

If you want to create movement, you have to ask this question: "What's the code that's causing that movement, and what are the important features that I have to simulate to reproduce it?" You did exactly this with the swarm movement, by breaking down the swarming by deconstructing its movement back to a set of rules to do with (x, y) properties that are followed to create the movement in the first place. Now on to the last point: collision.

Collision

Collision is a vital ingredient in a believable game world because most sprites have to know something is near them before they can interact or change their responses in some way. In the game you'll look at, collision means just that. In other, more sedate games, it may mean something more fundamental: the initiation of complex interaction between two sprites. In other words, sprites don't necessarily have to try to blow each other up!

In the Ecology game I mentioned at the end of Chapter 9, collision would mean that two creatures in significant proximity start interacting. The two sprites would have to be able to signal to each other and retrieve information about exactly what type of creature the other one is. This information would allow the sprite to decide whether the other sprite was a potential mate, food, a predator, or just another like-minded creature with which to swarm for safety.

Collision is something new, so I'll show you in practical terms how it works in Flash. The file for this FLA, `collision.fla`, is in this chapter's download file.

What is collision? Two things are in collision if their boundaries intersect. This is almost the same as a real-life collision. In real life, two things are in collision if their boundaries *touch*. Most collisions don't result in intersection because two solid things can't occupy the same space.

In the next exercise you'll create some basic collision detection. You'll make two circles and set up some dynamic text to tell you whether or not Flash sees a collision between them.

Creating the graphics

First you need to create the circle graphics.

1. Create a new FLA using the default settings (550×400, 12 fps, white background).

2. Now you'll create one of the two movie clips that will be colliding. Draw a simple filled circle on the stage. Press *F8* and make it a movie clip called hitArea. Give it the instance name `hitArea_mc`.

3. Next, you'll create the "hitter," the movie clip that will collide with the hit area. Draw another circle of about the same size as the first, and make it into a movie clip called `hitter`. Double-click this new movie clip to edit it in place. In the timeline of this new movie clip, rename the current layer as `circle` and create a new layer above it called `text`.

4. In layer `text`, put a dynamic text field just underneath the circle. This will contain a bit of dynamic text set up to display a message that will tell you if Flash thinks a collision has taken place.

Select the Show Border Around Text icon on the Properties panel so that the text has a border you can see. Deselect the Selectable button, and set it to display a single line. Give the text field the instance name `message_txt`.

5. Go back to the main timeline and give the `hitter` movie clip the instance name `circle01_mc`.

Let's recap. You now have two movie clips on the stage. The circle-only one has the instance name `hitArea_mc` and the circle-with-text one has the instance name `circle01_mc`.

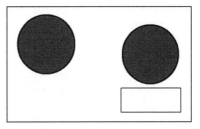

At the moment, the movie clips are some distance apart. You need to make one move toward the other somehow to cause the collision. The way you will do this is to make `circle01_mc` draggable, so you can drag and drop to move it.

Adding the code

Now follow these steps to add the code.

1. Back in the main timeline, create a new layer and call it `actions`. Rename the original layer as `graphics`. You now need to add some ActionScript to frame 1 of the `actions` layer. Enter the following code into the Actions panel:

```
function dragStarter() {
  this.startDrag("");
}
function dragStopper() {
  this.stopDrag();
}
detectCollision = function () {
  this.message_txt.text = "";
  if (this.hitTest("_parent.hitArea_mc")) {
    this.message_txt.text = "hit";
  }
};
attachHitterScripts = function () {
  this.onPress = dragStarter;
  this.onRelease = dragStopper;
  this.onReleaseOutside = dragStopper;
  this.onEnterFrame = detectCollision;
};
attachHitterScripts.apply(circle01_mc);
```

265

The code works by applying the functions listed in hitter to circle01_mc. The function dragStarter() becomes the onPress function, making hitter draggable when you click-hold over circle01_mc. The function dragStopper() makes it possible to stop dragging circle01_mc by releasing the mouse button.

> *Note that the* dragStopper() *function is assigned to both the* onRelease *and* onReleaseOutside *event handlers. This ensures that any mouse button release (with the mouse pointer either over the dragged clip or not over the dragged clip) will cause the clip to be dropped.*

The detectCollision() function is where the interesting code is. This function is used as the onEnterFrame of circle01_mc, and it will place the text hit in circle01_mc's text field if a collision is detected. If no collision is detected, the text is made to show nothing. The actual detection is made via this line:

```
if (this.hitTest("_parent.hitArea_mc")) {
```

The hitTest method will return true if "this" (that is, circle01_mc) hits the hitArea_mc movie clip, noting that hitArea_mc is on the parent timeline to "this" (that is, _root). The method returns false if no collision is detected, so in this case, the text remains blank.

You can try the code to see this. Drag the circle01_mc movie clip over hitArea_mc.

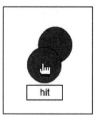

Some of you may be wondering why I used named functions and this:

```
hitter.apply(circle01_mc);
```

instead of this:

```
circle01_mc.onPress = function() {
   this.startDrag("");
};
circle01_mc.onRelease = function() {
   this.stopDrag();
};
circle01_mc.onReleaseOutside = function() {
   this.stopDrag();
};
```

and so on. The answer is coming up.

2. Add a new instance of the hitter movie clip called circle02_mc. You now have three movie clips on the stage.

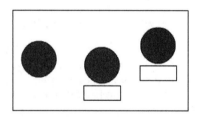

3. Give the new instance the instance name circle02_mc. At the end of the script so far, add the following:

```
attachHitterScripts.apply(circle02_mc);
```

If you test the FLA now, you'll see that both the existing and new hitter instances work. You've found a way to attach a number of events to any new movie clip with just one line!

What you've actually done is made your code more general. The functions that become event handlers don't care about the name of the movie clip—they use "this." The function hitter *also doesn't care for the same reason, but it does know which functions have to be assigned to which event to make the whole thing work. Finally, the* apply() *method makes the* attachHitterScripts() *function run with the scope (that is, which movie clip will be substituted for "this") equal to the argument—in this case,* circle01_mc *and* circle02_mc.

Also worth remembering is that apply() *isn't a method of the movie clip; it's a method of the* Function. *Yes, a function is also a class, just like* MovieClip. *That may seem a little odd, but if you think about it, it makes sense. Functions are created and are attached to timelines just like movie clips. They have instance names (*attachHitterScripts, dragStarter, *and so on). What they don't have is symbol names, but that's because they aren't symbols—they're purely code, and they don't need to live in the Library. This is all part of the general rule that almost everything that ActionScript knows about is a class. ActionScript doesn't understand much else apart from instances and classes.*

Remember, if at any time you get lost or just want to check that you're doing things correctly, open collision.fla *to check your work against the original file I created.*

This would make a nice drag-and-drop interface. You could have the user physically drag and drop products (which would be the equivalent of the circles) into a shopping basket, for example, or have an MP3 downloads page where the user chooses music through record icons he or she drops into a DJ's record bag.

There are some issues to note here:

- You have to name the item you want to detect the collision with, so you must know its instance name. This means that you can't just detect a collision with "anything" as the target (like you can in real life—if I walk into an obstacle, I'll hit it). To do this in ActionScript would require a loop that looked at all available instances, which would mean that you have to know the names of all available instances at any time.

- The two hitter movie clips don't detect collisions between each other; rather, they detect collisions between themselves and hitArea_mc.

- You use a general set of functions that control the individual parts of the problem, but individually these functions (dragStarter(), dragStopper(), and detectCollision()) don't do anything to solve the problem. This is left to the function attachHitterScripts, which knows which function to attach to which event for each movie clip it's applied to. The thing that tells it which movie clip is the *scope* that it's running in. The scope is defined by attachHitterScripts.apply(). This calling action is used by the attachHitterScripts function via the path this. Thus you have a hierarchy of code, starting with apply(), then attachHitterScripts, then the three functions that actually do the work.

- This exercise provided a good example of structured coding and included something new: black boxes within black boxes. At the apply() stage, you simply call attachHitterScripts, and you *don't need to know what the scripts* attachHitterScripts *will call are.* Inside attachHitterScripts, you see the names of the three scripts, because you've moved down a level into a box that needs to know the names.

An advantage of the last point is that if one of the animation functions, say detectCollision, *was large enough to warrant splitting into two because of new features you wanted to add, you wouldn't have to change either* attachHitterScripts *or the line that calls it via* apply().

You'll notice that the hit detection sometimes returns true when the circles are close but not touching. This is because you're checking the **bounding boxes**, which are the little outlines that appear around symbols when you select them in the Flash authoring environment.

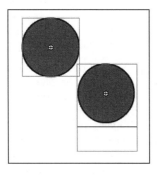

You can modify the hitTest method to check for movie clip outlines rather than the bounding box, but this is difficult and makes for a more complex collision-detection routine. Let's get it working with bounding box collisions for now.

There is one final area to consider in interactivity: performance. At the moment, the circles are updated at 12 fps, and this is a little slow. There are two ways around this. One is to increase the fps to something higher, but this makes Flash do *everything* faster, and it's a little inefficient. Good programming doesn't rely on making things better by using speed (because you'll soon find out that you can never have enough), but on making code *more efficient*.

*Increasing the frame rate to silly values because "it seems to run better" is a common technique. It's OK for small animated effects, but if you're building serious Flash applications, you need to accelerate only **some** of the things in the FLA. Accelerating them all makes the Flash player work harder and leads to posts on Flash message boards with questions like "Why is Flash so slow?" The answer is, of course, that the developer is expecting Flash to cover over inefficient code by running just that bit faster if the fps is set higher. If only everything was this easy!*

The Flash action updateAfterEvent() will add an extra screen redraw whenever it's invoked. You can use this action only inside (and at the end of) an event script, as the name of the action itself suggests. That kind of sounds useful, but where do you want to use it?

What you actually want to do is add extra frames only when the user is dragging a circle. You know when that occurs and for how long, because

- When the circle in question has been clicked *and* the mouse is currently moving, you know that the user is currently dragging.

- When the circle in question has been dropped, nothing is being dragged, so you can stick with 12 fps.

So once the mouse is clicked over a circle, you want to start looking for mouse movement and use updateAfterEvent() every time you detect this. In ActionScript, this converts to create an onMouseMove event that updates the screen when the mouse moves.

If the mouse button is released, then the user has stopped dragging. You no longer need to force Flash to use updateAfterEvent(), and the easiest way to do that is to delete the onMouseMove. Have a look at collision2.fla for an example of this in action. The updated code function is shown here, with new lines in bold:

```
function dragStarter() {
  this.startDrag("");
  this.onMouseMove = function() {
    updateAfterEvent();
  };
}
function dragStopper() {
  this.stopDrag();
  delete this.onMouseMove
}
detectCollision = function () {
  this.message_txt.text = "";
  if (this.hitTest("_parent.hitArea_mc")) {
    this.message_txt.text = "hit";
  }
};
hitter = function () {
  this.onPress = dragStarter;
  this.onRelease = dragStopper;
```

```
    this.onReleaseOutside = dragStopper;
    this.onEnterFrame = detectCollision;
  };
  hitter.apply(circle01_mc);
  hitter.apply(circle02_mc);
```

> *The way the* dragStarter() *function handles the issue of jerky drag-and-drop animation is to add extra frames only when the mouse is moving. This means that the "hit" text fields are still being updated at 12 fps, but the circle animation is animated much faster (it's animated as fast as Flash can run). Targeting only the stuff that you actually want to run faster has a cool side effect: because Flash doesn't update everything as fast as it can, the "as fast as Flash can" ends up being much higher!*

If you run this FLA, you'll see a marked improvement in the animation speed.

You've had a look at fairly simple examples thus far. Now it's time to delve into a bigger example, something more like the sort of project you'll want to create yourself.

Planning zapper

In this section you'll create a space invaders–type game, with swarming aliens at the top and the player's ship at the bottom. This is a pretty well-known setup, so I won't waste your time by showing you a design breakdown of a game that's been in the public domain since the late 1970s.

> *One of the most important issues with games is sound. I don't address sound in this chapter, but I'll discuss ActionScript-controlled sound in Chapter 12.*

Just because I'm not displaying a design breakdown doesn't mean I haven't thought it through. To shape my initial concept and develop an idea of what would happen, I thought of all the arena games I've played and broke down all the functions. I'll live and die by the statement I made in Chapter 2:

> *If it doesn't work on paper, it won't work when you code it.*

For simplicity's sake, I've decided that the player will be allowed only one life and one bullet (so that there's only ever one bullet on the screen). Also, I won't have the invaders attacking by firing on the player. This is entirely possible, but I feel a little uneasy about defining a game with too many sprites on the screen at the same time. Instead, the aliens will perform some form of swooping or diving attack, which calls for fewer sprites and makes for a faster game.

One of the major reasons that Flash is at a disadvantage when it comes to games is that it's forced to play its game inside a browser window and it can't control the screen attributes, such as what size the full screen will be. Unlike dedicated consoles that play games on fairly small screens, usually no bigger than about 600×400 pixels, Flash has to play on a screen of unknown bit depth. This could be a screen size of 1280×1024, on which currently only the highest specified desktop computers can render fast games acceptably, and then only with some form of graphic hardware support. Flash has to do this on the browser, a platform that wasn't built for speed. The Flash player itself doesn't do you any favors, as it doesn't grab all the available processor time for itself as most video games do. So, you'll keep things simple for the moment.

In the early arcade game machines, the games lasted a calculated amount of time for the average player. The difficulty level was graded so that the player would think she had gotten her money's worth. An important consideration at the planning stage—and one often overlooked by Flash games—is how long you want an average game to last. This affects all sorts of usability questions such as "Is the game too challenging?" "Does the game last long enough?" and "Does the player see enough of the game on the first turn to want to play again?" I generally assume that a good web game should last no longer than 1 minute for the first time, have immediately obvious controls, and have no long preloads that break up the game. The player should also be able to get better from her abysmal start by practicing.

The next step is to plan how the game will work from a programming perspective. The block diagrams that you see here relate to different aspects of the game and are taken directly from the three pages of handwritten notes and sketches that I scribbled down before I wrote the game.

You'll come back to look at each of these diagrams in more detail as you examine the ActionScript behind each section. I wanted to show them to you here so that you could see how they're as useful as the flowcharts that you looked at in Chapter 8, but on a slightly higher level. Flowcharts are more concerned with detailed logic, whereas these block diagrams are high-level overviews that helped me mesh together a game world with no logical flaws. Once I had these diagrams, I dropped down a level and began flowcharting the smaller ActionScript pieces of that world.

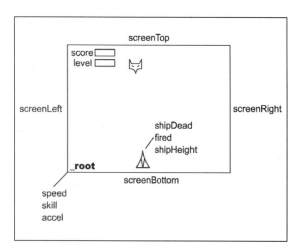

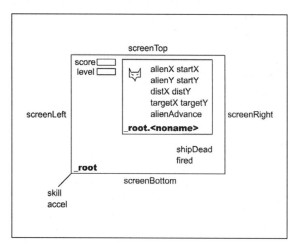

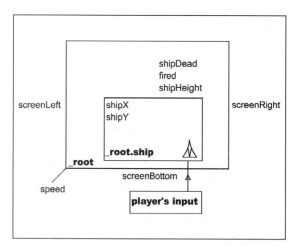

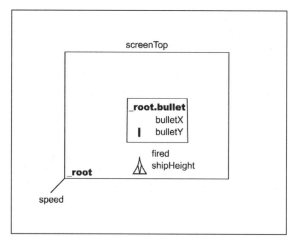

I found that these diagrams were a lot more useful than flowcharts because they imply *relationships* rather than logic, and they're easier to formulate. They show objects and their interfaces, which is useful for getting an overview of what each game piece can see and interact with in the game world, and what in the game world will influence each game piece's behavior.

It took me half an hour to create these diagrams, and by the time I finished, I knew I could complete this game because all the information was in front of me. This is the way you'll need to work if you want to reach this level of ActionScripting, and it's more or less mandatory if you expect to do it commercially. I wrote this game in around 8 hours, including planning, which isn't far from the timescale that you'll be used to in the real world. To turn ideas around that quickly, you must plan everything out first in the same way that I've done here. At first it may seem to slow you down, but with time you'll be able to home in on the important bits very quickly, and you'll find that the time you spend planning reaps massive savings when it's time to code.

I don't propose to go through the whole program as a tutorial in this section, because you should have developed far enough in ActionScript at this stage to be able to understand what's happening. I'm guessing that you're more interested in seeing how the plans are converted to ActionScript so you can go away and do the same thing with *Missile Command* or *Defender*. I'll break down the code and tell you what each bit does and my reasoning at every stage.

As I've said, you need to plan all aspects of a game before coding it. What I'm going to do here is show you the plans and the code separately for each section so that you get a clear view of what the ActionScript is doing in each section. Don't think for a moment that I planned only one section at a time!

> *One of the advantages of the friends of ED policy of providing downloads from its website rather than from book CD-ROMs is that you can look at the downloads for other books for free. If you want to see other game-related FLAs, try the download for* Flash MX 2004 Games Most Wanted *(friends of ED, 2003). The download for Chapter 7 of that book ("Retro Games") contains an advanced game based on the side-scroller* Defender *game. The code for this game is a logical progression of the zapper game.*

The game world (the main timeline)

One of the important issues in designing your game world is **approximation**. You want to concentrate only on those things that are important in your game. Deep space has all sorts of things that you aren't interested in, such as temperature, radiation intensity, and so on. These things won't affect anything in your game world, so you don't need them. This is an important thing to have a feel for, and it's one of the defining features of good simulation: knowing what to leave out and what to leave in.

The things your game will need to address are shown in the following image. You'll look at the player's ship, the aliens, the stage, and the score/level.

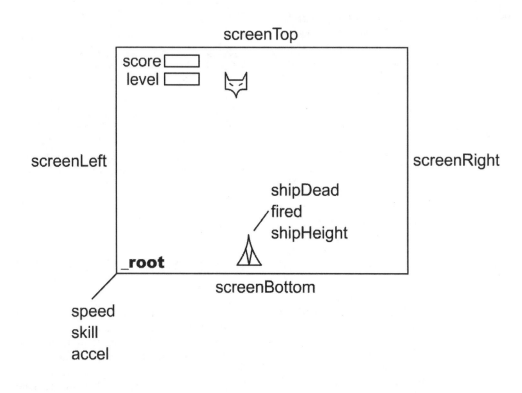

gSCREEN_TOP, gSCREEN_BOTTOM, gSCREEN_RIGHT, and gSCREEN_LEFT

These are the game world limits and represent the visible screen area. They're all constants, so in the final code they're shown in *CAPITAL_LETTERS*. I've also placed them in the _global level because they're universal constants for the game world (hence the lowercase g). You'll see later that the game allows some sprites to start off outside the game world, but their controlling code will force them to move back into the game world.

score

score is there for the player only and represents the carrot that keeps the player wanting to play again. In the final game, I've never gotten more than 700 points. So now you have an incentive. As you'll see, score also feeds into the level parameter.

level, skill, and accel

level is an important game world parameter, because it controls how well the SwarmAliens will play. It's derived from the score, and the higher the score, the higher the level. The longer the player survives, the harder the game gets. level works by feeding into several other parameters that control the alien behavior: skill and accel(eration). As the aliens get more skillful, they'll attack more, and as the accel parameter changes, the aliens will get to their top speed faster and therefore get from point A to point B quicker.

speed

speed is how fast things move in pixels per frame. The aliens will have a slightly different movement strategy, based on the equation in the last chapter, but the stars and player's ship will have movement based on this parameter.

shipDead, fired, and gSHIP_HEIGHT

These are some parameters for the player's ship that will be needed by the other sprites, so I decided it would be more convenient to make them global. shipDead represents whether the player's ship has died

or is still fighting the good fight. fired tells you whether a bullet is in the process of being fired (that is, the bullet is onscreen and visible). gSHIP_HEIGHT is an odd one. I put it in as a global constant because I could see it being important for at least some other sprites. One of these would be the bullet, which needs to start off at the top of the ship because that's where it's fired from.

I thought gSHIP_HEIGHT might also come in handy if the game runs too slowly—the aliens can't hit the ship until they're gSHIP_HEIGHT above gSCREEN_BOTTOM. You don't really need to test for collisions between the aliens and the ship until then. As it happened, the game ran fast enough and I didn't need to do this, but if you decide to develop the game further—and I hope you do—then you have this option to consider.

Let's have a look at how I've coded this game.

The timeline

Open zapper.fla from the download for this chapter and have a look at the main timeline (shown below). The first thing to notice is that the frame rate is set to 18 fps. This is a normal frame rate when smooth graphical movement is at a premium.

The reason frame 1 of the timeline is blank has to do with preloading. You want everything to be in the Library before the scripts start running; otherwise, the game may not work properly.

Normally in online Flash content, the next frame on the timeline isn't played until all content required to display and animate that frame (movie clips, graphics, buttons, scripts, and so on) has been loaded into the browser. This loading occurs in the current frame. Frame 1 is special because it has no frame before it for this loading to take place, and for advanced Flash content (games and other ActionScript-heavy content), this can occasionally cause problems.

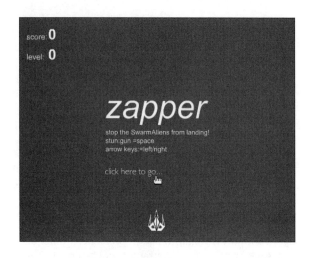

Most of the game plays out in the first five frames of layer actions:

Almost all the code is on frame 2 (comment label gameInit) of layer actions. This frame initializes the game, setting up the functions and events that drive zapper.

*A **comment label** is a keyframe with a label that starts with //. A comment label isn't exported into the SWF. Like comment lines in ActionScript, comment labels are there for your benefit.*

Frames 3 (label attractor), 4 (label gameStart), and 6 (label gameEnd) contain the three main phases of the running game.

attractor is the start screen. The game is paused at this frame, waiting for you to click the start button (an invisible button over the click here to play text) and begin a new game.

The introductory screens in coin-based arcade machines are called the "attractor" because they're designed to entice folks to put their money in the slot and play the game.

gameStart defines the start of the game. In terms of code, this frame initializes each new game. Some values (such as the player's score) need to be reset on starting a new game.

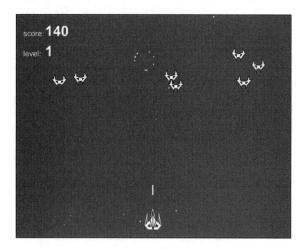

gameEnd indicates the end of the game. This is signified by a variable (shipDead) being set to true, telling you that the player has been hit.

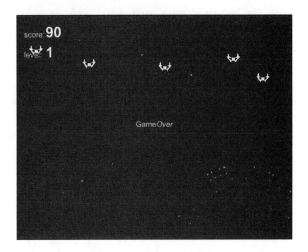

The code

The majority of the code is attached to frame 2 of layer actions. Select that frame to see the script in the Script pane of the Actions panel.

As usual, the main code starts at the bottom of the script, given that it's normal for functions to be defined first. Let's skip to the main code.

Global constants

Scroll down to about line 210 to see the following code:

```
// set up screen extents
_global.gSCREEN_LEFT = 20;
_global.gSCREEN_RIGHT = 530;
_global.gSCREEN_TOP = 20;
_global.gSCREEN_BOTTOM = 380;
_global.gSHIP_HEIGHT = 40;
```

This code sets up the global or "universal" values, and they are constant. They're universal in the sense that they're the things that define how the game world will work, much like physical constants define the real world. They're therefore defined in the _global scope. You can see how they affect the game by doing the following:

1. Test the SWF. You'll see the game start playing on the main stage. While you play the game, notice that all the sprites stay within the stage. In particular, they seem to know when they're near the right side of the stage, and they don't go outside it.

2. When you lose, close the SWF and do another test in Debug mode (*CTRL+SHIFT+ENTER/CMD+SHIFT+ENTER* or Control ➤ Debug Movie). Click the ▶ icon on the debugger to start the SWF. Using the debugger, find the global variables by selecting _global in the top-left pane and then selecting the Variables tab in the pane below it.

You can see that the global gSCREEN_RIGHT is 530. Double-click the 530 and change it to 300. Now play the game. You'll notice that *everything* in the game now sees a different right edge and reacts differently.

The variables you've chosen as universal all have this property of being able to change the way *everything* in the game works, and this is why they're in _global: everything important in the game uses them, so they need to be available everywhere.

*In most modern games, any particular title is built in two parts: the **game engine** and the **game data**. The game engine is general and can be used to build several different games or to emulate different environments in the same game. One of the ways this is achieved is the same way you changed a global variable just now to change how the game world reacts. For example, if your hero moves from planet earth to the low-gravity alien home world in the final level, you can modify the effects of gravity by changing one thing: the global constant that controls gravity.*

The "start game" trigger

The main code in the game appears directly after the global constants. The first thing you do is set up the event handler for the button that starts the game. Notice that this isn't the simple gotoAndStop("home") type of event handler you may have used in the past. The event handler is a whole series of function calls, and these will result in *hundreds* of lines of ActionScript running.

```
// event handler for invisible button
invisible_btn.onRelease = function() {
  this.enabled = false;
  initGo();
  makeStar(15);
  makeAlien(10);
  bullets.apply(bullet);
  starShip.apply(ship);
  gotoAndStop("gameStart");
};
```

You'll look at the more complicated individual functions in turn a little later, but here briefly is what the button script does.

First, the button disables itself. Why? Well, once the game starts, you no longer need the button, but if you remove it from the timeline, you also remove the event handler shown. Rather than the beginner "move to a keyframe where it doesn't exist" way of removing content from a timeline, you're now using a more ActionScript-centered way of controlling things. You don't use timelines as much, but you change the thing by varying its properties. In this case, you simply disable the button.

```
this.enabled = false;
```

The button is invisible, but if it wasn't, you could make it invisible as well as disabled by adding the code this._visible = false;*.*

Next, you initialize for a new turn of the game by calling the function initGo(). This sets up the variables that need to be reset every time so the player miraculously lives again with a zeroed score (shipDead = false rather than true, score is zeroed), the aliens revert from the super-killers they became at the end of the last game to the pussycats they always seem to begin as (speed = 10, skill = 0.04, accel = 20), and so on. The function itself starts at about line 200 and looks like this:

```
function initGo() {
  // reset variables for this turn
  speed = 10;
  skill = 0.04;
  accel = 20;
  score = 0;
  level = 1;
  fired = false;
  shipDead = false;
  // clear score and level text
  score_txt.text = score;
  level_txt.text = level;
}
```

So to recap, the start game button has been clicked, and so far you've run the code to set up your game data (variables). What you haven't yet done is create the graphics. You do this via the next two lines:

```
makeStar(15);
makeAlien(10);
```

This does exactly what it implies: it creates 15 stars (as can be seen scrolling in the background) and 10 aliens. Play around with these values, adding higher values if your computer is fast enough to handle them—and if it isn't, consider reducing them!

> This is, of course, modularity at work again. Although you have no idea how the code to create stars or aliens works (or even, at this stage, where it is) you can use it via its black-box interfaces. All you need to know is how many and the code that sits in the makeAlien box will do it all for you! You'll look at the makeStar() and makeAlien() code in a moment, so don't worry, you'll peep inside the boxes eventually.

So now you have variables, stars, and aliens. All you need to do is get your ship powered up and your lasers online to thwart the invasion. You do this via the last two lines in the button event handler:

```
bullets.apply(bullet);
starShip.apply(ship);
```

The first line attaches the function called bullets to the movie clip called bullet, and the second line attaches a function called starShip to the movie clip ship. By the magic of modular code, you don't have to know what the functions bullets and starShip do just yet, except that the first makes the bullet movie clip act like a bullet, and the second makes the ship act like a starship in a space invaders game. There—done!

Um, not quite. You've set up all the different *parts* of the game: stars, aliens, player, and bullets. What you haven't done is tie them all together so the game can be played. Rather like a baseball game where the players are dressed for the part but nobody knows how to *play* baseball, nothing much will really happen in your game—or rather it will, but not in a coherent way. For example, the aliens will dive at the player, but the game doesn't know what should happen when an alien actually hits the player.

What you need are some *rules*. You implement these rules in the zapper game via an onEnterFrame script that keeps track of what's happening via a check every frame.

```
// set up rules
this.onEnterFrame = gameRules;
```

The actual function called up as the umpire script is on line 185 onward and looks like this:

```
function gameRules() {
  // game rules...
  if (score>(level*200)) {
    skill = skill*2;
    accel = accel/1.5;
    level = ++level;
    level_txt.text = level;
  }
  if (shipDead == true) {
    shipDead = false;
    delete this.onEnterFrame;
    gotoAndPlay("gameEnd");
  }
}
```

There are two rules in the game:

- **As the game progresses, the aliens should get more aggressive**. The first if checks the current score and sets up variables that will make the aliens more aggressive based on it. The visual indication of this aggressiveness is the game level. At level 1, the aliens are placid, but they get impossible by level 5.

- **If the player's ship gets hit, it should explode and the game should end**. The second if checks the variable shipDead, which is set elsewhere if the ship is ever hit by an alien. If shipDead is true, you set up conditions for the game to end: make it possible for the ship to live for the next game (shipDead = false), make the main timeline play from label gameEnd, and stop the umpire script (this.onEnterFrame) from running (it will start again the next time a game starts via the start button).

> *onEnterFrame is attached to this, where* this *is the timeline you're currently on,* _root. *As* _root *is the game world inside which all other movie clips exist (and inside which all your game-control variables exist), it seems reasonable that this should be the timeline that controls the game. The game world (* _root*) maintains itself!*

Finally, you set up the timelines so that the appropriate graphics show. The ship movie clip has a tween explode sequence on its timeline that you want to play when the ship is destroyed. You don't want to play this sequence just yet, so you stop its timeline. You also move the main timeline to the start of the game proper: the **attractor** frame.

```
// move timelines...
ship.stop();
gotoAndStop("attractor");
```

> *Note that although the scripts are defined at frame 2, they actually start working on the attractor screen. The first frame on which the user can click the start button is frame 3.*

Now all the main code is sorted out. Next up are the individual sprites.

The player (the ship)

The player's sprite has no intelligence of its own; rather, it takes its movements from the player's keypresses. All it has to do is move left and right, and fire on demand from the player. It also has to check that it's always within the game world.

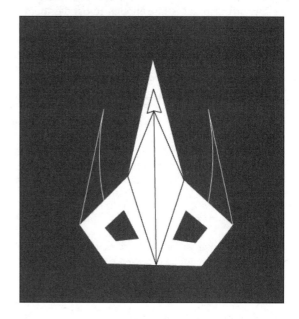

That's not enough information to actually write code, though. For that you need a diagram that tells you the same thing in terms of what ActionScript knows—that is, *data*, or in this case, variables.

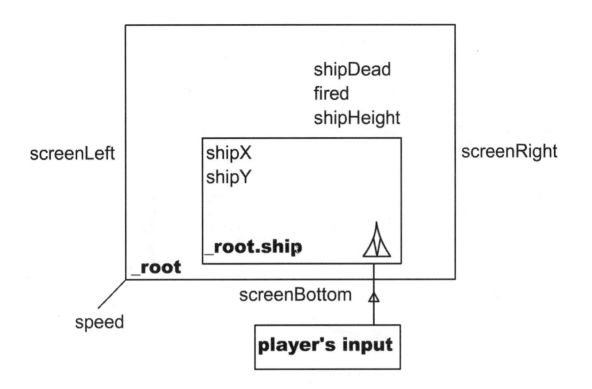

This diagram defines your ship sprite in terms of its data. There are several things of note on this diagram:

- **The data that's used to control the ship**. All variables used are shown here. You can also see where they are (that is, their scope) in the final SWF by where they are in this diagram. You know shipDead is on _root and shipX is in ship because they're in their appropriate movie clip "boxes." You also see that screenLeft is a global variable because it isn't in a box (that is, it has no scope, which makes it _global and available everywhere).

- **Important external variables**. All variables outside ship that are particularly important are placed in the bottom-left corner, with a label showing where they come from. The variable speed is very important, and you can see that it's in _root.

- **The hierarchy**. You can see that the ship movie clip is inside _root because the ship box is inside the _root box.

From the diagram, you can see that the ship movie clip is controlled by its own variables, shipX and shipY, and that the variable speed (on _root) is also particularly important. Other variables used include shipDead, fired, shipHeight, screenRight, screenLeft, and screenBottom (rather, the *CAPITAL_NAME* versions in the code). You can also see that the ship control code uses inputs from the player. Best of all, you see this *graphically*.

Although you'll probably learn about flowcharts in programming class, the graphical diagrams you're most likely to see in real industrial code are more complex versions of the diagram shown previously. This type of diagram goes by several names, but the one that best describes it is **object block diagram**. *It shows the relationship between all the objects (instances) in your code. It's also very useful for debugging your code.*

For example, if you find that your ship isn't firing properly, you could look on this diagram and quickly note that there's a fired *variable. You could then look at all the other diagrams to see where* fired *is coming from (sourcing) and where else it's going (sinking). By looking at what the other sink instances are doing, you can capture a lot of information about the error behind this simply by looking at the object block diagram,* **before** *you start looking at any code. Examining high-level object block diagrams and working down graphically toward the actual code is called* **system engineering** *in some fields. It involves treating code (and most other things) as blocks and working out what's going on by looking at the interfaces between the blocks.*

Put a different way, it's easier to follow the script if you assume all the code inside the function starShip *is attached to frame 1 of the ship movie clip timeline. It isn't in the FLA, but scope will make it act as if it's in the SWF when you run the game. As the code on the main timeline had a "functions first, then main code that actually uses the functions" structure, you'll see that the code in* starShip *has exactly that same structure.*

This is a very powerful concept. It allows you to write code that will relocate to where it's needed in the final SWF, even though all the code is in one manageable and easy-to-find script in the original FLA.

The ship code is split into two different sets of code (both of which are within the main function starShip): the onEnterFrame handler and some initialization code. Then you apply starShip to the ship movie clip, and you can assume that the code contained in starShip is on the ship timeline (even though the code is actually on _root; scope is a wonderful thing in Flash when you master it!). Thus, the function startShip is not so much a function in its own right, but more like a code block that will eventually be scoped to the ship timeline.

The main code for the ship instance is at the bottom of the starShip function (line 90 onward):

```
// Initialize ship on first run...
this.leftArrow = 37;
this.rightArrow = 39;
this.space = 32;
this.shipX =
➡ (gSCREEN_RIGHT-gSCREEN_LEFT)/2;
this.shipY = gSCREEN_BOTTOM;
this._x=this.shipX, this._y=this.shipY;
this.gotoAndStop(1);
```

leftArrow and rightArrow are key codes that will be used later to detect presses of the spacebar, the left arrow key, and the right arrow key on the keyboard. They're used to get the user inputs coming from the Player's Input block in the object block diagram.

You can see a list of all the key code values in the Help panel. Search on the phrase "keyboard keys and key code values".

The variables shipX and shipY contain the (x, y) position of the ship. They're set to initial values by looking at the world size constants. To actually move the movie clip to this position, you set the _x and _y properties of the ship movie clip at frame 1.

The main code controlling the ship is contained within the onEnterFrame definition starting at about frame 70:

```
this.onEnterFrame = function() {
    if (Key.isDown(this.leftArrow) &&
➥ (this.shipX>gSCREEN_LEFT)) {
        this.shipX -= speed;
    }
    if (Key.isDown(this.rightArrow) &&
➥ (this.shipX<gSCREEN_RIGHT)) {
        this.shipX += speed;
    }
    if (Key.isDown(this.space) &&
➥ (!fired)) {
        fired = true;
        bullet.bulletX = bullet._x =
➥ this.shipX;
        bullet.bulletY = bullet._y =
➥ this.shipY-gSHIP_HEIGHT;
    }
    if (shipDead) {
```

```
        this.gotoAndPlay("explodeMe");
        this.onEnterFrame = undefined;
    }
    // ship movement
    this._x = this.shipX;
};
```

Although the code looks a little long, it's just four conditions plus a line at the end to actually animate the ship. In plain English, the code is saying this:

> *If the player is pressing* the right arrow
> ➥ key *and I am not too far left already,*
> ➥ *go left.*
> *If the player is pressing* the left arrow
> ➥ key *and I am not too far right already,*
> ➥ *go right.*
> *If the player is pressing the spacebar and*
> ➥ *I am not firing already, fire.*
> *If I am dead, start my dying animation and*
> ➥ *kill my controlling script.*

If you look in the ship's timeline (sp.ship in the timeline, with sp being my chosen identifier for "sprite"), you'll see that it contains three keyframes in its actions layer:

The timeline will stay on frame 1 (the "ship is OK" graphic) until the controlling scripts make it play. When this happens, the ship's timeline will play from frame 2, resulting in the "blink and explode" animation, then it will stop at the last frame and wait until the ship is made to restart at frame 1 of its timeline, and do the whole thing again.

The SwarmAlien

In many ways, the SwarmAlien is the only thing in the game with intelligence. Its movements are based around a real motion that uses acceleration, and it defines its own motion (as opposed to the spaceship,

which is really no more than a puppet controlled by the player), attacking or swarming based on a fairly advanced script.

The SwarmAlien also advances down the game world as time goes on, getting closer and closer to the hapless player. It's only a matter of time. . . .

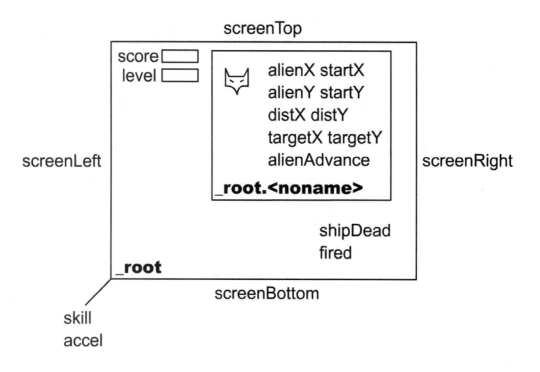

The SwarmAlien makes all the collision detections in the game, which is fairly impressive considering it's the main target. Altogether, it's quite an intelligent life form!

In logical terms, in this game the aliens are hitting the bullets rather than the other way around. It's easier to do it this way because each alien has to make one check for one bullet, rather than the single bullet having to check for all aliens. This seems a bizarre way to model the bullet-hitting detection, but it actually results in less code.

The SwarmAlien uses the four global constants that define the stage extents to make sure it stays onscreen as much as it can (it starts offscreen, so its first action is to zoom into the visible stage area as soon as it can). It has a number of internal variables (alienX, alienY, startX, startY, distX, distY, targetX, targetY, and alienAdvance), although you've seen most of them before in another form. They're very much like the swarm code you saw earlier; the SwarmAlien is based around the inertia/flocking motion. The alien has no name because both the alien and its name are generated dynamically at runtime.

In terms of external variables, the alien is highly dependent on the variables skill and accel (which define how fast it moves), and shipDead and fired (which tell the alien if the player has died or a bullet has been fired). The alien is controlled by the spaceAlien() function, which starts at about line 100.

Before you look at the detailed code, let's explore what each of the functions that control the aliens are. (You can find them all within the spaceAlien() function.)

alienSpawn()

This function initializes the alien when it first appears on the screen and every time it reappears after being shot.

onEnterFrame

The onEnterFrame event initially calls alienBrain(), which is the main alien-controlling script. When the alien dies, this script is overwritten by alienReincarnate(). This second script is what the dead alien does; it simply waits until it can be respawned.

alienBrain()

This script is the main script that controls the alien. It's a modified version of the swarm script you saw earlier in the book, so although it looks a little complicated, you've already seen most of it. It consists of a few distinct phases.

It first applies the inertia equation to the alien's movement, moving toward the target point (targetX, targetY) in much the same way as the swarm FLA does. If the alien has reached the current target position, the function alienInitialize() is called to decide on where the alien will move next.

It also checks to see whether this alien has been hit by the player's bullet:

    (this.hitTest(bullet) && fired)

and whether this alien has managed to hit the player's ship:

    this.hitTest(ship)

alienReincarnate()

This function runs when the alien has been hit by the bullet. It hides the alien and waits for a random amount of frames. It actually waits until Math.random()<0.005 or, put another way, it has a 1 in 1/0.005 (1 in 200) chance of respawning from the top of the screen every frame after it has died. On average, each alien will therefore reappear 200 frames after it has been hit.

To respawn an alien, the `alienReincarnate()` function calls `alienSpawn()` (to reinitialize the alien) and then reattaches `alienBrain()` to the `onEnterFrame` event, causing the reincarnated alien to start living and breathing again. Spooky!

The `alienInitialize()` function handles the alien's decision making. The alien moves in a set of straight-line paths, and this function initializes each path. This function decides whether the alien will swarm to a random position or whether it will swarm toward the player's ship. The latter is when the alien seems to dive toward the player's ship, and the former is when the alien mills around (swarms) at the top of the screen.

The aliens become more aggressive as time goes on because the deciding factor between dive and swarm is based on the current skill level:

(skill<Math.random())

As skill goes up, the aliens are more likely to dive toward the ship.

> *Unlike the code for the player's ship, which has to initialize only once per game, the alien code has to initialize the alien many times, which is why you have a separate initialization function for the alien.*

The `alienHit()` function handles the alien being hit. It updates the score and changes the `onEnterFrame()` script from `alienBrain()` to `alienReincarnate()`. This has the effect of changing the movement of the alien from "living" to "dead."

`makeAlien()` is a function outside the main `spaceAlien()` template. It is used to . . . well . . . make aliens. It takes an argument, quantity, which changes the number of aliens in the game. Setting this argument to a higher value will increase the number of aliens.

An important (but subtle) point to notice is that `makeAlien()` will *not* be attached to each instance of the alien sprites. This is because it's outside the `spaceAlien()` function. Instead, this function is on `_root`.

OK, back to the detailed code.

The SwarmAlien code

The first surprising thing to notice about the SwarmAlien is that it doesn't actually have to have an instance name for the game to work. This is because each alien doesn't divulge any information to the other sprites, so there's no need to reference it. You give each alien an instance name, though: `alien0` to `alien9`.

The SwarmAlien has a scary number of local variables. `alienX` and `alienY` are its positions on the screen, and `startX` and `startY` are its starting positions. The starting positions are used because the SwarmAlien never actually dies. Once it's hit, it waits a short time and respawns at the original start position, which is just offscreen (actually, it's 500 pixels above the visible screen). There are *always* the same number of aliens about at any one time. It's futile to attempt to kill them all, but you'll have fun trying!

`distX` and `distY` are variables that you've met before—they're the *where you are* terms in your real motion equation from Chapter 9. `targetX` and `targetY` are your *where you want to go* terms. The `alienAdvance` variable is a modification to the swarm code you saw in Chapter 9, which the aliens will be using. It represents the distance from the top of the screen that the alien is allowed to swarm in. As the game progresses, this variable increases and the alien swarms lower down the screen, making it closer to its target, the ship.

As soon as the alien has been shot, the respawned alien has to start again from the top, and `alienAdvance` is reset to its start value to make this happen. The secret of the game is for the player to shoot at the lowest aliens, because they will, on average, have the highest alienAdvance, and therefore give the player the biggest headache.

So how does each alien move and attack? Well, you'll be using the swarm code that you defined in Chapter 9. That had a *target* set of variables, which was your *where you want to go* term. Each alien moves much like the flies in the swarming animation you created in the last chapter.

If the alien decides to swarm, your target is a random position somewhere in the top 1/alienAdvance of the screen. alienAdvance is 4 to start off with (it's set to this in the function alienInitialize()), so you're initially looking at the alien swarming somewhere in the top quarter of the screen, well away from the ship and posing no real threat (the words "sitting" and "duck" come to mind). You'll thus see swarming motion such as the motion shown in the following image between point 1 and point 2, and between point 3 and point 4.

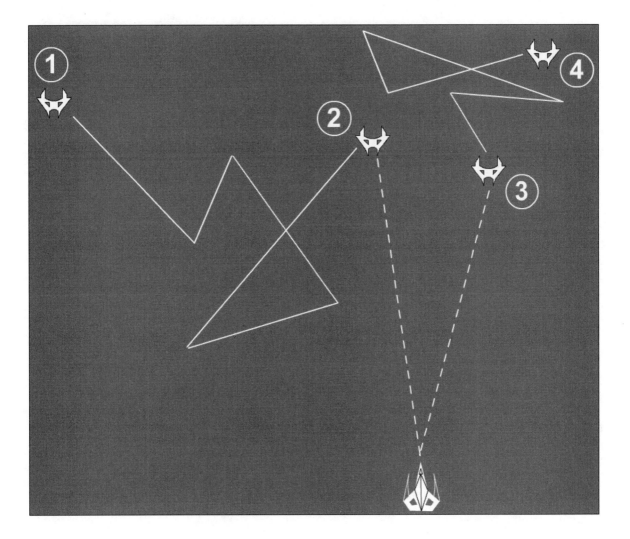

This motion is set up by the first leg of the if (highlighted in the following code) in the function alienInitialize(). If the skill variable (which is between 0 and 1) is less than a random number between 0 and 1, the next path will be defined as one that leads to swarming (that is, moving to a random position at the top of the screen). As skill goes up (which it does as the game progresses), the alien is less likely to swarm and more likely to take the alternative, more aggressive diving motion.

```
this.alienInitialize = function() {
  if (skill<Math.random()) {
    this.targetX = Math.random()*
➥ (gSCREEN_RIGHT-gSCREEN_LEFT);
    this.targetY=gSCREEN_TOP+Math.random()*
➥ (gSCREEN_BOTTOM/this.alienAdvance);
    } else {
      this.targetX =
➥ ship._x+((Math.random()*100)-50);
      this.targetY = ship._y-5;
    }
  if (targetY>gSCREEN_BOTTOM) {
    targetY = gSCREEN_BOTTOM+10;
  }
};
```

The else part of the same if is what causes the alien to dive (that is, movement such as the one shown between points 2 and 3 in the preceding image). If the alien isn't swarming, then you cause it to dive toward the player's ship by making the alien take a path that has a destination that's close to the current player's position.

```
  } else {
    this.targetX =
➥ ship._x+((Math.random()*100)-50);
    this.targetY = ship._y-5;
  }
```

The second if caters to the fact that there's no bottom limit to how far down the aliens can advance. If the alien intended to go lower than the bottom of the screen, it's constrained to just above the bottom of the screen. In this way, if the alien intended to move across and behind the ship, it will actually now sweep toward the ship on a collision course:

```
if (targetY>gScreenBottom) {
  targetY = gScreenBottom+10;
}
```

The alienInitialize() function defines only the *where you want to go* part of the alien motion. It doesn't actually cause the animation. This is done by the other major function, alienBrain().

The alienBrain() function is the big one. This is where the modified swarm comes in. You can really see code reuse at work here, because it's essentially the same idea with a few tweaks. The first five lines are almost the same as the ones you saw for swarm, except you add a *1/constant* term that's now 1/accel. As accel gets smaller, the aliens will get quicker and more efficient. The first block of code works out how far away the alien is from where it wants to be and stores this distance as the dist variable. This is then used in the movement equations to create a new position partway toward the target position, alienX, alienY.

```
this.alienBrain = function() {
  this.distX = this.targetX-this.alienX;
  this.distY = this.targetY-this.alienY;
  // Apply inertia equation
  this.alienX =
➥ this.alienX+(this.distX/accel);
  this.alienY =
➥ this.alienY+(this.distY/accel);
```

In the next few lines, the if checks whether the alien has reached the bottom of the screen, or "landed." If so, the code jumps to the alienLanded() function:

```
if (this.alienY>gScreenBottom) {
  this.alienLanded();
}
```

The second if looks at whether you're close to the target. If you've reached the destination (rather, if you're within 15 pixels of it), you allow the alien to swarm a bit further down the screen in recognition of its bravery in getting so far by reducing alienAdvance by 0.05. This variable decides which fraction of the screen the alien can swarm in, and reducing its value will increase that fraction.

> *Sanity check: one-third is less than one-half. As the bottom number decreases, the fraction goes up in value.*

You then jump to alienInitialize(), which will set a new target for the alien to move to. This will, on average, be slightly lower down the screen and closer to the ship. In this way, the alien will slowly advance down the screen toward the hapless ship, and it's also more likely to dive the lower it gets.

```
if ((this.distX<15) && (this.distY<15)) {
  this.alienAdvance -= 0.05;
  this.alienInitialize();
}
```

The final part of this block of code performs the sprite movement and checks to see whether the alien has hit either the bullet or ship in its movement. If the bullet and this alien collide, you jump to the alienHit() function and set fired to false (which allows the user to fire again). If you've hit the ship, you want the ship to die (and you communicate this by setting shipDead). For added realism, you could also make the alien explode by going to alienHit(), but I think the alien deserves a break for its bravery.

```
// perform animation
this._x = this.alienX;
this._y = this.alienY;
// check for collisions
if (this.hitTest(bullet) && fired) {
  fired = false;
  this.gotoAndPlay("explodeMe");
  this.alienHit();
}
if (this.hitTest(ship)) {
  shipDead = true;
  this.targetY = 100;
}
};
```

The alienHit() function (line 165) is called when the alien is hit. This is a simple script that adds the points for this kill to the score. You get 10 points for each alien, which is multiplied by the current level, so you get more points the longer you last.

```
this.alienHit = function() {
  score += level*10;
  score_txt.text = score;
  this.onEnterFrame =
➡ this.alienReincarnate;
};
```

As well as the code, the alien graphic has a timeline (shown below). Have a look in the Library at symbol sp.alien. Normally, the alien's timeline will stay at frame 1. When the alien is hit, the alien timeline will start playing, and you'll see the explosion. onEnterFrame is changed to alienReincarnate(), which causes nothing to happen for a random period before the alien starts again.

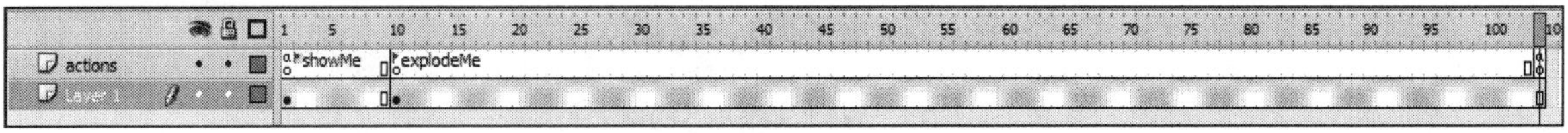

The bullet

The bullet is what comes out of the player's gun. There's only one bullet in the game—the player is always firing the same one, although it's no less potent with each use. I hope for humanity's sake that your aim is better than the joker's in the following image . . . miles away from the target! (Well, OK, it was me.)

You can tell that the bullet is controlled by some basic code just by looking at its object diagram:

Visually, the bullet is equally bland. It's just a long white rectangle, as you can see in the Library (sp.bullet).

When the game starts, you'll see the stationary bullet somewhere just outside the top-left corner of the stage. Although you can see the bullet in Test Movie, you won't be able to see it when you view the SWF in the browser (press *F12* to see the game in your default browser).

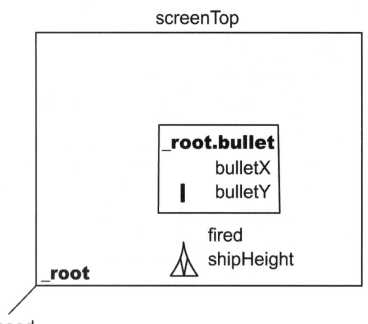

When the game is running, the bullet just sits on the stage, but it's invisible (its _visible property is set to false). As soon as you fire the laser by pressing the spacebar (thus making fired = true), the bullet is made visible and moved up the screen, starting at the current position of the ship. This will continue until either the bullet makes it to the top of the screen or an alien detects it has been hit by the bullet, in which case the bullet will simply turn itself invisible again and stop. That's all the bullet does!

> *The collision checking between the aliens and the bullet is carried out by the aliens rather than the bullet. See the code under the check for collisions comment in the function alienBrain() on line 129. This is easier, because the process then doesn't need to know how many aliens there are. As you add extra aliens, you also add more running scripts per alien to make the collision check, so neither the aliens nor the bullet know how many aliens there are.*

Let's see how this is implemented as code.

Inside the function bullets(), you'll see an onEnterFrame definition. The code that runs if fired is true (highlighted in the following listing) is the main bullet animation code. It will move the bullet up at 3 times speed until the bullet gets to the top of the screen (this.bulletY<gSCREEN_TOP) or fired becomes false (which will occur if an alien detects it has been hit via the alienBrain() function). The else part of the if (fired) is run if the bullet is *not* currently fired (fired = false), and it turns the bullet invisible.

After the end of the bullet's onEnterFrame code, you'll see a couple of lines setting bulletX and bulletY to 0, which is the position the bullet will take at the start of the game (at the top-left corner of the stage).

```
bullets = function () {
  //
  // Function to animate bullet...
  this.onEnterFrame = function() {
    if (fired) {
      this._visible = true;
      this.bulletY = this.bulletY-speed*3;
      this._y = this.bulletY;
      if ((this.bulletY<gSCREEN_TOP) ||
 (fired == false)) {
        fired = false;
        this.bulletY =
 gSCREEN_BOTTOM-gSHIP_HEIGHT;
      }
    } else {
      this._visible = false;
    }
  };
  this.bulletX = 0;
  this.bulletY = 0;
};
```

The debris of war

No laser battle in space is complete without some level of pyrotechnics. This game includes separate explosions for the aliens and the ship. The following image shows the SwarmAliens victoriously moving through the expanding plasma cloud that was once my spacecraft.

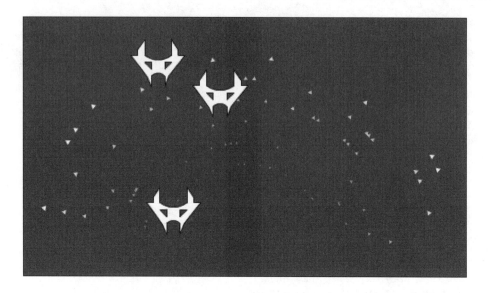

This is all about the scrolling star field that's the back-drop for the battle. No space game is complete without one. The star field is controlled by the starDot() and makeStar() functions. These are just very dumbed-down versions of the alien scripts.

> You might also want to look at Chapter 12, where you'll learn how to add scripted sound to the game.

Now that you've had a look through the code for the zapper game, take a few minutes to play the game. Go on, pretend you have a stack of quarters in your hand and you're back in the video game arcade you used to spend all your time in when you were a kid. Once you've played the game, think about how relatively simple the ActionScript that made it possible is.

Book project: Navigation event handling

You've nearly reached the end of the book, and you've learned an awful lot. I hope you realize just how far you've come. There are just three parts of the Futuremedia site left to take care of.

- **The forward navigation**, which is what happens when you click one of the colored strips

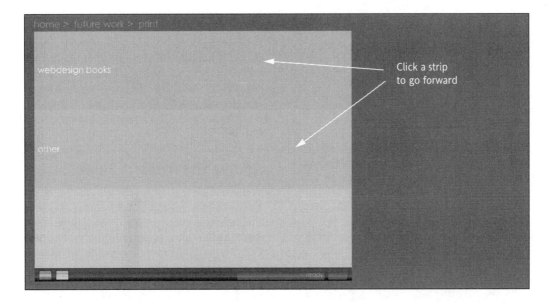

Click a strip
to go forward

- **The reverse navigation**, which is what happens
  when you click one of the icons (at the bottom of
  the screen) to move backward

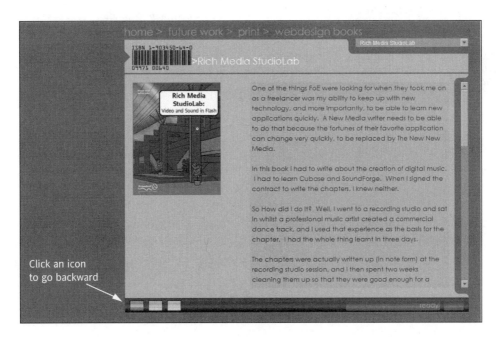

Click an icon
to go backward

■ **The content** you'll need to add to the site

In this section, you'll begin looking at the navigation.

> *There's no hiding the fact that the code in Futuremedia will start getting a little tricky from here onward.*
>
> *Unlike site design projects you may have seen in other books, in this book project my intention has been to avoid the "now put this bit of code at this keyframe without really knowing why you need to do this" teaching method or, even worse, the "this site is so easy that it needs no explanation (which also makes it totally useless because it teaches nothing about ActionScript)" school of thought. Instead, I've tried to explain my thought process as I went along in the design to show the* **why** *behind the design, and I've also used a moderately complex Flash ActionScript site.*
>
> *So, as the code gets more and more esoteric, you'll see more and more sketches and asides. They aren't there to simplify the code for you. They're there because they're the tools I used to actually write the code. An understanding of the sketches is more important than an understanding of the code, because the former will teach you to think like an ActionScript coder, whereas the latter will only enable you to type in the code for the Futuremedia site.*

Sanity check #1

Because you'll be playing around with a lot of code, there's a full printed listing of the final FLA at the end of this project section. You'll also find two FLAs that contain the working files, `futuremedia_code01b.fla` and `futuremedia_code02.fla`, at the midpoint and end of this part of the project in the download for this chapter.

Adding the basic UI animation

In the last section of the project you ended your work on the DEFINE EVENT SCRIPTS part of the listing with a simple script that returned which strip you clicked. You'll have a look at extending this and creating the first, very basic event-driven code to start animating the UI.

In the process, you'll take a look at how I started planning this via **UI storyboards**, little sketches that gave me an idea of how the interface should move and how to achieve this movement. The storyboards are the actual FLAs I used early on in the design to visualize how to convert the ideas I had in my head into code. Here's a complete example:

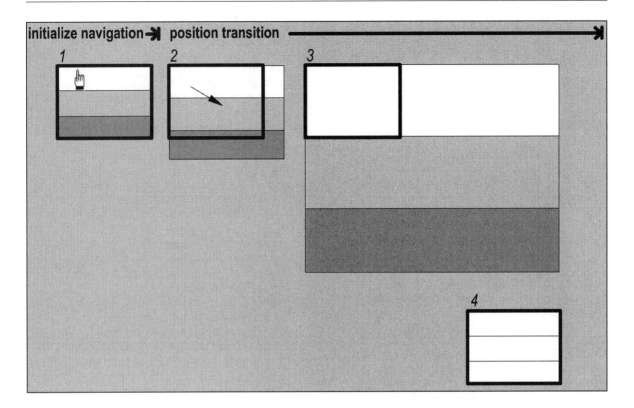

This proves that coding is a visual process. My code was written to a set of drawings, and this is true of commercially written code in anything from long-range missile global positioning/navigation systems with low-level flying Nap of the Earth (NOE) digital autopilots to all but the simplest web scripts.

If you didn't look at the diagrams and you just went straight to the code for Futuremedia, you'd probably just look at it and think, "Whoa! Where do I start with this?" With the diagrams, you should start to see the intent behind the site and, more important, you should see how the code is just a symbolic representation of my drawings that the computer can understand. Coding and drawing are closer than most graphic designers may suppose—it's just a well-kept secret!

So far you have the three strips outputting a message when you click them. What you actually want to do is something like this:

1. When you click a strip, you need to **initialize the navigation**. This is what the current navigate function will eventually do (step 1 in the storyboard). You then need to animate the navigation. You can split this into two separate parts.

2. The first transition is the zoom/pan **position transition**. This is where the selected strip zooms and pans so that it fills the screen (step 3 in the storyboard). There's actually a trick at the end where the three strips flick back to their original positions as well, and this involves a color change so that all three strips take on the selected strip's color and look the same as a single strip on its own (step 4 in the storyboard). This step requires you to be really sneaky, because the user isn't supposed to see it!

3. You need to fade the strips into three new colors via a **color transition**, and this takes you back to

step 1. If you want to display content at step 4 rather than present further navigation options, you simply leave the three strips as the same color, as shown in step 4 in the storyboard.

Let's build the core events that will handle these transitions. At the moment, you should have a file that contains the following code under the comment DEFINE EVENT SCRIPTS at the top of the script (you can also look at the file futuremedia_code01.fla).

```
// DEFINE EVENT SCRIPTS
navigate = function () {
  // initialize navigation event
  // handler here
  trace("");
  trace("you pressed me and I am"),
➥ trace(this._name);
  trace("but you need to fully define me");
  trace("before I start doing anything
➥ else!");
};
```

At the moment, navigate is a button event script. It will run only once, which isn't useful for the smooth animations you want. What you'll do instead is use navigate to start *other* events. What do you need these other events to do? Well, you need

- An onEnterFrame that performs the zoom and pan effect
- An onEnterFrame that performs the color fade effect once the zoom and pan effect has finished

Yeah, I know, you probably thought the site zooms and fades at the same time, but if you look at the finished site carefully, you'll see that the color fading doesn't happen until *after* the zoom.

> *A button event that starts up a whole series of other events running isn't something new. You did exactly the same thing when you created the* click here to play *button in the zapper game.*

At the moment, navigate is a simple stub that doesn't do anything. You'll stick to the same stub structure, but you'll expand navigate to include your zoom/pan and color transition animations. Delete the current navigate function and replace it with the following code:

```
// DEFINE EVENT SCRIPTS
navigate = function () {
  // initialize navigation here
  trace("");
  trace("you pressed me and I am"),
➥ trace(this._name);
  trace("I am initializing this
➥ navigation...");
  // then start navigation graphical
  // transition...
  this.onEnterFrame = posTransition;
};
posTransition = function () {
  // now do the actual animation...
  trace("I am now animating the zoom
➥ and pan effect");
  // we have now done the
  // position transition...
  this.onEnterFrame = undefined;
  // we next do the color transition...
  tricolor.onEnterFrame = colTransition;
};
colTransition = function () {
  // We finally do the color transition
  // that makes the tricolor split
  // back into 3 here
  trace("I am now animating the color
➥ transition");
  // finally, remove all event scripts...
  trace("I have finished this navigation");
  tricolor.onEnterFrame = undefined;
  trace(""), trace(""), trace("");
};
```

If you test this FLA, you still won't see any animation, but all the steps in the storyboard are being output to the screen in the order in which you want them. Each event handler runs, calls the next one in the sequence, and traces what it should eventually be doing to the Output window.

```
you pressed me and I am
strip1_mc
I am initializing this navigation...
I am now animating the zoom and pan effect
I am now animating the color transition
I have finished this navigation
```

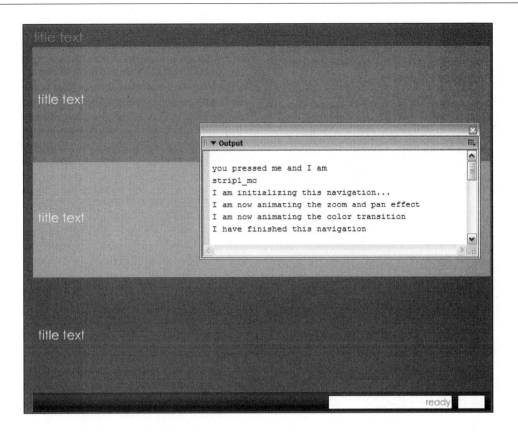

You've arranged the events in the correct order before you start adding the actual functionality. This is an important feature of using functions—you can add them as placeholders to define the structure. These placeholders define a basic framework (or skeleton, or you might even want to think of them as empty black boxes) for your final code. Once you have the framework right, you can go ahead and look at each function in isolation, fleshing (or should that be "Flashing"?) out the code as you add meat to the skeleton.

So you now have a skeleton. The next step is to define each event so that it starts moving things. In each function, the process is the same:

1. Draw or otherwise visualize what it is you want to happen.

2. Convert it into code.

navigate and posTransition

You'll add the meat to the two stub functions next. You're better off doing them in the order in which they'll run.

First up, the button event, navigate. navigate has to initialize the animation. It has to define the start and end position of the animation. Let's call the start position (x, y) and the end position (targetX, targetY). To initialize, you have to know what (x, y) and (targetX, targetY) are in terms of things you understand, and then in terms of things your computer understands.

First, you need to visualize this graphically.

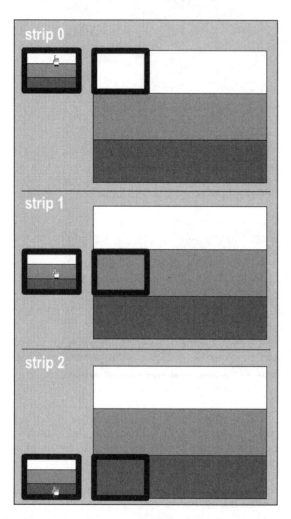

In each strip, the small image is what the site looks like before you click a strip, and the large image is what the site will look like after the position transition has occurred. The solid black frame is the visible screen area. It looks like an IQ test, and that's what it probably is. See how well you do. . . .

Question 1: What is the relationship between the three small images and the three big images next to them, expressed in terms of anything you can see in the picture?

No peeking! You have 1 minute. OK, time's up.

Answer 1: When you click any strip, the top-left corner of that strip moves to the top-left corner of the visible screen area. As it does this, the tricolor *clip trebles in size.*

Question 2: For an extra 3 points (and the game), express the transition mathematically in terms of what you already know.

Now it gets a bit trickier! At the risk of stating the obvious, you know the transition is a position-based one, but less obviously, you also therefore have to express the answer in terms of positions you already know only.

The starting position of `tricolor` is the top-left corner (`border, border`). At the risk of stating the obvious again (I have to, because I'm simply reiterating my thought process in designing this site to provide insight), the final position must be *related* to something that has to do with the three strips, because that's the only known thing that changes. I knew half the answer fairly quickly by looking at the existing drawings so far. The tricolor has to move a distance equal to the distance `l` *(lowercase "L")*.

- If you click `strip0_mc`, the distance `l` (shown as `l0` in the following diagram) is 0.
- If you click `strip1_mc`, the distance is `l1`, and if you click `strip2_mc`, the distance is `l2`.
- This distance is always actually the same—it's the *distance the selected strip is from the top-left corner*.

It took me a while to work this out, because one of the lengths was actually 0; the top strip is already at the top-left corner point, which threw me.

> The moral of this is that 0 is never a special case. It's a number just like any other, and if your logic assumes it's a special case, it's probably because your logic is flawed.

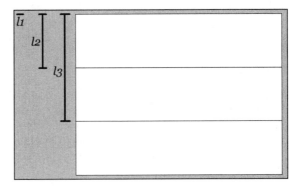

The distance of the center point of any given strip to the corner point you want to move it to is *always*

`-this._y`

where `this` is the strip you've selected *inside* tricolor, and you're taking into account the *direction* you have to move as well (that's what the - sign does). However, the tricolor is also scaled up by 300% so that a single strip grows enough to fill the screen. You therefore also have to increase this length by the same amount.

`-3*this._y`

You'll use this to move `tricolor` rather than the selected strip (so that all three strips move rather than just one), and you also need to take into account the fact that you don't want to move to the top-left corner of the screen, but to the border:

`(-3*this._y)+border`

or simply

`-3*this._y+border`

Note that you don't need to worry about the x position—the elements are already at the required x position.

So you have your answer.

Answer 2: You already know which strip you've selected from the last chapter, because the script prints this in the Output window every time you click a strip. If you call this strip this, *then the position you want to move to, relative to the center point, is as follows:*

    -3*this._y+border

And you also need to scale the movie clip containing the three strips, tricolor, *from 100% to 300%.*

Now replace the navigate function with this:

```
navigate = function () {
    // set up target for animation
    // transition...
    scale = 100, x = BORDER, y = BORDER;
    yTarget = -3*this._y+BORDER;
    scaleTarget = 300;
```

```
    // attach the animation transition to the
    // strip that has just been clicked...
    this.onEnterFrame = posTransition;
};
```

Replace the posTransition function with this:

```
posTransition = function () {
    scale = scaleTarget
    y = yTarget;
    tricolor._y = y;
    tricolor._xscale =
➡   tricolor._yscale = scale
};
```

When you click a strip, that strip fills the screen. You can do this only once at the moment (as soon as you click a strip, the other strips disappear offscreen, so run the SWF three times, clicking one of the three strips each time). Don't worry about all the stuff that appears off the stage area. If you test the site in the browser (press *F12*), you'll see that this content isn't displayed.

The following images show the before and after when a user clicks the top strip, strip0_mc.

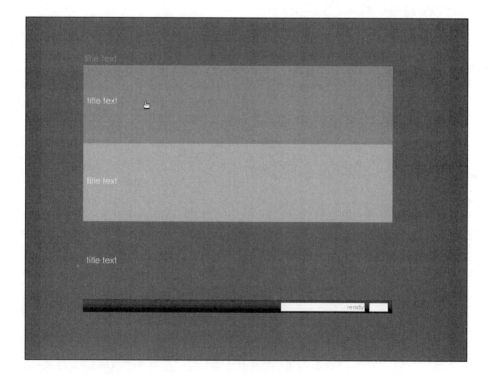

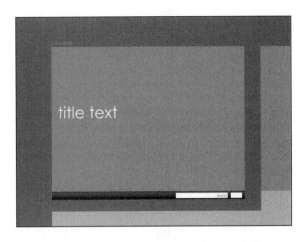

To keep things simple, you're developing only the forward navigation to start with; you won't be able to go backward yet. At this stage, you'll have to run the FLA again if you want to test navigating forward from a different starting point. To create the ability to go backward through the navigation requires you to be able to store the path you take when moving forward, and this means that you need to make sure you have the forward bit sorted out first.

So now that you've run this (as yet still basic) animation, let's have a look at the code you just added. `navigate` sets up your starting position (y) and size (s), and your target destination (yTarget) and size (sTarget). `navigate` is your onRelease event, and this starts up the `posTransition` animation. `posTransition` simply makes `tricolor` go to the final destination in one shot.

Adding typing

You've just added a load of variables without really defining them properly, so let's do that now. In the main code, add the following highlighted code (you need to add the first line below the existing line 66).

```
// Define navigation strip variables...
var NAVSTRIP_X:Number = BORDER;
var NAVSTRIP_Y:Number = BOTTOM;
```

```
// Define animation variables
var scale:Number = 0, x:Number = 0,
➥ y:Number = 0;
var yTarget:Number = 0,
➥ scaleTarget:Number = 0;
// Initialize UI...
stripPage.apply(tricolor);
```

Sanity check #2

Since you've added a lot of code so far, I've created a working intermediate FLA for those who aren't seeing the effect so far (or who just want to check that they're seeing the right thing). Have a look at `futuremedia_code01a.fla` if you have any worries.

For those having trouble with the code so far, here are a few words that might make more sense of the situation. `scale` is the current scale factor. At the moment, you set it to 100% in navigate and 300% (which is the same as scaleTarget) in posTransition. That, on the face of it, looks a bit silly. Why not forget scale and just use scaleTarget? Well, scale will be varied between 100 and 300% *gradually* in the final site design, and this is what gives you the smooth transition. You'll look at creating a smooth transition next.

Creating a smooth transition

At the moment you have a single-step animation. As soon as you click a strip, the clicked strip scales to its final size immediately.

Let's slow it down a little. In this section you'll add the inertia effect to the scale. This is very easy to do, because you've already set up all the variables you need. Rather than make scale and y equal to the *where you want to go* values scaleTarget and yTarget, you make them change via an inertial effect in the movement function, posTransition. Change the following lines currently in posTransition:

```
scale = scaleTarget
y = yTarget;
```

to the following:

```
posTransition = function () {
  scale -= (scale-scaleTarget)/3;
```

299

```
   y -= (y-yTarget)/3;
   tricolor._y = y;
   tricolor._xscale=tricolor._yscale=scale;
};
```

If you've taken my advice and installed the really useful "center in browser" extension way back in the book's introduction, you'll be able to publish the site as per the final Futuremedia site on the Web, www.futuremedia.org.uk.

In the HTML tab of the File ➤ Publish Settings dialog box, set Template to Flash only (centered) and set Dimensions to Match Movie.

OK, you now need to do a little trick to put the tricolor back to the starting position without anyone knowing. In the function posTransition, add the following lines:

```
posTransition = function () {
   scale -= (scale-scaleTarget)/3;
   y -= (y-yTarget)/3;
   tricolor._y = y;
   tricolor._xscale=tricolor._yscale=scale;
   if (Math.abs(scale-scaleTarget)<5) {
      // if so, disconnect this function
      // from onEnterframe...
      delete this.onEnterFrame;
      // then place tricolor back at
      // start position...
      tricolor._y = BORDER;
      tricolor._xscale=tricolor._yscale=100;
   }
};
```

This returns tricolor to its original position, but it's a little obvious to say the least! What you need to do is find out the color of the selected strip and apply it to all three strips. The color of each strip, stripn_mc, where n equals 0, 1, or 2, is held in variable colorn, where n equals 0, 1, or 2.

Obviously, then, n is the key. To get n from the name of the selected strip, you use the following method of the String object:

```
substring(5, 6)
```

You apply that to the name of the current strip:

```
selectedStrip = this._name.substring(5, 6);
```

This will return 0, 1, or 2.

To form the required colorn variable (or, more specifically, _root.colorn), you use this:

```
selectedCol = _root["color"+selectedStrip];
```

If selectedStrip is 2, _root["color"+selectedStrip] will give you _root.color2.

OK, you're almost there. Add the following code to posTransition:

```
posTransition = function () {
   var selectedStrip:String;
   var selectedCol;
   scale -= (scale-scaleTarget)/3;
   y -= (y-yTarget)/3;
   tricolor._y = y;
   tricolor._xscale=tricolor._yscale=scale;
   if (Math.abs(scale-scaleTarget)<5) {
      // if so, disconnect this function
      // from onEnterframe...
      delete this.onEnterFrame;
      // then place tricolor back at
      // start position...
      tricolor._y = BORDER;
      tricolor._xscale=tricolor._yscale=100;
      selectedStrip =
➥ this._name.substring(5, 6);
      selectedCol =
➥ _root["color"+selectedStrip];
      tricolor.setCol(selectedCol,
➥ selectedCol, selectedCol);
   }
};
```

Note that the selectedCol variable hasn't been given a type. It's a path (or a reference to an instance rather than an instance itself) so it's typeless. If you're having trouble with that concept, think of it as a variable name rather than a variable itself, which means it's really just a pointer to a number (color0, color1, or color3, all three of which are of type number), rather than a number itself.

If you test the FLA now, you'll see the color of all three strips change on the snapback. You're calling the previously defined function setCol. You used this in the last section to turn the gray strips to the three colorful ones.

In the following image, you can see a before (top) and after (bottom) image of a user clicking the middle strip.

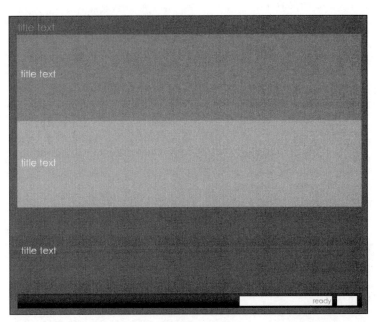

The title text text on each strip gives the game away a little, but you can soon fix that by hiding it.

You'll fade the text while the transition occurs. To do this, you need a value that goes from 100% alpha to 0% as the transition takes place. You already have one that goes from 100% to 300%, and that's the scale value that controls scale. It's a good idea to follow the scale value, turning it to what you want, because then your text fade will be in synch with the transition itself.

To change the 100% to 300% of s to 100% to 0% of your new variable (say fadeAlpha), you use this:

```
fadeAlpha = 300-scale;
```

You also need to change all three text fields' _alpha values according to the preceding equation, so let's create a function to do this. If you're hiding the text, you'll more than likely have to unhide it again later, so you might as well make your code reusable!

Add the following new lines in the function posTransition:

```
posTransition = function () {
  var selectedStrip:String;
  var selectedCol;
  var fadeAlpha:Number;
  scale -= (scale-scaleTarget)/3;
  y -= (y-yTarget)/3;
  fadeAlpha = 300-scale;
  tricolor._y = y;
  tricolor._xscale=tricolor._yscale=scale;
  fadeText(fadeAlpha);
  if (Math.abs(scale-scaleTarget)<5) {
    // if so, disconnect this function
    // from onEnterframe...
    delete this.onEnterFrame;
    // then place tricolor back at
```

```
    // start position...
    tricolor._y = BORDER;
    tricolor._xscale=tricolor._yscale=100;
    selectedStrip =
➥ this._name.substring(5, 6);
    selectedCol =
➥ _root["color"+selectedStrip];
    tricolor.setCol(selectedCol,
➥ selectedCol, selectedCol);
  }
};
```

Here you use a new function called fadeText with your new fadeAlpha variable. You still need to define the function, though. After the end of colTransition, add the new function fadeText as shown:

```
fadeText = function (fadeValue) {
  var fadeValue;
  tricolor.strip0_txt._alpha = fadeValue;
  tricolor.strip1_txt._alpha = fadeValue;
  tricolor.strip2_txt._alpha = fadeValue;
};
```

If you run the FLA now, you'll see that your sneaky switch is successful. You should test the site in a browser to see the full deception (press *F12*), and then run it in normal test mode (*CTRL+ENTER/CMD+ENTER*) to see what's going on behind the scenes.

Here's what you'll see. You're first presented with the start screen, the by now familiar orange, green, and blue page.

As soon as you click any strip, you'll see the interface slowly morph in a smooth, organic transition until the whole center area becomes the color of the strip you just clicked. The FLA for this point is included as futuremedia_code02.fla and implements the storyboards so far.

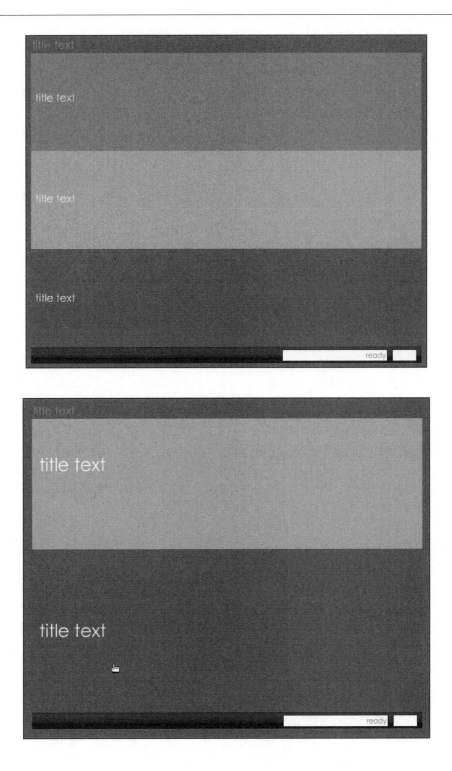

Next you'll create a *new* tricolor full of three new strips. You'll save that until the end of the next chapter.

Before we move on, here's a full listing of the site so far:

```
// DEFINE EVENT SCRIPTS
navigate = function () {
  // set up target for animation
transition...
  scale=100, x=BORDER, y=BORDER;
  yTarget = -3*this._y+BORDER;
  scaleTarget = 300;
  // attach the animation transition to the
  // strip that has just been clicked...
  this.onEnterFrame = posTransition;
};
posTransition = function () {
  var selectedStrip:String;
  var selectedCol;
  var fadeAlpha:Number;
  scale -= (scale-scaleTarget)/3;
  y -= (y-yTarget)/3;
  fadeAlpha = 300-scale;
  tricolor._y = y;
  tricolor._xscale=tricolor._yscale=scale;
  fadeText(fadeAlpha);
  if (Math.abs(scale-scaleTarget)<5) {
    // if so, disconnect this function
    // from onEnterframe...
    delete this.onEnterFrame;
    // then place tricolor back at
    // start position...
    tricolor._y = BORDER;
    tricolor._xscale=tricolor._yscale=100;
    selectedStrip =
➥ this._name.substring(5, 6);
    selectedCol =
➥ _root["color"+selectedStrip];
    tricolor.setCol(selectedCol,
➥ selectedCol, selectedCol);
  }
};
fadeText = function (fadeValue) {
  var fadeValue;
  tricolor.strip0_txt._alpha = fadeValue;
  tricolor.strip1_txt._alpha = fadeValue;
  tricolor.strip2_txt._alpha = fadeValue;
};
```

```
colTransition = function () {
  // We finally do the color transition
  // that makes the tricolor split
  // back into 3 here
  trace("I am now animating the color
➥ transition");
  // finally, remove all event scripts...
  trace("I have finished this navigation");
  tricolor.onEnterFrame = undefined;
  trace(""), trace(""), trace("");
};
// DEFINE MAIN SETUP SCRIPTS
stripEvents = function () {
  // attach button events to the 3 pages...
  this.strip0_mc.onRelease = navigate;
  this.strip1_mc.onRelease = navigate;
  this.strip2_mc.onRelease = navigate;
};
stripCols = function () {
  this.colStrip0 =
➥ new Color(this.strip0_mc);
  this.colStrip1 =
➥ new Color(this.strip1_mc);
  this.colStrip2 =
➥ new Color(this.strip2_mc);
  this.setCol =
➥ function(col0, col1, col2) {
    var col0, col1, col2;
    this.colStrip0.setRGB(col0);
    this.colStrip1.setRGB(col1);
    this.colStrip2.setRGB(col2);
  };
};
stripPage = function () {
  // note use of Function inheritance
  this.inheritEvents = stripEvents;
  this.inheritCols = stripCols;
  this.inheritEvents();
  this.inheritCols();
};
// Define screen extents for later use...
Stage.scaleMode = "exactFit";
var BORDER:Number = 30;
var BOTTOM:Number = Stage.height-BORDER;
var TOP:Number = BORDER;
var RIGHT:Number = Stage.width-BORDER;
var LEFT:Number = BORDER;
Stage.scaleMode = "noScale";
// Define initial screen colors
```

```
// (further colors will use these
// colors as their seed)
var color0:Number = 0xDD8000;
var color1:Number = 0xAACC00;
var color2:Number = 0x0080CC;
// Define navigation strip variables...
var NAVSTRIP_X:Number = BORDER;
var NAVSTRIP_Y:Number = BOTTOM;
// Define animation variables
var scale:Number = 0, x:Number = 0,
➥ y:Number = 0;
var yTarget:Number = 0,
➥ scaleTarget:Number = 0;
// Initialize UI...
stripPage.apply(tricolor);
// Set UI colors...
tricolor.setCol(color0, color1, color2);
// now sit back and let the event scripts
// handle everything ;)
stop();
```

Parting shots

You still have a pretty unfinished site, but you're moving forward at a good pace now. You only need to bring in the colTransition event script to complete the main site graphic transitions.

The use of diagrams that define how the code works and what it actually needs to do is one of the cool things about programming in Flash. You don't put away the drawing pencils when you start coding. Most of the time you'll need to sharpen them and get ready for half an hour of playing around and experimenting on paper before you try out your ideas in ActionScript and the Flash environment.

This can be an exciting and rewarding pastime in itself because, unlike with traditional graphic design, with Flash you don't end up with pretty logos and typography—you end up with things that *move*.

> At some point, the navigation will have to display pages of content as well as simply linking to new pages, but you'll come to that part in due course. At the moment you're really only concerned with getting the main concept working.

I remember the first site I put together. For ages it was a bunch of ideas on paper and graphic mockups in Photoshop, but over a few days something changed as it got fed into Flash: *it started to come alive*. It moved and reacted.

That's where Flash is totally different from static media such as bitmaps or HTML, and if you're just looking over the diagrams and sketches in this section, you'll never get the feel of Flash. It's all about motion and saying "Look at that move! Cool—this is going somewhere!"

Summary

Once you have your head around the way ActionScript works, you'll see that even complicated-looking projects (like the zapper game) are quite simple when you break them down into their constituent parts.

You've seen the same thing in the Futuremedia project, where you've concentrated on one function (posTransition), leaving all the other code alone while you got this one code module working. Although the Futuremedia script is still under 100 lines long, think how much more difficult it would be to add things to the code now that it has grown in length beyond a little trick FLA! All that careful timeline and graphic planning and construction is really paying off now, because you don't have to worry about seeing showstopper problems appearing out of the blue as you build the site, and your use of functions to modularize the code keeps everything manageable.

As well as covering the practical use of code, this chapter also delivered a philosophical message. Coding is not just about knowing what to do. You saw how I developed my ideas as sketches before I started coding, and the harder the code became, the more sketches I produced.

Code is never created in isolation. For every ten lines of code, there's probably a rough sketch or diagram somewhere. Those of you who have looked at scripts created by some of the masters and thought "Wow, I could never do that!" are probably beginning to realize that the written code is only a small part of the process. *That's why code appears hard, not because it actually is hard*! The way you've developed the ideas behind the code by finding clever ways around logical and practical problems in a graphic way is the way forward. Code writing is a *creative process*, and as creative designers, you should really be as at home with ActionScript if statements as you are with the Flash Pen tool or Photoshop Quick Masks.

The main point I'd like you to take away from this chapter is that you've moved from easy, beginner-level tasks to more advanced tasks you would probably never have contemplated. *You can now do these tasks on your own*. Think how far you've come since I showed you the stop() command at the beginning of the book! This is the beauty of ActionScript. It's not really that difficult, and yet you can achieve the most amazing things with it when you think in terms of code *and* the concepts behind what you're trying to achieve.

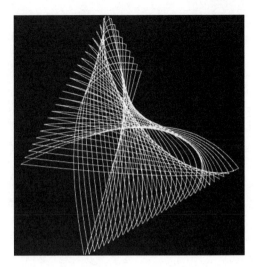

Chapter 11

DRAWING API

What we'll cover in this chapter:

- Using the drawing API in Flash MX 2004 to dynamically create lines, curves, fills, and pattern effects
- Working with scripted color
- Understanding data-driven sites

One of the coolest features of Flash is the **drawing API**, which allows you to create new content within your movie clips. You can now go straight to the engine room of the movie clip and produce new sketches *on the fly*. In fact, you can create three things:

- Lines
- Curves
- Fills

Although you could emulate lines in previous versions of Flash, you couldn't control the movie clip with clever scripting to create controlled curves or fills, so this feature is totally new. As you'll learn in the next section, it all started with a turtle.

Turtle graphics

Flash's drawing API is based on something called **turtle graphics**. In this section, you'll take a quick look at what that is before getting down to business, because the drawing API can get a little complicated.

Turtle graphics is an old graphics language used back in the day to control a little robot with a pen attached to it. The turtle was the robot, which typically looked like an upturned bowl on wheels (hence the name). The robot could do a few basic things:

- Lift the pen up (*penUp*).
- Put the pen down (*penDown*).
- Rotate without moving forward.
- Travel forward (but not at the same time as rotating, so it could travel only in a straight line).

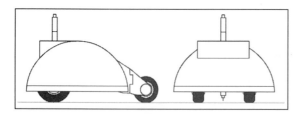

I can't swear on the details because I'm sketching from memory here (and I was young when I first saw one—I'm a lot older now), but I think the turtle kind of looked as shown the preceding drawing. The pen fit

between the middle of two big wheels at the front, and the wheel at the back was like that of a shopping cart: it could twist on a hinge, allowing the turtle to turn on the spot. Because the pen was situated at the center of rotation between the two front wheels, the turtle could rotate without moving the pen tip, and if the turtle moved forward with the pen down, it left a line describing its path.

The turtle had two basic commands:

- *move(x, y)*: This was a *penUp* followed by a rotate until (x, y) was directly in front of the turtle. The turtle would then move forward in a straight line as far as (x, y). This command didn't result in a line being drawn.
- *draw(x, y)*: This consisted of rotating until (x, y) was in front of you, followed by a *penDown* and moving forward in a straight line as far as (x, y). This command resulted in a line being drawn from the start point to (x, y).

Sometimes the teachers put software on the turtle that allowed you to enter angles and distances, so you could say "rotate 90, move 5, rotate 45, move 6," and so on, but that was for the nursery kids. You used it with the Cartesian (x, y) scale. The deal was you put a piece of paper under the turtle and did stuff like working out how to draw a cube or (even harder) an equilateral triangle. If you could work out the latter, they would even let you attempt to write your name with the turtle. "Sham" was the shortest name in my class, so I aced it, but the surname was going nowhere!

Turtles were really cool in the early 8-bit computer days. Kids actually ran to math class to use them, and they found out later that the turtle had fooled them into learning Cartesian geometry.

So anyway, what does this have to do with Flash? Well, Flash uses something that's recognizable as turtle graphics. In fact, most vector graphics actually *are* turtle graphics at the most basic level, and thinking in terms of the little turtle trundling around on cheap paper in real time is easier than imagining the Flash graphics engine drawing stuff with scripts and events firing off, running at 12 fps. Indeed, the turtle makes it easy to visualize. Kids were learning the Pythagorean theorem at the age of 5 with these things, so it must be true!

Drawing lines

Flash has a virtual turtle that controls the drawing API. It can move to a point (x1, y1) and then draw to a point (x2, y2). To draw a line from (50, 50) to (100, 100), you do the following:

1. Move to (50, 50).

2. Draw to (100, 100).

Easy, huh? Let's get some practice by working through an example. The following code is included in the download for this chapter as `lines01.fla`. In a new movie, you'll add a script on frame 1 of the timeline. You don't have to rename the layer or anything. You're going to do everything in ActionScript, and you need only that one layer and one keyframe.

1. Open a new FLA with File ➤ New. Select frame 1 of the timeline and pin the Actions panel to this frame. The tabs at the bottom left of the Script pane of the Actions panel now look like this:

Layer 1 : 1   Layer 1 : 1

The first thing you need is some paper. Let's create some virtual paper—a movie clip, to be precise.

2. In the Script pane, type the following:

```
var paper:MovieClip =
➥ this.createEmptyMovieClip("paper", 100);
```

This creates an empty movie clip called paper at depth 100, plus a reference (path) to it also called paper. I chose 100 in case you want to go and add some other stuff onscreen later.

Where is this clip? Well, it's at (0, 0), the top-left corner on the stage, and on timeline _root (because the _x and _y properties of a newly created clip are 0, and the scope of the code is _root, the timeline it's on).

Here's an important point: as long as you leave the clip where it is now, the coordinate space of the main timeline is the same as the local coordinates of the movie clip. As soon as you move the clip, however, the position of a turtle on the piece of paper called _root becomes different relative to a turtle on the piece of paper called paper, even if

they head for the same point (x, y). As shown in the following image, the internal coordinates of paper will show a different origin (0, 0) from that of _root after being moved:

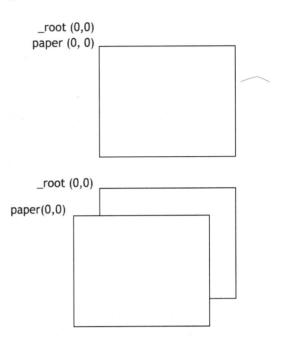

There are times when having the paper in a different place is a good thing, but not while you're coming to grips with the drawing API, so leave it where it is for now.

> *Don't forget that the y-axis is "down" in Flash, not "up" as it is in math. This is because web design is based around web pages, and they read from top to bottom.*

3. Next, you want to define your pen. A turtle could draw different lines depending on which pen you had in it, and the drawing API is no different. You select the line style of the turtle on the movie clip myClip with this:

```
myClip.lineStyle(thickness, color, alpha);
```

The pen will have a thickness of 3, a color of red (0xFF0000), and an alpha value of 100% for the turtle on paper, so type the following line under the script you already have:

```
paper.lineStyle(3, 0xFF0000, 100);
```

4. You now have to move to the start point. The method to do this is moveTo(x, y). So if you want to move to (50, 50), you use this line:

```
paper.moveTo(50, 50);
```

Add this line to the end of what you have so far.

The turtle is now in position at the start of the line. It needs to put the pen down and draw a line as it travels to (100, 100). The method you use to draw is lineTo. Here's the code so far, plus the new line you need at the end:

```
var paper:MovieClip =
➥ this.createEmptyMovieClip("paper", 100);
paper.lineStyle(3, 0xFF0000, 100);
paper.moveTo(50, 50);
paper.lineTo(100, 100);
```

On testing this code, you should see a short diagonal line in the top-left corner that points to the bottom-right corner. That's fine, but there's not much happening after the initial elation. Time for a little interactivity. Instead of moveTo to a fixed distance and then lineTo to another fixed distance, you'll use lineTo (_xmouse, _ymouse), and you'll do this every time the mouse moves.

5. Change your script to the following (the second line is new, and the moveTo and lineTo arguments have changed), which you'll find in the source code folders as lines1.fla:

```
var paper:MovieClip =
➥ this.createEmptyMovieClip("paper", 100);
paper.onMouseMove = function() {
  paper.lineStyle(3, 0xFF0000, 100);
  paper.moveTo(50, 50);
  paper.lineTo(_xmouse, _ymouse);
};
```

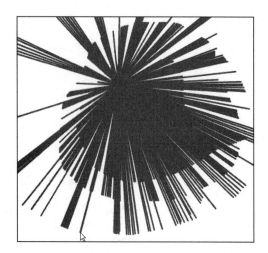

Wow, an explosion in a paint factory!

Notice that this script gets slow if you allow a large number of lines to be drawn. You should really clean up the excess lines every now and then. You can't *undraw* lines, but you can *clear* the whole movie clip with myClip.clear().

Change your script as follows:

```
var maxLines:Number = 100,
➥ lines:Number = 0;
var paper:MovieClip =
➥ this.createEmptyMovieClip("paper", 100);
paper.onMouseMove = function() {
  lines++;
  if (lines<maxLines) {
    paper.lineStyle(3, 0xFF0000, 100);
    paper.moveTo(50, 50);
    paper.lineTo(_xmouse, _ymouse);
  } else {
    paper.clear();
    lines = 0;
  }
  updateAfterEvent();
};
```

Here you're limiting yourself to a maxLines of 100. As long as lines<maxLines, you do the original moveTo/lineTo actions in the clip paper. As soon as you see more than 100 lines, you clear the paper movie clip with paper.clear() and reset lines back to 0. You also add updateAfterEvent() at the end of the onMouseMove to make Flash redraw the stage on every mouse movement, rather than on every frame. This should make the animation much smoother.

6. You can also make your lines into one continuous line simply by commenting out or removing the moveTo action. You'd then see something like this:

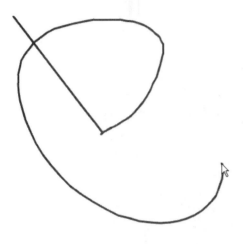

If you can't visualize what's happening here, think back to the turtle. Rather than going back to the center of the screen after every mouse move, the turtle just waits for you to move the mouse, and then it goes to the last position you were *from where it is now*. It's effectively following you. If it does this fast enough, all your straight line segments get short and therefore start to look like curves.

You have the beginnings of a drawing tool here, and you'll develop this idea in a while. First, though, you need to think about curves.

Drawing curves

The curve functionality of the drawing API is best understood through a demonstration. It's time for another script! Add the following script to the first frame of a new movie. You're again going to use ActionScript only, so you need just the script and a single frame.

Create a new movie with File ➤ New ➤ Flash Document, and select and pin frame 1 of the only layer (as you did before). Add the following script in the Script pane:

```
var paper:MovieClip =
➥ this.createEmptyMovieClip("paper", 100);
paper.onMouseMove = function() {
  paper.clear();
  paper.lineStyle(3, 0xFF0000, 100);
  paper.moveTo(100, 200);
  paper.curveTo(_xmouse, _ymouse, 400,
➥ 200);
  updateAfterEvent();
};
```

You can find this script in the file curves01.fla.

Note that you're now using a new method, curveTo, in place of lineTo. You're moving the turtle to point (100, 200), center-left of the stage, and then drawing to (400, 200), center-right of the stage. But something happens to the turtle in between. It's almost as if the mouse was some sort of turtle magnet. The turtle tries to get to point (400, 200), but it's attracted to the "magnet" and gets pulled away toward the mouse. The turtle's new path is a *curve*:

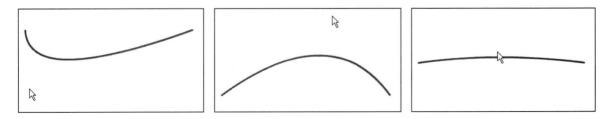

Notice that you're also clearing the paper every time. This means you delete the previous line and draw a new line every frame, and the resulting curve looks animated. Comment out the `paper.clear()` command to see all the individual curves that make up the animation. Isn't that pretty? I have a feeling that lots of geometrical screen savers and "Please wait . . . loading" eye-candy screens are in the cards!

Looking at the difference between the `lineTo` and `curveTo` arguments, you can see what's going on:

```
moveTo(100, 200);
lineTo(400, 200);
moveTo(100, 200);
curveTo(_xmouse, _ymouse, 400, 200);
```

The first two lines of code cause a line to be drawn. The turtle moves to (100, 200) and then draws to (400, 200). The second pair of lines contains the curveTo

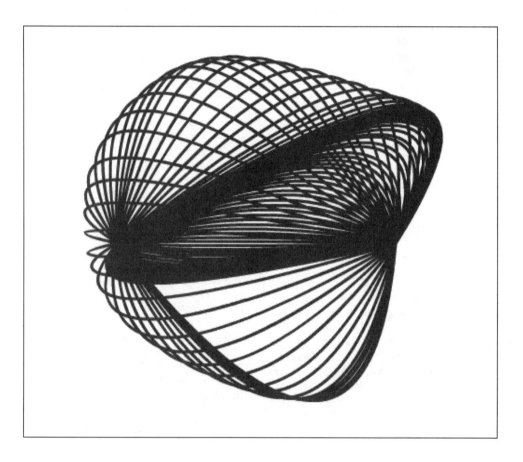

action, which has the (400, 200) point specified but also has a new set of control points (_xmouse, _ymouse). That explains why the mouse is doing stuff to the curve: its position is being used somehow.

So you have

```
curveTo(controlPointX, controlPointY,
➡ x, y);
```

curveTo is just like lineTo in that it causes the turtle to go to (x, y) with the pen down, drawing a line as it goes. Unlike lineTo, however, curveTo has a control point made up of (*controlPointX*, *controlPointY*) that affects the path the turtle takes. The turtle seems to want to go through the control point, but it doesn't do it, so it *tends toward* the control point. OK, that's fine, but you really need more information than that to know what the control point is well enough to actually create a curve you can predict.

There are two ways I can tell you about this. I can discuss quadratic Bezier curves and stuff like that for a couple of pages (and probably alienate half of my readership in the process), or I can tell you what the curveTo method actually does in nonmathematical words and pictures. The pretty pictures option wins hands down every time for me. Let's look at a quick example.

Create a new movie and attach this script to frame 1 of the main timeline (or just open the file curves03.fla):

```
var red:Number = 0xFF0000;
var blue:Number = 0x0000FF;
var paper:MovieClip =
➡ this.createEmptyMovieClip("paper", 100);
paper.onMouseMove = function() {
  paper.clear();
  // draw curve…
  paper.lineStyle(3, red, 100);
  paper.moveTo(100, 200);
  paper.curveTo(_xmouse, _ymouse,
➡ 400, 200);
  // draw control point tangent…
  paper.lineStyle(0, blue, 100);
  paper.moveTo(100, 200);
  paper.lineTo(_xmouse, _ymouse);
  updateAfterEvent();
};
```

This gives you the picture you want, and it's interactive as well. The thin line is the control line. It's a line joining the start point to the control point, and the curve forms itself so that it's *tangential* to the control line:

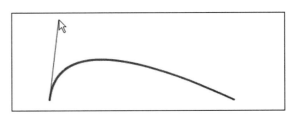

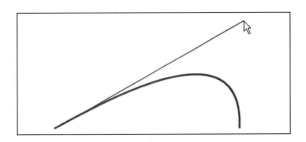

Also worth looking at is the file drawAPI.fla. This FLA contains fully interactive versions of a line and curve to show you what the lineTo and curveTo methods are capable of. Click any control point and you'll find you can drag it to change the shape of the attached line or curve. Adventurous readers may also want to look at the code, which is written in modular motion graphics code and contains a rather nifty trick for drawing circles with a single line. See if you can work it out!

You now have everything you need to construct a simple interactive drawing tool. Create a new movie yet again and attach the following script to the first frame of the main timeline, or just open the file elasticBand.fla:

```
function spaceBarPress() {
  endX = end2X=_xmouse;
  endY = end2Y=_ymouse;
  penToggle = false;
}
function penHandler() {
  this.clear();
  if (!penToggle) {
    // if penToggle is false, use line pen
    this.lineStyle(0, blue, 100);
```

```
    this.moveTo(endX, endY);
    this.lineTo(_xmouse, _ymouse);
  } else {
    // penToggle must be true,
    // so use curve pen
    this.lineStyle(0, red, 100);
    this.moveTo(endX, endY);
    this.curveTo(_xmouse, _ymouse,
➥ end2X, end2Y);
  }
  updateAfterEvent();
}
paperHandler = function () {
  if (!penToggle) {
    // first press...
    // toggle to curve pen
    // and set second endpoints of curve
    penToggle = true;
    end2X = _xmouse;
    end2Y = _ymouse;
  } else {
    // second press...
    // Draw the curve to the paper...
    this.lineStyle(0, black, 100);
    this.moveTo(endX, endY);
    this.curveTo(_xmouse, _ymouse,
➥ end2X, end2Y);
    // reset pen back to line pen...
    penToggle = false;
    endX = end2X;
    endY = end2Y;
  }
};
//
// Initialize Objects & Variables...
var keyboard:Object = new Object();
var endX:Number = _xmouse;
var end2X:Number = _xmouse;
var endY:Number = _ymouse;
var end2Y:Number = _ymouse;
var penToggle:Boolean = false;
var red:Number = 0xFF0000;
var blue:Number = 0x0000FF;
var black:Number = 0x000000;
// Create clips...
var paper:MovieClip =
➥ this.createEmptyMovieClip("paper", 100);
```

```
var pen:MovieClip =
➥ this.createEmptyMovieClip("pen", 101);
//
// define handlers...
keyboard.onKeyDown = spaceBarPress;
Key.addListener(keyboard);
pen.onMouseMove = penHandler;
paper.onMouseDown = paperHandler;
```

There are two movie clips: paper and pen. The pen clip is where the cursor lines sit—that is, where curves and lines in progress are drawn. When you're ready to fix a curve, it's transferred to the movie clip paper. You have to do this because to animate your lines in progress (your "pen"), you have to constantly clear the pen movie clip. This means that you can't draw anything permanent in it as well, so the movie clip paper is where you place your lines once you want them to be indelible.

To draw a line, you move the blue line around to the first point to which you want to draw. Click when you have your mouse at the right place.

> Notice that if you split the paper into several movie clips, paper01, paper02, paper03, and so on, you'll have the beginnings of drawing layers right away, with no fuss.

The line will then turn red. If you click again without moving the mouse, you'll get a permanent black line. If you want to draw a curve, move the cursor while the line is red to form a curve. Once you're happy, simply click again and the red curve will become a permanent black curve. So, double-click to make a straight line, single-click to bend the line, and single-click again to make a curve.

Also, to move your cursor without drawing, just press and hold any key while you move. By doing this you can easily make a simple drawing consisting of lines and curves. Not quite enough to make Picasso jealous, but pretty neat anyway.

How the sketching code works

As it stands, the basic code works as follows: all lines are drawn from point (endX, endY) to either the mouse position (_xmouse, _ymouse) for a line or to (end2X, end2y) with the mouse position as the control point for the curve:

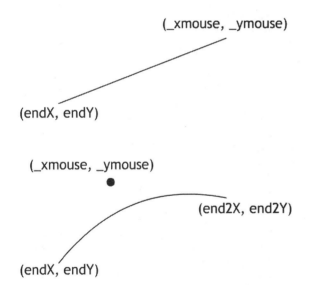

When you draw the current line style permanently to paper, the pen has two states: you've either clicked once (so the pen draws a blue line) or twice (so the pen draws a red curve). This is controlled by the variable penToggle.

Filling shapes

OK, you're moving on to the final bit of the drawing API: **fills**. Obviously, the poor virtual Flash turtle can draw only lines, so how do you visualize it drawing a fill? The answer is that it trundles around the *perimeter* of the area you want to fill and then politely asks the drawing API to fill the area it just defined.

This perimeter is called the **fill path**, or just **path**. Although the detail of the fill part of the drawing API is a little hairy, the fundamental principle is easy. As usual, I'll present an example to show you how to use it.

1. First you create a movie clip object to draw into. In a new FLA, attach the following script to frame 1:

```
var paper:MovieClip =
➡ this.createEmptyMovieClip("paper", 100);
```

2. Now that you have something to draw into, you want to draw around the edge of your shape. Here, you'll draw the following square:

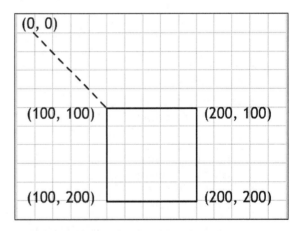

You have to move from the origin (0, 0) and draw out your square path. To do this, add the following lines:

```
paper.lineStyle(3, 0x000000, 100);
paper.moveTo(100, 100);
paper.lineTo(200, 100);
paper.lineTo(200, 200);
paper.lineTo(100, 200);
paper.lineTo(100, 100);
```

You've given the turtle a pen of thickness 3, a color of black (0x000000), and an alpha of 100%. The turtle then moves from the start position to (100, 100) and proceeds to draw around the perimeter in a clockwise direction. If you run the movie, you'll see the finished path drawn.

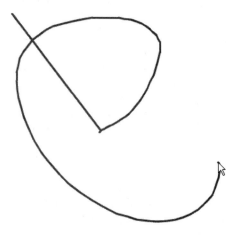

An important point to notice is that you must get the order of the corner points that you make the turtle visit correct. If the points are out of sequence, the turtle will draw incorrectly, as the following script demonstrates:

```
var paper:MovieClip =
➥ this.createEmptyMovieClip("paper", 100);
paper.lineStyle(3, 0x000000, 100);
paper.moveTo(100, 100);
paper.lineTo(200, 200);
paper.lineTo(200, 100);
paper.lineTo(100, 200);
paper.lineTo(100, 100);
```

This looks like an hourglass or a rotated bow tie—clearly not what you want! Flash would still fill the path if you asked it to, but it would fill out the two enclosed triangles rather than the square you want filled.

3. To fill the square, you first need to define the fill color. You do this via the beginFill method.

```
myClip.beginFill(color, alpha);
```

color refers to the color of the fill, and you can also set alpha. beginFill tells Flash one other important thing. Essentially it says to the drawing API "I'm setting my turtle off on the path I want you to fill." To tell Flash that the turtle is done, you simply include an endFill(x, y).

4. Enter the following code:

```
var paper:MovieClip =
➥ this.createEmptyMovieClip("paper", 100);
paper.lineStyle(3, 0x000000, 100);
paper.beginFill(0xFF0000, 100);
paper.moveTo(100, 100);
paper.lineTo(200, 100);
paper.lineTo(200, 200);
paper.lineTo(100, 200);
paper.endFill(100, 100);
```

The first and second lines create a movie clip to draw into and set the line style. Line 3 tells Flash you've started defining your path, and it also tells Flash to use a red fill (0xFF0000) when the path is completed. Lines 4 through 7 define the area to be filled. The last lineTo is now replaced by an endFill. This tells Flash to draw to the point (100, 100) and to fill the path defined by the turtle since the initial beginFill. You'll see the red square with black border as shown in the following image if you run this FLA (or open fillSquare.fla):

You can also use curves instead of lines:

```
var paper:MovieClip =
➡ this.createEmptyMovieClip("paper"π,
100);
paper.lineStyle(3, 0x000000, 100);
paper.beginFill(0xFF0000, 100);
paper.moveTo(100, 100);
paper.lineTo(200, 100);
paper.lineTo(200, 200);
paper.lineTo(100, 200);
paper.curveTo(50, 150, 100, 100);
paper.endFill(100, 100);
```

This code creates the following shape:

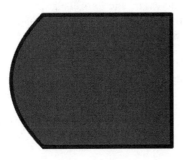

Notice that because you have to end your path definition with an endFill, and the line you want to end with is now a curveTo, you're a little stuck with the endFill since there are no more lines to create in the path. Instead, you simply endFill to the point you're already at, (100, 100).

You can, of course, animate the filled shapes using clear() and redraw a transformed version of the same shape every frame. You'll find the following code within the file fillCartoon.fla:

```
var paper:MovieClip =
➡ this.createEmptyMovieClip("paper", 100);
var vertexX:Array =
➡ new Array(100, 200, 200, 100);
var vertexY:Array =
➡ new Array(100, 100, 200, 200);
paper.onEnterFrame = function() {
  for (i=0; i<4; i++) {
    vertexX[i] += (Math.random()*10)-5;
    vertexY[i] += (Math.random()*10)-5;
  }
  paper.clear();
  paper.lineStyle(3, 0x000000, 100);
  paper.beginFill(0xFF0000, 100);
  paper.moveTo(vertexX[0], vertexY[0]);
  paper.lineTo(vertexX[1], vertexY[1]);
  paper.lineTo(vertexX[2], vertexY[2]);
  paper.lineTo(vertexX[3], vertexY[3]);
  paper.endFill(vertexX[0], vertexY[0]);
};
```

This time you assign the four points of your square to a couple of arrays. The points are now (vertexX[0], vertexY[0]) to (vertexX[3], vertexY[3]), and you're varying their positions by a small random value every onEnterFrame (try different random increments for vertexX and vertexY, and different frame rates to find a nice organic animation).

Flash also allows you to define gradient fills. I recommend that you don't do this for dynamic animation until you're fully up to speed with the solid color fills. Flash uses a number of objects to define the gradient and, as with gradient fills in general, it's a little slow if you try to animate your shapes as you've just done with solid fills.

Now that you have an idea of how the drawing API works, you'll get your hands dirty and start playing. One of the cool things about the drawing API is that you can build a generalized bit of code to draw something (the **draw engine**), and then just go ahead and start playing around and experimenting. That's what the experts do in the *Flash Math Creativity* book (friends of ED, 2003)—much of which is still relevant to Flash MX 2004. You'll do something similar, although you'll keep the math rather closer to the ground, so don't worry!

First, though, you need a starting point.

Creating a kaleidoscope

My partner, Karen, has a little kaleidoscope on a string. You can twist it around and it creates lots of pretty patterns. It's all done with mirrors, of course. In a kaleidoscope, only one segment (the grayed-out one in the following diagrams) actually contains the colored beads. The others are just reflections of that segment. I thought maybe I could do something similar with Flash, although to keep the math simpler I'll base it on quadrants rather than the kaleidoscope's eightfold symmetry.

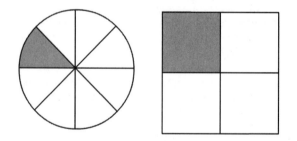

Let's go with this and have a look at the math.

Kaleidoscope math

To set up a kaleidoscope, you first need to understand how a real kaleidoscope works. A kaleidoscope works via *reflections*. In math-speak, a reflection is simply a *copy*. There's a difference between the original and the reflections in a real kaleidoscope: the reflections are *rotated*. You rotate the original segment to create copies that form a circle. To achieve this effect in Flash, you need to perform a similar operation.

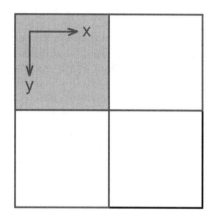

So, if the original segment has the orientation and position shown in the preceding image, you need to *rotate* the other three copies. Generally, you need to rotate by 360/number of segments per segment. So if you have four segments, you need to rotate the first copy by 90 degrees, the second by 180 degrees, and the third by 270 degrees.

The next step is to put all that into code.

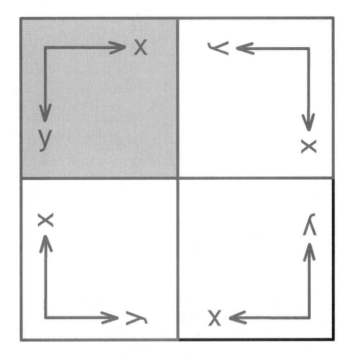

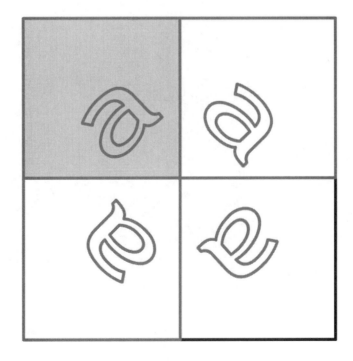

Building the kaleidoscope engine

You'll start off by drawing a simple shape (a rectangle) in a movie clip. To do that, you need to select a line style and a fill color, and then move between the corner points within a beginFill...endFill set of actions. To define the corner points, it would be wise to hold them in an array, because you can then easily add more corner points later if you want to extend the code.

This function will draw out a general rectangle as shown in the following image. It will draw it within a movie clip specified by the argument clip, with a white border and a fill color defined by the argument color.

```
function drawQuad(clip:MovieClip,
➥ color:Number):Void {
  clip.lineStyle(0, 0xFFFFFF, 100);
  clip.beginFill(color, 100);
  clip.moveTo(x[0], y[0]);
  clip.lineTo(x[1], y[1]);
  clip.lineTo(x[2], y[2]);
  clip.lineTo(x[3], y[3]);
  clip.endFill(x[0], y[0]);
}
```

It's not obvious how to create a rectangle without a border. To do this, you can set a line style with an alpha of 0, but this means that Flash will still draw a border (it's just that you can't see it). That's cool, but it means

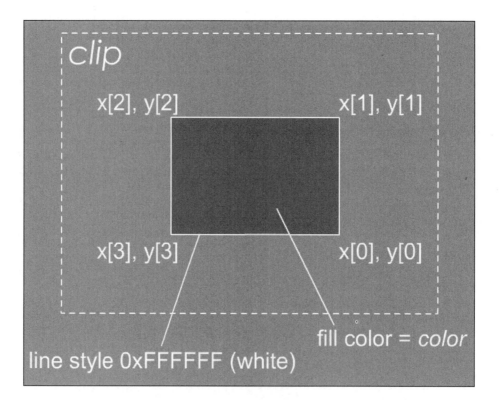

that it slows Flash down, and when you get to the heady heights of creating a 3D vector engine, you'll want all the performance you can squeeze out of the Flash player. A better but somewhat obscure way to create a rectangle so that Flash doesn't even draw the lines is to set a line style of undefined. If you replace the following line:

```
clip.lineStyle(0, 0xFFFFFF, 100);
```

with this line:

```
clip.lineStyle(undefined, 0, 0);
```

Flash won't draw the lines at all, and your code will run faster because of it.

Let's use this function in a bit of code.

1. Create a new FLA. Select Modify ➤ Document and set the background color to a light gray and the frame rate to 24 fps.

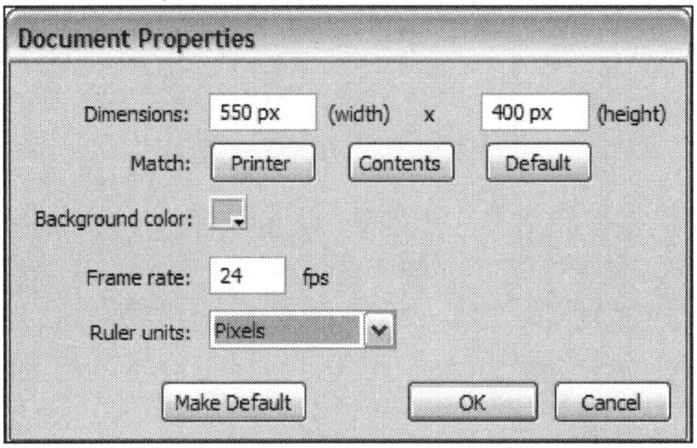

2. Select frame 1 of the only layer and enter the following code in the Script pane (or have a look at pattern01.fla):

```
function drawQuad(clip:MovieClip,
➥ color:Number):Void {
  clip.lineStyle(0, 0xFFFFFF, 100);
  clip.beginFill(color, 100);
  clip.moveTo(x[0], y[0]);
  clip.lineTo(x[1], y[1]);
  clip.lineTo(x[2], y[2]);
  clip.lineTo(x[3], y[3]);
  clip.endFill(x[0], y[0]);
}
```

```
//
// Define colors
var color1:Number = 0xDD8000;
var color2:Number = 0xAACC00;
var color3:Number = 0xFFF287;
var color4:Number = 0x6699FF;
// Define screen extents for later use
Stage.scaleMode = "exactFit";
var middleX:Number = Stage.width/2;
var middleY:Number = Stage.height/2;
Stage.scaleMode = "noScale";
// create clip...
var quad1:MovieClip =
➥ this.createEmptyMovieClip("quad1", 100);
quad1._x = middleX;
quad1._y = middleY;
// Initialize points...
var width:Number = 100;
var height:Number = 100;
var x:Array = new Array();
var y:Array = new Array();
x[0] = 0;
y[0] = 0;
x[1] = 0;
y[1] = -height;
x[2] = -width;
y[2] = -height;
x[3] = -width;
y[3] = 0;
drawQuad(quad1, color1);
```

The additional code will create an empty movie clip called quad1 and place it in the center of the screen. It will then draw out a rectangle of height height and width width.

OK, that's one static square. You're in the game of creating motion graphics, though, so how do you make the drawing API create animated content? Well, you can clear all the content in a movie clip and redraw it. Change the function to include the clear line as shown here (you can see the full effect for this in pattern02.fla):

```
function drawQuad(clip:MovieClip,
➥ color:Number):Void {
  clip.clear()
  clip.lineStyle(0, 0xFFFFFF, 100);
  clip.beginFill(color, 100);
  clip.moveTo(x[0], y[0]);
```

```
      clip.lineTo(x[1], y[1]);
      clip.lineTo(x[2], y[2]);
      clip.lineTo(x[3], y[3]);
      clip.endFill(x[0], y[0]);
   }
```

Also, delete this line from the end of the listing:

```
   drawQuad("quad1", color1);
```

Replace it with this:

```
   this.onEnterFrame = function() {
      for (i=0; i<4; i++) {
         x[i] += Math.random()*4-2;
         y[i] += Math.random()*4-2;
      }
      drawQuad(quad1, color1);
   };
```

So what does this new code do? It draws a new rectangle every frame, changing the position of the corner points every time and producing a "wobbly" square.

To create the kaleidoscope pattern, you need to make another three rotated versions of quad1. That's actually very easy. Change the "create clip" section of the code (which currently creates only one movie clip, quad1) as follows:

```
   // create clip...
   var quad1:MovieClip =
   ➥ this.createEmptyMovieClip("quad1", 1);
   quad1._x = middleX;
   quad1._y = middleY;
   var quad2:MovieClip =
   ➥ this.createEmptyMovieClip("quad2", 2);
   quad2._x = middleX;
   quad2._y = middleY;
   quad2._rotation = 90;
   var quad3:MovieClip =
   ➥ this.createEmptyMovieClip("quad3", 3);
   quad3._x = middleX;
   quad3._y = middleY;
   quad3._rotation = 180;
   var quad4:MovieClip =
   ➥ this.createEmptyMovieClip("quad4", 4);
   quad4._x = middleX;
   quad4._y = middleY;
   quad4._rotation = 270;
```

You also want to draw content into the new clips, so change the onEnterFrame:

```
   this.onEnterFrame = function() {
      for (var i = 0; i<4; i++) {
         x[i] += Math.random()*4-2;
         y[i] += Math.random()*4-2;
      }
      drawQuad(quad1, color1);
      drawQuad(quad2, color2);
      drawQuad(quad3, color3);
      drawQuad(quad4, color4);
   };
```

Instead of drawing in just quad1, you're now drawing in all four quadrants, using different colors.

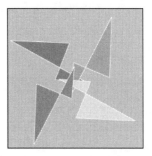

By changing the alpha values of the (now skewed) rectangles, you're drawing via the function drawQuad, and you can create some pretty overlapping patterns.

```
   function drawQuad(clip:MovieClip,
   ➥ color:Number):Void {
      clip.clear();
      clip.lineStyle(0, 0xFFFFFF, 70);
      clip.beginFill(color, 50);
      clip.moveTo(x[0], y[0]);
      clip.lineTo(x[1], y[1]);
      clip.lineTo(x[2], y[2]);
      clip.lineTo(x[3], y[3]);
      clip.endFill(x[0], y[0]);
   }
```

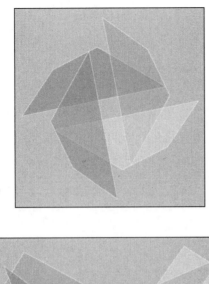

Have a look at pattern03.fla, which develops this train of thought further, except this time you create a separate speed value for each point on the quad, which will "bounce" around within a 200X200 square rather than change direction randomly.

```
function drawQuad(clip:MovieClip,
➥ color:Number):Void {
  clip.clear();
  clip.lineStyle(0, 0xFFFFFF, 70);
  clip.beginFill(color, 50);
```

```
  clip.moveTo(x[0], y[0]);
  clip.lineTo(x[1], y[1]);
  clip.lineTo(x[2], y[2]);
  clip.lineTo(x[3], y[3]);
  clip.endFill(x[0], y[0]);
}
//
// Define colors
var color1:Number = 0xDD8000;
var color2:Number = 0xAACC00;
var color3:Number = 0xFFF287;
var color4:Number = 0x6699FF;
// Define screen extents for later use
Stage.scaleMode = "exactFit";
var middleX:Number = Stage.width/2;
var middleY:Number = Stage.height/2;
Stage.scaleMode = "noScale";
// create clip...
var quad1:MovieClip =
➥ this.createEmptyMovieClip("quad1", 100);
quad1._x = middleX;
quad1._y = middleY;
// create clip...
var quad1:MovieClip =
➥ this.createEmptyMovieClip("quad1", 1);
quad1._x = middleX;
quad1._y = middleY;
var quad2:MovieClip =
➥ this.createEmptyMovieClip("quad2", 2);
quad2._x = middleX;
quad2._y = middleY;
quad2._rotation = 90;
var quad3:MovieClip =
➥ this.createEmptyMovieClip("quad3", 3);
quad3._x = middleX;
quad3._y = middleY;
quad3._rotation = 180;
var quad4:MovieClip =
➥ this.createEmptyMovieClip("quad4", 4);
quad4._x = middleX;
quad4._y = middleY;
quad4._rotation = 270;
// Initialize points...
var width:Number = 100;
var height:Number = 100;
var x:Array = new Array();
```

```
var y:Array = new Array();
var sX:Array = new Array();
var sY:Array = new Array();
x[0] = 0;
y[0] = 0;
x[1] = 0;
y[1] = -height;
x[2] = -width;
y[2] = -height;
x[3] = -width;
y[3] = 0;
for (var i = 0; i<4; i++) {
  sX[i] = Math.random()*4+4;
  sY[i] = Math.random()*4+4;
}
this.onEnterFrame = function() {
  for (var i = 0; i<4; i++) {
    x[i] += sX[i];
    y[i] += sY[i];
    if (Math.abs(x[i])>200) {
        sX[i] = -sX[i];
      }
      if (Math.abs(y[i])>200) {
        sY[i] = -sY[i];
      }
  }
  drawQuad(quad1, color1);
  drawQuad(quad2, color2);
  drawQuad(quad3, color3);
  drawQuad(quad4, color4);
};
```

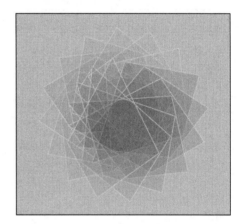

You now have something that has its moments, but the effect is simple. You can generalize the effect to cater to any number of shapes instead of the current four, and this has been done for `pattern04.fla`. Here, the number of shapes (or "petals," as the pattern now looks like a flower) is defined by the value sectors, and loops are used to produce the required number of clips.

Groovy!

The final two files in the download for this section start to move away from the concept of the kaleidoscope (but they use what is essentially the same code) to create a totally new effect that users of the Windows platform may recognize as similar to the "mystify" screen savers that ship with their operating system. There are two versions, **flashMystify**, which uses filled curved shapes, and **mystifyRetro**, for those who (like me) enjoy the old-school stuff, complete with simple vectors:

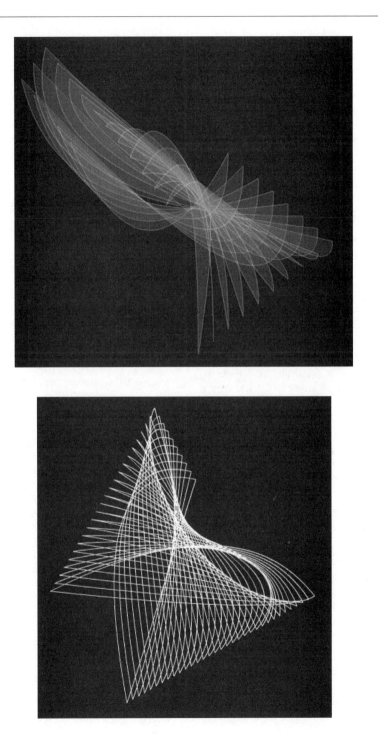

This sort of experimentation with Flash to create new effects is one way you can create code that you may one day repurpose as part of a new site's navigation. By making such experimentation open source, designers like Joshua Davis made a name for themselves early in Flash's history.

More to the point, you will have noticed that, although this stuff has nothing to do with web design, it's a good way of practicing ActionScript. Also, as with my experience with the turtle all those years ago, you'll forget you're using advanced code techniques because the whole thing is so much *fun*!

That's not to say that the drawing API isn't useful. It's a great way to create some nifty UIs. If you look at the Futuremedia site, you'll see that the expanding rectangle effect could have been created using the drawing API, so rather than all that painstaking hand-drawing you did at the beginning of the project, you could have made Flash draw the tricolor from scratch at runtime. A big advantage of doing this is that the code would have a much lower file size than the hand-drawn graphics in the final SWF. The disadvantage is that you would have had to learn the drawing API at the beginning of the book, and given that it's an advanced technique, Marlene the technical editor would have told me that it wasn't a good idea (which is true). There's nothing stopping you from doing some stuff with the drawing API once you have a finished Futuremedia site at the end of the book, though!

Book project: Color transition event handling and data

In this section, you'll complete the event-driven site animations in the Futuremedia site by adding the final part of the transition that occurs when you click a strip: the color fades. You'll then start to think about adding some data to allow Flash to create the site structure.

So far you have the position transition sorted out, but the color transition isn't implemented. At the moment, when you click a strip, the selected strip zooms in correctly, but it doesn't split off into three new strips to present further navigation options to take you deeper into the site.

Wiring the colTransition function

The starting point of this section is your work-in-progress file. You can also use the file `futuremedia _code02.fla` if you want to double-check your work or play it safe.

At the moment, the function `colTransition()` is neither complete nor linked up to the previous events, `navigate()` and `posTransition()`. Let's link `posTransition()` up to `colTransition()` first.

At the end of the last chapter, the end of `posTransition()` you had this in the file `futuremedia_code02.fla` (you'll change the high-lighted lines in a moment) looked like this (line 23 onward):

```
        delete this.onEnterFrame;
        // then place tricolor back
        // at start position
        tricolor._y = BORDER;
        tricolor._xscale=tricolor._yscale=100;
        selectedStrip =
➥ this._name.substring(5, 6);
        selectedCol =
➥ _root["color"+selectedStrip];
        tricolor.setCol(selectedCol,
➥ selectedCol, selectedCol);
      }
    };
```

You need to wire up the `colTransition()` function to your animation sequence so far. At the end of the position transition code (function `posTransition()`), you'll extend the animation to include your (as yet unwritten) function stub `colTransition()`. To do this, you need to change the following line in `posTransition`.

```
    this.onEnterFrame = undefined;
```

to

```
    this.onEnterFrame = colTransition;
```

The game plan

So what do you want to do? You guessed it, it's story-board time! Everyone sitting comfortably? Then I'll begin. . . .

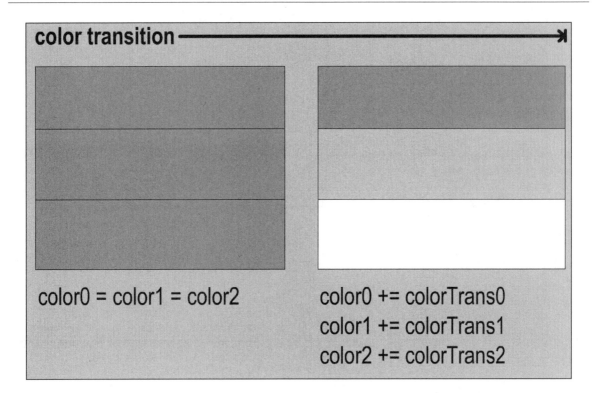

color0 = color1 = color2

color0 += colorTrans0
color1 += colorTrans1
color2 += colorTrans2

At the end of the position transition, which is the point you are in (looking again at `futuremedia_code02.fla`) after you click any strip, all three strips are the same color. If you click the top strip, you'll end up with an orange rectangle. In this case, color0 = color1 = color2 = orange (or, in numbers, 0xDD8000).

You need to fade the three strip colors to three new different colors that are based on the *original* color of the strip you clicked (in this case, orange).

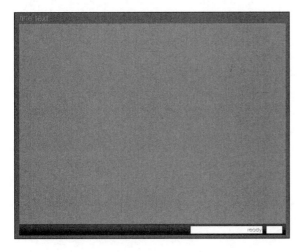

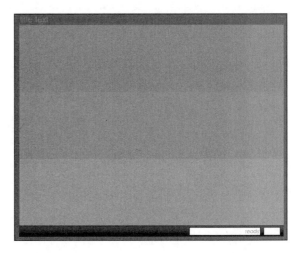

You'll do this by making all three final colors brighter, which you can achieve by adding something to the current color value. The preceding storyboard shows the addition of the three values colorTrans0, colTrans1, and colorTrans2. So the colTransition() code has to fade from the three monocolored strips to the three uniquely colored strips.

OK, that's the direction you'll take. You now need to know how to implement it. You need to ask yourself the following two questions:

- How do I perform the fade so that it's smooth?

- What will my target colors (color + colorTrans) be?

Fading color

If you want to fade between black (0x000000) and white (0xFFFFFF) in a gradual transition, how would you do it? Well, you could simply add 1 to the starting color every frame until you reach the final target color, white. That doesn't actually work. You don't get a smooth transition from black to white through all the grays; you get a transition from black to white that goes through all the colors of the rainbow.

The way to do it is similar to the way you mix colors in the Color Mixer panel when you create new colors with the RGB model: you treat the red, green, and blue components *separately*. So to move from black to white while only sticking to the colors that are actually between black and white (that is, all the grays) rather than different hues (red, blue, green, and so on), you have to add 1 to the red component, 1 to the green component, and 1 to the blue component every time. You can see this effect if you try it manually in the Color Mixer panel.

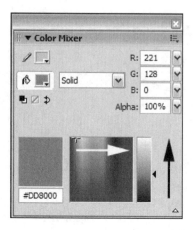

If you click the crosshairs in the color swatch and drag it in the direction of the white arrow, you'll see that the color changes through the colors of the rainbow (or the colors of the visible spectrum for the physicists in the house). As you do this, you'll see that the R, G, and B values change in sequence, and the hex color value at the bottom left goes up linearly. That isn't what you want. You want a more subtle effect, where color is maintained and the only thing that changes is brightness. You can do this if you click-drag the little left-facing arrow to the right of the color swatch upward in the direction of the black arrow. You'll see that the R, G, and B values all go up at the same rate, and *all* the digits of the hex value seem to change at the same time. This is closer to the effect you want.

Red tends to add "warmth" to an RGB color. Keeping this value the same will make for pages that seem to have a consistent "mood." So what you really need to do is change the green and blue channels without varying the red channel.

> Although I talk about fading color, the code actually goes toward brighter colors, so you're creating "fade to white" rather than the usual "fade to black."

Coding the color transition

Let's start coding. You first need to define your color variables.

1. Add the following code to the INITIALIZE section (around line 80):

```
// Define initial screen colors (further
// colors will use these colors
// as their seed)
var color0:Number = 0xDD8000;
var color1:Number = 0xAACC00;
var color2:Number = 0x0080CC;
// Define transition colors
var colTrans:Array = new Array();
colTrans = [0x000880, 0x001100, 0x002280];
var fadeColor:Number = 0;
// Define navigation strip variables...
```

This defines your target colors when you want to recolor your strip; color0's target becomes color0+colTrans[0], color1's target is color1+colTrans[1], and so on. Notice that color0 is the closest to the original color, and color2 is the furthest away (because you're adding a bigger value to it). You'll also use a variable, fadeColor, that will allow you to slowly add the transition value over time, resulting in a fade effect.

2. Next up, you'll add lines to the functions posTransition and colTransition to use the new variables. Add the following line to the end of posTransition. This sets fadeColor to 0, so you reset the fade effect at the start of every new transition.

```
    selectedStrip =
➡ this._name.substring(5, 6);
    selectedCol =
➡ _root["color"+selectedStrip];
    tricolor.setCol(selectedCol,
➡ selectedCol, selectedCol);
    fadeColor = 0;
  }
};
```

3. Add the following code to completely replace the existing colTransition:

```
colTransition = function () {
  fadeColor += 0x000202;
    if (fadeColor<colTrans[0]) {
      tricolor.colstrip0.
➡ setRGB(selectedCol+fadeColor);
    }
    if (fadeColor<colTrans[1]) {
      tricolor.colStrip1.
➡ setRGB(selectedCol+fadeColor);
    }
    if (fadeColor<colTrans[2]) {
      tricolor.colStrip2.
➡ setRGB(selectedCol+fadeColor);
    } else {
      // we are now at the new page...
      color0 = tricolor.colStrip0.getRGB();
      color1 = tricolor.colStrip1.getRGB();
      color2 = tricolor.colStrip2.getRGB();
      delete this.onEnterFrame;
    }
};
```

So what does this code do? Well, it slowly increments fadeColor, which increases from 0x000000. This means fadeColor starts off as black and slowly gets brighter. You add this color to the starting colors, color0, color1, and color2, and using the color objects colStrip0 through colStrip2 you defined earlier via the function stripCols (and which are inside tricolor), you gradually add fadeColor to the existing strip colors. You stop adding this new color to each strip once it has reached its target color, colTrans.

Because strip 2 is the one with the highest colTrans value, you know all three color transitions are complete when this one is done, so that's when you stop. When you've completed the full color change, you replace the original colors with the new strip colors.

```
color0 = tricolor.colStrip0.getRGB();
color1 = tricolor.colStrip1.getRGB();
color2 = tricolor.colStrip2.getRGB();
```

This means that the colors are unique for each page in the site, and these colors tell you something about where you are in the navigation. In fact, if you look at the finished site (you can find the link to this site from either the friends of ED site, www.friendsofed.com, or the Futuremedia site, www.futuremedia.org.uk), you may notice that everything else is tied in to the navigation: the colors, the text—in fact, *everything except the content*! There are no little graphical extras to make it look nice, and this is part of its charm. The pared-down design has a very modern feel to it (the fact that the core UI comes in at about 12 to 15K once it's on the Web is also cool).

As you navigate through the FLA with the new code in place, you'll notice two things:

- You've forgotten to bring the text back once the new page is created.
- If you navigate too far into the site, the colors start to break up, and you lose the graded color scheme.

You'll sort out the first problem in a moment. The second problem is something you're seeing because you're currently allowed to go much further into the navigation than would normally be expected. Usually the **three-click rule** applies: if the user can't get where he or she wants to go within three clicks, your site has poor navigation. You'll arrange the content later so that all pages can be reached within three clicks, and users will never see the color breakup.

> *The technical reason for the breakup is that you've overflowed on one of the color channels. One of the channels (blue or green, because those are the ones you're changing in the transition) has gone over 0xFF. You lose the subtle tonal changes when this happens because you've suddenly shifted to a different position on the color spectrum.*

Finishing the text transition

Bringing the text back again is remarkably easy because you already have the function to fade text (fadeText). All you have to do is set up the variable you used to fade the text out so that this time you fade back in. There are two places you need to add new code. First, you need to add some code to the end of posTransition:

```
selectedStrip = this._name.substring(5,
➥ 6);
selectedCol = _root["color"+
➥ selectedStrip];
tricolor.setCol(selectedCol, selectedCol,
➥ selectedCol);
fadeColor = 0;
fadeAlpha = 0;
}
```

Second, you need to add the code to actually create the transition via the function colTransition:

```
colTransition = function () {
  fadeColor += 0x000202;
  fadeAlpha += 6;
  fadeText(fadeAlpha);
  if (fadeColor<colTrans[0]) {
    tricolor.colStrip0.
➥ setRGB(selectedCol+fadeColor);
  }
  if (fadeColor<colTrans[1]) {
    tricolor.colStrip1.
➥ setRGB(selectedCol+fadeColor);
  }
  if (fadeColor<colTrans[2]) {
    tricolor.colStrip2.
➥ setRGB(selectedCol+fadeColor);
  } else {
    // we're now at the new page...
    color0 = tricolor.colStrip0.getRGB();
    color1 = tricolor.colStrip1.getRGB();
    color2 = tricolor.colStrip2.getRGB();
    fadeText(100);
    this.onEnterFrame = undefined;
  }
};
```

At the end of colTransition, you explicitly set the text alpha value to 100. This is to make sure that you end up with fully faded-in text even if you make the other transitions quicker (in which case the alpha fade wouldn't finish in time).

Reviewing the code so far

If you look at the FLA in test mode, you're able to see the full color transition of the UI and how the variables and events change as the animations progress. Test the FLA in debug mode and take a look at the Variables tab of root (_level0). You'll see that the various color and fade variables change in two distinct ways as posTransition and colTransition are at work. It's almost like watching a clock mechanism!

When using the debugger, you may find that the variables change in a blur of activity. A good trick is to temporarily change the frame rate to 1 fps to 5 fps when debugging.

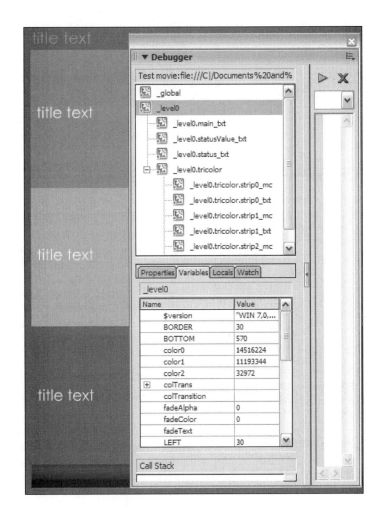

You can also see the true relationship between tricolor and the three strips inside it by checking the Variables tab for their timelines.

The tricolor movie clip is simply a carrier of the three strips and the background functions to drive it all. The individual strip movie clips control and initiate the animation (via the onRelease events, which are always attached to the strips), and control the onEnterFrame events that become attached to the strip (you'll see them as _level0.trocolor.strip0_mc to strip2_mc in the debugger) that was clicked once animation takes place.

Notice also that the onEnterFrame events that control the animation disappear as soon as the animation navigation has completed. So what does Flash do when there are no animations going on?

Nothing! It just sits there, waiting for a mouse click on one of the three strips. That's actually a *very good thing*. Some Flash designers blame Macromedia for sluggish graphics, but that's usually because their UI

code is always running in the background, and this makes the final content sluggish. The Futuremedia UI takes up none of the Flash player's precious performance budget when it isn't doing anything, and that makes the site processor-friendly. It will never be the cause of performance bottlenecks that the final content may experience. Flash UIs that are always animating even when users aren't interacting with them are cool as long as they know when to stop and get on with the important task of providing quick and responsive navigation, and then let the content do its stuff once it's reached.

Speaking of content and site structure, the site so far is very colorful. It has the look of a Pantone swatch book (the kind of book graphic designers look at and say "Wow, that looks kind of cool—if only I could actually do something that looks as colorful as that!"). Guess what, that was one of the influences of this site. I've always wanted to somehow design a site that looked like a swatch book or a paint swatch brochure. However, you don't really seem to be going anywhere in this site. You always end up at pages marked *title text*.

In the final part of this section, you'll turn your attention to adding some structure to the navigation. Unlike the sort of beginner Flash sites you may have tried before now, you'll notice that this site doesn't move up and down a timeline when jumping between pages. Instead, it stays on the same frame (frame 1) and changes the appearance of that frame. To change the pages to include content and titles, you need to define one more major part for the site: **data**.

Data-driven sites (and why you need to understand them)

A beginner **timeline-driven** site is easy to understand because the concepts behind it are simple to grasp. The Futuremedia site is a **data-driven** site. Rather than changing the appearance of the site by moving up and down a timeline, you'll get the UI to look at a set of data that defines how the new page should look.

Although the way this second type of site works is harder to grasp, it's easier to maintain once built. To change pages in a timeline-driven site, you have to physically change the timeline and UI by adding new navigation buttons and keyframes. In short, you have to change everything. To change pages in a data-driven site, you can leave the UI alone—you just change the data associated with the content.

This is your old friend modularly at work again. In a data-driven site, you have two parts (modules), both of which are separate from each other:

- UI
- Data and content

The user requests a page via the interface, and the interface uses this click to do the following:

1. Animate itself to provide feedback.
2. Retrieve the data associated with the requested page.
3. Use the data to build the content associated with the page.

> *Thus far, you've only looked at creating step 1, which is why the Futuremedia site still looks like it's missing a lot of details that a full site should have.*

The UI is thus separate from the data and content (and, incidentally, the data and content are separate from each other because they're different; one is code based, and the other consists of graphics and text), which means that if you want to add new pages, you don't have to change the UI. You instead change just the parts of the module that actually need to change— that is, data and content.

Not only are data-driven sites much easier to maintain than timeline-driven sites, but such sites are also much

better in cases where the content can't be known when you build the UI. This "can't be known" bit is usually because the content is **dynamic**, or changeable from day to day. Looking at my contact list of Flash web designers, I know that the people making the real money are the ones who can build dynamic sites (also called **web application front-ends** or **rich Internet applications**).

The Futuremedia site is built the way it is because I want you to be able to take the concepts taught in this book and actually make money. That's why Futuremedia is a data-driven site. It doesn't get its data from a server (as a real web application would, although you can easily modify it so it does), but it's still an important type of site for your development into a designer who can build Flash sites that further your career. It's the stepping-stone that takes you from timeline-based sites to web applications.

Now that the preamble is out of the way, let's get on with it and get your hands dirty.

Defining data for Futuremedia

The whole site navigation so far looks like this:

There's a home page, and clicking any strip zooms you into a new page, which then magically splits again into another tricolor. This goes on forever, taking you down an endless series of three-way crossroads. You need to add some information here to tell Flash how to do this in a structured way that allows you to do the following:

- Add unique titles to each page.
- Form definite paths. This includes the ability to close off certain paths where you don't want all three strips to take you somewhere.
- Allow you to add a new type of page that doesn't turn into more linkPages, but enables you to display content (contentPages).

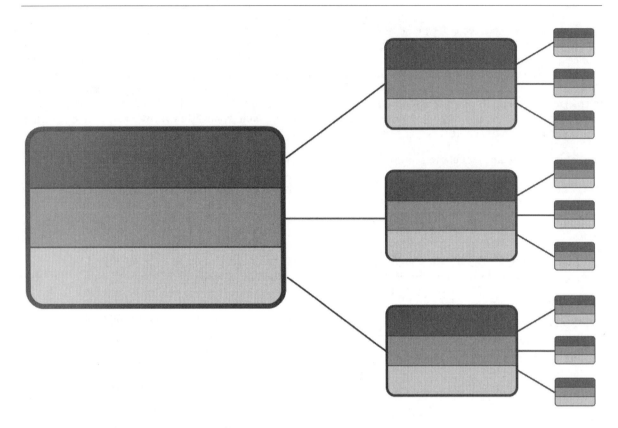

And while you're at it, you might as well push the boat out and add some other cool stuff that normal tween-based sites can't do. You'll make the content general with the following:

- The ability to define the content as something that's currently in the Library
- The ability to define content that needs loading as a SWF file

Wow! That's a lot of stuff. There are two ways you could do this. One way is by defining a set of arrays for each full page. The other way is by having all the information for the full site in one place. You're moving forward in leaps and bounds, so you'll go for the latter, because you're feeling confident about all this.

There's a third way you could do this: you could define the data as an XML file. I'm assuming you won't know much about XML at this stage, so you won't go down this route, but there's nothing stopping you from doing so later.

The Futuremedia site is structured on at least two levels. On one level, the code itself is written in a structured way using functions, and on another level, the data that drives the content is itself also structured.

To define the required information of each page, you need to set up a **record** per page. Within each record, you'll have **fields** that define each page, covering all the preceding information in a structured way.

So exactly what bits of information do you need to know? Well, for the pages you've seen so far (pages that link to other pages, or linkPages) you have this:

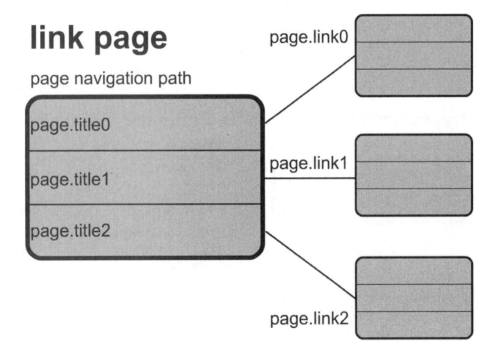

You need to know the following:

- Three items that define links to other pages.
- Three page title strings plus one page navigation path. You can either get the UI to work this last one out or just put up a string that you've defined (you'll go for the latter).

If the page will show some content, you'll want another game plan that looks something like this:

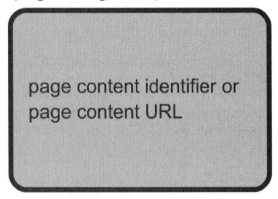

content page

page navigation path

page content identifier or
page content URL

Here, you're more concerned about the content you'll show. You need to know the following:

- The movie clip linkage identifier if you're going to pull content from the Flash Library
- The URL that the content lives at if it's a SWF

Now here's the big question. If you want to represent all this information as a *general* set of data that Flash could understand, how would you do it? Well, you know about arrays from Chapter 3, but you couldn't really use them, because arrays store only *lists*. You need something more structured. The answer is that you need to produce an *object*.

As you learned earlier in the book, objects have properties that describe them. Properties are just raw data, and it's up to you to decide what they mean.

You have some information you want to define for the site, so how about you do that? **Property** is just a fancy programmer way of saying "something that describes a thing." You have a bunch of things that you want to describe on your web pages, so how about you do that with this odd **object** thing?

You need several properties, but there's a problem. You have two kinds of pages! How do you do it? Well, you can have two objects, one for the content pages and one for the link pages. That isn't how programmers think, though—programmers like to *generalize*. In this context, "generalize" means "what you have to do for there to be only one kind of page." See if you can guess without peeking at the answer. . . .

The answer is *you make the page type a property as well*!

So you'll have something called page with the following properties (all of which I've taken from the previous diagrams):

- Page type
- Page links
- Page titles
- Page content linkage identifier
- Page content URL

And that's everything you need to define your site's pages. In fact, in principle, it's almost enough to define *any* web page!

> *The final product of this little trial is included in the download as* futuremedia_database.fla.

Let's create an object in Flash that has these properties. Open a new FLA (you can do this even if you have something else open in Flash), select frame 1 of the timeline, and type the following code in the Script pane of the Actions panel:

```
var page:Object = new Object();
page.pType =
➥ "this is the page type; content
➥ or linking";
```

```
page.plink =
➥ "this defines all the page links";
page.pTitle =
➥ "this is the page navigation title";
page.pID =
➥ "this is the content linkage
identifier";
page.pURL = "this is the content URL";
```

Test the FLA in debug mode (Control ➤ Debug Movie). Click the ▶ icon to start the SWF, and then select _level0 in the top-left pane. Click the Variables tab to see the data structure you've just created.

Name	Value
$version	"WIN 7,0,14,0"
⊟ page	
pID	"this is the content linkage identifier"
plink	"this defines all the page links"
pTitle	"this is the page navigation title"
pType	"this is the page type; content or linking"
pURL	"this is the content URL"

Now you're probably thinking, "That's fine, but some of the properties of my pages have properties of their own. For example, the pLink part will need three links, one for each strip."

So you're stumped, right? Well, sort of. There are two ways to fix this problem. One way is to build a constructor function that creates subproperties. The other, much simpler, way is to use the fact that properties can be *any* primitive data type themselves, and that includes strings, numbers, Booleans, and arrays.

If you go through and define your properties as the actual *types* you need, and make those that contain multiple subproperties into arrays, you can encapsulate all your descriptive data for a single page into a single object. Let's do that now. Change the code as follows:

```
var page:Object = new Object();
page.pType = new String();
page.plink = new Array();
page.pTitle = new Array();
page.pID = new String();
page.pURL = new String();
```

This gives a structure to your properties, but it doesn't put in any data. You should do that next. Add the following lines to what you have so far:

```
// add the data for a general page...
page.pType = "linkPage or contentPage";
page.pLink = ["strip0 link", "strip1 link",
➥ "strip2 link"];
page.pTitle = ["navigation",
➥ "strip0 title", "strip1 title",
➥ "strip2 title"];
page.pID =
➥ "content library identifier (optional)";
page.pURL =
➥ "content URL (optional)";
```

Now run the FLA in debug mode again. This time you'll see a much larger structure of properties. In fact, there are enough branches on the tree to fully define the two kinds of pages. You have all the titles, the locations from which to get the content, and the list of links (including the back button link) of each page.

Name	Value
$version	"WIN 7,0,14,0"
⊟ page	
pID	"content library identifier (optional)"
⊟ pLink	
0	"strip0 link"
1	"strip1 link"
2	"strip2 link"
⊟ pTitle	
0	"navigation"
1	"strip0 title"
2	"strip1 title"
3	"strip2 title"
pType	"linkPage or contentPage"
pURL	"content URL (optional)"

In the same way that the folder in which your doctor keeps your medical history is called your medical record, this structure is a page record. Your medical record defines your health history since birth. The Futuremedia site's page record fully defines the page.

You have one last problem. You have only one record, but you have many pages in your site. You need some way of building more of these records. The doctor's staff can look up a patient's medical history in a filing cabinet of medical records before the patient is treated, and you need to be able to do the same for the current page the UI needs to display, so that Flash knows what to show, where to link to, when a strip is clicked, and so on for all the properties of every page.

Suppose there are 50 pages. You need 50 of the previous structures. How many lines do you think that you'll have to add to your listing so far? Guess!

OK, it's not many. Handling large quantities of repetitive data (or, to use a polite programming term, **structured data**) is something computers are very good at. You have to add only three new lines (and one of them is a brace, so it's really two lines!). You also have to change all references to page to page[i]:

```
var page:Array = new Array();
for (i=0; i<50; i++) {
  page[i] = new Object();
  page[i].pType = new String();
  page[i].plink = new Array();
  page[i].pTitle = new Array();
  page[i].pID = new String();
  page[i].pURL = new String();
  // add the data for a general page...
  page[i].pType =
➥ "linkPage or contentPage";
  page[i].pLink = ["strip0 link",
➥ "strip1 link", "strip2 link"];
  page[i].pTitle = ["navigation",
➥ "strip0 title", "strip1 title",
➥ "strip2 title"];
  page[i].pID = "content library identifier
➥ (optional)";
  page[i].pURL = "content URL (optional)";
}
```

So what have you done? Well, you created an array of size 50 called page. You made each array element, page[i], an object, which allows you to add the properties of page number i.

Cool! So now you have a data structure (it's actually a simple **database of records**) that you can use to make Flash create all your page titles and links. You can see it in the debugger if you debug the FLA one last time. You'll see that there are now 50 sets of records (0 to 49). If you open any of them, you'll find the familiar page-definition structure.

Name			Value
⊞	35		
⊟	36		
	⋯	pID	"content library identifier (optional)"
	⊟	pLink	
		0	"strip0 link"
		1	"strip1 link"
		2	"strip2 link"
	⊟	pTitle	
		0	"navigation"
		1	"strip0 title"
		2	"strip1 title"
		3	"strip2 title"
	⋯	pType	"linkPage or contentPage"
	⋯	pURL	"content URL (optional)"
⊞	37		
⊞	38		
⊞	39		
⊞	40		

Going back to the medical record analogy, you've just created a filing cabinet full of records. Your patients are labeled 0 to 49, and you've filed the records numerically. At the moment, each record is filled with basic default information, but you'll soon make the records specific to each page in your site.

Some of you may recognize the preceding tree structure as something you could define via a separate XML file that the final SWF will load at runtime. You've come a *very* long way here!

In the book project section in Chapter 12, you'll integrate the page data structure into the Futuremedia site, and then you'll start to use it to produce real navigation.

Parting shots

I've thought long and hard about building a site that was based around a set of records. Many existing Flash designers would see this as advanced.

Times have changed since the days of Flash 4 and 5, when a nice bit of Flash eye candy would have been termed "cool." In the modern Flash world, you have to look beyond graphics to build a cool website. You need to have structured and extensible code, and sites that are easy to manage.

Something you may have noticed is that you've used almost all of the information you've acquired so far in the book: variables, objects, loops, arrays, and even that inertial effect that you thought would be of use only in a "for fun only" flies-chasing-the-mouse-pointer FLA (which has actually become a fundamental part of the Futuremedia site—the site zooms with the same inertial effect!). Like the approach to the final scene of a movie, all the elements of the plot are finally starting to come together.

Summary

You've learned in this chapter that by using the drawing API, it's possible to *create* motion graphics via ActionScript, not just *manipulate* graphics that you previously created in Flash.

It's somewhat ironic that you started out with Flash working in a purely visual way, with all tweens with no code. And yet here you've produced quite impressive visual effects purely by using ActionScript—there's nothing else in the FLAs. I bet that when you began this book, you never thought you'd end up here!

In the next chapter, you'll finish up the data structure that you've defined in this chapter. You'll populate the structure with real data, and you'll start using it to drive the site, finally making the Futuremedia site truly "data driven."

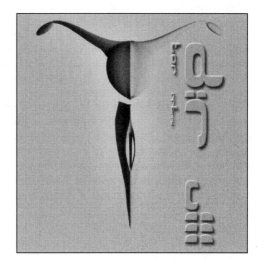

Chapter 12

SOUND

What we'll cover in this chapter:

- Importing sound clips into the Library
- Converting a sound clip into a sound object that ActionScript can control
- Using sound object event-handling to synchronize sounds
- Adjusting sound objects to pan and change the volume of a sound effect
- Dynamically loading sounds

This chapter is about using sound to enhance your Flash movies, a feature that will really start to open up the world of Flash multimedia in your designs. Multimedia websites, in HTML for example, have usually separated the sound content from the rest of the site. However, the introduction of sound in previous versions of Flash has dramatically improved the overall user experience. Clever use of music and sounds in your designs allows for a high degree of interactivity and usability, and at the very least produces a pleasant atmosphere within your sites. With Flash, you can now begin to push the limits of using sound in your websites, from streaming sound in parallel with video to actually sequencing and mixing completely new pieces of music online.

In the past, sound on the Web was problematic, but then **MPEG Audio Layer-3 (MP3)** came along. Before the advent of MP3, there were limited options for the web designer: **Musical Instrument Digital Interface (MIDI)**, which isn't a universal (web) standard and tends to be of variable quality depending on your hardware, and **sampled sound files** of various formats (like WAV, SND, and AIFF), which can be rather bulky—a major headache during download!

MP3 is a sound format that compresses sounds intelligently via several different filters to give a much smaller file size for a given quality than any other sound compression system currently available. It's now *the* standard for music files on the Web, in the same way that Macromedia Flash is the standard for high-impact, highly interactive websites. It therefore comes as no surprise that Flash now supports MP3.

OK, that's enough of the background details for now. Let's start, quite naturally, with the very basics: importing and using sounds in Flash.

Adding sound to Flash movies

Compared to what I've covered so far in this book, working with sound in Flash can be quite complicated. In fact, there are so many options to choose from that even advanced Flash users often don't know when to use one over another. Don't worry, though—you're

going to start from the absolute basics and build up gently from there. I won't go into every detail, but by the end of the chapter you should have a good enough grasp of the basics to confidently start exploring the more advanced options yourself.

Attaching sounds to a timeline

The simplest way to add sounds to a Flash movie doesn't involve using any ActionScript at all. It's fairly limited in terms of what it lets you do, but you'll use it as a starting point so that you can see what's going on.

1. Open a new document in Flash and select File ➤ Import ➤ Import to Library to import some sound files. You can find an FLA with some sounds already imported in the download file `sounds.fla`. You'll use this file as a starting point for several examples, so if you decide to save it partway through the next few tutorials, save it with a different filename via File ➤ Save As.

2. Once you've imported all the files (or opened `sounds.fla`), press *Ctrl+L* to call up the Library panel:

The image shown for each item depicts the **sound wave** it contains, which shows you roughly how the sound's volume varies over time. You can listen to a selected sound right away by simply clicking the play button (the ▶ icon) in the top-right corner of the wave preview.

3. You can attach the sounds to any keyframe you like. Select the item called Plastic Button and drag it onto the stage. You won't see anything appear on the stage itself, but take a careful look at frame 1 on the timeline and you'll see a small horizontal line running through the middle.

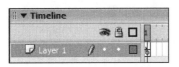

4. Now insert a frame (*F5*) at frame 10, and you'll see that this horizontal line runs right across the first few frames of the timeline—it's actually a tiny picture of the sound wave you just attached to frame 1.

The sound will play whenever the playhead hits the keyframe it's attached to. As you can see from the timeline, the Plastic Button sound will begin playing when frame 1 is entered, and it will finish playing by frame 3. Test the movie now, and you should hear the sound repeated every couple of seconds as the movie loops around its ten frames.

Attaching sounds to button keyframes

You're not limited to putting sounds on the root time-line. You can just as easily attach them to keyframes on a button, so that a sound plays every time a particular button state occurs. Say you attach a sound to the *down* state. The sound will play every time the button is clicked.

1. Close the current FLA and start again using the initial file, sounds.fla. Open the Macromedia Buttons Library (Window ➤ Other Panels ➤ Common Libraries ➤ Buttons) and drag an instance of any button that strikes your fancy onto the stage. I've used the blue arcade button (which you can find in the Arcade buttons Library folder).

2. Drag an instance of the button onto the stage. Double-click the button to edit it in place. Add a new layer called sounds, and insert keyframes in the Over and Down frames on the new layer:

			Up	Over	Down	Hit
haze	X · ■		•	☐	•	
shine	X · ■		•	☐	•	
hazy ring	X · ■		•	☐	•	
ring	X · ■		•		▯	
gradients	X · □		•	☐	•	•
color	· · ■		•		▯	
shadow	· · ■		•		▯	
sounds	∥ · · □		○	○	○	☐

At this point, you could easily drag sounds from the Library straight onto the stage—like you did before—to attach them to the currently selected keyframes on the timeline. However, there's another way to do it that's well worth knowing about because it's more precise and also allows you to *remove* sounds from keyframes as well as add them.

3. With the Over keyframe selected, take a look at the Properties panel. You'll see a drop-down menu labeled Sound. Select Plastic Button from the Sound drop-down menu to attach a sound to the keyframe. Repeat this process for the Down keyframe using the Plastic Click sound.

4. Now test the movie. You'll hear the two sounds play as you roll over or click the button. Note that it's not normal practice to add sounds to the Up state, and attaching sounds to the Hit state is effectively the same as attaching sounds to the Down state (so you need to attach a sound to only one or the other, not both).

None of this should really be new to you, but it does serve to emphasize an important concept: sounds must always be **attached** to something. Attaching sounds to keyframes on a timeline is a cool and simple way to put them in your movies, but it's fairly inflexible.

ActionScript gives you a powerful and more versatile approach. You can attach sounds dynamically at run-time, and you can attach sounds to non-timeline-based events (such as the pressing of a key or a mouse button) or any more complex events that your code has been wired up to recognize (such as "site has finished loading" or "spaceInvader12 has just been hit"). Let's start making some noise with ActionScript.

Using the Sound class

This is where you step into new territory and start using **sound instances** so that you can truly program your sound effects. Sound instances are the fundamental building blocks that you use to work with sound in ActionScript. There are three simple steps involved in using a sound instance in your movie:

1. Define a sound object.

2. Attach sound data to the sound object.

3. Use the sound object's methods to control how and when the sound is produced.

As you'll learn shortly, these methods give you some pretty neat ways to control sound. For instance, you'll discover that you have enough control to produce a stereo soundscape, so that if you have a car moving from left to right on the screen, you can write some ActionScript to make the car's engine sound pan from left to right at the same rate. In the same way, if the car moves into the distance, ActionScript can make the sound fade.

All of this is possible in Flash, and you even have some other sound features to play with:

- The onSoundComplete event for detecting when a sound has finished playing. This allows you to do something called **sound sequencing**, which allows you to create (among other things) interactive mixing boards.

- The loadSound() method for loading sound files directly into movies at runtime.

- The ability to load MP3 sounds dynamically to create video jukeboxes.

You use all these features to manipulate the sound instance. Creating this instance is quite easy, but it can also be very fiddly, and you can easily forget what you're doing if you blink in the middle of the process. In the next section, you'll learn how to create a sound instance and use it to vary sounds dynamically.

Playing sounds from ActionScript

You can add and manipulate sounds in your movies at two distinct stages, just as you can with movie clips:

- At design time (using the Flash authoring tool to drag, drop, import, and so on)
- At runtime (writing ActionScript that will do all the hard work while the finished SWF is running)

When there's no ActionScript involved—as has been the case in the examples so far—it's safe to say that all the hard work is done at design time. Play the movie and it hums. Click the button and it beeps. All safe, all predictable . . . all pretty boring! Add a little ActionScript into the mix and things get interesting quickly.

With ActionScript, you can make all sorts of subtle changes to your sounds, perhaps in response to user input, *while the movie is running*. That doesn't mean you don't have to make any design decisions—quite the contrary, in fact. It means that you can design complex, flexible soundtracks that can adjust themselves to all sorts of different situations.

The possibilities are truly fantastic. In fact, the only way to convey the scope of what this means for your movies is to show some of those possibilities being put into practice. So, once you've walked through the basics, that's precisely what you'll do.

Attaching sounds to a sound instance

In the last example, you attached sounds to keyframes on the timeline. This time, you'll attach them to a sound instance, so your first step is to create that sound object.

1. Open the file `sounds.fla` yet again, and then rename Layer 1 as actions (alternatively, take a look at `soundObject1.fla`, where you'll find the completed code for this example). Select frame 1. Pin the Actions panel to this frame and put the following ActionScript on the first line of the Script pane:

   ```
   var mouseSound:Sound = new Sound(this);
   ```

Unlike some other constructors, you must give the new Sound() constructor an argument. The Sound() constructor always looks like this (assuming you are using typing):

```
var instanceName:Sound = new Sound(target);
```

or this (if you aren't using typing):

```
var instanceName = new Sound(target);
```

where *target* is the scope of the sound instance *instanceName*. Usually, you just make the target this, which means that the sound instance will be created on the current timeline.

2. Next, you must attach some raw sound data to this object. There are two ways to do this. The first way is to load an item from the Library with the attachSound() method. The second way is to load the sound directly from an external file. You're going to concentrate on the first approach for now, as it's similar to what you did with movie clips in the last chapter.

> *Don't panic—you'll take a look at the second approach (which is a very cool feature of Flash) later on when you explore ActionScript and streaming.*

3. Remember that an item's name (as shown in the Library) isn't used by ActionScript (it's there as a reminder for you only), so you'll need to give your sounds a **linkage identifier** before you can call them up from your code. To do this for your sounds in the Library, right-click/*Ctrl*-click the sound you'll be using in turn (Plastic Button) and select Linkage from the context menu that appears. You'll see the Linkage Properties dialog box appear. Select the Export for ActionScript check box. This will automatically also select the Export in first frame check box (don't uncheck this box!) and make the Identifier and AS 2.0 Class text input boxes active. You're interested only in the Identifier field; leave the AS 2.0 Class field blank.

In the Identifier field for your two symbols you'll see Plastic Button and Plastic Click as the defaults. You're less likely to get the linkage identifiers wrong in your code if you make these names more like the sort of thing you would expect to see as variable names, in camelCase. Change the identifier for Plastic Button to plasticButton and the identifier for Plastic Click to plasticClick.

In the Library, you should now see the linkage identifiers appear in the Linkage column. You may have to increase the width of the Library to see this column.

*For every sound clip you use, you have three names to consider: the name of the **file** the sound came from, the name the sound is given in the **Library**, and the **linkage identifier** it's given so that you can refer to it from ActionScript. If you mix any of them up, your ActionScript may not work!*

Another point to bear in mind is the reason you have to check the Export for ActionScript *and* Export in first frame *check boxes in the Linkage Properties dialog box. Normally, Flash optimizes the SWF during compilation, so that only those symbols and assets that you use appear in the final SWF. The Flash compiler decides whether you use a symbol or asset by looking for it on the timeline at compile time. Symbols and assets that are used by ActionScript don't appear on the timeline at compile time; they're placed on the stage dynamically at runtime. The* Export for ActionScript *check box is your way of saying "I actually use this symbol or asset at runtime via ActionScript, so make sure it's exported in the final SWF."*

That's all well and good, but Flash also has to know on which frame you need the symbol or asset. For normal Flash content, the compiler will look on the timeline, check for the first frame each symbol/asset is used, and try to arrange content in the SWF so that everything is loaded into the browser by the frame it's first required. For ActionScript, it isn't usually obvious when the code will place the content on the timeline. For example, the frame in which the "all aliens are dead, you have won" sound is required in a Flash video game will depend on how good the user is at playing space invaders. To make sure that ActionScript will be able to load content from the Library as and when required, select the Export in first frame *check box to ensure the content is available at the first frame it can be requested by ActionScript: frame 1.*

4. If you test the SWF (Control ➤ Test Movie or *CTRL+ENTER*), you'll find . . . nothing happens! That's because you've only *created* a sound instance. You can't hear the instance (because it has nothing to start playing), though, and you can't see it either (because . . . uh, it's a sound). You *can* see its data

representation, however, if you use the debugger. To check for this, select Control ➤ Debug Movie and then start the debug session (click the ▶ icon at the top right of the Debugger panel). You'll see the sound instance you've just created at the correct scope (look for it on _level0 under the Variables tab).

5. Back to the code. You need to attach the Flash Library's sound clip to the ActionScript sound object. In line 2 of your code, add the following:

```
mouseSound.attachSound("plasticButton");
```

The argument for attachSound is a literal string (you know this because it's enclosed in double quotes " "), and this means it must be **exactly** the same as the linkage identifier you just defined in the Linkage Properties dialog box.

One of the most off-putting things about ActionScript-based sound is that if you get this step wrong, the sound file won't be attached to the sound instance, and you won't hear anything when you try to start the sound. Worse still, Flash doesn't tell you if this has happened; it is what's called a **silent failure**. The only way to tell if a sound has been correctly set up is to start it. Add the new line 3 as follows:

```
var mouseSound:Sound = new Sound(this);
mouseSound.attachSound("plasticButton");
mouseSound.start();
```

This new line causes the sound to start. It will play once, and you should hear a single click when you test the movie (Control ➤ Test Movie). If you don't hear it, check that the linkage identifier in the code matches the one in the Library panel.

Note that I use the word "start" rather than the more common word "play" when I talk about making a sound begin. This is because the play() method only works for movie clips. To play a sound, you use mySound.start(), not mySound.play() (which doesn't work!). Getting into the habit of saying "start the ActionScript sound" rather than "play the ActionScript sound" will help you avoid using the wrong method.

6. You should now have a working sound instance. At the moment, your sound starts on frame 1, which is cool, but not really any advantage over simple timeline sounds. The advantage of ActionScript-driven sound is that it can be interactive and dynamic, so let's add some of those magic ingredients now. To this end, you use the start() method, specifying two arguments. The first argument indicates where in the sound you want to start playing, and the second argument indicates how many times the sound will repeat. Change your code as follows:

```
var mouseSound:Sound = new Sound(this);
mouseSound.attachSound("plasticButton");
this.onMouseDown = function() {
  mouseSound.start();
};
```

Those of you who remember vinyl records know that you could start playing a record some way into a song by lowering the needle arm anywhere other than the start of the recording. The first argument of the start() method does exactly the same thing: it specifies how many seconds into the recording you want to start listening.

Press CTRL+ENTER/CMD+ENTER to test the movie. You should hear the plasticButton sound start whenever you click your mouse button.

As you're probably beginning to realize, Flash sound is full of little tricks that you need to follow, and it can seem a little overly fussy and pedantic (especially when the darn thing just doesn't work!). Here's a quick checklist to memorize to avoid problems.

- Always define a target for your sound instances. Use new Sound(this) rather than new Sound(), even though the latter seems to work. You'll find that there are a number of situations in which the latter will mysteriously stop working, especially when you're building sites with multiple SWFs (you'll look at this when you start adding content to Futuremedia later in this chapter).

- Remember to check that the linkage identifier in the code is the same as the linkage identifier in the Library.

- Use mySound.start(), not mySound.play(). You'll be amazed how often even longtime Flash users make this mistake (myself included!).

Controlling sounds via the Sound class

Short sounds are great because they don't require much control. Longer sounds, though, bring with them problems of their own. To investigate this, import the sound file songLoop.mp3 (File ➤ Import ➤ Import to Library).

1. Right-click/CTRL-click the new sound (soundLoop) in the Library and select Linkage from the context menu. In the Linkage Properties dialog box, select Export for ActionScript and make sure songLoop appears in the Identifier field:

Notice that making sure that the filename of any sound you import into Flash is in camelCase will cause the default name Flash picks for your sound's linkage identifier to be in camelCase too, so you don't have to change a thing!

2. Change the code to use the new sound:

```
var mouseSound:Sound = new Sound(this);
mouseSound.attachSound("songLoop");
this.onMouseDown = function() {
  mouseSound.start();
};
```

If you press the mouse button now, you'll hear a funky beat. Foot-tapping stuff to be sure, but listen to what happens if you press the mouse button a few times without waiting for the current sound to stop.

If you input multiple quick mouse presses, you'll hear a number of different versions of the sound. Flash has **eight-channel sound**, which means you can hear up to eight versions of the sound at the same time.

If all eight channels are already playing something, Flash will ignore any new sounds.

This can produce some cool and unexpected effects, but it isn't really ideal for your purposes. You would prefer the sound started every time the mouse button was pressed and restarted (rather than playing several sounds at the same time) when multiple mouse buttons were entered. The simplest way to do this is to stop the sound just before you start the next one.

It's always a good idea to do this when attaching sounds to an event that could be triggered many times in quick succession. If you're not careful about stopping unwanted sounds (especially if they're long), you may run out of sound channels and prevent other sounds in your movie from starting at all. In addition, you may get that unwanted echo-noise effect you just experienced, which is something that can make your site appear a little buggy and amateurish when it comes to audio.

You can stop the sound with the ActionScript command mouseSound.stop("songLoop"). You could be forgiven for wondering why you can't just use mouseSound.stop(), as you're simply telling Flash to stop playing sound from the mouseSound instance. Since you already told it that mouseSound is attached to plasticButton, why should you have to specify it again? Well, it may seem pointless, but that's how it works.

- If you do add the linkage identifier in a sound.stop(), then only that sound object is stopped.
- If you don't add the linkage identifier, then **all** sound is stopped in the SWF.

The start() method also has optional arguments, so let's look at those while you're in an exploratory mood. The start() method when written with arguments is as follows:

```
mySound.start(offset, loops);
```

The *offset* value (in seconds) defines how far into the audio you want to start, and the *loops* value defines how many times you want to play the sound. If you specify more than one loop, each one will start at the offset value.

Let's put all this into practice.

1. Add the following new lines in the onMouseDown event handler:

```
var mouseSound:Sound = new Sound(this);
mouseSound.attachSound("songLoop");
this.onMouseDown = function() {
  mouseSound.stop("songLoop");
  mouseSound.start(0, 2);
};
```

Any sounds associated with mouseSound that are currently playing will be stopped, ensuring that you don't fill all eight sound channels with duplicates. If mouseSound isn't producing any sound for you to stop, the extra line will have no effect. The code will then start a sound consisting of *two* loops of songLoop.

2. Test the FLA again, and you'll find that you no longer get any odd echo effect. The stop()

command now prevents you from filling up every available sound channel with a new version of the same sound.

3. What if you want to make sure that the triggered sound plays right through before it can be triggered again (instead of restarting every time the event occurs, whether or not the sound has finished)? You might do this, for example, when you want the user to hear the full sound (if it's a voice giving some information, for instance). It also feels more professional, because you don't get that awful "scratching" interruption effect. Fortunately, Flash gives you the onSoundComplete event, which occurs whenever a sound completes all the loops specified in sound.start().

So, to make your mouse-driven sound play right through following a mouse click (and ignore subsequent clicks until it's done) you need to modify the script to look like this:

```
// set up the sound object
var mouseSound:Sound = new Sound(this);
mouseSound.attachSound("songLoop");
//
// set up the sound finished flag
var soundFinished:Boolean = true;
//
// set up a onSoundComplete event
mouseSound.onSoundComplete = function() {
  soundFinished = true;
};
//
// set up a handler function for the
// onMouseDown event
this.onMouseDown = function() {
  if (soundFinished) {
    mouseSound.start(0, 1);
    soundFinished = false;
  }
};
```

As you can see, the code has really started to expand. I've added in comments so that you don't forget what each bit does.

You use a Boolean called soundFinished to indicate whether the mouseSound sound is currently stopped (true if it's stopped; false if it's playing). As soon as soundFinished becomes false, the onMouseDown event can no longer trigger new sounds because the main event handler code is inside an `if` statement that will only run if soundFinished is true.

This situation will continue until the sound runs through the specified number of loops, whereupon the onSoundComplete event handler sets it back to true, allowing the onMouseDown event to start new sounds.

*This is a very useful bit of code because it contains a common advanced coding structure (known as an **interlock**, **semaphore**, or **inhibit flag**, depending on the context in which it's being used). Essentially, you're using one event (onSoundComplete) to modify a value (soundFinished) that governs what actions are triggered by another event (onMouseDown).*

In fact, this is the same sort of structure that your operating system uses in multitasking. For example, when two programs want to access the same hard drive, the first will lock the second out until it has finished. The fact that each program limits its usage to very short periods of time gives humans the impression that both are actually using the same hard drive simultaneously. Sneaky, huh? As you can probably imagine, it's possible to set up some very sophisticated responses to user events when you organize things in this way.

Creating dynamic soundtracks

While you're looking at the onSoundComplete event, let's do something fun with it. You now have a way to spot when a sound finishes playing, so why not use that event to trigger another sound? You should be able to link several sounds together quite seamlessly and create an ongoing soundtrack that can jump from one sound clip to another (in response to the user or whatever's going on in the movie) without any audible joins or, in other words, a **dynamic soundtrack**.

Dynamic soundtracks are becoming a big talking point in the video games market and on the menu system of interactive DVDs. You'll often hear the background music change as you move from one area to another to reflect the changing mood of the interactive content.

*In the past, you'd often have to put up with having one piece cut off halfway through choices or the soundtrack fading in and out, as if under the control of a third-rate dance club DJ. Nowadays, you'll be much harder pushed to spot the joins, as designers create soundtracks in lots of tiny sections that can be played together in a whole variety of different sequences, but nevertheless sound like a continuous piece of music. Such sections are called **loops** because they can be seamlessly repeated to form longer compositions. The sound file you just used, songLoop, is a good example of a loop.*

Creating dynamic soundtracks from scratch can be a tricky process, mainly because you need to find (or create) a number of sound clips that will sound OK together, no matter what order you play them in. Fortunately, I've done the hard bit for you. Check out the following files in the download:

- beats01.wav
- beats02.wav
- beats03.wav
- beats04.wav

The actual ActionScript isn't too hard: you basically need to trigger each new sound with the onSoundComplete event that's generated by the last sound finishing. Let's start putting together the movie.

1. Create a new document in Flash. Select Modify ➤ Document to bring up the Document Properties dialog box and set the document dimensions to 250 pixels wide by 150 pixels high. Now use File ➤ Import ➤ Import to Library to import the four sound files listed previously into the Library. (Note that you can select them all by *SHIFT*-clicking.)

In the Library, right-click/CTRL-click each sound in turn to set its linkage properties, exactly as you did for the songLoop clip in the previous example, giving each the same linkage identifier as the original filename (beats01, beats02, beats03, and beats04).

When you've finished, the Library panel should look like this:

2. Now it's time to set up the main timeline. You need two layers: actions and interface (you should be able to guess what you're going to do with them!). Use *F6* to insert keyframes on frame 5 of each layer.

In fact, you're going to put **everything** into frame 5, and not into frame 1 as you might have expected. There's a very good reason for this: some versions of the Flash player seem to take a few frames to "settle," and since your movie depends on accurate sound timing, you want to make sure that the player doesn't compromise this accuracy.

Here's a useful rule of thumb: if your movie relies a great deal on the accurate timing of events, it's always a good idea to start adding code a few frames in.

3. Let's build up the interface now. This will consist of four buttons (for selecting sound clips) and two dynamic text fields (to show which sound is currently playing and which one is up next), with a label for each (simple static text fields). Here's how frame 5 of your interface layer might look:

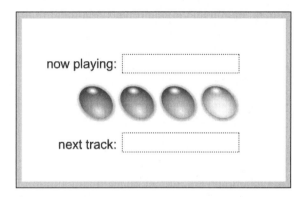

Here's how it will work. When you click any of the buttons, the sound file being played will only change when the current audio loop has finished, *not* when you click a button. If all your loops are of the same length and musical properties (beats per minute and style), this results in a seamless transition from one loop to the next, allowing you to interactively create a soundtrack of your own choosing.

Note that the buttons I use in this example come straight out of the Ovals folder in the Macromedia Buttons Library (Window ➤ Other Panels ➤ Common Libraries ➤ Buttons).

4. The next step is to use the Properties panel to name each of the instances you'll want to use in your ActionScript. Begin by naming each button after the sound clip you want it to trigger. Select the first button, and give it the instance name beats01.

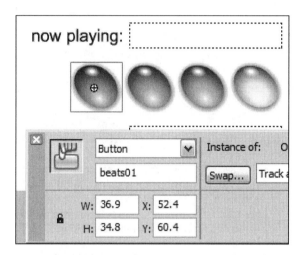

5. Repeat the process for each of the other buttons, naming them beats02, beats03, and beats04, respectively.

So what's going on here? Why aren't you calling them beats01_btn, beats02_btn, and so on, as recommended by Macromedia? Well, there's a good reason for this: you're going to use a sneaky shortcut to keep your code to the minimum. You'll use an ActionScript variable called soundNext to indicate which track you want to play next. You therefore want it set to beats01, beats02, beats03, or beats04, depending on which button was last clicked. The simplest way to do that is to name the buttons beats01, beats02, and so on, and set soundNext to the name of the button each time. Don't panic if you're not quite following this—it should all become clear soon!

6. You must now do the same for the dynamic text fields. Using the Properties panel, name the fields nowPlaying (top text field) and nextTrack (bottom text field).

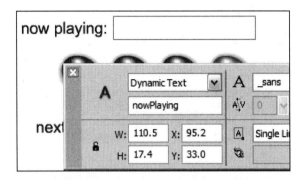

OK, now that the stage is set, let's write the ActionScript that will bring it to life. All the following code needs to go into frame 5 of the actions layer, so it's a good idea to select this keyframe and pin the Actions panel to it before you start.

7. You'll begin by initializing the soundNext variable, which (as you've already noted) you'll be using to indicate which track you want to play next:

```
// initialize starting track
var soundNext:String = "beats01";
```

8. Next, you create your sound instance, attach the specified sound clip, and tell it to play through once. You also update the nowPlaying text field with the name of the clip:

```
// set up dynamic sound object
var dynamicSound:Sound = new Sound(this);
dynamicSound.attachSound(soundNext);
dynamicSound.start(0, 1);
nowPlaying.text = soundNext;
```

9. Now you wire up the buttons with a rather strange-looking event handler:

```
beats01.onRelease = beats02.onRelease=
➡ beats03.onRelease=beats04.onRelease=
➡ function () {
  soundNext = this._name;
  dynamicSound.attachSound(soundNext);
  dynamicSound.start(0, 1);
  nowPlaying.text = soundNext;
};
```

Actually, all this does is assign the same handler function to the onRelease events for each of the buttons. You could have written it out as four identical event handlers, one for each button, like this:

```
beats01_btn.onRelease = function(){
    soundNext = this._name;
    dynamicSound.attachSound(soundNext);
    dynamicSound.start(0, 1);
    nowPlaying.text = soundNext;
};
beats02_btn.onRelease = function(){
    soundNext = this._name;
    dynamicSound.attachSound(soundNext);
    dynamicSound.start(0, 1);
    nowPlaying.text = soundNext;
};
beats03_btn.onRelease = function(){
    soundNext = this._name;
    dynamicSound.attachSound(soundNext);
    dynamicSound.start(0, 1);
    nowPlaying.text = soundNext;
};
beats04_btn.onRelease = function(){
    soundNext = this._name;
    dynamicSound.attachSound(soundNext);
    dynamicSound.start(0, 1);
    nowPlaying.text = soundNext;
};
```

Clearly, the first technique saves a lot of repetition. I know which way I'd rather do it if I had to type it all in!

But what about the function itself? Let's go through it.

```
soundNext = this._name;
```

Well, this is how you refer to whatever generated the event that called this function. For instance, if the function got called because the beats02 button generated an onRelease event, then this refers to the beats02 button. In that case, this._name gives you the instance name of the beats02 button (beats02—logical, huh?), which is precisely what you want to make the sound instance play next:

```
dynamicSound.attachSound(soundNext);
dynamicSound.start(0, 1);
```

You also update the top text field to signify which sound you've just requested:

```
nowPlaying.text = soundNext;
```

So clicking any of the four buttons makes nextSound equal to one of four string values. These string values are the same as the four linkage names for our sound clips, so you can safely feed soundNext into the attachSound method on your sound instance.

Finally, add a stop to the end of the script so far, so you don't go looping around the five-frame timeline:

```
// stop the timeline
stop();
```

The script so far should look like this:

```
// initialize starting track
var soundNext:String = "beats01";
// set up dynamic sound object
var dynamicSound:Sound = new Sound(this);
dynamicSound.attachSound(soundNext);
dynamicSound.start(0, 1);
nowPlaying.text = soundNext;
// define handler for button events
beats01.onRelease = beats02.onRelease =
➥ beats03.onRelease=beats04.onRelease =
➥ function () {
  soundNext = this._name;
  dynamicSound.attachSound(soundNext);
  dynamicSound.start(0, 1);
  nowPlaying.text = soundNext;
};
// stop the timeline
stop();
```

Try this out (CTRL+ENTER/CMD+ENTER) for a taste of what can happen when Flash sound goes wrong. Each sound is **musically unsynchronized**. It plays when you click a button and, unless you're rather more tuned in to hitting sounds "on the beat" (to use the remix DJ terminology), the overall track created is less than musical!

10. Well, you know what needs to be done. The whole point of this exercise was to put the onSoundComplete event through its paces, so let's see that put into practice. Change the button event handler as shown:

```
beats01.onRelease = beats02.onRelease =
➥ beats03.onRelease = beats04.onRelease =
➥ function () {
  soundNext = this._name;
  nextTrack.text = soundNext;
};
```

This time, the buttons don't change the sound immediately; they only set the soundNext variable to the next sound file that has been requested. What you want to do is change to the requested sound "on the beat," or when the current sound has completed. You guessed it—onSoundComplete. Add the following code between the end of the button script and the stop() as shown.

```
  soundNext = this._name;
  nextTrack.text = soundNext;
};
// trigger next sound
dynamicSound.onSoundComplete = function() {
  dynamicSound.attachSound(soundNext);
  dynamicSound.start(0, 1);
  nowPlaying.text = soundNext;
};
// stop the timeline
stop();
```

Test run the movie again, and you'll hear quite a difference! When you listen to it, you'll understand why it's so ingenious. The sounds won't just change as soon as you click one of the buttons—they'll change only after the track that's currently playing has finished. This means that your little techno tune stays in a musical beat sequence no matter what you do!

When you first click one of the buttons, you'll see the nextTrack text field updated immediately, but there's no change to the nowPlaying field and, more important, there's no change in the sound. However, once the current clip has played through, both will change to match the clip shown in nextTrack.

This is sequencing to the nearest beat in a four-beat sequence. A dance DJ or remix artist would call this **mixing in on the beat**, *and most other musical types would call it a* **sequencing loop**.

Controlling sound from ActionScript

Thanks to the Sound class, you can use ActionScript to manipulate your sound clips in more subtle ways than you've looked at so far (where all you've really done is control the start and stop instant). In particular, you can alter two aspects of the original sound: the **volume** (how loud the sound is) and the **panning** (the balance of sound you hear in each speaker). The ActionScript Sound class has two methods that allow you to make the changes that you want: setVolume() and setPan().

setVolume()

This method allows you to vary the total volume produced by a sound object. The values that change this are pretty obvious:

- sound.setVolume(0): This value gives you 0% volume (silence).
- sound.setVolume(100): This value gives you the maximum volume, which largely depends on your speaker setup.

setPan()

The sound object's setPan() method allows you to vary the sound level in each speaker—that is, the

balance between them. The values that you can apply to it alter the sound accordingly:

- sound.setPan(0): This value gives an equal balance in the left and right speakers.
- sound.setPan(-100): This value gives the full current volume in the left speaker, and nothing in the right.
- sound.setPan(100): This value gives the full current volume in the right speaker, and nothing in the left.

Let's put this information to use and design a simple sound control system.

Building sound controls

When you look at the following images, imagine the black square is a stage as viewed from above. The black dot is you sitting in front of the stage, and the white dot is a musician on the stage. As you drag the white dot around the stage area, you want ActionScript to dynamically alter the stereo image, or panning, and the volume of the music to reflect the performer's movement around the stage.

Say the musician is standing right in front of you by the footlights. You'll hear the sound at a maximum volume, in your left and right ears equally.

If the musician then moves toward the back of the stage—assuming, of course, that he or she isn't using a microphone—and plays at the same level, the sound will become equally faint in both of your ears.

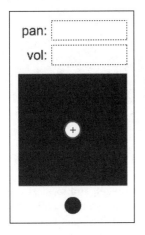

If the musician moves down and across to stage left, you'll hear more sound in your left ear than in your right ear (and vice versa if the musician moves to stage right).

Let's go to work.

You'll reproduce this setup, creating a draggable white dot. This dot will control a sound instance via the setVolume() and setPan() methods. The effect of this will be that the sound you hear from your computer (assuming you have stereo speakers appropriately connected and placed) will be exactly the same as if you stood in the same position as the black dot in the preceding description.

1. This example is called controls.fla in the download for this chapter if you get stuck. Once again, set up two layers called actions and interface, and use File ➤ Import ➤ Import to Library to import any one of the loop files you've used before into the Library. Right-click (CTRL-click on a Mac) to select Linkage from the context menu and set the sound clip to Export for ActionScript with a linkage identifier of loop. Your Library should look something like the following image, the important thing being that the Linkage column for your sound file is the same as the one shown (Export: loop).

2. You'll create some symbols that need to be centered on the symbol registration point. By default, all measurements shown on the Properties panel are from the top-left corner. To change this so that measurements are shown from the center, bring up the Info panel (Window ➤ Design Panels ➤ Info). In the 3×3 matrix (the cursor is pointing to it in the following image), select the middle square. This forces Flash to measure position from the center of each item.

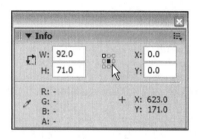

3. Select Insert ➤ New Symbol and create a new movie clip called puck. Draw a circle with a white fill and black stroke of 1.5, and then select it (double-click the fill to select both the fill and stroke). Using the Properties panel, give the circle a height and width of 15 pixels and a position of (−7.5, −7.5).

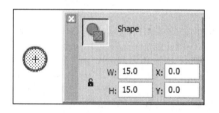

4. Return to the main timeline. Now create a second movie clip (again with Insert ➤ New Symbol) called controller, and place a strokeless black square, 100 pixels across, in the center of the stage. You can use the Properties panel to fine-tune its size and position as before.

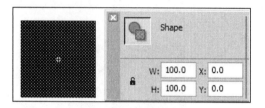

5. Add a small black circle just below the black square (to indicate where you're listening from at the front of the stage), and make sure it's placed centrally. (Selecting the circle and using the Properties panel to give it the same values shown in the following image should do this.)

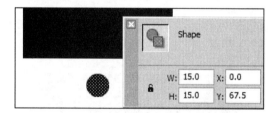

6. Now rename the current layer (which will be called Layer 1) to back. Add new layers called drag button and text. Into layer drag button, drag a copy of the puck movie clip from the Library, place it center stage (that is, give it a position of (0.0, 0.0)), and give it the instance name puck (so now its symbol name and instance name are the same):

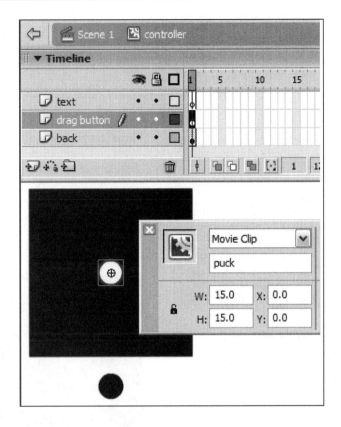

7. In layer text, add a pair of dynamic text fields, giving them the instance names pan and vol. Label the two text fields with static text to the left of each.

Here's how the controller movie clip should look when you're done:

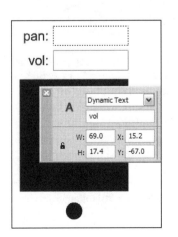

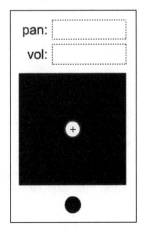

8. Back in the main timeline, drag the controller movie clip from the Library into frame 1 of the interface layer, and give it the instance name controller.

9. Select frame 1 in the actions layer and pin the Actions panel to it.

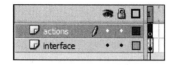

10. You now want to make the percussion sound start playing and loop forever (actually, the maximum number of times that Flash will let you loop a sound is 214,748, so for a sample that's only 1 second long, this amounts to almost 60 hours of looping, which is easily enough for most purposes). Add the following code in the Script pane of the now pinned Actions panel.

```
var loopSound:Sound = new Sound(this);
loopSound.attachSound("loop");
loopSound.start(0,1000);
```

If you test the movie now, you'll hear the sound playing, but you'll have no control over it. Let's fix that.

11. The next step is to wire up the puck so that you can use the mouse to drag it about:

```
function drag() {
  this.startDrag(false, -50, -50, 50, 50);
    this.onMouseMove = function() {
      updateAfterEvent();
    };
}
function drop() {
  this.stopDrag;
  delete this.onMouseMove;
}
var loopSound:Sound = new Sound(this);
loopSound.attachSound("loop");
loopSound.start(0, 1000);
controller.puck.onPress = drag;
controller.puck.onRelease = drop;
controller.puck.onReleaseOutside = drop;
```

> *Notice that you use dot notation here to refer to the movie clip* puck *inside the timeline* controller, *hence the dot notation path* controller.puck.

Although there's a lot of new code, it isn't that hard to see what's going on. The function drag() is used to define what happens when puck is click-dragged, and drop() defines what happens when the puck is dropped.

The function drag()includes the line this.startDrag(false, -50, -50, 50, 50). This line is used to constrain the dragging within the black rectangle that is part of controller.

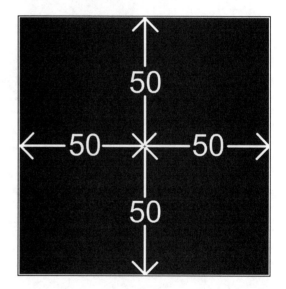

The values I've used represent distances from the center point of controller (which is the position the puck initially starts off at on your stage). Remember that the y direction is measured such that *down is positive* (as is the stage).

OK, the puck now works properly, but it makes no difference to the sound you hear. Nor does it give you values for volume and pan in the dynamic text fields. Hold on, though, you're nearly there! You just need to do a little elementary math.

You need to evaluate setVolume() and setPan() values for the sound object, from the x- and y-coordinates of the drag button. The button can be dragged 50 pixels to the left and 50 pixels to the right from its initial starting position. You need to scale this to −100 to +100 for use in the setPan() method. This is simply a question of doubling the x-coordinate of the button:

(-100 to 100) = (-50 to 50) x 2

So, more generally:

pan level = (button x-coordinate) x 2

Likewise, you can drag the button 50 pixels up and 50 pixels down from its starting position. This must be translated to a range of 0 to 100% for use with the setVolume() method. To do this, you just need to add 50 to the button's y-coordinate:

(100 to 0) = (50 to -50) + 50

That is

volume level = button y-coordinate + 50

Now you're ready to start producing the effects you want.

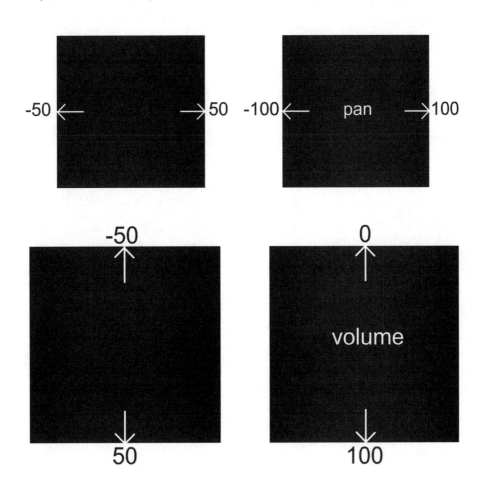

12. The final code adds an onEnterFrame event to the puck every time you click-drag it. This new event converts the puck's position into two variables (pan and vol), which are used to control the panning and volume of the sound instance loopSound. You also update the two text fields to show the current pan and volume values. Here's the finished code:

```
function drag() {
    this.startDrag(false, -50, -50, 50, 50);
    this.onEnterFrame = function() {
        pan = 2*this._x;
        vol = 50+this._y;
        loopSound.setPan(pan);
        loopSound.setVolume(vol);
        this._parent.pan.text = pan;
        this._parent.vol.text = vol;
    };
    this.onMouseMove = function() {
        updateAfterEvent();
    };
}
function drop() {
    this.stopDrag();
    delete this.onEnterFrame;
    delete this.onMouseMove;
}
var pan:Number = 0;
var vol:Number = 0;
var loopSound:Sound = new Sound(this);
loopSound.attachSound("loop");
loopSound.start(0, 1000);
controller.puck.onPress = drag;
controller.puck.onRelease = drop;
controller.puck.onReleaseOutside = drop;
```

Try the movie once again, and you should find that it works. Drag the puck around the stage and you'll hear the sound move from side to side, rising and falling in volume as you move it up and down.

Also worth noting is the way you're dynamically creating events in the code.

- Rather than allow the onEnterFrame to run all the time, you run it only as long as the puck is being dragged.

- The puck is redrawn every time you move the mouse, which is much faster than the frame rate. The text fields are updated at the slower frame rate. This makes for a much more efficient and responsive SWF, as Flash spends more time creating a smoothly animated puck. The user won't notice that the sound methods and text fields are being controlled at a much slower rate than the puck, and they'll get the impression that the whole thing is silky smooth. This is one way to overcome the relative slow speed of the Flash player—cheat!

These sound variations are occurring in real time, in response to how you drag the button. This is a template for creating a dynamic soundscape for your websites or Flash games. As the sound source moves around the screen, you can create the appropriate sound effects on the fly with the sound object and ActionScript. If you convert your simple controller graphic into something that looks like a sound-board control (shown right), you can also very quickly build up an interactive soundboard, allowing users to mix in several loops to create their own remix. You can see a version of this concept in action (although the code is Flash 5) if you download mixer.fla *(7.7MB) from the book* Flash 5 ActionScript Studio *(friends of ED, 2001) from* www.friendsofed.com. *If they get enough requests, maybe friends of ED will also put up a Flash MX 2004 version!*

Dealing with large sound files: Compression and streaming

As you've probably noticed by now, most sound files tend to weigh in on the heavy side. A lot of information goes into making a small snippet of sound, and the size of your audio files will most likely reflect this. If you're making local movies for a non-web audience using stand-alone kiosks, for example, or you're blessed with clients who all have limitless bandwidth via a fast intranet, then this might not be a problem.

If you're designing anything for the wider realms of the Web, you must think carefully about the size of files you work with. Most folks simply aren't going to stick around long enough to see the fruit of your labor if that fruit takes 20 minutes to download. This is one reason sound on the Web hasn't been as common in the past as it might have been.

In recent years, though, two technologies have helped change things for the better: **compression** and **external sound files**.

Compression

Compression is a process involving squishing big files into smaller files, and figuring out what information is important and what can be thrown out, so that you end up with a version of the file that's still adequate for the job, but isn't so large. The best-known form of audio (sound) compression is MP3, which typically squeezes sound files down to one-tenth (or less) of their original size without much audible loss of quality.

As I mentioned at the start of this chapter, Flash can work with MP3 files—along with many other compressed sound formats too numerous to discuss here—in just the same way as uncompressed WAVs and AIFFs. However, in general you'll rarely use anything other than MP3 because the others are really just legacy formats included for backward compatibility.

Here are some points to keep in mind when you consider compressing Flash files that include sound:

- Flash has the option to compress the whole SWF (File ➤ Publish Settings ➤ Flash), and this takes up performance bandwidth of the player for other things during streaming. If the SWF content is already compressed (that is, it consists of lots of sound), then you should consider not compressing it.

- You'll typically use high compression rates (for small file sizes) for sound, and you should consider using sound files that compress well. Generally, low, bassy sounds compress much better than high-frequency sounds.

- Rather than accept the default compression settings, you should look at each sound file separately and find the best compression settings for each. Sound is bandwidth heavy, and it can be the biggest part of your SWF file, so take every precaution to minimize the file sizes. To compress sounds individually, right-click/CTRL-click a sound in the Library and select Properties from the context menu that appears. Change the Compression drop-down setting from Default to one of the other options (usually MP3). You can see the effect of your changes to file size via a line of text at the bottom of the dialog box that compares the original file size with the compressed one. You can also listen to the compressed sound by clicking the Test button.

So, there are things you can do to bring down file sizes using compression, but that's only one part of the solution.

> *Note that the* Quality *setting has no effect on file size. It simply changes the trade-off between compressed sound quality and the amount of time it takes to turn your FLA's sound files into compressed SWF assets. For most modern computers, consider setting this to* Best, *unless doing so makes SWF compilation unacceptably slow.*

External sound files

Flash allows you to load sounds as individual files. By "individual" I mean separate from the SWF that actually plays them. The advantages of this include the following:

- Your sound files don't increase the size of the SWF, which would otherwise cause the initial site download to be much longer.

- You can load sound files only when they're requested. For example, if you're developing a Flash jukebox that allows the user to select from a number of different song files, you don't want to load the songs until they're selected to be played. To do otherwise may involve SWFs that run into MBs!

- You can choose which versions of a sound file to load at runtime. You can select between high-quality and low-quality files to cater to users utilizing different bandwidths.

Flash can load a sound file in two ways: it can load a streaming sound or an event sound.

- A **streaming sound** is just that: it streams from the Web. It's downloaded from the Web every time you want to play the associated audio, and the associated audio can begin before the sound is fully loaded.

- An **event sound** is associated with events, that is, a sound you want to start playing as soon as something happens, such as a button click. For the sound to be able to play immediately on receipt of the event, it can't wait to download, so event sounds must have fully loaded before they can be played. The upside of event sounds is that you have to load them only once; the downside of event sounds is that the sounds have to be fully loaded before you can hear any of them.

> *Generally, you should use streaming sounds for long pieces of audio, such as songs for a jukebox. Event sounds are more useful for spot effects, such as UI click sounds.*

A streaming sound will start playing as soon as enough of it has loaded in to fill a sound buffer, which is 5 seconds by default. You can change the buffer duration by changing the _soundbuftime of any movie clip. (Note that this will change the buffer time of the whole Flash player, not just that of the current movie clip.) Once the buffer has filled to the minimum level, the sound will continue to load the sound file, playing it at the same time. Once the sound has completed, you need to load it again to hear it again.

An event sound needs to load in fully before it can start playing. Once the event sound has loaded, though, you can use it much like a sound in the Library; you don't have to reload it every time you want to start the sound again.

Many people seem to have trouble with loading external sound files, so here are a few tips:

- You can load only external MP3 files into Flash. Flash is very picky about exactly which MP3 files it will load. If you can import the file into the Flash authoring tool (File ➤ Import), chances are good that the file will also load without problems at SWF runtime.

- Another issue to watch out for is that your operating system may show MP3 files and WAV files using the same file icon, so be sure you're asking Flash to load an MP3! In my Windows XP–based machine, MP3s and WAVs appear with the two following icons because I've set up my operating system to open MP3 files with iTunes and WAV files with Windows Media Player. If you don't want to do something like this, you need to view the properties of the file (right-click and select Properties in Windows XP) to see what the file type actually is.

songLoop   songLoop

Let's have a look at using both streaming and event sounds.

Loading a streaming sound

You'll need the files `soundLoader.fla` and `song.mp3` from the download for this chapter. For the effect to work properly, you need to perform these steps:

1. Publish `soundLoader.fla` (File ➤ Publish).

2. Copy the files created, `soundLoader.swf` and `soundLoader.html` to the Web. Copy the file `song.mp3` to the same location.

3. Browse to `soundLoader.html` to view the SWF over the Web.

You can also view the files locally, but you won't see the full effect.

When you view the HTML, you'll see the following button:

Clicking this button will make a loading message appear. Once the percent loaded reaches a certain value (around 5%), you'll begin to hear the song play over the Web. The percentage loaded message will continue to advance as you listen to the song.

Once the song has fully loaded (a few seconds after you see the loading value reach 100%), you'll see the message change to tell you the song has finished loading. You'll most likely continue to hear the song for some time after this message has appeared. If you run the SWF from your local hard drive, the fully loaded message (shown in the following image) will appear immediately.

The thing to notice here is that the MP3 file is 2.5MB, but you don't have to wait for 2.5MB worth of

downloaded SWF before you see the button, and neither do you have to wait for the full 2.5MB file to load before you see something.

> *If you listen to the song over a 56K or lower band-width connection, you may hear the song occasionally pause. This is because the MP3 is loading at a slower rate than that needed to play through the song without any pauses. You'll look at how to prevent this in a moment.*

What happens here is something very much like a streaming SWF. The song starts playing before it's fully loaded in. You've created a simple web music player using streaming sound!

Let's have a look at how it works. Open `soundLoader.fla` and have a look at the main timeline. This consists of two layers, actions and interface. Layer interface contains a button, `startLoad`, plus a dynamic text field loaded and associated static text.

The main meat is, of course, in the code on layer actions:

```
function loadProgress() {
  loaded.text = "loading: " + Math.round
➥ (100*song. getBytesLoaded()/
➥ song.getBytesTotal())+"%";
}
function loadDone() {
  loaded.text = "loaded";
  delete _root.onEnterFrame;
}
var song:Sound = new Sound(this);
song.onLoad = loadDone;
startLoad.onRelease = function() {
```

```
    song.loadSound("techno.mp3", true);
    _root.onEnterFrame = loadProgress;
};
```

The main code starts by defining a new sound called song. You then define an onLoad event for song that will run the function loadDone when the sound file associated with song is fully loaded into the SWF. loadDone enters the text loaded into the text field and deletes the onEnterFrame that updates the percent loaded message in the same text field.

The final few lines of the main code set up an onRelease script for the button. This runs the line to load the MP3:

```
    song.loadSound("techno.mp3", true);
```

The loadSound() method has two arguments: the URL of the MP3 file you want to load and whether you want to stream the sound file (that is, load it as a streaming sound). For a streaming file, the second argument is true.

The button script also defines the function loadProgress() as the onEnterFrame for the main timeline, and this function generates the percent loaded status message until the file is fully loaded. Easy!

Sometimes you may want to stop a loadSound(). *There is no method to do this. The best way to handle this is to delete the sound instance you're loading into (in this example, with a* delete *song; line within a "stop download button"* onRelease *script).*

Loading an event sound

Loading your event sounds rather than placing them into a Library and using linkage identifiers has several advantages:

- You can decide when to load the event sounds. Using the Library/linkage identifier way means that you have to load all the sounds at frame 1 of your site, which can be undesirable.

- You can choose which set of sounds you load. This allows you to change the site sounds dynamically. For example, you might want a different set of sounds for low-bandwidth users and high-bandwidth users. Where you're creating an international site with spoken words, you have the ability to choose from a number of different regional speech samples.

- You can easily modify the sounds. Keeping the sound files separate from the SWF means that you (or even the client) can modify the sounds after the site is up very easily. You simply replace the sound files—no SWF redesign necessary!

To load an event sound, set the second argument of the loadSound() method to false, as shown in the following listing:

```
var clickSound:Sound = new Sound(this);
  clickSound.onLoad = function() {
  this.start(0, 1);
};
clickSound.loadSound("beats01.mp3",
➥ false);
```

The only downside of using loaded event sounds is that the sounds have to be loaded in before they can be sounded, so the earliest you can listen to a sound is after the onLoad event has triggered. Any start() methods you attempt before this event won't sound. Also worth noting is the fact that you must define the onLoad event handler *before* you attempt the loadSound(), otherwise the onLoad event handler will never run in some cases. If the clickSound.loadSound line appeared in the preceding code before the clickSound.onLoad definition, the code would not work online (although you would probably get away with it offline).

If you want to check whether a sound file has actually loaded (for both event and streaming sound), you can add a parameter called success to the onLoad event handler. To modify the preceding code so that you can detect a failure of the sound file to load, use something along the lines of the following code:

```
var clickSound:Sound = new Sound(this);
clickSound.onLoad = function(success) {
  if (success) {
    this.start(0, 1);
```

```
    } else {
      // code to handle failure to load
      // the sound
    }
  };
  clickSound.loadSound("beats01.mp3", false);
```

A final point to note when you use separate MP3 files is the issue of *security*. When you embed MP3 files into the SWF, the user can't easily use the MP3 files for his or her own use (because you can't listen to a SWF on an iPod!).

Many recording artists shy away from making MP3 files of their records available on a traditional website, because the listener might just burn the MP3 onto a CD-ROM, make it available on file-sharing networks, or save it onto an iPod. Flash allows a much greater level of protection when the MP3 is embedded within a SWF (although it can still be extracted using the right tools and a bit of know-how).

When you load MP3 files separately, they become accessible (the user will be able to find the MP3 files in the browser cache, which the user can find by searching his or her computer for "mp3" after visiting the site). To avoid this, you can rename the MP3 files in one of the following two ways:

- Your MP3 files don't have an .mp3 file extension. So instead of this:

  ```
  clickSound.loadSound("beats01.mp3", false);
  ```

  you would use this:

  ```
  clickSound.loadSound("beats01", false);
  ```

  and place the file beats01 instead of beats01.mp3 on your web server. The user wouldn't be able to play the MP3 file on his or her iPod unless the user knew he or she had found an MP3 file and added the .mp3 extension to the file.

- Your MP3 files have an extension other than .mp3. If you're particularly devious, you could rename your MP3 file to *anything* else that a user would be

expected to see in a browser cache. Renaming your MP3 file to top_bar.gif, for example, would totally confuse everyone!

```
mySound.loadSound("top_bar.gif", false);
```

This will work perfectly if top_bar.gif is actually an MP3 file, because Flash ignores file extensions. Flash needs to see extensions as part of the file-name string, but it doesn't actually recognize them in any other way. Your operating system, however, will try to prevent you from attempting to play this file on your iPod.

Book project: Adding data to the Futuremedia site

So far you've thought about adding navigation structure as data, but you haven't implemented it. You've also given users a way to move forward in the site, but they still can't move backward. There's a very good reason for this: without data that defines the forward path, you can't go back

Something you may have picked up on is that in defining navigation links as data, you separated the data from the actual content. Normally, you create a web page, adding all the links on the individual buttons within the page, and the linking data is therefore part of the content and site graphics.

In Futuremedia, you're going to add the links on a site that's still free of *any* content. Although this may go against the grain when compared with simple sites you may have designed before, it actually leads to a very flexible design. The Futuremedia site UI and navigation links are separate from the final content, so you can define the overall UI separately from the client content.

The fact that the Futuremedia site currently appears to let you go forward is an illusion. It shows only the forward animation, but it doesn't actually go anywhere.

Obviously, there's the issue of the graphics—the UI look and feel has to match seamlessly with the content. This isn't an issue for the code, though, which will stay the same.

You need to make the final connections that turn the UI from a pretty set of interactive color swatches into something you can actually use as a website. Here's a to-do list of steps you need to perform:

- First, you'll create the data structure. You did that in the last chapter (via the separate test file futuremedia_database.fla), so all you really need to do is transfer the data structure into the site.

- Second, you'll populate the data structure with your navigation data.

- Third, you have to get Flash to use the data, so that when you click a strip, the site takes you to the appropriate page.

Creating the data structure

The first of the three to-do list tasks is creating the data structure. You've already more or less defined this in the previous chapter, so the only thing to do is write a function that creates the structure and put it somewhere appropriate in your code.

You need to continue working on the FLA you ended with last chapter with. If you want to use my FLA, use the futuremedia_code03.fla file from last chapter. The end result of this chapter is futuremedia_code04 .fla, if you get stuck.

You'll define your data array, page, and then create a new function, navigationData(), that uses page. You also need to call navigationData(), so you can also add a line for that while you're here. Add lines as shown to the end of the script (just before the last stop()):

```
// Set UI colors...
tricolor.setCol(color0, color1, color2);
// Define and populate database
var page:Array = new Array();
navigationData();
// now sit back and let the event scripts
// handle everything
stop();
```

The place to add the following function is after the DEFINE MAIN SETUP SCRIPTS block of functions (that is, after the end of the stripPage() function at line 84 in futuremedia_code03.fla):

```
// DEFINE SITE NAVIGATION DATA
navigationData = function () {
// define and populate page data structure
//
  for (var i=0; i<50; i++) {
    // define structure...
    page[i] = new Object();
    page[i].pType = new String();
    page[i].pLink = new Array();
    page[i].pTitle = new Array();
    page[i].pID = new String();
    page[i].pURL = new String();
  }
};
```

The basic data structure is now in place. If you run the FLA in debug mode, you'll see this data structure appear on _level0. Clicking the little + icon will reveal 50 page entries.

OK, you've set up your data structure. Now comes the tricky part: what to put in it!

Defining your data

A number of parameters define the website, and you need to decide what values each should take. Some of you might be thinking, "Hey, this is a bit like the parameters in components. . . ." (which you'll look at next chapter). Well, if you *are* thinking this, congratulations! You're right on the money.

Components are dependent on parameters that define their look and feel. These parameters *configure* the components, and the full set of parameters is sometimes called the **configuration data**. You can think of what you're doing as the next level of this. The whole site is just one big component, and right now you're sorting out the parameter list on a rather large sitewide Properties panel!

Page type pType

This is one of the easier parameters, because you can have only two possible values: contentPage and linkPage. You'll therefore make the page type a string value, "contentPage" or "linkPage":

    pType = "contentPage" or "linkPage"

Page links pLink

This is a difficult parameter to tie down because there seems to be so many possible configurations. Each strip can link to another page, or there's the possibility that there is no link. So you can have any number of links, from zero to the maximum number of links, three.

How do you represent that? Well, the Romans had the same problem. They could represent any positive number, but they didn't see the logic in representing "no number" (what we now call zero) as a number. Arabic includes a zero, and that's why we use the Arabic digits 0 to 9 when we count—*doing so allows us to fill the spaces where there is no value.* The Romans didn't appreciate the beauty of this concept and had a strange number system that's useless for representing large numbers because it requires so many different symbols. In the same way, as long as you treat "no link" the same as an actual link, *you always have the same number of links, and your link data for each page becomes the same.*

How do you represent a nonlink? Well, a common programming trick is to give "nondata" a special value. You'll make a nonlink point to a page that doesn't exist, page –1 (you can't use 0, because that's a valid page). If a –1 is seen by the code, then you should write the code to recognize that this actually means "no link." If any other number is seen (such as 23 or 2), the link should be taken as valid.

    pLink[0] = link for strip 0 (number or -1
    ➥ for no link)
    pLink[1] = link for strip 1 (number or -1
    ➥ for no link)
    pLink[2] = link for strip 2 (number or -1
    ➥ for no link)

> *Some programmers prefer to use the value* null *instead of –1. The* null *value is a special constant that represents "no value set."*

OK, that's a rather esoteric set of information. Let's see how this works through an example. Suppose page 6 links to

- Page 4 if you click strip 0
- Page 3 if you click strip 1
- Nowhere if you click strip 2

You could represent this with the following line:

    page[6].pLink = [4, 3, -1];

page[6].pLink[0] tells you that when you click strip 0, you need to jump to page 4, and page[6].pLink[2] tells you that if you click strip 2, no navigation should occur because the link points to page –1.

Page titles title

You need four titles:

- One for the navigation title (at the top left)
- One for each of the three strips

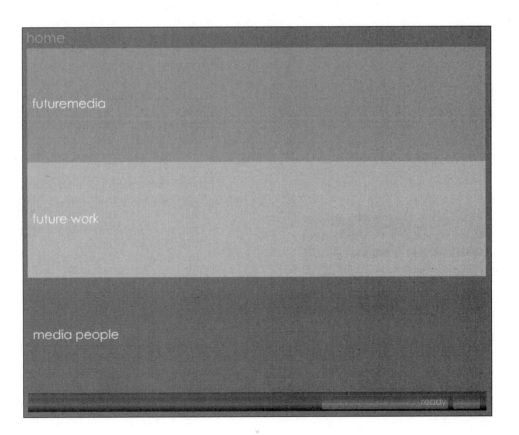

That's four in all, and because you need four separate strings, you'll need to use another array.

```
title = [mainTitle,titleStrip1,
➥ titleStrip2, titleStrip3]
```

The home page of the final site has titles as shown in the following image. It has a main title, home, and the three individual strip titles futuremedia, future work, and media people.

To define the titles for this page (noting that the home page is page 0), you use this:

```
page[0].titles = ["home","futuremedia",
➥ "future work","media people"];
```

Setting the content linkage identifier and URL

These final two parameters define where to get the content from. They need to be used only if the current page is a contentPage, and they'll all be string values. A minor issue is what to set them to if they're unused. You'll set them to "non", although you could just as easily leave them undefined or set to null.

Some of you may notice that you're actually defining more information than you need to—Flash can infer the values of some of the parameters from other parameters. For example, if a page is a contentPage, then you know that you won't link to anywhere via the strips, so pLinks 0, 1, and 2 will all be –1. Although you could do it that way, I prefer to always define enough data to make it clear to me and not just the computer. Code clarity is usually more important than efficiency when you're writing large amounts of code.

Redundant data can also act as an aid in debugging. In fact, all error detection relies on redundant data, and spoken human languages are full of redundancy. That's why you can still understand someone with an accent dissimilar to yours—you only have to understand every other word that person says, because around 50% of spoken language is redundant.

Populating the data with default values

You next need to populate your data with default values. Why? Well, it's actually efficient to do so. Not only does it make debugging easier (everything has a definite value rather than being undefined), but it also shows the final data structure before any real data is entered.

Add the following code to navigationData() to initialize each piece of data as you define it:

```
// DEFINE SITE NAVIGATION DATA
navigationData = function () {
  // define and populate page data
➥ structure
  //
  for (var i = 0; i<50; i++) {
    // define structure...
    page[i] = new Object();
    page[i].pType = new String();
    page[i].pLink = new Array();
    page[i].pTitle = new Array();
    page[i].pID = new String();
    page[i].pURL = new String();
    // populate with default values...
    page[i].pType = "non";
    page[i].pLink = [-1, -1, -1];
    page[i].pTitle = ["warning > unlinked
➥ page > site error", "error", "error",
➥ "please contact the site owner"];
    page[i].pID = "non";
    page[i].pURL = "non";
  }
};
```

If you now look at the database entries (select Control ➤ Debug Movie and look at the Variables tab for _level0), you'll see that each one has a set of default values:

Name	Value
⊞ 4	
⊟ 5	
pID	"non"
⊟ pLink	
0	-1
1	-1
2	-1
⊟ pTitle	
0	"warning > unlinked page > site error"
1	"error"
2	"error"
3	"please contact the site owner"
pType	"non"
pURL	"non"
⊞ 6	
⊞ 7	

Populating the actual data values

You're finally ready to start defining the data. It should be noted that, because this is a book on ActionScript rather than Flash site design, I won't go too much into the reasoning behind the pages, page content, and the nature of the general site page structure, although it's fairly self-evident.

Although you'll introduce all the data for your site, during actual development, I added pages as they were needed (one of the advantages of the design is its flexibility). For the purposes of continuity, I've included the full site data up front.

*Another point worth mentioning is the use of the word "**field**." It's identical in meaning to the term "**property**," although "field" is used when describing databases. The reason for this is that the records that describe each page are obviously objects. "Obviously" comes from the fact that every bit of data (apart from the low-level primitive data types String, Number, and Boolean) is invariably an object whenever you use any modern computer language.*

Even the low-level primitive data types are usually objects (because they have an associated class), but most languages don't force you to treat them as such for purely historical reasons. Most computer languages are based on non-OOP versions some way down the line, and these all had strings, numbers, and Booleans, but not the classes to make them objects.

To begin, let's have a look at how the pages will look and how they'll link. You have three links and four titles for each page's page[pageNumber].

page[pageNumber]

pTitle[0]

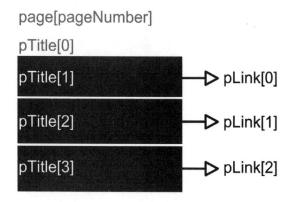

The home page will look like this in terms of data:

page[0] *home page*

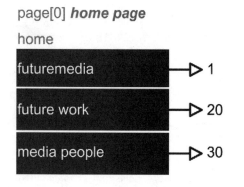

I decided on three main areas for the home page:

- futuremedia tells users what Futuremedia is all about.
- future work includes a client list and links to personal work.
- media people includes information about the Futuremedia designers.

You can tell that this will be a link page from the diagram, because it has, um, *links*.

The data to define this page is as follows:

```
page[00].pType = "linkPage"
page[00].pLink = [01, 20, 30]
page[00].pTitle = ["home", "futuremedia",
➥ "future work", "media people"]
```

The futuremedia strip will send users to page 1, and the links from the other two strips will take users to pages 20 and 30, respectively, as shown in the preceding diagram.

Pages 1, 20, and 30 look like this:

page[1] *futuremedia*

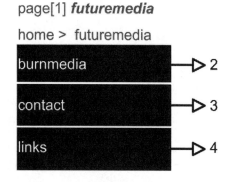

```
page[01].pType = "linkPage"
page[01].pLink = [02, 03, 04]
page[01].pTitle = ["home > futuremedia",
➥ "burnmedia", "contact", "links"]
```

page[20] *future work*

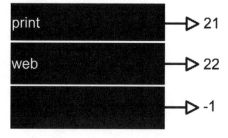

```
page[20].pType = "linkPage"
page[20].pLink = [21, 22, -1]
page[20].pTitle = ["home >  future work",
➥ "print", "web", ""]
```

page[30] *media people*

home > media people

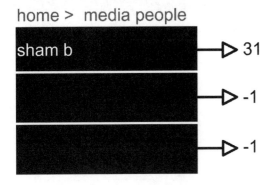

There are a couple of things to notice here:

- Unused strips are given a link of –1.
- Unused titles are given a text string of "".

To add this data to the code, simply add it to the end of the function navigationData(). You *could* just add it directly to the code, but let's think about this first. At the end of this book, you'll end up with the Futuremedia site. Hopefully, you don't want your home site to look like mine. You want to start adding your own pages and content to replace mine. So what you really want is to have the configuration data that goes into the database be easily editable. When you start changing the site, you probably don't want to go around changing the code. You would rather change just the configuration data.

Let's fix it so that you can do this. You'll create a **configuration file** that contains the site database. Add the following line at the end of the function navigationData():

```
    page[i].pID = "non";
    page[i].pURL = "non";
  }
  #include "config.as"
};
```

The new line containing #include *must not* have a semicolon (;) at the end of it *because it's not a part of ActionScript*. It's a compiler directive. During the process of turning the FLA into a SWF, Flash will compile the script into something called **byte code**, which is what the Flash player reads at runtime. Without going into specifics, byte code is a highly optimized version of the original ActionScript listing. The compiler will do this conversion for each line in turn. When it encounters #, the compiler will realize that this line isn't a line of ActionScript, but is an order (or **directive**) to the compiler itself. The compiler will read on and encounter the include "config.as" part. This line tells the compiler, "Go and find the file config.as and insert its contents at this point in the listing. Then continue compiling."

The SWF will turn out the same as if you had simply added the lines in config.as in the listing itself, but you have an advantage: you've created two files.

- One that defines the site UI, futuremedia_codexx .fla
- One that defines the configuration for any given site, config.as

You've done that thing again—you've modularized the code! You now have two separate bits of code, and you can manage the project much better for it.

You should note that the AS file is merged with the SWF at compile time and isn't separate when you look at the final (runtime) site files. You could make the configuration separate during runtime, something that has definite advantages, because it allows you to change the configuration dynamically, which gives you a much more complex site design. For now, you'll stick to the one SWF because it's easier.

If you test the FLA now, you'll see this error:

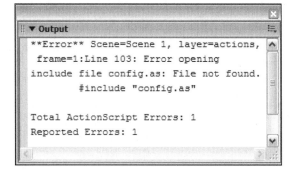

```
▼ Output
**Error** Scene=Scene 1, layer=actions,
  frame=1:Line 103: Error opening
include file config.as: File not found.
        #include "config.as"


Total ActionScript Errors: 1
Reported Errors: 1
```

This is the Flash compiler telling you it can't find the file `config.as`. Well, of course it can't—you still need to write it!

Creating the Futuremedia configuration

Those of you who are using the Professional edition of Flash will have a slightly easier time in this section, because you have a dedicated full-screen editor for writing AS files. The non-Professional folks don't need to worry too much, though—they can still do everything, it's just a bit less intuitive.

If you're using the Standard edition of Flash, you can skip the next section and catch up with the rest of us at the exercise titled "Creating the configuration file: Standard edition."

Creating the configuration file: Professional edition

If you own the Professional edition, you'll create the file `config.as` as follows:

1. Select File ➤ New. In the New Document dialog box, select ActionScript File.

> **New Document**
>
> General | Templates
>
> Type:
> - Flash Document
> - Flash Slide Presentation
> - Flash Form Application
> - ActionScript File
> - ActionScript Communication File
> - Flash JavaScript File
> - Flash Project

2. A new document window opens. You'll notice that all the other major panels are now grayed-out, and the only active thing is a very large Actions panel. This is the Professional user's dedicated script editor:

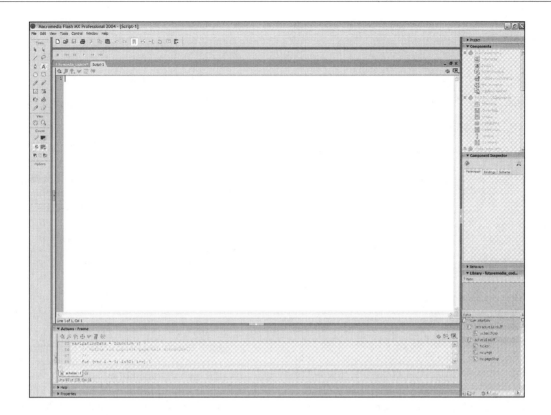

3. Save the file in the same folder as the FLA in progress as config.as. You now have two tabs at the top of the screen: one for the FLA and one for the AS file (currently called Script-1). This allows you to edit both pretty much at the same time.

4. Now that you have a professional-grade set of files to manage in the Futuremedia project, you should have some professional file management going on. If you don't already see the Project pane, select Window ➤ Project to bring it up (shown right). Click the new project link.

Flash will prompt you to name a new file of type FLP (Flash Project). Call it futuremedia and save it in the same place as the other two files. You can save this file anywhere, but you'll save it in the same place as the other stuff for now so that everyone's on the same page.

379

5. You're now ready to define your project files. The Project panel looks like this:

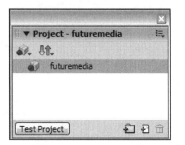

At the top are two icons. The one to the left (the yellow box) is the Project icon. Select this icon to switch between projects. If you've never used the Project panel before, you should have only one project displaying so far: futuremedia. The next icon (the up and down arrows) is for version control. This icon allows you to manage your site once it's online, so you can make sure you have all the latest files uploaded and so on. It's particularly useful for sites with many different files, which is what the Futuremedia site will become by the end of the book—just wait and see!

At the bottom of the panel are a button and three icons. The Test Project button makes Flash compile all your project files to create a finished site. The Add Folder to Project icon does just what its name suggests. Rather like layer and Library folders, it allows you to tidy up your project structure. The Add File(s) to Project icon and Remove from Project icon (which is currently grayed-out because there are no files to delete) allow you to add and delete files from the project, respectively.

To add your two files to the project, select the Add File(s) to Project icon, and choose futuremedia_code04.fla (or whatever you're calling your version) and config.as. The Project panel should now look like this:

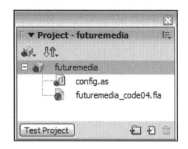

Next you need to define a **default document**. This is the document that Flash will compile first. Select futuremedia_code04.fla and right-click/CTRL-click it. Select Make Default Document from the context menu. The futuremedia_code04.fla file will now change to the default document icon.

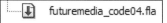

6. You can now test the project. First, save any changes made so far in futuremedia_code04.fla and config.as. You can check if there are any changes to save per file by looking for an asterisk (*) at the end of the tabs at the top of the editor. For example, the config.as file needs saving in the tab in the following image.

Although some multiple-file compilation systems will raise an error if any files have unsaved changes in them, Flash doesn't. It's up to you to check! You can quickly save all unsaved files by clicking all tabs with an asterisk (*) showing and pressing CTRL+S/CMD+S.

At the moment, the `config.as` file is empty, so there's nothing new in the way of code created by the steps you've taken so far. What *will* happen is that the "file not found" error for `config.as` will now not appear.

> Those of you with some experience in other programming environments are probably thinking, "Hey, you could have made the whole code listing an AS file, and within this AS file called out to the `config.as` file. That way you would have a FLA containing the graphics only, an AS file containing the ActionScript, and a second AS file containing the configuration."
>
> The reason I didn't do this is I wanted to teach you how to use the Actions panel before I introduced the Professional edition's file-management features. If you have the Professional edition and you'll modify Futuremedia for your own ends, the "one FLA file and two AS files" is a setup you might consider changing over to.

You can skip to the "Populating the configuration file" section if you don't want to know how the Standard edition users will set up their AS files.

Creating the configuration file: Standard edition

If you own the Standard edition of Flash, to create the file `config.as` you need to follow these steps:

1. Select File ➤ New. In the New Document dialog box, select Flash Document.

2. Pin the Actions panel to frame 1 of the main timeline of the new file. Without entering anything in the Actions panel, click the Actions panel's menu (the icon at the top-right corner of the Actions panel). Select Export Script from the menu that appears. Call the file `config` and save it in the same folder as the main Futuremedia site (in this case, `futuremedia_code04.fla`).

3. You can now test the project. Select the tab corresponding to the FLA at the top of the screen, and then select Control ➤ Test Movie.

> Every time you make changes to `config.as`, *you need to resave the file as you did in step 2. Flash will compile the last saved version of this file when it encounters #include, not the version you're currently editing.*
>
> To load the `config.as` *file into the Standard edition of Flash, use the Actions panel's menu again, but this time select* Import Script.

At the moment, the `config.as` file is empty, so there's nothing new in the way of code created by the steps you've taken so far. What *will* happen is that the "file not found" error for `config.as` will now not appear.

Populating the configuration file

The finished Futuremedia site has a large number of pages defined as per the process outlined earlier. To enter this data you can do one of the following:

- Type the following listing into your `config.as` file (this is *not* recommended!).

- Load the `configuration.txt` file in a text reader (such as Notepad if you're a Windows user). Copy the entire text, paste the text into `config.as`, and save `config.as`.

- Use your version of `config.as`.

> Advanced readers who know XML will realize that, instead of using a compile-time #include file, they can use a runtime XML file. This second option is very easy to set up—all you have to do is parse the XML data into the local database. Using XML, of course, has advantages over using an #include because the XML can be dynamically generated, allowing you to create pages on the fly and making the Futuremedia UI a quick and easy front-end to a web application.

Anyway, here's the data that Futuremedia uses (as of this writing):

```
// define data...
//
//
// HOME LEVEL
//
// Page 00 -  home (linking page)
page[00].pType = "linkPage";
page[00].pLink = [01, 20, 30];
page[00].pTitle = ["home", "futuremedia",
➥ "future work", "media people"];
//
//
// FIRST STRIP NAVIGATION TREE
//
// Page 01 - futuremedia (linking page)
page[01].pType = "linkPage";
page[01].pLink = [02, 03, 04];
page[01].pTitle = ["home >  futuremedia",
➥ "burnmedia", "contact", "links"];
//
// Page 02 - burnmedia (content page)
page[02].pType = "contentPage";
page[02].pLink = [-1, -1, -1];
page[02].pTitle = ["home >  futuremedia >
➥ burnmedia", "", "", ""];
page[02].pID = "futureTV";
//
// page 03 - contact (content page)
page[03].pType = "contentPage";
page[03].pLink = [-1, -1, -1];
page[03].pTitle = ["home >  futuremedia >
➥ contact", "", "", ""];
page[03].pID = "map";
//
// page 04 - links (content page)
page[04].pType = "contentPage";
page[04].pLink = [-1, -1, -1];
page[04].pTitle = ["home >  futuremedia >
➥ links", "", "", ""];
page[04].pID = "links";
//
//
// SECOND STRIP NAVIAGATION TREE
//
// Page 20 - future work (link page)
```

```
page[20].pType = "linkPage";
page[20].pLink = [21, 22, -1];
page[20].pTitle = ["home >  future work",
➥ "print", "web", ""];
//
// Page 21 - print (content page)
page[21].pType = "linkPage";
page[21].pLink = [23, 24, -1];
page[21].pTitle = ["home >  future work >
➥ print", "webdesign books", "other",
""];
page[21].pID = "placeholder";
//
// Page 22 - web (content page)
page[22].pType = "contentPage";
page[22].pLink = [-1, -1, -1];
page[22].pTitle = ["home >  future work >
➥ web", "", "", ""];
page[22].pID = "placeholder";
//
// Page 23 - public (content page)
page[23].pType = "contentPage";
page[23].pLink = [-1, -1, -1];
page[23].pTitle = ["home >  future work >
➥ print > webdesign books", "", "", ""];
page[23].pID = "books";
//
// Page 24 - personal (content page)
page[24].pType = "contentPage";
page[24].pLink = [-1, -1, -1];
page[24].pTitle = ["home >  future work >
➥ print > other", "", "", ""];
page[24].pID = "draconis";
// THIRD STRIP NAVIGATION TREE
//
// Page 30 - media people (linking page)
page[30].pType = "linkPage";
page[30].pLink = [31, -1, -1];
page[30].pTitle = ["home >  media people",
➥ "sham b ", "", ""];
//
// page 31 - sham b (content page)
page[31].pType = "contentPage";
page[31].pLink = [-1, -1, -1];
page[31].pTitle = ["home >  media people >
➥  sham b", "", "", ""];
page[31].pID = "shamb";
```

Once you save your `config.as` file, you can test whether the data has been accepted by looking at the compiled SWF in debug mode.

Regardless of which version of Flash you're using, once you've saved the `config.as` file, you can test that the data has been accepted by following these steps:

1. Switch to the FLA file (in this case, `futuremedia_code04.fla`) via the tabs.

2. Debug the FLA by selecting Control ➤ Debug Movie. Click the ▶ icon on the debugger panel to start the session.

3. In the debugger, access the main timeline (`_level0`) by using the Variables tab. You should find that the first and last page array items used, page[0] and page[31], are populated as shown in the images below.

You can also double-check other page items against the preceding listing if you want to make sure all your data is correct.

Assuming you're happy that your `config.as` file is correct, you can now save it and forget about it. You'll concentrate on the code again and edit the FLA.

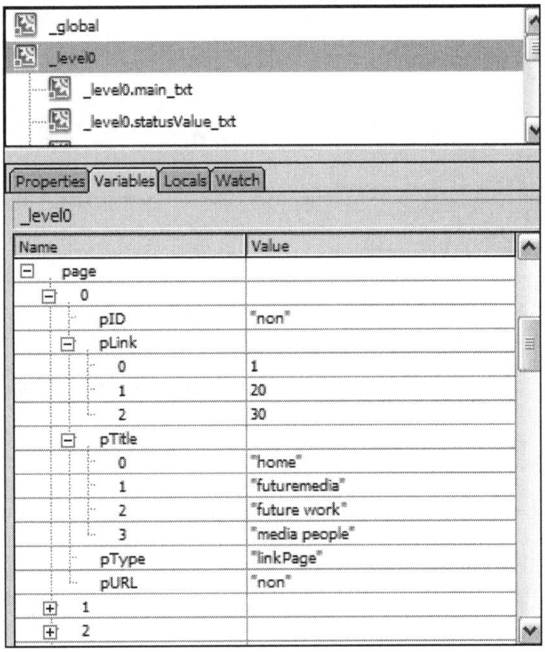

_global
_level0
_level0.main_txt
_level0.statusValue_txt

Properties | Variables | Locals | Watch

_level0

Name	Value
⊟ page	
⊟ 0	
pID	"non"
⊟ pLink	
0	1
1	20
2	30
⊟ pTitle	
0	"home"
1	"futuremedia"
2	"future work"
3	"media people"
pType	"linkPage"
pURL	"non"
⊞ 1	
⊞ 2	

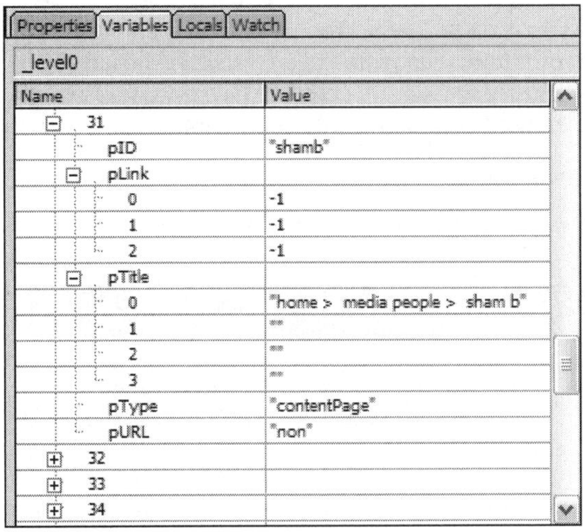

Properties | Variables | Locals | Watch

_level0

Name	Value
⊟ 31	
pID	"shamb"
⊟ pLink	
0	-1
1	-1
2	-1
⊟ pTitle	
0	"home > media people > sham b"
1	""
2	""
3	""
pType	"contentPage"
pURL	"non"
⊞ 32	
⊞ 33	
⊞ 34	

Obviously, being able to forget about your `config.as` *file is the main advantage of using a separate AS file for configuration data. By separating configuration data from the code, you can totally forget about the data when you modify the main code. All you really have to remember is the format the data is in.*

This has another advantage. If you ever decide to update or even totally change the Futuremedia UI, you can still use the old configuration file as long as the new site design can load and read the `config.as` *file. Cool!*

Getting Flash to read the data

OK, let's quickly recap. You've just defined all the navigation data into the page object. This object is a large, multiproperty data structure. Your next task is to get Flash to start reading it. You need to pull a number of bits of information from page to successfully create a new display for your UI. Let's first have a look at two of the easiest tasks you need to accomplish:

- Populate the titles.
- Add the link data to the current page.

Populating the titles

You'll create a new block of functions called BUILD PAGE AND DYNAMIC UI ELEMENTS to do this. You need three functions:

- One function called `populateTitles()` adds all the text titles.

- One function stops the three strips from acting like buttons if there's no need for them (that is, you don't want the strip to act as a link because there is none defined), and another function makes them act like links when you do. You can see two examples of this in the final site. The page home > future work doesn't have a link for the third strip. If you navigate to this page and mouse over the three strips, you'll see that only the first two show the hand cursor (signifying they're active links). The third doesn't act like a link because there is nowhere to go for this strip.

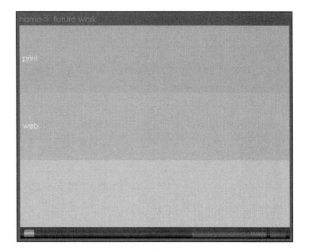

The page home > future work > print > other (shown next) shows content rather than links. Although when you first looked at the final site, you may have thought that such pages no longer contained the three strips, you now know that *all* pages contain the three strips. The three strips are disabled when they don't need to act as links. The function that does this disabling is the same one that disables the *one* strip in home > future work.

So, you'll define one function, populateEvents(), to make strips act like links, and another, unpopulateEvents(), to make the strips stop acting like links.

1. Add this code after the existing DEFINE EVENT SCRIPTS block (that is, after the end of the function colTransition(), around line 59):

```
   ...
   ...
      fadeText(100);
      delete this.onEnterFrame;
   }
};
// BUILD PAGE AND DYNAMIC UI ELEMENTS
populateTitles = function (pageIndex) {
  main_txt.text =
➥ page[pageIndex].pTitle[0];
  tricolor.strip0_txt.text =
➥ page[pageIndex].pTitle[1];
  tricolor.strip1_txt.text =
➥ page[pageIndex].pTitle[2];
  tricolor.strip2_txt.text =
➥ page[pageIndex].pTitle[3];
};
// DEFINE MAIN SETUP SCRIPTS
stripEvents = function () {
  ...
  ...
```

The new function populateTitles() takes an argument, pageIndex, and uses it to retrieve the titles for page page[pageIndex]. It then populates the four text fields with the appropriate text strings, as specified by the data you defined in the last section.

OK, apart from the fact that you don't have a pageIndex argument generated anywhere yet, the text titling is sorted out. Next stop: the linking.

2. Add the following code below the populateTitles() function you just added:

```
populateEvents = function (pageIndex) {
  if (page[pageIndex].pLink[0] != -1) {
    tricolor.strip0_mc.onRelease =
➥ navigate;
    tricolor.strip0_mc.useHandCursor =
➥ true;
  }
  if (page[pageIndex].pLink[1] != -1) {
    tricolor.strip1_mc.onRelease =
➥ navigate;
    tricolor.strip1_mc.useHandCursor =
➥ true;
  }
  if (page[pageIndex].pLink[2] != -1) {
    tricolor.strip2_mc.onRelease =
➥ navigate;
    tricolor.strip2_mc.useHandCursor =
➥ true;
  }
};
```

All this function does is look at the current page (page[pageIndex]) and add an onRelease event that's defined as your old friend navigate(), so that if a link exists for a strip, it's made to act like a button (thus enabling the user to follow the link). It does this *unless* any strip has a –1 link defined for it.

3. Now add this function (directly below populateEvents()), which does the reverse of the previous function—it *removes* all the events:

```
unpopulateEvents = function () {
  delete tricolor.strip0_mc.onRelease;
  delete tricolor.strip1_mc.onRelease;
  delete tricolor.strip2_mc.onRelease;
  tricolor.strip0_mc.useHandCursor = false;
  tricolor.strip1_mc.useHandCursor = false;
  tricolor.strip2_mc.useHandCursor = false;
};
```

This function deletes all the button events, so that the UI no longer responds to button clicks on the three strips. This in itself doesn't get rid of the hand cursor, though. To stop that, you have to change a property, useHandCursor, to false (and when you give the three strips button events again

via populateEvents, you make this property true for those strips that are links in the new page). You now need to modify your existing functions to use the new events.

The first thing you don't yet know is the page you're on. Well, actually, you know what page you're on to start off with—you always start at the home page, and that is page 0. When you navigate to another page, you should be able to tell where you are from the link data.

> *Although some of you may see immediately which bit of data will give you this information, using data in a website in this manner will be new to many, so I'll move slowly so that I don't lose anyone.*

If you look at the sketch for page 0 again, you see immediately the bit of data you need: *the link number*. This tells you the page number right away.

page[0] *home page*

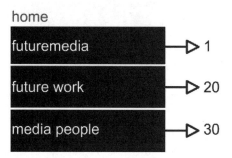

For example, if you click strip 2 (media people), you go to page 30, and that becomes the new page number. When you use the populateTitles (pageIndex) and populateEvents(pageIndex) functions, you want pageIndex to hold the value 30. This causes page 30 to be built as the next page.

Looking at the following, more general diagram, it becomes obvious that the current page is page 0 when you start. As soon as you click a strip, the new page becomes pLink[strip], where strip is the strip number (0, 1, 2).

page[pageNumber]

pTitle[0]

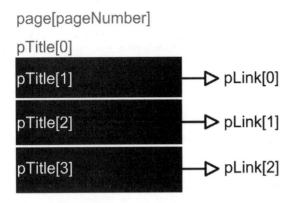

pTitle[1] → pLink[0]

pTitle[2] → pLink[1]

pTitle[3] → pLink[2]

Let's try the page 0 bit. Given that you know you're on page 0 to start with, you'll assign this value to a variable that tells you the current page number, currentPage. Add this to the INITIALIZE section (at the end of the listing):

```
...
// Define and populate database
var page:Array = new Array();
navigationData();
// Build first page...
var currentPage:Number = 0;
populateTitles(currentPage);
// now sit back and let the event scripts
// handle everything
stop();
```

4. Test your FLA. You'll see that you now have titles correctly showing on the home page. The only trouble is that when you click a link, the titles don't change. Well, they shouldn't—you haven't added that part yet.

5. The next step is to ensure that you *always* see the correct titles. You need to do this by changing currentPage when you see a new page and populating the page based on the new value. The place to do this is at the end of posTransition(), once the position transition has occurred and the current titles have faded out. Add the following highlighted lines:

```
posTransition = function () {
  var selectedStrip:String;
  scale -= (scale-scaleTarget)/3;
  y -= (y-yTarget)/3;
  fadeAlpha = 300-scale;
```

```
    tricolor._y = y;
    tricolor._xscale = tricolor._yscale=
 scale;
    fadeText(fadeAlpha);
    if (Math.abs(scale-scaleTarget)<5) {
      // if so, disconnect this function
      // from onEnterframe
      this.onEnterFrame = colTransition;
      // then place tricolor back at
      // start position
      tricolor._y = BORDER;
      tricolor._xscale = tricolor._yscale =
 100;
      selectedStrip =
 this._name.substring(5, 6);
      selectedCol =
 _root["color"+selectedStrip];
      tricolor.setCol(selectedCol,
 selectedCol, selectedCol);
      currentPage =
 page[currentPage].pLink[selectedStrip];
      populateTitles(currentPage);
      fadeColor = 0;
      fadeAlpha = 0;
    }
};
```

If you test the FLA, you'll see your titles appear. Unfortunately, you can still navigate to pages you shouldn't be able to (page –1, or empty links), and to fix that you need to look at integrating populateEvents() with the main code.

Populating the events

You'll change the way the strips work as follows:

- As soon as the user clicks a strip, you'll remove all events from all the strips via unpopulateEvents(). You thus have a blank slate.

- When the new page appears, you make those strips that should have a link into active buttons. If you don't do this to one or two strips, those strips will stay inactive.

So, the first step is to remove all button events as soon as any of the strips are clicked. How do you know when a strip has been clicked? Easy! navigate() is the onRelease event handler for each strip. A strip has been clicked *as soon as* navigate() *runs*.

Add the following call to unpopulateEvents() to the start of the function navigate():

```
navigate = function () {
  unpopulateEvents();
  // set up target for animation transition
  scale=100, x=BORDER, y=BORDER;
  yTarget = -3*this._y+BORDER;
  scaleTarget = 300;
  // attach the animation transition to the
  // strip that has just been pressed
  this.onEnterFrame = posTransition;
};
```

This removes the button events from all strips in the tricolor. Once you're at the new page, you want to add the events back in, but only for those strips that are valid links.

All you have to do now is put the new events back onto the strips when the navigation has completed, and that occurs at the end of colTransition(). Add the following call to populateEvents() at the end of colTransition() (around line 60 in the script):

```
    ...
    color1 = tricolor.colStrip1.getRGB();
    color2 = tricolor.colStrip2.getRGB();
    fadeText(100);
    delete this.onEnterFrame;
    populateEvents(currentPage);
  }
};
```

The FLA to this point is saved as futuremedia_code04.fla.

If you test this file, you'll see that you're *almost* there. Although the pages now work for link pages, as soon as you hit a content page, the site messes up, because it still changes to the three strips. On a content page, the UI should simply act as a dumb background until the content is loaded, so you don't want it to split into the three colored strips. You need to make the UI read the pType value and act accordingly.

> You have to do this because your page always remains the same. You never really go to a new page—you simply keep reusing the tricolor.

Reading content pages

You want to use colTransition() only if the new page happens to be a link page. If it isn't, you don't need to fade the three strips in again. To make this change, add the following code at the end of posTransition():

```
posTransition = function () {
  var selectedStrip:String;
  scale -= (scale-scaleTarget)/3;
  y -= (y-yTarget)/3;
  fadeAlpha = 300-scale;
  tricolor._y = y;
  tricolor._xscale = tricolor._yscale =
➥ scale;
  fadeText(fadeAlpha);
  if (Math.abs(scale-scaleTarget)<5) {
    // if so, disconnect this function
    // from onEnterframe
    this.onEnterFrame = colTransition;
    // then place tricolor back at
    // start position
    tricolor._y = BORDER;
    tricolor._xscale = tricolor._yscale =
➥ 100;
    selectedStrip =
➥ this._name.substring(5, 6);
    selectedCol =
➥ _root["color"+selectedStrip];
    tricolor.setCol(selectedCol,
➥ selectedCol, selectedCol);
    currentPage =
➥ page[currentPage].pLink[selectedStrip];
    populateTitles(currentPage);
    // if this is a link page,
    // create another tricolor
    if (page[currentPage].pType ==
➥ "linkPage") {
```

```
        fadeColor = 0;
        fadeAlpha = 0;
      } else {
      // otherwise place the content
      placeContent();
      }
    }
};
```

If the current page happens to be a link page, you continue as before. If it isn't, you go to a new function, placeContent(). Don't worry—this is a very short function, and then you'll be done for this section. Add the following function below unpopulateEvents():

```
placeContent = function () {
  _root.attachMovie("placeholder",
➥ "placeholder", 10000);
  _root.placeholder._x = border;
  _root.placeholder._y = border;
};
```

This time, if you get to a page that has content in it, the whole UI stops working—it acts like a background to the content. Because the content isn't actually there, you see just a blank content area, but you haven't yet defined the content, so not to worry.

Try this out by navigating from home to futuremedia, and then to links.

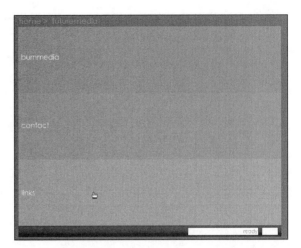

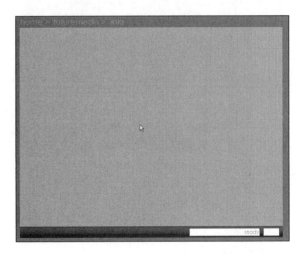

The last screen is a blank, light-orange screen in the site in progress. In the final site, the only real difference is that this page has some content on it.

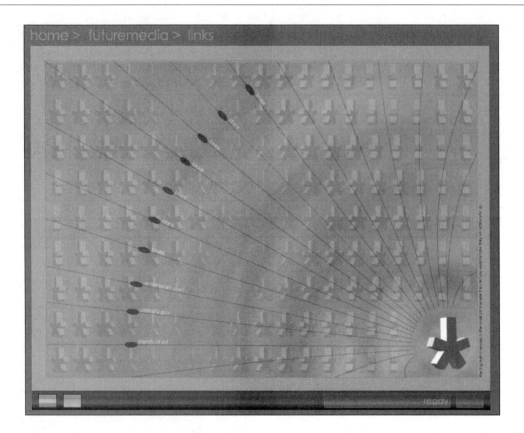

OK, you might see a world of difference graphically here, but in terms of code, there's only one difference: the site in progress doesn't attempt to load the content because you don't have any yet. There is at most a couple of lines difference!

Parting shots

I know what you're thinking at this point in the book: *"Phew!"*

This section was hard. That's because the concept covered in the section was hard. You've learned one of the major differences, if not *the* difference between a Flash beginner and an ActionScript master: how to keep Flash's graphics, code, and data environments totally separate. The navigation for the Futuremedia site isn't hard-coded into the timelines. It isn't even contained in the code. It's in a separate file altogether.

You've done the navigation data in terms of separate files, but in this part of the book project, I've tried to force you to see them as different parts of the design. You started by defining the graphics for the UI, and then you forgot about them. Next you wrote a longish script to animate the UI.

The way you defined a text file (which is what an AS file is at the end of the day) that contained all the navigation data, added it to your project, and just moved on with other problems is the way advanced programmers think about problems, and the way they tend to structure them.

The only remaining problem left is how to fully integrate the code and data, so that you can finally move backward as well as forward in the site, and load content. You'll also need to look at adding sound.

That's the technical message of this section. There's a more philosophical issue to think about as well. Notice that the site looked really unfinished for almost the entire book, but now, right at the end, it is all coming together *quickly*. Simply add two lines, and every page starts to show titles. Add a couple more lines and the navigation moves forward in massive leaps toward completion. The reason the project is going this way is the way it has been built: with careful planning. I knew how the site should work right at the beginning, created copious sketches and tests, and stuck with it through all the "nothing much happening" stages, because I knew what to look for behind the scenes: the way the data was changing even though the graphics were not budging.

I've learned one thing from having worked for many years in software, and that is that the difference between a senior programmer and a novice is the level of planning the senior programmer does and the confidence the senior programmer places in the planning. It can take a long time before you actually start to see stuff begin to move the way you want it to in a complex interface. Without a high level of confidence, you'll always be stuck with simple timeline sites that show results immediately.

Don't worry if you're thinking, "Heck, Sham, I just couldn't keep going this long! I would have given up well before this point." I'll let you into a secret. The Futuremedia site design didn't always go as smoothly as this book implies. A few times I had to go back a number of steps to fix a small problem. The things that kept the whole thing moving were the fact that the code is well structured (so it's easy to modify even though there's lots of it and the fact that I knew it would work because my planning said it should. That's partly a result of that "confidence" word again.

Rest assured that it comes quicker than you think—it's a bit like riding a bicycle. The first time you get it right with your own site design, you'll have that confidence to keep it going straight without losing your balance. And like riding a bicycle, once that happens, you'll have it for life.

Summary

This chapter has taught you something that a lot of people seem to be struggling with: how to understand and tame the Sound class. Believe me, this took me some time, so you're benefiting from my late nights, and you can use the time you've saved building your own Academy Award–winning soundtracks.

In this chapter you learned

- How to create a new sound object and control it with ActionScript
- How to add pan and volume controls
- How to load sound dynamically

You've also reached and passed a crucial point in the Futuremedia site design. You know how to treat the different parts of a site (graphics, code, and data) differently, and you know how to structure both design and implementation along the same lines. With this structured way of coding (and building multimedia generally), you've laid the foundations for building truly epic Flash applications with ease.

Although you still may not know every action, method, and class in the ActionScript Dictionary, that doesn't matter. The important thing is that you're no longer a beginner. In the next chapter, I'll stop treating you like one.

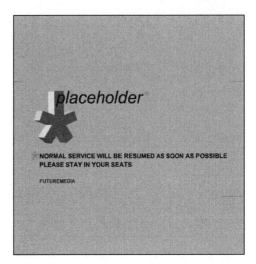

Chapter 13

ADVANCED
ACTIONSCRIPT

What we'll cover in this chapter:

- Using Flash components and the listener event model
- Extending ActionScript with prototypes
- Extending ActionScript with classes

So far in this book you've created a lot of Flash content that relies on ActionScript. You've done some clever things with a very small subset of the ActionScript language, but there will come a time when you need to go further. At the moment you're playing by the rules. You're taking Flash building blocks such as the movie clip and using them to create your content. Instead of playing by the rules, how about if you change the building blocks themselves or even build some new building blocks of your own?

Instead of accepting the standard movie clip in a series of video games you're going to create, for example, you could say, "Hey, my games would be much easier to create if I changed the movie clip so that it acts a bit more like a sprite in a video game." In Flash you can do this in two ways, both of which involve changing the MovieClip class itself so that the class better reflects the application you're building.

As well as changing the built-in classes, you can create your own new classes. In the video-game building example, you could add a collision class that looks after all collisions in your games, so you just use that in all your games.

In short, instead of using ActionScript to build an application, you change ActionScript itself first, so that it's better suited to the application you want to create. You add new classes to Flash or alter some of the existing classes such that the available methods and properties are better geared toward solving your problem.

Macromedia has already done this "extending ActionScript with new classes" deal in creating **components**. Components are a series of self-contained movie clips that allow quick creation of common UIs and other cool stuff—everything from components that create scrollbars to components that define totally new software classes that are "added on" to Flash.

> *This ability to extend the Flash environment is one of the big selling points of Flash MX 2004. It's easier than ever to alter Flash so that it's better configured to solve your problems. This* **extensibility** *takes several forms. You can create your own classes to redefine ActionScript, and you can change parts of the Flash interface because much of it is defined via XML (which you're allowed to modify). You can also define new tools and commands via a dedicated language, JavaScript Flash (JSFL), that allows you to redefine the way the Flash interface works.*
>
> *It's always the way, isn't it? You're getting comfortable with ActionScript, and then I go and tell you that there's another language hidden in the Flash interface that you may have to learn if you want to get the most out of Flash, plus the fact that learning XML is probably also a good idea!*

Components

A component is a special type of movie clip. It can be given an icon other than the standard movie clip icon shown in the Library panel, and it isn't editable when you place it on the stage (that is, you can't edit in place with a component). A component can also be **precompiled**, which means that you can't open it at all to take a peek inside. This makes the component a perfect black box. The component takes the idea of "you don't have to look inside the box to make it work" a step further: sometimes you can't take a peek inside even if you want to!

You can see the components that Macromedia provides by looking in the Components panel (Window ➤ Development Panels ➤ Components). The components are shown in a tree diagram, with each branch representing a particular component set or type of component. The following image shows the UI components. You use these to quickly add common UI elements, such as radio buttons or alert windows, to your site.

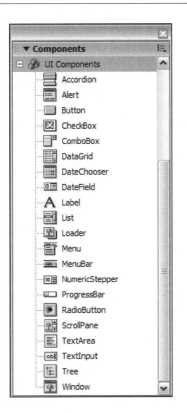

So what's so special about components? Let's try one and see.

The Professional edition of Flash contains a couple more default UI components (the Alert *and* Accordion *components) than the Standard edition. The Professional edition also contains many data and media components that aren't available in the Standard edition.*

Adding a component

So far in this book, you've used text fields. They're great but they're a little basic. They don't have a lot of the niceties of text fields in commercial applications, such as scrollbars and the like. If you wanted to build that sort of thing, you *could* build it by yourself, but why go to all that trouble?

1. In a new blank document, open the Components panel if you need to (Window ➤ Development Panels ➤ Components). Find the TextArea component (it's part of the UI Components branch of the tree). Click-drag the TextArea component from the Components panel (in the same way you would drag a movie clip from the Library) and place it onto the stage. You'll see a little rectangle appear on the stage. This is an instance of the TextArea component.

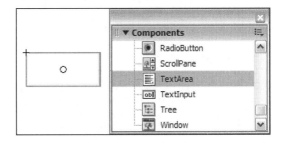

You can also place a component onto the stage by double-clicking the component in the Components panel.

You'll see a new symbol appear in the Library panel. Note that its Kind is listed as Compiled Clip. You can't edit it or view its timeline, no matter what you do!

2. Keep the rectangle selected. In the lower-right corner of the Properties panel, you'll see two tabs: Properties and Parameters. Click the Properties tab. You'll see a number of properties appear, as shown in the following image. Select the text field, and in it type enter some text here!

editable	true
html	false
text	enter some text here
wordWrap	true

Properties | Parameters

As soon as you press the *ENTER* key or deselect the text field, you'll see the component change to reflect the changes in its properties. Previous versions of Flash had components with a feature called "live preview." Flash MX 2004 components go a step further: they're totally WYSIWYG, and unlike standard movie clips, they can sometimes start working as soon as they're on the stage (rather than when they're part of a running SWF). As an example of this, change the text to enter some text here and see what happens! When you've entered the text and deselected the component, the instance will change to reflect that the new text needs scrollbars. The scrollbars won't actually work just yet, but you have a good idea of how the final component will look with your chosen text entered in it.

Enter some
text here and

3. You would be better off with a larger text area. Select the TextArea instance on the stage, and then click the Properties tab of the Properties panel. You'll see the standard Properties panel layout.

Change the Height value to 200 and the Width value to 100. You'll see the component text area change as you would expect . . . or does it? If you did this to a regular movie clip, *everything* would get bigger—the text would get larger, and the scrollbar would still be there. What actually happens is what you would expect a text field to do when you want to make it bigger: only the actual text area gets bigger, while the text remains the same size and reflows into the new available space. You also lose the scrollbar because it's no longer needed.

> *You can also use the Free Transform tool to resize the component.*

4. Finally, test the movie. The scrollbar will appear when needed, making the input or display of large areas of text easier. Much more useful than a regular text field!

5. The Properties panel contains *some* of the ways you can control the component, but it doesn't list them all. For that, you need to look at the Component Inspector panel (Window ➤ Development Panels ➤ Component Inspector). Select the TextArea instance on the stage and you'll see a fuller set of parameters on the Parameters tab. As an example, set the enabled parameter to false.

6. When you test the movie now, you'll see that the TextArea component is grayed out (it isn't enabled).

Components and ActionScript

That's a good introduction to using components manually, but you don't want to do things manually—you want to use ActionScript. You know that this makes the whole process much better.

For example, rather than manually place the text area onto the stage, what if you could dynamically attach instances of the TextArea component onto the stage, so that you could create interactive forms? You could do all that resizing and other stuff you entered into the Properties panel at runtime via code, and gray out TextAreas on a form unless they're actually appropriate. You know that everything in Flash is really controlled by OOP, so you possibly already suspect that there are some classes and properties behind all this magic, and if there are, you should be able to do the following:

- Change the way the component instance *works or looks* by changing its properties.
- Make the component *do things* by using component methods.
- Make the component instance *respond to interaction* and other events by defining event handlers.

The cool thing about components is that once you know how to work with one of them, you more or less know how to work with them all.

To find out the full list of ActionScript applicable to the TextArea component, search on the phrase "TextArea class" in the Help panel (press *F1* to bring up the Help panel, and click the magnifying glass icon at the top of the panel to search). You can find out more about any of the default components by searching on the name of the component followed by the term "class." You'll be presented with up to three tables of ActionScript associated with the component:

- A property summary
- A method summary (if applicable)
- An event summary (if applicable)

The tables will take you to more detailed entries. Simply click the light blue link text:

Property summary for the TextArea class

Property	Description
TextArea.editable	A Boolean value indicating whether the field is editable (true) or not (false).
TextArea.hPosition	Defines the horizontal position of the text within the scroll pane.
TextArea.hScrollPolicy	Indicates whether the horizontal scroll bar is always on ("on"), never on ("off"), or turns on when needed ("auto").S
TextArea.html	A flag that indicates whether the text field can be formatted with HTML.
TextArea.length	The number of characters in the text field. This property is read-only.
TextArea.maxChars	The maximum number of characters that the text field can contain.
TextArea.maxHPosition	The maximum value of TextArea.hPosition.
TextArea.maxVPosition	The maximum value of TextArea.vPosition.
TextArea.password	A Boolean value indicating whether the field is a password field (true) or not (false).
TextArea.restrict	The set of characters that a user can enter into the text field.
TextArea.text	The text contents of a TextArea component.
TextArea.vPosition	A number indicating the vertical scrolling position
TextArea.vScrollPolicy	Indicates whether the vertical scroll bar is always on ("on"), never on ("off"), or turns on when needed ("auto").S
TextArea.wordWrap	A Boolean value indicating whether the text wraps (true) or not (false).

Event summary for the TextArea class

Event	Description
TextArea.change	Notifies listeners that text has changed.

All components also use a set of common component properties derived from an associated class called UIObject. This class allows you to handle lower level properties, such as height, width, color, and position. Search on the phrase "UIObject class" to view the help for this class. (And don't worry, it isn't as daunting as it looks—you'll work through examples using important parts of this class later.)

Another basic class, UIComponent, provides basic event handling. Search on the phrase "UIComponent class" to find more information. (Again, don't worry, it isn't as daunting as it looks.)

Using component properties and methods

You change component properties in much the same way as you do with other class instances (such as movie clips). Simply use dot notation.

*Some of you may have dabbled with Flash MX components before moving on to Flash MX 2004. Flash MX 2004 (or **v2**) components are a big step up from the older (**v1**) components because you can access v2 component properties directly. With v1, you had to do everything through methods, and sometimes this led to long-winded code to do apparently simple things.*

Let's see this in action. Delete the component currently on the stage. You'll now have a TextArea component in the Library. Rather than use the component in the Components panel, this time drag the version in the Library onto the stage to create a new default instance (shown next). Using the Properties panel, give the instance an instance name of myText.

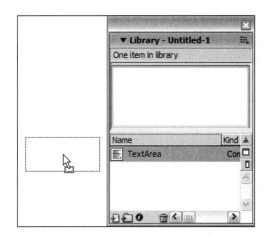

> When you drag a component from the Components panel to the stage, Flash imports the component into the Library. You should therefore drag subsequent components of the same type from the Library. If you don't want to use a component in a FLA anymore, be sure to delete it from the Library as well as from the stage, otherwise the component will be exported in the final SWF, regardless of whether it's actually used in the SWF. The quickest way to stop this from happening is to delete the component from the FLA completely.

Looking at the help text for the TextArea class, you can see that there are several properties you can use. Rename the current layer component. Add a new layer called actions.

In the first frame of actions, attach the following script:

```
myText.html = true;
myText.editable = true;
myText.text = "This text area allows
➥ <b><i>HTML formatting</i></b>";
```

This makes the TextArea instance display HTML text, makes it editable, and adds some HTML-formatted text inside it. If you test the movie, you'll see this:

Cool, except it's small. Add the following new lines to make it larger:

```
myText.html = true;
myText.editable = true;
myText.text = "This text area allows
➥ <b><i>HTML formatting</i></b>";
myText._height = 100;
mytext._width = 200;
```

Whoops—not quite what you had in mind!

What happened? Well, when working with classes, you're working with black-box modules and you need to communicate with them using the specified interfaces. What you're doing here is looking into the black box itself. You're changing the properties of one of the building blocks inside the component black box, the MovieClip class. Rather like wanting to extend your house and doing it by replacing all the bricks and woodwork with bigger versions, you don't get what you want. What you actually want is a house with extra rooms, not one with *everything* bigger.

> When working with components, you should never communicate with them using movie clip properties. Instead, use the properties and methods of the component class and UIObject.

399

You should have changed the size via the UIObject class instead. This class forms the property interface with the component black box. Replace the last two lines in the previous code snippet with the last line in the following code:

```
myText.html = true;
myText.editable = true;
myText.text = "This text area allows
➥ <b><i>HTML formatting</i></b>";
myText.setSize(200, 200);
```

That's better! Rather than scaling the whole component by resizing everything, the setSize() method of UIObject makes the TextArea bigger by making the text input area bigger. The scrollbar now appears when needed and resizes itself to fit the new area when it does. The text font stays the same size and reflows to fill the new area. You can also enter text of your own into the TextArea.

Although this looks intuitive, there is a *lot* of code needed to create such a component. The way the component recognizes HTML-formatted text alone could take more code than you have time for.

At the moment, you have something that works well graphically, but you have no efficient way to work with the text that the user inputs into the TextArea. For that, you need to know how to set up your component to respond to events.

Components and event handling

Components use a more advanced version of the event model you've looked at so far for movie clips and buttons. They use **listeners**.

Rather than the event/event handler pair you've looked at so far, a listener-based event model consists of a **broadcaster** and **listeners**. A normal event/event handler pair is a one-way channel, rather like a telephone conversation. The event propagates like someone talking down the phone line. There's only one recipient: the event handler on the other side of the connection. So, if a button is clicked, there can be only one callback function that acts as the event handler.

A listener is more like a radio broadcast. This time the event is broadcast everywhere. The number of recipients isn't just one person, but everyone who is listening in. Listeners offer greater flexibility when compared with the restrictions of a single event/event handler pair:

- **The number of listeners per event is unlimited.** This means that you can set off *multiple event handlers* in response to some of the more important events. For example, suppose you put a "clear everything, I want to start again" button on a page. It makes sense to have everything listening to the "I have just been clicked" event of that one button, so that all the various UIs can be cleared or reset. With an event/event handler pair, the event handler would be the only thing to respond, something that makes the code for it difficult to manage (it has more to do). Instead, you can have lots of listeners looking out for the quit and clearing their own specific part of the application.

- **Where the broadcaster is sending out multiple events, the listeners can choose to respond to only some events.** This is rather like a human listening to a radio station only when music from the alternative rock charts are being broadcast, because adult-oriented rock music and boy bands aren't suited to this particular music fan. In the same way, a particular Flash listener can choose to respond to those events that involve TextArea resizing only, because that's what it's written to handle. The advantage of this is that you get to *structure your event handling*.

- **A listener can respond to several different events**. In an event/event handler model, the event handler is limited in what it can respond to, because the link to available event sources is less flexible. A listener can respond to *any* broadcast event, because *all* of them are available to it; it can simply pick what it wants. This allows you to *generalize more*. A listener could be set up to listen to all events that would need the current SWF to quit. The "quitter" listener is thus not just listening for events, but more generally it's handling all events that lead to a particular outcome.

- **Listener-based events aren't attached to the instance broadcasting the event, which makes for better extensibility**. Adding a listener event doesn't affect the instance creating the event. This is very useful when you want to update code. Adding new listeners to a movie clip doesn't change what the movie clip does, but adding a new onEnterFrame deletes any onEnterFrame already attached to the movie clip.

When setting up a listener, you do the following:

1. Set up a new object to listen.
2. Attach event handlers to the new object.
3. For each event you want to listen to, define the event handler you want it to be linked to.

That's a lot of information to take in without an example to back it up. I feel a few examples coming on! You'll fix that TextArea example with some listener-based event handling before exploring the listener event model in general.

Listeners are the way of controlling component event handling for v2 components. They're also the preferred way of defining events when you're building new classes (for the reasons listed previously). This is why I'm laboring the point with listeners—they're a fundamental change in emphasis in the transition between Flash MX scripting and Flash MX 2004 scripting, and you need to know how to use them if you want to write code in the preferred ActionScript 2.0 style. As you'll see, this has advantages that aren't often realized currently, but I expect these advantages will soon become mainstream.

Adding an "in focus" event to the TextArea

In this exercise, you'll add a listener to the TextArea, so that when you click inside it the existing text will be cleared.

1. First, you need to add a new object that will become your listener. Edit the code so far as shown, adding line 1 and changing the second-to-last line. You create a new object instance, myListener, and change the displayed text. Notice that myListener is just an ordinary object—you don't have to do anything special to it to make it a listener.

```
var myListener:Object = new Object();
myText.html = true;
myText.editable = true;
myText.text =
➡ "Enter some text <i>here!</i>";
myText.setSize(200, 200);
```

2. You want something to happen as soon as the user clicks inside the TextArea. This is a general event for all UI components (rather than a specific, specialized event for the TextArea class), so it makes sense that the event should be part of the general UI component class. The event you want is UIComponent.inFocus (you can search for it in the Help panel if you'd like more information). You need to add an event handler to deal with this event, as shown here:

```
var myListener:Object = new Object();
myListener.focusIn = function(){
  trace("you clicked inside something!")
}
myText.html = true;
myText.editable = true;
myText.text =
➥ "Enter some text <i>here!</i>";
myText.setSize(200, 200);
```

3. The function will trace a message every time it is run. At the moment, it will never run because myListener isn't listening for any event broadcasts. To make it listen to the focusIn event for myText, add the following line at the end of the listing:

```
myText.addEventListener("focusIn",
➥ myListener);
```

4. Test the movie. When you click inside the TextArea, you'll see the message you clicked inside something pop up in the Output panel. That's progress, but you actually want to do something with the particular component you clicked inside. To do so, you'll pass a parameter to the event handler. Change the event handler as follows:

```
myListener.focusIn = function(ui) {
  trace("you clicked inside "+ui.target);
};
```

> *The important thing to remember when you're using listeners is that you can't use your old friend* this, *because the event handler is attached to something other than the instance creating the event.*

Test the movie. The message will now tell you what you've clicked inside when you clicked inside the component, because the target property of the parameter (called ui) tells you the name of the broadcasting instance. .

```
┌─────────────────────────────┐
│ ▼ Output                ≣  │
├─────────────────────────────┤
│ you clicked inside          │
│  _level0.myText             │
│                             │
└─────────────────────────────┘
```

You can now make the event handler clear the text inside the broadcasting component. Change the event handler as shown and test the movie:

```
myListener.focusIn = function(ui) {
  ui.target.text = "";
};
```

This time, as soon as you click inside the TextArea, the existing text is cleared. The chain of events for this operation is as follows:

1. You click inside the TextArea instance myText.

2. myText broadcasts its inFocus event.

3. myListener is listening in to this broadcast and responds.

Compare this to what would have happened for a regular event/event handler pair:

1. Flash sees an event.

2. Flash looks to see if there is an event handler defined to handle this event.

3. If Flash finds an event handler defined to handle this event, the event handler is executed.

The listener event involves two instances, the broadcaster and the listening object, whereas the event/event handler pair requires only the event handler to be set up. The latter is an easier system to set up, but it's less flexible if you want to do something clever.

So what do I mean by "clever"? The beauty of listeners is that the event is *broadcasted* rather than sent to one handler only. This means you can have multiple listeners (among other things). Change the code as follows:

```
var textHandler:Object = new Object();
textHandler.focusIn = function(ui) {
  ui.target.text = "";
};
var soundHandler:Object = new Object();
soundHandler.focusIn = function() {
  trace("beep!");
};
myText.html = true;
myText.editable = true;
myText.text = "enter why you want to
➥ <b>win $1,000</b> here!";
myText.setSize(200, 200);
myText.addEventListener("focusIn",
➥ textHandler);
myText.addEventListener("focusIn",
➥ soundHandler);
```

This time when you click inside the TextArea, the chain of events is as follows:

1. You click inside the TextArea instance myText.

2. myText broadcasts its inFocus event.

3. textHandler is listening in to this broadcast and responds by sorting out the text handling.

4. soundHandler is listening to this broadcast and responds by sorting out the sound handling.

You can have as many different handlers as you want listening, and this allows you to make your event handling *modular*.

This may not be a big deal for this example, and you may well be thinking "Um, Sham, I think I prefer the simpler event/event handler system for now." Well, I'm sure you do—it's far easier to come to grips with. When using components, you won't be using multiple handlers, and you can get away with thinking that this listener deal is just another way of writing event/event handler pairs. Let's take a look 6 months down the road, though, assuming you embrace the event listener model.

Suppose you've been asked to build an online teaching application, which will create many text-based screens. To make the project easier, you've created several listeners, each looking at a particular type of event:

- An input listener, inMan, which manages user input events

- A navigation listener, navMan, which manages user navigation events

- And so on

All your managers are *general* listeners that aren't written to be attached to *specific* instances, but *the general events they create*. Your advanced multimedia event-handling code is no longer a set of simple cause and effect systems, but a true data-broadcasting network. Events aren't one-way; rather, they're made open to any other code module that requests them.

A Flash UI

When you were young you probably went through the **teenage deep** phase. That's the one where you think you know everything and are a true individual. Painting your bedroom black and wearing funky haircuts seems like a good idea for asserting yourself (given you're too young to have actually done anything else to prove individuality). It works, until many years later when you realize that *everyone* else did *exactly* the same thing. Darn.

Well, it doesn't stop there, because there's also the **office deep** phase, which occurs later in life when you think you're past teenage introspection. Not many people miss out on the first deep phase, but you may have been lucky and missed the second one. I didn't, so I'll tell you all about it.

It involves management training courses and lots of whiteboard diagrams to try to convince everyone that they don't go to work to get paid, and companies don't exist to make stuff, but to promote personal growth. Managers tend to inflict such courses on young workers on the premise that it's actually a good thing. It's really cool when you're there at the course, but the desire to give your coworkers a group hug at the end of each day tends to disappear fairly quickly.

Anyway, during the courses you're given questionnaires and tests to see what kind of person you are and to fool you into thinking you're a unique and valued asset. In the following FLA, you'll create an online version of one of the better questionnaires. By "better" I mean the one that everyone agreed is right on the money and tried on their coworkers the Monday morning after the course, thus totally negating any productivity gains caused by the management training for the rest of the week.

As with most personality tests, knowing the answers in advance negates the test, so if you want a slice of office deep, load and run the file form.fla before moving on. Be honest in your replies!

OK, now that you know a bit more about yourself, let's see if you can also learn a bit more about component listeners.

Forms

You create what is essentially a **form**, a page that allows structured input from the user.

> *Point-and-click interfaces are all very well, but there's only so much information that can be captured from the mouse pointer. For any complex application, at some point you'll need the user to input some more complex data, and that's when you need to turn to a form-based approach. Forms have many more uses than helping you buy this book from Amazon.com!*

When you run form.fla, you'll be presented with two TextArea components. The top one presents a question, and the bottom one is where you enter your response.

Work through the questions as quickly as you can. Answer with the first thing that comes into your head for the best results.

Click button to start.

Start...

There's also a button that appears in the bottom right of the top TextArea. It appears in a contextual way—when it isn't required, it isn't there. When it does appear, the text changes to reflect what will happen when you click it.

The lower TextArea contains a prompt to make it obvious where the response needs to be entered. As soon as you click this TextArea, the prompt disappears.

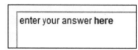

enter your answer **here**

The scrollbars appear when needed on both TextAreas.

Let's have a look behind the scenes. The main stage contains *nothing*. The timeline contains only one layer and one frame with an attached script. The secret is in the ActionScript!

> *The use of v2 components can get a little confusing because the methods used can come from several classes. You can find help on any method by right-clicking/CTRL-clicking it in the Script pane and selecting* View Help *from the context menu that appears. This clarifies whether the methods are coming from the component class (TextArea, Button), UIObject, or UIComponent.*

The main code starts at line 31 by initializing your variables: .

```
// Initialize
var answerListener:Object = new Object();
var btnListener:Object = new Object();
var question:Array = new Array();
var prompt:Array = new Array();
var answer:Array = new Array();
var qNumber:Number = 0;
question[0] = "<br>One of the scenes in the
➥ list below will appeal to you the
most.";
question[0] += "<br><b>Q: Describe why your
➥ chosen item appeals the most.</b>";
question[0] += "<ul><li>A slow moving
➥ river</li><li>A large lake</li>"
```

```
question[0]+= "<li>A waterfall</li>
➥ <li>A fast moving stream</li></ul>";
question[1] = "<br>You will be
➥ re-incarnated as an animal,
➥ but can pick which one."
question[1] += "<br><b>Q: Which animal do
➥ you choose and why</b>?";
question[2] = "<br>You wake to find
➥ yourself locked in an empty and
➥ dark room.  ";
question[2] += "After a time you realize
➥ there is no way to escape.<br>";
question[2] += "<b>Q: What is your first
➥ thought</b>?";
prompt[0] = "Next question";
prompt[1] = "Next question";
prompt[2] = "View results";
answer = ["", "", ""];
```

The two objects answerListener and btnListener are used later to listen to your components. You have three arrays, one for the questions, one for the prompts (they appear on the button), and one for the answers. Finally, you have a number, gNumber, to track the current question number.

The next section of code dynamically builds the interface by attaching versions of the components to the stage (on _root). The createObject function creates three instances shown in the following image:

■ The two TextAreas, questionField and answerField

■ The button instance enterButton

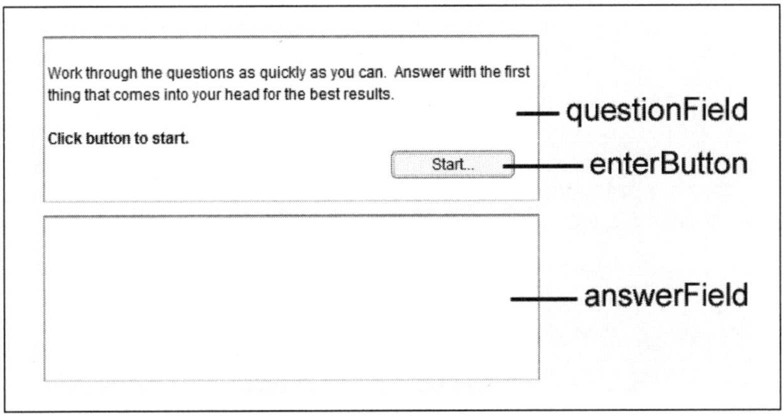

405

```
// Build UI
this.createObject("TextArea",
➡ "questionField", 0);
this.createObject("TextArea",
➡ "answerField", 1);
this.createObject("Button",
➡ "enterButton", 2);
```

To dynamically attach your components to the stage, you have to know the linkage identifiers of the two components. These are added automatically when you add any component to an FLA. To see what the linkage identifiers are, simply look at the Linkage column in the Library (you may have to increase the width of the Library or use the left-right scrollbar to see the column).

The three components are set to their default size and position when they're first attached to the stage, so you need to set their position, scaling, and other properties. You do this via two functions. setTextField() is written for the TextAreas, and setButton() looks after the button.

```
setTextField(questionField, 80, 10, false);
setTextField(answerField, 80, 150, true);
setButton(enterButton, 360, 100);
```

You can see these two functions at the top of the listing. setTextField()has four arguments and returns nothing.

```
function setTextField(fieldName:MovieClip,
➡ x:Number, y:Number, edit:Boolean):Void {
```

- fieldName is the instance name of the TextArea. Notice that it is of type MovieClip rather than TextArea.

- The x and y values are the position you want to move the TextArea to (the registration point is measured from the top-left corner of the components).

- The edit value defines whether you want the TextArea to be editable. The questionField instance needs to be noneditable (it will display the questions and present the results). The answerField instance needs to be editable (the user needs to be able to enter answers).

The setButton() function is much simpler. It sets the position of the instance buttonName to (x, y):

```
function setButton(buttonName:MovieClip,
➡ x:Number, y:Number):Void {
```

Have a look inside these functions if you want to see the methods used.

The next step in the code is to populate the components with their initial text. I've set the two TextAreas to display HTML text, so the text uses HTML formatting.

```
// Initialize UI
questionField.text = "<br>Work through the
➡ questions as quickly as you can.  ";
questionField.text += "Answer with the
➡ first thing that comes into your head";
questionField.text +=
➡ " for the best results.<br><br>
➡ <b>Click button to start.</b>";
enterButton.label = "Start...";
```

Flash HTML text tends to do odd things at times if you use the paragraph tag, <p>, so although it looks a little retrograde to the HTML folks in the house, use of the break tag <br> is usually more predictable.

Next up are the listener event handlers. The answerListener object will listen to events broadcast by answerField (the lower TextArea). When you click inside this field, the answerListener.focusIn function deletes the current contents of the TextArea, which is how the enter your answer here text is made to disappear.

```
// Set listener event handlers
answerListener.focusIn = function(ui) {
  ui.target.text = "";
};
```

The button is kept invisible if answerField contains fewer than ten characters. This is checked every time you make a change via the next function:

```
answerListener.change = function(ui) {
  if (ui.target.length>10) {
    enterButton.visible = true;
  } else {
    enterButton.visible = false;
  }
};
```

When the button is clicked, the btnListener.click function is run. If all three questions have been answered (qNumber ==3), the showResults() function is run, which displays the results. If all answers are in, there's also no longer a need for answerField, so it's disabled (this also prevents answerField from broadcasting any further events).

If question 3 hasn't been reached, the next question is asked by incrementing qNumber and running the function askQuestion():

```
btnListener.click = function() {
  answer[qNumber-1] = answerField.text;
  if (qNumber == 3) {
    showResults();
    answerField.text = "Finished!";
    answerField.enabled = false;
  } else {
    askQuestion();
  }
  qNumber++;
};
```

The final part of the code tells your listeners what they need to be listening to. This process is also called **subscribing** or **registering** the listeners to the broadcast (rather like pay-per-view TV/movies in the real world!).

```
// Tell listeners what to listen to
answerField.addEventListener("focusIn",
➥ answerListener);
answerField.addEventListener("change",
➥ answerListener);
enterButton.addEventListener("click",
➥ btnListener);
```

Components allow you to build complex interfaces quickly. You've looked at only two components here, but there are many more to play with. All the UI components follow the same sort of coding patterns you've explored in this chapter.

The only things the previous code doesn't show you are how to remove components and how to remove listeners. Let's look at that before moving on to the coding style that allows you to create your own components and other clever stuff.

> You can also populate your components with dynamic data, so that the personality test would be generated by a remote server, but that's a topic for another book.

Removing components

Suppose you want to remove answerField rather than disable it at the end of the personality test. To do this, you would use the UIObject.destroyObject() method. To see this method in action, change the btnListener.click function as follows:

```
btnListener.click = function(ui) {
  answer[qNumber-1] = answerField.text;
  if (qNumber == 3) {
    showResults();
    _root.destroyObject("answerField");
  } else {
```

```
    askQuestion();
  }
  qNumber++;
};
```

The destroyObject method looks for the answerField instance on the _root timeline and destroys (removes) it. Although the component is now no longer broadcasting, the listeners will continue to listen for the missing broadcasts, so it's a good idea to know how to stop a listener from listening as well.

Removing listeners

Sometimes you don't want to remove a component, but you want to stop some events from being handled. To do this, simply unregister the listener from the broadcast using removeEventListener:

```
btnListener.click = function(ui) {
  answer[qNumber-1] = answerField.text;
  if (qNumber == 3) {
    showResults();
    answerField.text = "";
    answerField.removeEventListener(
➡ "focusIn", answerListener);
    answerField.removeEventListener(
➡ "change", answerListener);
    enterButton.removeEventListener(
➡ "click", btnListener);
  } else {
    askQuestion();
  }
  qNumber++;
};
```

If you think about what you've written and learned here, it's actually fairly advanced. You generate a UI on the fly, and then you create an efficient, event-based control structure that runs the interface. You know how to change the text fields and buttons around on the screen so that the form is truly interactive. The input elements can reconfigure themselves to suit the current task, pulling in any interface components required dynamically. There must be a downside to all this advanced interface creation, right?

Components and bandwidth

Components are very versatile, and they achieve this versatility by creating a large number of general classes that are added to ActionScript. These classes (plus the actual component graphics) must be loaded on frame 1 of the SWF to add the component code framework, and this takes up around 30KB. Not so much of a pause for broadband users, but it might be significant for others, particularly users with a 56K modem.

There are ways around this. For one thing, you can make the component classes load on a frame other than the first frame (File ➤ Publish Settings ➤ Flash, click the Settings button, and then change the Export frame for classes from frame 1 to another frame number), but the fact remains that it's not really worth using components at all for some Flash sites where bandwidth is a limiting factor.

> *The additional 30KB for component classes is reused as you add more components to your SWF (the download for the first component is 30KB, but the additional download is less for subsequent components you add), so it makes sense to use components only when you can see the need for a few different component types.*

Components use advanced coding structures and lots of them. Nevertheless, the same coding structures are available to you, and that's the final thing you'll look at: object-oriented programming, or OOP.

Revisiting classes, objects, methods, and properties

Classes, objects (or instances, which means the same thing), methods, and properties are something you know how to use by now. You know that the MovieClip class provides you with a number of methods and properties that allow you to control a movie clip on the stage.

You know that you create instances of the movie clip by dragging it from the Library onto the stage, or by doing the same thing through code. For nonvisual objects, you use a constructor. The following line creates a new array:

```
var myArray:Array = new Array();
```

You can use all your arrays and movie clips with the structured code techniques you already know about, so a couple of questions immediately come to mind:

- What new features will OOP coding styles give me?
- Will OOP help me write code quicker or more efficiently?

Contrary to popular opinion in some quarters, writing object-oriented code will give you *no* new features to play around with. All it gives you is a more structured development environment.

In terms of speed, using OOP coding styles will actually *slow you down* for small projects, unless you take the time to get proficient in it. Object-oriented code requires well-defined interfaces in your code, and this can also make your code longer.

Um, I feel a third question coming up:

- Why the heck do I need to learn OOP, then?

In many cases, you don't need OOP. Small projects can be created using the styleless but structured code you've been using throughout the book so far. If your code won't be reused in anything else (that is, you'll start your next web project from scratch), then OOP isn't appropriate.

Here are the instances when OOP *is* appropriate:

- **When you're building large applications**. Writing the first thing that comes into your head is a good way of getting a small, 30-line ActionScript trick-shot working, but for anything bigger, you need a more structured approach. Something like the Futuremedia site is about as big as you can get with a general modular coding style that doesn't use OOP before you need to rethink your strategy

- **When you want to reuse your code**. If you're going to use the same code often, it makes a lot of sense to make that code a class or part of an existing class. When you do this, the interfaces to your code become methods and properties, both of which are totally recognizable to you *and* any other ActionScript coder. This makes your code easy to use in new Flash FLAs—you can simply treat the new features provided by the code as an add-on to ActionScript. A good example of this process is components. They're class based, and this makes them easy to add to your code. All the new features of components are accessed by calling methods or changing properties.

> You may have assumed that the methods and properties that you used to access the TextArea and Button *components are part of ActionScript. They aren't; instead, they're the interfaces to the code that drives the components. That provides a good example of how closely integrated a class-based add-on can be. It can begin to look like you're using a new part of ActionScript itself, rather than code written by someone else!*

Hopefully you're now sold on OOP and know when to use it. The next issue is what flavor of OOP to use. Flash has two available:

- **Object based**: Flash 5 was the first revision of Flash to include ActionScript with classes, but it didn't include any features that would allow you to build your *own* classes. The way you have to do it is take an existing class and add new stuff to it. This type of class isn't really a class at all (although it's closely related). Programmers call this "class-like" structure a **prototype**, and the programming style associated with prototypes is called *object based* rather than *object oriented*.

- **Class based**: This is the real deal—true OOP. It's available only in Flash MX 2004 (both Standard and Professional editions). Unlike the prototype-based approach, it allows you to create totally new classes.

It's also much more structured than the prototype approach. This makes it overkill for small bits of code, but as your applications get bigger, this structure starts to give real advantages.

Enough talk—let's have a look at prototypes.

Prototypes

Prototypes are cool. They allow you to extend existing classes quickly and simply. Suppose you want a function that allows you to move a movie clip to a new position on the stage, (x, y).

> **Creating the "mover" function using standard code**

You could create a function much like the following one to do this.

1. In a new FLA, call the existing layer actions, and then select frame 1 and attach the following script to it:

```
function mover(x:Number, y:Number,
➥ clip:MovieClip) {
  clip._x = x;
  clip._y = y;
}
```

> *This code uses typing (where the data type is specified as well as the data value) but, of course, this isn't mandatory.*

2. Lock layer actions. Create a new layer called graphics.

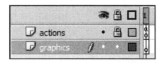

3. Select frame 1 of layer graphics and draw a circle about 20 pixels in diameter, roughly in the middle of the stage. Select it and make it into a movie clip (*F8*) called circle. Give the instance on the stage the instance name myClip.

4. To use the function to move the movie clip myClip, select frame 1 in layer actions and add the new line below your existing function mover, as follows:

```
function mover(x:Number, y:Number,
➥ clip:MovieClip) {
  clip._x = x;
  clip._y = y;
}
mover(10, 10, myClip);
```

The last line calls the function mover and causes myClip to move to the top-left corner of the stage, to coordinates (10, 10).

Although this script is OK as it stands, mover is a cool function to have around. It would be great if Macromedia had added this as a method to the movie clip so you could have done something like this:

```
myClip.mover(10, 10);
```

In this case, you assume a method called mover that is part of the movie clip class, in much the same way as you assume a method called play() exists in ActionScript when you use myClip.play(). The trouble is that there is no method called mover . . . yet!

5. Change the script as follows:

```
MovieClip.prototype.mover =
➥ function(x:Number, y:Number) {
  this._x = x;
  this._y = y;
};
myClip.mover(10, 20);
```

Although the innards of the function are still the same, you change the way the function is called and the way it's defined. The definition line now looks like this:

```
MovieClip.prototype.mover =
➥ function(x:Number, y:Number) {
```

You attach the function mover to somewhere (or something) called MovieClip.prototype. What's that? Well, the MovieClip part doesn't refer to just *any* movie clip, but *the* movie clip: the MovieClip class.

> *Whenever you're referring to a class in Flash (or any other programming environment), by convention you should start the reference with a capital letter.*

So you aren't referring to a particular timeline or instance when you write MovieClip, but to *all* movie clips! OK. Next up, you'll see prototype. A prototype is a definition of what a movie clip *is*.

Let's break this down a little. Suppose you're working in the auto industry, and you're the production manager at the factory where the cars are actually built. For every car production line, the scientists and engineers over in the research and development (R&D) department have built a **prototype car**. The prototype car is a one-off vehicle that has been fully tested to work, and you see the results of this as a series of drawings (blueprints) that specifies what you need to build.

Now and then, you need to make minor corrections to the design, because during production meetings, your process and production engineers will say things like "We need to reduce the amount of steel in the car, because the price of steel is rising." It's up to you and the team to make changes to the prototype design in line with the changing economic or social constraints. Whatever you change, though, your remit is to build essentially the same car—the basic prototype remains unchanged.

Using prototypes in Flash is similar. You can alter bits and pieces of the prototype to make slightly different cars, but the blueprint for the car (the *class*) remains essentially the same.

You've gotten as far as MovieClip.prototype. The next part is mover. This is the bit you're adding to the prototype. Like the auto-factory production manager, you take the basic prototype and tweak it slightly. The only real differences are as follows:

- You're building movie clips, not cars.
- The R&D team is Macromedia. Macromedia defined the MovieClip prototype for you to build standard movie clips. Macromedia doesn't expect you to change the MovieClip significantly, so rather than allow you to build totally new classes, Macromedia has given you the ability to make changes to the existing class by making additions to the basic prototype.

Creating an inertial movement method using prototypes

Suppose you want to create an animated inertia effect for a movie clip. You could simply write an event handler to do this. Inertial motion is a common motion effect, though, so it would be cool to have a new and general movie clip method, MovieClip.moveInertia(x, y), where (x, y) is the position that you want a clip to move to. The completed FLA for this exercise is included in the chapter download as prototype01.fla if you get stuck.

1. Create a new FLA and set the frame rate to 18 fps (Modify ➤ Document).

2. Rename the current layer as graphics. In this layer, draw a small square of width and height 35 pixels, in the middle of the stage. With the square selected, press *F8* and make it a movie clip called square.

3. With the movie clip square instance on the stage still selected, use the Properties panel to give it the instance name myClip:

4. Create a new layer called actions. Pin frame 1 of this new layer. Time to get scripting!

5. Enter the following script in the Script pane of the Actions panel:

```
MovieClip.prototype.moveInertia =
➡ function(x:Number, y:Number) {
  this.onEnterFrame = function() {
    var distX:Number = x-this._x;
    var distY:Number = y-this._y;
    this._x += distX/4;
    this._y += distY/4;
    if (Math.abs(this._x-x)<1) {
      if (Math.abs(this._y-y)<1) {
        this._x = x;
        this._y = y;
        delete this.onEnterFrame
      }
    }
  };
};
myClip.moveInertia(10, 10);
```

The first line of this script defines the new moveInertia(x, y) method of the MovieClip class. All the code within this definition sets up an onEnterFrame that's attached to the movie clip this method is called for. The final line calls this method for the movie clip myClip.

6. If you test this movie, you should see the movie clip move with inertia to the top-left corner of the stage. Cool. You have a problem, though. Methods must be **transparent**. A transparent method is one that does its thing without disturbing anything else.

> You should avoid creating methods that aren't transparent to other code. When changing prototypes, you're making low-level changes to the way Flash works, and you should be careful not to upset anything else. For example, you should avoid overwriting anything. A prototype should not, for example, add event handlers to the this movie clip, because this may already have an onEnterFrame attached to it. There are several ways around this, but the easiest is to create a dummy movie clip to attach an event to, which is what you'll do next.

7. You can see why this method isn't transparent. Add the following code to the end of the script so far. This code adds an onEnterFrame to myClip to cause it to rotate.

```
myClip.onEnterFrame = function() {
  this._rotation += 5;
};
```

When you test the movie now, you'll see that because you've tried to attach two onEnterFrames to the same movie clip, one of them gets overwritten. A well-written method shouldn't do this—you should see the movie clip rotate *and* move with inertia at the same time.

8. Change the script as shown:

```
MovieClip.prototype.moveInertia =
➥ function(x:Number, y:Number) {
  var clip:MovieClip = this.
➥ createEmptyMovieClip(
➥ "moveIntertiaHolder",
➥ this.getNextHighestDepth());
  clip.onEnterFrame = function() {
    var targetClip:MovieClip=this._parent;
    var distX:Number = x-targetClip._x;
    var distY:Number = y-targetClip._y;
    targetClip._x += distX/4;
    targetClip._y += distY/4;
    if (Math.abs(targetClip._x-x)<1) {
      if (Math.abs(targetClip._y-y)<1) {
        targetClip._x = x;
        targetClip._y = y;
        this.removeMovieClip();
      }
    }
  };
};
myClip.moveInertia(10, 10);
myClip.onEnterFrame = function() {
  this._rotation += 5;
  if (this._x == 10) {
    this.moveInertia(400, 300);
  }
};
```

This time, you create a prototype that sneaks in, does its job, cleans up after itself, and sneaks away again, so much so that the onEnterFrame you define is oblivious. You see the movie clip move around under control of the moveInertia() method at the same time as it's rotated by the onEnterFrame.

How does this work? Well, the easiest way to see what happens is to use the debugger. Select Control ➤ Debug Movie. Don't click the debugger's ▶ icon until you've set it up as shown in the following image (select the _level0.myClip timeline and make sure the Variables tab is selected), because things will move fairly quickly when it all starts.

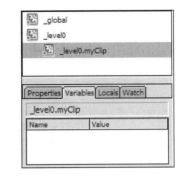

You can temporarily reduce the frame rate to 1 or 2 fps if you want things to move slower.

When you start the movie, a new movie clip, myClip.moveInertiaHolder, is created. The method attaches the onEnterFrame to the new clip, and this allows any other onEnterFrame to work unhindered on myClip. There's a chance that the user has placed a movie clip with the same name and position as your new clip, but you've made this highly unlikely by basing the created movie clip's name on the method calling it. If the user had a same-named movie clip on the time-line, it would most likely be because the user is doing something similar to your method and wouldn't need to call your method.

When the method has finished (it's called twice, so you should see two inertial moves in the animation), the moveInertia() method cleans up. It deletes moveInertiaHolder from the timeline of the target clip (myClip, in this case). Because you're creating local variables (that is, you use var within the functions), none of the variables exists outside the function blocks that make up your method.

So, using the same style of coding, you could create several animation methods:

```
MovieClip.rotater()  rotates a movie clip
MovieClip.fader()  fades a movie clip
Etc.
```

These methods will be transparent to each other, so you can have more than one running at the same time to create some very complex animations.

Hang on a minute, though—all this looks remarkably familiar! When you looked at creating modular ActionScript earlier in the book, you created a drag-and-drop component that turned the target clip into a mouse follower. The difference here is that you're going deeper into ActionScript and adding new features to ActionScript itself. You aren't using graphical stuff like drag-and-drop building blocks, but you're changing the Flash environment itself.

You can make your prototypes modular in a much better way by making them an include file, as follows:

1. Select lines 1 to 17 (that is, your entire prototype definition). In the Flash Standard edition, select File ➤ New and open a new Flash file. In the Professional edition, open a new AS file (File ➤ New ➤ ActionScript File).

2. If you're using the Standard edition, select a keyframe in the new FLA, paste the script into the Script pane of the Actions panel, and then select Export Script from the Actions panel's Panel menu (the icon at the top-right corner) to save it as moveInertia_prot.as. If you're using the Professional edition, paste the script in the full-screen script window and save it as moveInertia_prot.as.

3. You can now load the prototype in your main FLA by changing your script as follows:

```
#include "moveInertia_prot.as"
//
myClip.moveInertia(10, 10);
myClip.onEnterFrame = function() {
  this._rotation += 5;
  if (this._x == 10) {
    this.moveInertia(400, 300);
  }
};
```

When you use the MovieClip.moveInertia() method, you need to know its syntax (MovieClip.moveInertia(x, y)), and you need to include the file moveInertia.as if you want to use it. What does that give you? To the professional scripter, it gives *lots* of possibilities:

- If you want to use other methods, you can just include the AS files for those as well, and then use them as if they were always a part of ActionScript.

- You can arrange all your prototype definitions into a common directory, building up a library of common and useful prototypes.

- Because you're pulling in prewritten bits of code that have already been fully tested and are transparent to the current FLA, not only are those code bits bug-free (so you don't have to keep reinventing the wheel), but also they *won't affect your existing code* because they're transparent to it. This makes development much faster, particularly when you're building large applications.

- Splitting up the code like this makes it easier to divide the workload. An ActionScript coder can concentrate on writing the prototype libraries (the #include files). Because the prototypes use the same interfaces as standard ActionScript methods, it's easy for the designers to simply load them into any FLA in progress and start using them *without knowing how they work*.

See that? *You're creating modular code without needing any black boxes.* You've abstracted so far away that the concept of black-box containers holding your code becomes irrelevant. Using the prototype level, you bypass all that modularity and use the inherent low-level modularity of the class structures that underpin ActionScript itself.

Although you've built a simple method, here the way you have done it is important. This is powerful stuff. You're moving away from writing code that uses ActionScript to writing code that changes ActionScript itself, so that rather than writing code that does stuff, you're first writing more general code that changes ActionScript so that it's closer to your solution. This means that your **application-specific code** is shorter, which in turn leads to less time spent on coding, fewer errors, and the ability to manage larger overall scripts.

You're almost at the summit, but you have one steeper slope to climb: true class-based coding.

ActionScript 2.0 classes

The difference between prototype-based or object-based coding and true OOP coding can be explained using the car production analogy. In prototype coding, you're given a basic design from the R&D department, and you can build on this basic design to make minor variations. In a true class-based language, you can also fully define the design yourself. You can create your own prototypes, and these are now called *classes*.

In this more integrated car-manufacturing company, you aren't only the production manager—you also have direct control of the R&D department. The benefits of this are as follows:

- You're better suited to building cars that take into consideration both the technical aspects *and* the production aspects, which results in a better design.
- You have the ability to design things *other* than just cars. You have control of the R&D team, so you could tell the team to build an aircraft, for example. The team would use its expertise in car manufacturing to design items that are similar to cars, but the team would design totally new plans for stuff like avionics and wings, which aren't part of a car.

So what are the downsides?

- The flexibility comes at a cost. You have to consider R&D and production as part of the project every time, even if you aren't going to use R&D much. This creates waste for projects that don't really require this dual consideration. It's just overkill for designing a slightly new dashboard shape, for example (which is a production problem, with a little ergonomics and consumer testing thrown in).
- You have to know more. As soon as you're charged with leading both the R&D and production departments, you have to know what makes both tick.

So, in general, you have increased flexibility and structure versus the increased workload needed to set all this extra stuff up.

Another point worth mentioning now is that using class-based code doesn't make the final code any more efficient. In fact, Flash will convert a lot of your class-based code into simpler modular code as part of the conversion from FLA to SWF.

> *The Flash player doesn't think in terms of class-based code. Whether you've used prototypes or classes in the FLA is irrelevant as far as the Flash player (and, for that matter, the end user) is concerned.*

The only advantage of using one style over another relates to managing the coding project. Choose the one that best fits what you're comfortable with and the size of the task.

- Well-written modular code is good for most website design.
- Prototype-based design is good when you want to change one or two existing classes such as MovieClip. You can use well-written modular code along with prototype-based code.
- Class-based code is useful when you want to build major additions to ActionScript (such as components) or you want to build complex Flash sites.
- Some problems involve working with classes, so it makes sense to use classes in your solution. This works well when you're handling large amounts of information (such as databases) or you're working with fairly complex transmission protocols as part of your design. By integrating the class definitions (of the objects you're interfacing with) into your solution, you're better positioned to manage the interfaces.

It has to be stressed that there's no pecking order here. Suggesting that class-based code is better than function-based structured code is much the same as saying that a hammer is better than a screwdriver.

The statement is nonsense unless you also include *the task*. A hammer is good for hitting nails, but if you always think in terms of a hammer, all your solutions will involve hitting things, which may not always be appropriate.

How class-based coding works

Flash class-based programming involves the use of one or more classes that *extend* your code toward the solution. For example, if you're creating a general set of scripts to allow game programming, you might write

- A general movement class, Mover.

- A more aware class, Navigate. As well as moving the sprites, this class is able to know exactly where the sprite can and can't move, and take appropriate action.

- A final class, Animate. As well as moving and navigating, this class controls the appearance of the sprite, so an alien that has just been hit will be caused to explode.

The way to write class-based code would be to start with the simplest class, Mover. The Mover class would be rather like the moveInertia method in that it would contain methods that allow movement to specified points on the stage.

The next class, Navigate, would extend Mover by preventing any movement that stopped the movie clip, for example, from moving offscreen.

Finally, the third class, Animate, might be designed so that more advanced methods are available. You might have additional methods that can ensure a movie clip will always point in the direction it's traveling.

The cool thing about this is that you have different levels of problem solving:

- The low-level classes such as Mover are very general and would be used in *all* games.

- Classes like Navigate would be used in most games.

- Classes like Animate would be used in games in which you actually wanted sprites to point in the direction they're moving.

So, rather than a simple library of finished methods as you see via prototypes, you end up with different *layers* of problem solving in the class-based approach. You start at the foundation, building the simplest classes, and then you use these classes to build more complex classes.

The advantage of this is that not only do you have structured code, but you also have a structured way of splitting complex problems in a series of levels of problem solving, rather like building a house:

1. Build the foundation (the basic or core classes).

2. Extend the foundation by adding more functionality.

3. Keep repeating the last step, building new classes until you've solved your problem.

Let's try this out with a simple example. I recommend you try this using the Professional edition of Flash, although you'll be able to get by using the Standard edition.

Creating and using the low-level (base) class

The lowest level class is called Mover. This class will do much the same thing as the MovieClip.moveInertia() method you created using prototypes.

The first thing you'll do is create the class files. Rather than type these in, load your version. Professional edition users should use File ➤ Open and load Mover.as. Standard edition users will have to load the AS files via the Actions panel's Import Script option (it's on the Panel menu, which you can access via the icon at the top-right corner of the Actions panel).

Flash Standard edition users should note that they won't be able to autoformat or check the syntax of the AS files without raising an error. A class definition *must* be defined via an external AS file, and Flash won't like the fact that Standard edition users have loaded the class into an FLA.

```
class Mover {
  //
  // PROPERTIES
  private var target:MovieClip;
  private var clip:MovieClip;
  private var distX:Number;
  private var distY:Number;
  //
  // CONSTRUCTOR
  public function Mover(targetClip) {
    target = targetClip;
  }
  //
  // PUBLIC METHODS
  public function
➥ moveInertia(x:Number, y:Number):Void {
    clip = target.createEmptyMovieClip(
➥ "moveIntertiaHolder",
➥ target.getNextHighestDepth());
    clip.x = x;
    clip.y = y;
    clip.onEnterFrame = moveClip;
  }
  //
  public function getTarget():MovieClip {
    return target;
  }
  //
  // PRIVATE METHODS
  private function moveClip():Void {
    var me = this;
    var mc = me._parent;
    distX = me.x-mc._x;
    distY = me.y-mc._y;
    mc._x += distX/4;
    mc._y += distY/4;
    if (Math.abs(mc._x-me.x)<1) {
      if (Math.abs(mc._y-me.y)<1) {
        mc._x = me.x;
```

```
        mc._y = me.y;
        me.removeMovieClip();
      }
    }
  }
}
```

Hmm. This code is quite a bit longer and more complicated than the prototype version! There's a very good reason for this: the code is *very* structured, with extremely tight interfaces between the separate code modules, and this extra structure takes time to build. The core code is still the same, but the structure is now a substantial part of the code.

The general structure of a class definition named *className* is to create an AS file with the filename className.as and content as follows:

```
class className {
  //Define properties
  //Define constructor (function className)
  //Define methods
}
```

This is why your AS file is called Mover.as. It *has* to have the same name as the class, otherwise Flash won't be able to find it.

Within the base class definition, you define properties and methods. Both properties and methods can be one of two things: private or public.

■ A **public** part of the class definition is available to ActionScript outside the class file. A public variable becomes an instance *property* when using the class back in the world of the FLA, just like the _x property of a movie clip is a freely accessible (public) property, and all movie clips have one.

■ A **private** part of the class definition is *not available* to ActionScript outside the class file. A private property is used internally by the class, and it isn't for use by the main application. Think of a private part of the class as the part of the black box that you aren't supposed to see. It's the "black code" that you shouldn't use because it does low-level stuff that you don't really need to bother with.

The Mover class is defined in two parts: first the property definitions and then the methods. The first section defines the properties of Mover:

```
// PROPERTIES
private var target:MovieClip;
private var clip:MovieClip;
private var distX:Number;
private var distY:Number;
```

As you can see, all of them are private.

■ target: This is the name of the movie clip you're moving.

■ clip: This is the name of the dummy movie clip. As you'll recall, this movie clip exists in the prototype version to make the operations of the onEnterFrame transparent.

■ distX and distY: These are two internal values that are used to work out the inertia motion. Again, the main FLA isn't required to know about these values, so you hide them.

Next up, you have the constructor function. This function is called whenever the main code using this class creates a new instance with new and it must return nothing.

```
// CONSTRUCTOR
public function Mover
➥ (targetClip:MovieClip) {
  target = targetClip;
}
```

The constructor here accepts a movie clip as an argument.

The next part is the functions that define the methods. There are two public functions, moveInertia() and getTarget(). This first of these functions creates the dummy movie clip, sets the data that the dummy movie clip needs to know, and attaches the onEnterFrame script (moveClip()) to the dummy clip, clip.

```
// PUBLIC METHODS
public function
➥ moveInertia(x:Number, y:Number):Void {
  clip = target.createEmptyMovieClip(
➥ "moveIntertiaHolder",
➥ target.getNextHighestDepth());
  clip.x = x;
  clip.y = y;
  clip.onEnterFrame = moveClip;
}
```

The second function returns the name of the target movie clip that you're controlling with this class:

```
public function getTarget():MovieClip {
  return target;
}
```

The function moveClip() is defined next. Note that this is defined as private. It's used by moveInertia(), and nothing else needs to look at this code, so you make it inaccessible outside the class by making it private. Inside this function, you have your old friend, the inertia equation. You stop the animation when the target clip is within 1 pixel of its target position via the if statements at the end of the function, and you do this by deleting the dummy clip.

```
// PRIVATE METHODS
private function moveClip():Void {
  var me = this;
  var mc = me._parent;
  distX = me.x-mc._x;
  distY = me.y-mc._y;
  mc._x += distX/4;
  mc._y += distY/4;
```

```
if (Math.abs(mc._x-me.x)<1) {
  if (Math.abs(mc._y-me.y)<1) {
    mc._x = me.x;
    mc._y = me.y;
    me.removeMovieClip();
  }
 }
}
```

You need to notice a couple of other things:

- **There's an almost total lack of the** this **path**. Class-based code needs to be *very* modular, and it uses explicit interfaces. The this path is an implied argument and doesn't cut it in the mega-strict world of classes. I've used it only once, when I needed to know the scope of the onEnterFrame.

- **Everything is fully defined and explicit**. Everything has its place. The class may look a bit daunting, but once you get a feel for it, you'll find that this structure makes programming *easier*. Why? Well, in normal ActionScript, if you get no errors, you may or may not have a working FLA. The only way to know is to test it thoroughly. In well-written class-based code, if your code compiles with no errors, it's much more likely that this is because your code is working. This is the real payback of taking the time to use class-based code.

Phew! Yeah, I know. All this sounds like learning Vulcan at the moment. The main problem is that class-based code isn't ultra-difficult—it's ultra-simple. You need to define *everything*, and that can be difficult to do sometimes, because you know too much and assume the computer does too. That's the path that leads to errors.

Class-based coding stops you from assuming anything by acting like a 3-year-old. You as patient parents need to explain the problem, not to an advanced coding language, but to a *child*. The class-based structure acts like a curious preschooler, constantly pointing and saying "What is that?" and "Where does it come from?" It won't quit repeating these annoying but simple questions.

The real simplicity is revealed when you actually use the class. Open a new FLA and enter the following code:

```
var myClip:MovieClip;
var myMover:Mover = new Mover(myClip);
myMover.moveInertia(10, 10);
```

If you now create a movie clip with the instance name myClip on the stage, then save the FLA *in the same place as the* Mover.as *file*, the whole thing will work just like the prototype version did. The instance myMover (which is an instance of the Mover class) will take the movie clip myClip and control it without your having to do anything. You don't have to know about all those internal interfaces in the class or anything about all that private code.

Try adding this line:

```
trace(myMover.getTarget());
```

This uses the getTarget() method to remind you which movie clip you're controlling. Finally, try this:

```
var myClip:String;
var myMover:Mover = new Mover(myClip);
myMover.moveInertia("f", 10);
```

This code has two errors. You pass a string to the class when creating your instance in line 2, and you pass the string f instead of a number in the last line. You'll find that meaningful error messages come back. Flash tells you that you're sending the wrong type of data in both cases.

```
▼ Output
**Error** Scene=Scene 1, layer=actions, frame=1:
Line 2: Type mismatch.
     var myMover:Mover = new Mover(myClip);

**Error** Scene=Scene 1, layer=actions, frame=1:
Line 3: Type mismatch.
     myMover.moveInertia("f", 10);

Total ActionScript Errors: 2     Reported Errors:
2
```

Extending the class

The structure also allows you to easily *extend* your class, creating a more advanced class over the existing one, rather like building a high-tech and modern house starts with a simple concrete foundation.

> When you extend a class, the new class is called the **subclass**, *and the class that has been extended is the* **superclass**.

In this simple example, you'll create a new class, Navigator, which is the beginnings of a more complex set of motion routines based on the more primitive (**base class** or **lower level class**) Mover class. Navigator will allow you to limit the inertia movement within a bounding box. At the moment, you can use the Mover class to make your target clip go anywhere. What is more useful is a method that stops you from going outside a defined area as shown.

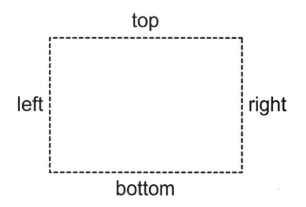

The constructor for the Navigator class has five parameters:

```
var myNavigator:Navigator = new Navigator
➥ (target, left, right, top, bottom);
```

target is the movie clip you want to animate, and *left*, *right*, *top*, and *bottom* define the rectangular area you want to keep *target* within.

The Navigator class extends the current method *Mover.moveInertia()* by never moving *target* outside the bounding box. Let's have a look at the class definition to do this. Open the AS file Navigator.as. As you can see, this has the same general structure as Mover except that it's *extending* an existing class rather than *defining* one from scratch.

```
class Navigator extends Mover {
  //
  // PROPERTIES
  private var left:Number;
  private var right:Number;
  private var top:Number;
  private var bottom:Number;
  private var x:Number;
  private var y:Number;
  //
  // CONSTRUCTOR
  public function
➥ Navigator(target:MovieClip,
➥ l:Number, r:Number, t:Number, b:Number)
  {
      super(target);
      left = l;
      right = r;
      top = t;
      bottom = b;
  }
  // METHODS
  public function moveClipTo(xPos:Number,
➥ yPos:Number) {
      x = xPos;
      y = yPos;
      if (xPos<left) {
        x = left;
      } else if (xPos>right) {
        x = right;
      }
      if (yPos<top) {
        y = top;
      } else if (yPos>bottom) {
        y = bottom;
      }
      moveInertia(x, y);
  }
}
```

The two important lines are highlighted in the preceding script. The line

```
super(target);
```

is the first line of the constructor, and it's telling Flash "Start with Mover, and add my new methods and properties to that class (to create a more advanced class)." Navigator *inherits* methods and properties originally belonging to Mover.

The function moveClipTo() has a set of if statements that make sure that the target position (x, y) the user specifies for the animation is never outside the bounding box. The last line of the function calls the method moveInertia() from the superclass. So how does this extend Mover in real terms, and what are the advantages of extending anyway?

Well, you add the "keep target within the bounding box" functionality. Rather than add more lines of code to the Mover class to do this, you bolt on a new code module. Even your updates to make your code more advanced are now modular! You don't have to stop with Navigator, though. You could extend Mover in other ways with other classes.

Although class-based code looks daunting right now, have a look at the differences between Mover and Navigator. You'll see that they're similar in general structure. All classes are similar, and this is the key, because once you build one and have it working, you can make others easily. Although there are all sorts of more advanced substructures and techno-speak to describe classes, the basic class definition isn't that difficult.

Book project: Finishing the Futuremedia site

You now have a UI that's starting to look like the finished version of the site. You need to add the following to the site you've created so far:

- A way to move backward as well as well as forward. In the final site, this is done via the icons that appear at the bottom of the site.

- The UI sounds.
- The content.

The starting point of this chapter's book project is the file you finished with in the previous chapter futuremedia_code04.fla.

Going backward

The file futuremedia_code05.fla is my version of the site with a working backward navigation. If you choose to use this file, remember that you must place it in the same location as the config.as file from the last chapter, otherwise it won't be able to find its configuration during compilation.

You now have a website UI that looks almost complete. There is, in fact, only one remaining thing you have to do before you can finally start thinking about finishing the site: you need to implement the backward navigation.

In this part of the project, you'll add the code to read the backward path, and you'll then build the backward animation into the existing code. This means that you also need to add the little icons representing the backward path (the breadcrumb trail).

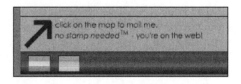

Adding the backward path

If you have a look at the final version of the site, you'll see that the back strip has a number of icons at the bottom left. Clicking one of these icons takes you back one or more pages through the current navigation, and clicking the first icon takes you back to the home page.

You already have the symbol for the icons built and ready in the Library (mc.icon in the User interface ➤ active UI stuff Library folder). This symbol is exactly the same as page, except there's no text.

During testing of the site, I found that the icon looked much better if it had a few separating lines on it, so you may as well add them now. Double-click mc.icon. It should have one layer at the moment, back. Add a new layer above it called lines. In this layer, you need to add hairlines around the perimeter, and two going across as shown in the following image. Give the ones that go across an alpha value of about 40%. I've made the colors of the following screenshot brighter so that you can see the lines (they're a little difficult to see against the grays!).

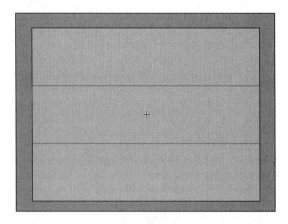

> To place the two lines that go across, it's easiest to draw two horizontal lines (hold down SHIFT as you drag them out using the Line tool), and then position the lines precisely vertically using the Properties panel, with Y values of −90 and 90 for the two lines.

You need to create the functions to drive the icons, and then you need to integrate them with the existing code so that the functions are called at the appropriate times. So what do you need? Well, there are a number of stages you need to consider.

Create each icon as new pages are added

Initially, at the home page, there are no icons. As soon as you click a strip, the icon to go back to the home page appears. As you click further strips that take you deeper into the site, more icons appear, each color-coded to look like a small version of the page

it represents. Thus, a breadcrumb trail that shows you the path you've taken is created.

Delete icons as they're used to navigate backward

A given icon can be used only once; as soon as you've used one to go backward, it's no longer needed and should disappear, as should the "back history" from that point onward. For example, if you click the second icon in a breadcrumb trail, you'll no longer need the second or third icon to remain. So clicking the home icon should result in all icons disappearing, because you've gone back all the way to the start.

Display a new animation transition that shows the effects of backward navigation

The final site has a separate animation to represent the user moving backward. Because this is different from the forward animation (the selected icon grows from the back strip to become the new page), you need to code a new function to handle the backward animation.

Make sure that the UI knows where it needs to return

An obvious point, but perhaps the hardest one so far: you need to re-create the page that the icon represents. You need three things to do this:

- You need to know the page number of the page each icon represents. This value is held in the variable currentPage when the page is being or has been displayed, so you need to somehow store this value so that each icon knows what the currentPage value was when the page you're going to was last displayed.

- You need to know the colors of the new page you'll be going back to. Remember that the color of each page (except the home page) isn't predefined; it's calculated on the fly. However, the icon already "knows" the page colors, because it's colored using the same scheme.

- If the current page contains content, you need to delete it from the screen before you go backward. An interesting question is "What if the new page you want to go back to also has content on it?"

Well, that one caused me some worry initially, but the answer is actually very simple: *that never happens, so you don't have to worry about it*. The navigation is designed so that only the last page in any navigation is a content page; all the others leading up to it are link pages.

> *Although the back strip functionality looks and feels totally simple and intuitive, and is one of the little touches that makes the navigation look so sweet, you'll have realized by now that it's actually one of the hardest parts to design. Ergonomic simplicity is usually one of the more difficult things to code for all but the most basic UIs.*

Now that you've defined the problem, let's turn to the coding solution. You'll split the functionality into two parts:

- The part that looks after the building of the icon (and related data and event handlers), buildIcon()
- The part that looks after the animation transition, iconTransition()

The starting point for adding the new code is futuremedia_code04.fla from the last chapter. The first FLA for this chapter, futuremedia_code05.fla, contains all the new code to handle the backward navigation, plus the change to the icon symbol.

You also need to keep a track of the number of icons you have, so the first thing to do is create a new variable, iconCount (it's in the INITIALIZE block):

```
...
// Define navigation strip variables
var iconCount:Number = 0;
var NAVSTRIP_X:Number = BORDER;
var NAVSTRIP_Y:Number = BOTTOM;
...
```

The next thing you'll look at is where you'll build the new icon. It's a good idea to build it as soon as a new page is created, and that means at the beginning of navigate() (right at the start of the listing):

```
// DEFINE EVENT SCRIPTS
navigate = function () {
  unpopulateEvents();
  // build icon to get back to current page
  buildIcon(currentPage);
  // set up target for animation transition
```

The buildIcon() function is similar to the code you've created for the tricolor, and you'll be using many of the same functions. Because of this, I'll go through it fairly rapidly and concentrate on the stuff that's unique to the icons.

OK, you'll now put buildIcon()directly after unpopulateEvents(). Here's the code:

```
unpopulateEvents = function () {
  delete tricolor.strip0_mc.onRelease;
  delete tricolor.strip1_mc.onRelease;
  delete tricolor.strip2_mc.onRelease;
  tricolor.strip0_mc.useHandCursor = false;
  tricolor.strip1_mc.useHandCursor = false;
  tricolor.strip2_mc.useHandCursor = false;
};
buildIcon = function (pageIndex) {
  // initialize
  var pageIndex:Number = 0;
  var iconDepth:Number =
➥ iconDepth=100+iconCount;
  var iconName:MovieClip =
➥ this.attachMovie("icon", "icon" +
➥ iconCount, iconDepth);
  // apply functions to icon
  stripCols.apply(iconName);
  // set colors, size and position
  iconName._xscale = iconName._yscale=4;
  iconName.setCol(color0, color1, color2);
  iconName._x =
➥ NAVSTRIP_X+(40*iconCount)+10;
  iconName._y = NAVSTRIP_Y+5;
  // update iconCount by one for next icon
  // and store current page details onto
  // the icon stack
  iconCount++;
  iconName.currentPage = currentPage;
  iconName.color0 = color0;
  iconName.color1 = color1;
  iconName.color2 = color2;
  iconName.iconCount = iconCount;
```

```
// add the animation functions to icon
// define icon button script
iconName.onRelease = function() {
  // delete all icons after this one
  for (i=this.iconCount;
➥  i<=iconCount; i++) {
    _root["icon"+i].removeMovieClip();
  }
  // delete any content on
  // the current page
  _root.createEmptyMovieClip("dummy",
➥  10000);
  // zoom icon into the new current page
  s=4, x=this._x, y=this._y;
  xTarget = BORDER;
  yTarget = BORDER;
  sTarget = 100;
  this.onRelease = undefined;
  this.onEnterFrame = iconTransition;
  };
};
```

Uh . . . what's all that about, then? Let's have a look around.

First, you have an argument for the buildIcon() function, currentPage. Looking at the code you added in navigate() just now, this is simply your old friend currentPage.

When you start, there are no icons on stage, and you'll have to place them on the stage with code. You have three ways to do this:

■ Drag an instance of the icon movie clip, icon, onto work areas and put it somewhere off stage where the user won't be able to see it. When you need icons to appear, you copy them via the duplicateMovieClip() method.

■ Copy the icon clips directly from the Library using attachMovie().

■ Create an empty movie clip and draw an icon inside it using the drawing API.

The first method is what folks used way back in the days of Flash 5, but you have better ways to handle this now. The third method is cool, but there's not really any reason for getting so complicated, so you'll opt for the second method.

To create movie clips dynamically, you need to put three things in place:

■ Set up the symbol to be attached properly in the Library by giving it a linkage identifier and getting Flash to export it correctly. More on this in a moment.

■ Give the movie clip you want to copy (or attach to the stage) an instance name. You'll have to give each icon a unique name because you'll need to selectively remove them later.

■ Give each icon a unique **depth**. Flash places everything onscreen using depth.

This defines the order that things are drawn in; the higher the depth, the more "in front" it is. This is rather like layers. I use the phrase "rather like layers" because there's one major difference: there can be only one thing at each depth. If you try to put a movie clip at depth 100 when there's already something occupying that depth, that something will be deleted and replaced by your new movie clip. The upshot of this is that when you assign depths, you have to make sure that you don't overwrite existing and already occupied depths. There's an easy way to do this: *make sure each depth value you use is unique.*

Layers don't actually exist in Flash SWFs—they're there as an authoring tool for us designers. Layer order is used to define the depth order (among other things), which is what the Flash player understands. Stuff placed on stage has a negative depth, and this is assigned by Flash itself during the process of converting an FLA into a SWF. When you attach content directly to the stage at runtime, the depth is positive, and this means that the things you attach will always be in front of any content placed manually during author time. Valid and supported depths that you can use are any integer between 0 and approximately 16,000.

So what does all that mean for you? Well, the linkage identifier and export options are set up for you in the files I've provided, but if you're working through your own FLA from scratch, you need to do the following:

1. In the Library, locate the `mc.icon` movie clip (it's in the User interface ➤ active UI stuff Library folder, remember?), and right-click/*Alt*-click it. Select Linkage.

2. Check the Export for ActionScript check box (the Export in first frame check box will also become checked when you do this). In the Identifier text entry box (which is now selectable), enter icon.

The reason you have to do all this is as follows. The identifier is simply the name Flash will use to recognize the movie clip when it's in the Library. Normally, Flash doesn't include any symbols that aren't used in the final SWF. By "aren't used in the final SWF" I mean that the symbol doesn't appear on any timeline of the FLA. That's cool, but if you're going to place content dynamically at runtime, *it won't appear on any timeline at the time when Flash creates the SWF* (as noted in the last chapter).

Left to its own devices, Flash wouldn't include such content in the SWF Library. By checking Export for ActionScript, you're overriding Flash and saying "Well, it's not on any timeline now, but put it in the SWF because I'll need it during runtime."

OK, so you've told Flash that you need a symbol. The next thing Flash needs to know is *when* the symbol will be needed. Flash usually arranges things in the SWF so that the symbols needed early on (that appear in the first few frames of the timeline) stream in first. Stuff that is exported for ActionScript will *never* appear on a timeline of the FLA, so Flash has no idea when it's required.

Flash therefore has two options: load stuff marked for Export for ActionScript first, or load it last. You're best off downloading the symbol on the first frame, because then at least you know that it's there right away. This is

why you should *always* leave Export in first frame selected when you select Export for ActionScript. There are a few advanced reasons you wouldn't do this, but they're few and far between, so it's a good rule of thumb.

Meanwhile, back at the ranch, the first few lines of `buildIcon()` do all the icon creation:

```
buildIcon = function (pageIndex) {
  // initialize
  var pageIndex:Number = 0;
  var iconDepth:Number = iconDepth =
➥ 100+iconCount;
  var iconName:MovieClip =
➥ this.attachMovie("icon", "icon"+
➥ iconCount, iconDepth);
```

The instance name is "icon" plus the value of the new variable, iconCount. The first icon you create will thus be called "icon0". If you increment iconCount every time you create a new icon, then the second icon will be called "icon1" and so on; in other words, the instance names are *unique*.

The depth is also based on iconCount. I've started the icon depths at 101 (there's a chance you may need to attach other, more permanent stuff on _root, so I've left free depths 0–100 for this purpose).

> *Within this function, this is actually _root. Why? Well, the function isn't attached to anything, so it must be scoping the timeline it's defined on: _root.*

The last line creates the icon movie clip by copying the movie clip with the linkage identifier "icon" to _root. You need to change the strip colors within the icon. Fortunately, you can do that using code you've already defined for tricolor. The icon and page movie clips are very similar, and this is the reason: *you can use the same code to control the color changes in both*. The next bit of code attaches the stripCols function to the icon you just created.

```
// apply functions to icon
stripCols.apply(iconName);
```

You then need to position and scale the icon. At the moment, the icon is the same size as the tricolor instance, so you need to make it much smaller. The following line does this by making it 4% of its original size:

```
// set colors, size and position
iconName._xscale = iconName._yscale=4;
```

Next, you need to color it:

```
iconName.setCol(color0, color1, color2);
```

Finally, you need to position it on the back strip. This took a bit of tweaking, but here are the values I came up with. Note that the position is dependent on the icon number, iconCount. As you add more icons, the position changes so that no two icons occupy the same position:

```
iconName._x =
➥ NAVSTRIP_X+(40*iconCount)+10;
iconName._y = NAVSTRIP_Y+5;
```

Now here's the important part: you need to store the current position so that you can get back to "here" if the icon is clicked later. You *could* be clever here and create an array a bit like page, which lists the backward path, but I prefer to keep it simple by being devious. I stored the values that allow me to build the current page again by storing the variable values *inside the icon itself*. More correctly, I copied the values that describe the current page on the timeline of the current icon. I also updated iconCount here, so the next icon after the home icon ("icon0") will be called "icon1", and so on.

```
// update iconCount by one for
// next icon and store current
// page details onto the icon stack
iconCount++;
iconName.currentPage = currentPage;
iconName.color0 = color0;
iconName.color1 = color1;
iconName.color2 = color2;
iconName.iconCount = iconCount;
```

> *Not only are the icons "visual breadcrumbs," but they're also "data breadcrumbs." I'm using the icon timelines to display the icon graphics, but I'm also using the icon timeline's scope to store data. Readers who are proficient in other languages should note that this is a feature not normally used in other web languages (JavaScript and so on). Flash has two levels of localization when it comes to data: code's localization (scope within a code block), and timeline localization or timeline variables (scope within a timeline).*
>
> *In Flash, you don't always have to create an object to store information describing a graphic element (usually a movie clip). In Flash, the graphic itself can store the data.*

The icons are actually buttons, and that means you have to attach a button script to them. This occurs via the next bit of code. The icon you just created is given an onRelease script.

```
// add the animation functions to icon
// define icon button script
iconName.onRelease = function() {
  // delete all icons after this one
  for (i=this.iconCount;
➥ i<=iconCount; i++) {
    _root["icon"+i].removeMovieClip();
  }
  // delete any content on the current page
  _root.createEmptyMovieClip("dummy",
➥ 10000);
  // zoom icon into the new current page
  s=4, x=this._x, y=this._y;
  xTarget = BORDER;
  yTarget = BORDER;
  sTarget = 100;
  this.onRelease = undefined;
  this.onEnterFrame = iconTransition;
};
```

What does this script have to do? Well, remembering what the icons do in the final site, when you click an icon, all icons to the right of it have to be deleted because they're no longer needed.

- Any content currently displayed has to be deleted.
- The icon has to grow to become the new page.

The first part is done here:

```
      for (i=this.iconCount;
➥ i<=iconCount; i++) {
          this["icon"+i].removeMovieClip();
      }
```

This deletes all icons between the local value of iconCount (that is, the value that iconCount was when this icon was created) and the current value of iconCount. This has the effect of deleting all icons that were placed onscreen since this icon was created.

You then delete any content that may exist. Rather than check if there's any content to delete, you'll simply delete it whether or not you need to. Deleting nothing does nothing, and it's easier to do than checking first.

```
      // delete any content on the current page
      // (note - 'this' is _root)
      this.createEmptyMovieClip("dummy",
➥ 10000);
```

The code to handle content is still code in progress, so don't get too worried about it at the moment. You'll have a look at that in the next section of the project.

The last part of the buildIcon() function is much like the navigate() function. You set up for the position transition and delete the current onRelease event (so that the animation can't be stopped once it has started). You set up the target size and position you want the icon to end up as (at position (border, border) and size 100%, which is what it has to change to before it looks like the tricolor in position and size).

```
          // zoom icon into the new current page
          s=4, x=this._x, y=this._y;
          xTarget = border;
          yTarget = border;
          sTarget = 100;
          this.onRelease = undefined;
          this.onEnterFrame = iconTransition;
      };
};
```

The last part of buildIcon() attaches the iconTransition() function as the onEnterFrame script for the icon. Add the following script immediately after buildIcon():

```
      iconTransition = function () {
        s -= (s-sTarget)/4;
        x -= (x-xTarget)/8;
        y -= (y-yTarget)/4;
        this._x=x, this._y=y;
        this._xscale = this._yscale=s;
        // have we reached the target?
        if (Math.abs(y-yTarget)<3) {
          // change page to new page
          tricolor.setCol(this.color0,
➥ this.color1, this.color2);
          currentPage = this.currentPage;
          populateTitles(currentPage);
          populateEvents(currentPage);
          // update page color variables
          color0 = this.color0;
          color1 = this.color1;
          color2 = this.color2;
          // update the icon count and
          // remove this icon
          iconCount = this.iconCount-1;
          this.removeMovieClip();
        }
      };
```

This new function animates the icon as it grows to cover the current page. It's similar to the previous function, posTransition(), with one subtle sting in the tail: when the icon totally covers the old page, it *doesn't* become the new page. Instead, the icon is deleted and the current tricolor changes so that it looks like the icon. It might look like the icon grows and becomes the new page, but this isn't the case.

Why do you do this? Well, the site UI is written to animate tricolor. Changing this clip for a new icon clip causes no end of problems, so you do the sneaky switch-around to keep life simple.

The last thing iconTransition() does is set iconCount to the value of iconCount held in the icon (this.iconCount). This has the effect of resetting the iconCount value so that it now reflects the fact that some icons have been deleted.

You can see the `iconCount` value and the way the icons store the current state of the navigation by debugging this FLA (or use mine, `futuremedia_code05.fla`, remembering that you must place it in a location containing `config.as` from last chapter before it will compile). When the site starts from the home page, you'll see that there are no icons.

As you navigate deeper into the site, you'll see the breadcrumb icon trail build up.

You can see the icon movie clips created in the debugger if you look at the movie clips created on the main timeline:

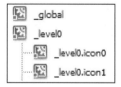

Look inside an icon (select an icon and then look at the Variables tab), and you'll see the local variables that are stored inside each icon instance (`color0`, `color1`, `color2`, `currentPage`, and `iconCount`). These variables are used to return to the page represented by the icon when the icon is clicked.

Also worth looking at is the way the variable `_level0.iconCount` changes as you interact with the icons.

Tidying up the UI

There are a few glaring differences between the interface you have at the moment and the final one. For example, notice the appearance of the back strip. In the site at the moment, you have a couple of ugly text fields to the right of the back strip.

The version of the back strip in the final site looks significantly better.

Also, the text fields do nothing at the moment, so you need to start driving them with code.

If you view the online version of the site with a slow- or medium-bandwidth connection, you'll see that the site has a preloader:

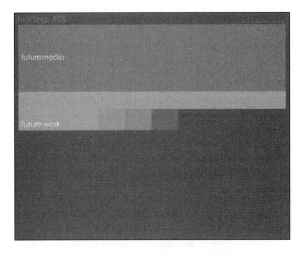
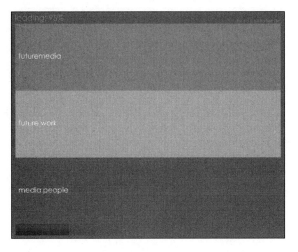

You'll see the site fade in as a series of colored blocks as content is loading. The percentage loaded is also listed at the top left via a text message.

Of course, if you have a high-bandwidth connection, you'll miss all of this. That's actually a good thing—nobody wants to wait for long downloads, so the site tries to make the best of it by giving the low-bandwidth users something to look at. High-bandwidth users see the main site immediately and miss the preload completely, which is good news for busy web surfers who tend to click away at the slightest hint of "Flash is bad" self-absorbed eye-candy.

Be wary of making your preloader or start screen too long. Whether you know it or not, a cool but long intro says you expect users to visit this site only once. I won't even try to talk about intro screens that are so big they need a preloader of their own!

One of the most important points about the final site design isn't so much what it *does* as much what it *doesn't do*. The UI shouldn't waste any valuable processor time when it isn't being used. You need to test that this is the case. Although you won't see this point in most programming books, it's important to remember that you're creating code for a very specialized application here—motion graphics—and performance and responsiveness are *everything*. You'll tackle these points in the sections that follow.

Tidying up the graphics

A text field's appearance is controlled by the TextField class. You can find out all about it by looking in the Built-in Classes ➤ Movie ➤ TextField book at the top-left pane of the Actions panel. Note that you can access help on any method or property by right-clicking/*Ctrl*-clicking any of the arrow icons and selecting View Help from the context menu.

You want to change two things:

■ The text field background color
■ The text field border color

> *Why don't you just change these properties via the Properties panel? Try it and see. (You can't.) Which brings me to an important point: there are some properties that you can't access unless you know ActionScript. You wouldn't be able to make the changes you're going to do next without using code.*

Add the following new lines, just after the point where you define and populate the database (around line 250):

```
// Define and populate database
var page:Array = new Array();
navigationData();
//Set up status text colors
status_txt.backgroundColor = 0x394444;
status_txt.borderColor = 0x5A5555;
statusValue_txt.backgroundColor = 0x394444;
statusValue_txt.borderColor = 0x5A5555;
// Build first page
var currentPage:Number = 0;
populateTitles(currentPage);
```

This sets the background and border colors for the two text fields on the back strip to dark shades of gray, in keeping with the overall design (subdued color everywhere except the two focuses of attention: the central tricolor and the back icons).

You still don't have exactly the same thing as the final site, though. The final back strip (below right) is shinier, with a subtle metallic effect.

This effect is created via a semitransparent movie clip that is placed over the back strip. You can see the symbol in `futuremedia_code05.fla`. **Look in the Library** and you'll find it in the User interface ~ non active UI stuff folder as the movie clip strip shine, which also has a linkage identifier of stripShine.

You need to create a similar clip. To do so, you can either take the easy route (drag-drop the clip from `futuremedia_code05.fla`'s Library to your work-in-progress FLA) or create a version of your own. To create your own version, follow these steps:

1. Create a new movie clip and call it `strip shine`. Inside it, draw out a black, strokeless rectangle (the dimensions aren't important). In the Properties panel, give the rectangle the settings shown in the following image. These numbers make the rectangle the same dimensions as the back strip.

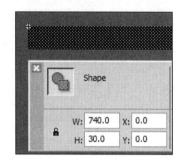

2. Next, you need to give your black strip a semitransparent shine. Using the Color Mixer panel (Window ➤ Design Panels ➤ Color Mixer), create a linear fill that is white with 35% alpha at the center, and white with 0% alpha at the edges.

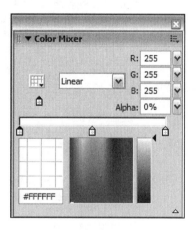

3. Apply this fill to the rectangle using the Paint Bucket tool. You'll see your rectangle fade from white (left edge) to transparent (right edge).

You need to rotate this fill so that it runs from top to bottom rather than from left to right as shown in the following image. Do this using the Fill Transform tool. You may have some difficulty to start off with, because some of the Fill Transform envelope will be offscreen. Move the center point to the left to make it fully visible if this is the case.

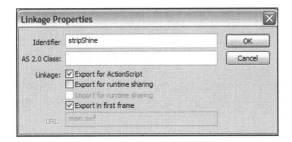

4. When you're done, give your strip shine movie clip a linkage identifier of stripShine.

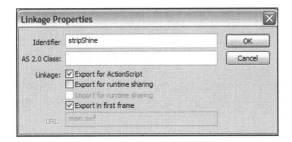

You can now use this strip to produce the metallic shine. Add the following lines after the code you've just added to set up the text fields:

```
//Set up status text colors
status_txt.backgroundColor = 0x394444;
status_txt.borderColor = 0x5A5555;
statusValue_txt.backgroundColor = 0x394444;
statusValue_txt.borderColor = 0x5A5555;
// place strip shine
this.attachMovie("stripShine",
➥ "shine", 200);
shine._x = NAVSTRIP_X;
shine._y = NAVSTRIP_Y;
// Build first page
```

Notice that you don't bother to equate the attachMovie to a movie clip reference, such as

```
var myClip:MovieClip =
➥ this.attachMovie("stripShine",
➥ "shine", 200);
```

This is because you don't need to access the strip shine instance once it has been created—it's a static part of the UI.

Some readers may be asking "Well, why did he go to all the trouble of attaching the strip shine movie clip to the stage dynamically, then?" The reason is you need the shine to appear above the icons that are also created dynamically. Unless you also place the shine strip dynamically, there's no way to make the shine appear above the icons.

Oh, if you're one of the readers asking that question, you can probably stop reading now and start making money from Flash web design, because you're certainly ready!

Adding sound and interface status messages

You've sorted out the appearance, so let's now turn to the more code-intensive dynamic stuff. You'll add some UI sounds and start animating the status text. To do that, you need to have a good understanding of what part of the code does what.

A great big sanity check

I'm guessing there are more than a few people out there who have been concentrating on each little thing they've done so far but can't step back and see the big picture. If you've just looked up after the "good understanding of what part of the code does what" sentence and, after a few moments of reflection, said *"Um . . . darn!"* or choice words to that effect, then this sanity check has your name written all over it.

Because the code is very large, it can be difficult to see what's what anymore, so let's do a little pruning and unearth the original skinny pup that this big animal of a listing started off as. If you ignore all the minor code sections, there are *only six main functions* that do everything. These consist of two functions for the initialization and four functions for the actual navigation. Let's break this down visually before looking at the code again.

The initialization phase goes like this:

1. The main code calls navigationData() to set up the database, page. The main code then calls stripEvents() and stops.

2. The main execution thread has now passed to stripEvents(). This function initializes the tricolor. In terms of program flow, the function's main task is to attach navigate() to each of the strips as the onRelease event handler.

3. Program flow then stops.

main code

calls **navigationData()**
calls **stripEvents()**

attaches **navigation()**
to strips as the *onRelease*

So how does stuff happen if no code is running anymore? The three strips within tricolor are now *buttons*. As soon as the user clicks one of the strips, the icons also appear, and these are also buttons. Program execution is kick-started by the user clicking any of these buttons. Clicking a strip takes the user forward in the navigation; clicking an icon takes the user backward in the navigation:

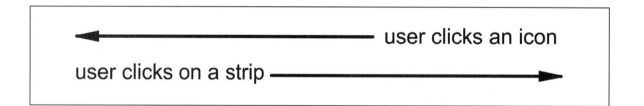

user clicks an icon

user clicks on a strip

If the user clicks a strip, the program flow is as shown in the following image. The onRelease event handler, navigation(), is invoked, and this calls buildIcon(). It then makes posTransition() run as an onEnterFrame to provide the first part of the navigation animation. Once it's finished, a decision is made on whether colTransition() needs to run (it does need to run if the new page is a link page, because you want to fade in the three strips again). At the end of this flurry of execution, you have an icon created to go backward and either a content page or another link page.

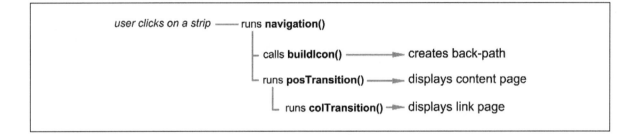

If you're a little unsure about what's happening here, it's worth following this diagram while you test the UI so far.

You can now put together a full picture of what happens in the code:

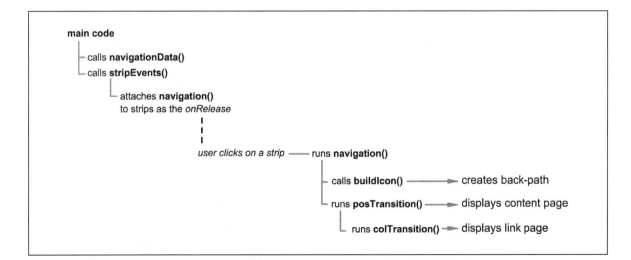

You can now also explain in words how the code works:

- The main code runs first, calling navigationData() and then stripEvents(). The first initializes the *data* for the site, and the second sets up the structures (events and objects) to *use this data.*

- One of the things stripEvents()does is attach an onRelease event to each strip. The associated event handler, navigation(), runs every time the user clicks a strip, and this event handler does the following:

  - Always sets up an icon to take the user back via buildIcon()

  - Optionally displays a content page via posTransition(), based on the data set up in navigationData()

  - Optionally displays a link page via colTransition(), again based on the data set up in navigationData()

> *Note that the preceding diagram shows what happens in code execution order, top left to bottom right. It also shows the time order from left to right. Finally, it shows the basic structure of the entire site design in terms of major building blocks (or, to use the terminology I've used previously, it shows you the relationships [interfaces] between all your black boxes). Quite a useful diagram to refer to!*

You should now be able to understand the listing better by looking at the preceding diagram and picking out each function in the code listing. You can probably even recognize that skinny puppy again. For those who can't, here's a quick helper: it's *very* useful to read this listing while looking at the preceding image to see how it all fits together.

```
// DEFINE EVENT SCRIPTS
navigate = function () {
    I am the onRelease handler for the
    three strips.  I set everything off
    when you click a strip.
};
posTransition = function () {
    navigate() makes me the onEnterFrame
```

```
    for the tricolor.
    I perform the first part of the
navigation
    animation - position and scale.
    I also set off the loading of content
    if required.
};
colTransition = function () {
    Once posTransition() has finished, it
    makes me the onEnterFrame for the
    tricolor if I am needed (i.e. if the
    current page is a link page)
};
buildIcon = function(){
    I create icons to allow the user
    To move backward through the
    navigation, and I am called
    at the start of every forward
    navigation by navigate()
}
// DEFINE MAIN SETUP SCRIPTS
stripPage = function () {
    I initialize the tricolor.
    In particular, I attach navigate() to
    each strip so that it becomes a button.
    This sets the whole site in motion.
};
// DEFINE SITE NAVIGATION DATA
navigationData = function () {
    I set up the configuration data that
    drives the whole site user interface.
};
I am the main script.  I call stripPage()
and then navigationData(), and then I
sit back and let the event scripts handle
everything ;)
```

I hope that has quelled any growing panic. Let's move on and start using this information.

Adding sound

It's always a good idea to add audio feedback to a UI because

- **Real-world experience has conditioned users to expect it**. You expect a click noise when you use most real switches and buttons. Adding sound to a virtual button is a very good way of making it appear "real."

- **Sound is a good way to create mood and atmosphere**. Choosing sounds that are in tune with your site design will increase the impact of the site. Of course, choosing the *wrong* sounds can sometimes have the opposite effect!

The UI uses two sounds, pad1.wav and pad2.wav. Import them into the FLA so far using File ➤ Import ➤ Import to Library. To keep your Library tidy, create a new Library folder (click the second icon from the left at the bottom of the Library panel) called sounds and drag the folder over the existing Library folder User interface to get the same folder structure as shown in the following image. Drag the two sound files into the sounds folder.

Finally, give pad1 a linkage identifier of pad1, and give pad2 a linkage identifier of pad2. The two check boxes Export for ActionScript and Export in first frame should both be checked when you set the linkage.

You can (and should), of course, alter the sounds if you want to create your own site based on Futuremedia, but for now you'll stick to my files.

Sound is totally undersold in most web design books, mainly because few web designers are also musicians. Well, I think that's no excuse. Given that I spent time talking about the graphics of the Futuremedia site UI, I think it's only fair that I share a few choice secrets on the sound creation of the UI as well.

- Most sites tend to use generic sounds taken from sound collections or public domain sites. I created my own sounds, but for those who aren't musically inclined, an alterative place to get high-quality (and free) UI sounds is from **abandonware**, games and applications that are no longer commercially viable and/or the original copyright holder no longer exists. You can find many websites and FTP sites that host abandonware simply by doing a search on the word "abandonware" using your web search engine of choice (mine is the totally under-rated http://vivisimo.com, which clusters the search results). Older games tended to use WAV files, which are perfect for immediate import into Flash (rather than the more recent MP3 file format, which can sometimes cause problems with Flash import because there are so many different MP3 settings).

- Another source of UI sounds is time-stretched audio. The UI sounds for Futuremedia were created in part using this rather sneaky technique. **Time stretching** allows you to increase or decrease a sound's duration without changing the pitch, so you could (for example) change the duration of a compete CD from 1 hour to 20 seconds without ending up with something with more squeaks than a mouse on amphetamines. Your CD will *still sound the same,* it will just last 20 seconds!

- The Futuremedia sounds were created from a personally written 7-minute electronic music ambient track that was time compressed to about 1 second. The sounds still have the "feel" of the original ambient track because pitch is maintained. This means that the atmosphere of that ambient track is now there in the Futuremedia site.

- As a final trick, I needed a matched pair of sounds, one that sounds like a "forward" sound (to be played when the user clicks a strip) and one that sounds like a "backward" sound (to be played when the user clicks an icon). I did this by reversing one of the two stereo channels of pad1 to create pad2. They're actually created from the same sound.

It all goes to show that code isn't the only thing you can be clever with, and graphics aren't the only things you can be creative with. Don't forget audio!

Time stretching has real possibilities for the web designer who knows everything about graphic design but has no clue about creating music. Suppose you want a set of UI sounds for a site that requires metallic and hard techno sounds. Time compressing different sections of a piece of music that "matches" your site design will create UI sounds with the same feel, without your having to know anything about creating techno sounds.

Time stretching is an option on many digital audio manipulation applications (it may also be called **time/pitch stretching***).*

On to the code. To control the two sounds through scripting, you need to start by using the Sound class and create a couple of sound instances. Add the following lines in the main code section (toward the end of the existing var definitions, around line 245):

```
// Define animation variables
var scale:Number = 0, x:Number = 0,
➥ y:Number = 0;
var yTarget:Number = 0,
➥ scaleTarget:Number = 0;
// Define sound instances
var pad1:Sound = new Sound(this);
var pad2:Sound = new Sound(this);
pad1.attachSound("pad1");
pad2.attachSound("pad2");
```

Those who want to experiment will find that the code will still work if they remove the this *arguments. You can usually get away with doing this, unless your site consists of more than one SWF— and guess what you're going to do in a few pages?*

You'll find that when you split the site into two SWF files (a preloader SWF and main site SWF . . . doh! I've given the game away), the sound instances will suddenly stop working unless you add the this *as shown.*

Next, you need to make the sounds start as required. Given the great big sanity check you encountered not so long ago, you should be able to look at the code block diagrams and say where you need to add the sounds. For those too lazy to turn back a few pages, here's the lowdown:

- The forward sound needs to be heard as soon as a strip is clicked. The best place to add code to do this is on the strip onRelease event handler, navigate().
- The backward sound needs to be heard every time an icon is clicked. The place to do this is in the onRelease event defined for each icon, which can be found in the buildIcon() function.

First, the forward sound (pad2). Add the following lines at the end of the function navigate():

```
// attach the animation transition to the
// strip that has just been pressed
this.onEnterFrame = posTransition;
// UI forward navigation sound
pad2.start(0, 1);
};
```

Next, the backward sound (pad1). Add the following lines at the end of the buildIcon() function:

```
sTarget = 100;
this.onRelease = undefined;
this.onEnterFrame = iconTransition;
// UI backward navigation sound
pad1.start(0, 1);
};
};
```

If you test the site now, you'll hear the sounds play at the appropriate time when you click a strip or icon.

Adding the status text messages

Although you've set the color of the two text fields at the bottom right of the back strip, they still don't do anything. In particular, the first one just sits there telling you it's "ready." Time to fix that. You'll change the message so that

- When the UI is animating, the status message will be navigating.
- When the UI isn't doing anything, the status message will be ready.

Looking at the diagrams of how the code works (in the section "A great big sanity check"), there are two ways to start a navigation and two ways to end a navigation:

- A navigation can start when the user clicks a strip (function navigate()) or an icon (function buildIcon()).

- A navigation can end at the end of posTransition() or colTransition(), depending on what kind of page the user is navigating to.

So, you need to add a navigating message in navigate() and buildIcon(), before the forward/backward animations start. In addition, you need to return the message text to ready at the end of both posTransition() and colTransition(). You also need to return it to ready at the end of the iconTransition() event handler.

Another sanity check

A few pictures should help here for the almost-lost. The following two diagrams summarize the concepts just described graphically. The top illustration is the forward navigation, and the bottom illustration is the backward navigation.

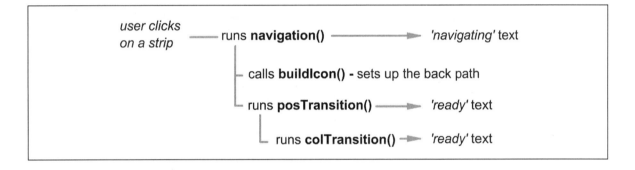

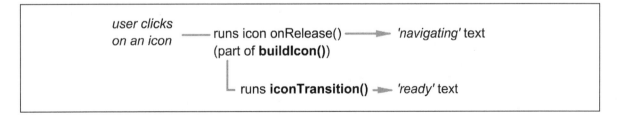

Let's implement this in the code, starting with the forward path.

Forward path

The status text reads ready at the start of the site (because you've manually entered this into the status_text text field). As soon as the user clicks a strip, you want to change the text to navigating. To do this, add the following new lines at the end of the function navigate():

```
    // UI forward navigation sound
    pad2.start(0, 1);
    // Set status text
    status_txt.text = "navigating...";
  };
```

When the navigation has completed, the text needs to return to ready. Add the following code to the last part of posTransition() (the final else):

```
    } else {
      // otherwise place the content
      // and set status to 'ready'
      placeContent();
      status_txt.text = "ready";
    }
  }
};
```

If this else doesn't run, then colTransition() has been called instead, and you need to update the status text the last time this function runs. Add the following line to the last else in colTransition():

```
    } else {
      // we are now at the new page
      color0 = tricolor.colStrip0.getRGB();
      color1 = tricolor.colStrip1.getRGB();
      color2 = tricolor.colStrip2.getRGB();
      fadeText(100);
      delete this.onEnterFrame;
      populateEvents(currentPage);
      status_txt.text = "ready";
    }
  };
```

Backward path

If the user clicks an icon, you need to make the text read navigating. The code that runs when the user clicks an icon is the onRelease defined within buildIcon() (it's anonymous, so it has no name). To do this, add the following to the end of buildIcon():

```
      // UI back navigation sound
      pad1.start(0, 1);
      // set status to 'navigating'
      status_txt.text = "navigating...";
    };
  };
```

You want to return the text to ready at the end of the onEnterFrame that controls the icon transition from "little icon" to "full screen." This occurs at the end of the last if in iconTransition() (which runs on the last onEnterFrame in the animation). Add this to the bottom of iconTransition():

```
      // update the icon count and
      // remove this icon
      iconCount = this.iconCount-1;
      this.removeMovieClip();
      // update status text
      status_txt.text = "ready";
    }
  };
```

The status text will now switch between ready and navigating when the interface is running. Not the biggest feature of the UI, but it does have one very big advantage. In placing these text changes into the code, you've been forced to understand how the (nearly complete) code hangs together, and this is, after all, a teaching exercise!

> *The status text actually started out as a bit of diagnostic text that told me what was happening to the UI as it ran. I thought it was a cool feature for showing what the code is doing at any time that I put it into the design (see next figures).*

There's a second text field that you haven't looked at: the statusValue_txt text field. In the final site, this gives you numeric feedback, such as the percent loaded during content load operations. You can't use this text field just yet, because the site isn't capable of such operations.

Testing the site

You should really do some testing on your site. You'll notice that there's a config_test.as file in the download for this chapter, and the file futuremedia_code05.fla has a set of files in the Library that I haven't talked about yet.

placeholder stuff	Folder		
placeholder	Movie Clip	0	Export: placeholder
placeholder assets	Folder		

The file placeholder also has a linkage identifier placeholder, and if you look at config_test.as, you'll see that this loads the same file for each content page: placeholder.

Here's a typical entry from config_test.as:

```
// Page 02 - burnmedia (content page)
page[02].pType = "contentPage";
page[02].pLink = [-1, -1, -1];
page[02].pTitle =
➥ ["home > futuremedia > burnmedia",
➥ "", "", ""];
page[02].pID = "placeholder";
```

The page.pID property gives the name of a linkage identifier, and it's this value that decides what's loaded as the content per page (at the moment—you'll change it to make the whole thing much more flexible later).

The function that handles loading is placeContent(). Here's a reminder of what it looks like:

```
placeContent = function () {
  _root.attachMovie(page[currentPage].pID,
➥ "content_mc", 10000);
  _root.content_mc._x = BORDER;
  _root.content_mc._y = BORDER;
};
```

Content is loaded in at the end of posTransition() via a call to placeContent(), and the content is deleted as soon as you click an icon via this line in buildIcon():

```
// delete any content on the current page
_root.createEmptyMovieClip("dummy",
➥ 10000);
```

The only thing you need to change in futuremedia_code05.fla so that the site starts showing the placeholder is the line that includes the configuration. Change the following line (around line 220):

```
#include "config.as"
```

to

```
#include "config_test.as"
```

If you test the site now, you should see content appear in the previously blank content pages:

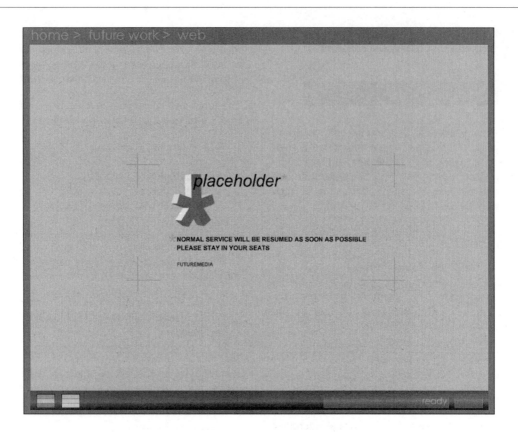

Cool, the site is now really starting to take shape!

You may have guessed that you've already done the performance testing. The status text is a big clue that tells you that the site only does things when it's making a UI transition. The site is designed such that these transitions never occur when there's content present; content is either not loaded or deleted before a UI transition takes place.

The content is kept separate from the UI code, and the case is the same in terms of everything else. The UI animations are kept separate from anything the content may want to do, so that when either content *or* the UI want to do something, there is nothing else going on in the background to slow it down—the site is always *doing only one thing at a time*.

Although the site may have started to look a little sluggish when you test it in Test Movie, try viewing the site in the browser and you'll see a different story. It's much quicker because Flash doesn't have to draw anything that ends up offscreen.

The Futuremedia design has been relentless in its approach—everything is modular. This is paying real dividends now at the end. Sticking almost pedantically to structured code has meant that you've been able to totally bypass one of the biggest issues with complex motion graphics: performance. The code modules work in a structured and sequential manner, and that means the site is fast.

If you don't follow this approach, you'll most likely ace the early stages of development, moving along at two or three times the speed. Only right here at the end game would you start to have problems. You would know your site is working, but you might be unsure of what bit of code is doing what, and whether it's running at times it shouldn't.

The Futuremedia site is designed in terms of the six major code functions, and all of them have distinct interfaces. Among other things, the point at which each function starts running and stops is as regimented as an army on the march. When you say "stop," everything really does!

OK, so that's one important part of the development that you don't even have to consider. What you should do, though, is confirm correct operation.

You're almost there. You have one final thing to do before the UI is finished and you can start adding the final content.

Adding a preloader

The site so far looks pretty, but you have no idea what the final content will look like or how bandwidth heavy it will be. Without a preloading strategy, you'll be stuck if this content turns out to be bandwidth heavy. All of your site currently lives on frame 1 of the timeline, which is bad news if the site has to load a significant amount of content on that frame, as the user will see a blank screen until the content is loaded and the first frame of Futuremedia can be shown. You have two ways around this:

- You can create a preloader within the current FLA.
- You can create a separate preloader file.

The first option isn't recommended, because you don't know how much content will have to be loaded in frame 1 (particularly if some of your content requires the loading of class definitions, which are always loaded at frame 1 by default. You can change this, of course, but it's better to cater for the default).

Have a look at the second new file in the download for this section, `index.fla`. This is your preloader. Some of you may have been wondering how the final site loads the tricolor as a series of fading blocks, when the tricolor isn't made out of blocks; it's a single complete graphic. This is how it's done—as usual, you cheat. You actually cheat big-time, because everything you assume about the preloader is incorrect.

- The site that appears slowly during the preload is *not* the Futuremedia site—it's a copy.
- The site that does appear during the preload doesn't load over time—it loads *immediately*. You simply reveal it over time to give the impression that it's loading over time.

When you open `index.fla`, you'll see something that looks exactly like the home page of the Futuremedia site. That's it, though; the tricolor is just some static graphics, and nothing on this version of the site actually works. Because it does nothing, this doppelganger has one very cool feature: it will load almost instantaneously.

When `index.fla` loads, it's hidden behind a set of blocks that are created dynamically. These are set up as a grid. At this point, the code tells the Flash player to start loading the main (working) site that you've been building so far.

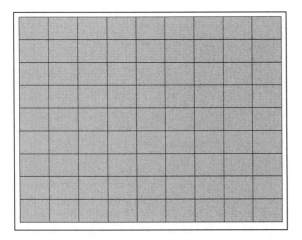

As loading of the real site progresses, the blocks are removed to reveal the nonfunctioning doppelganger. The blocks are removed by code that looks at the percentage loaded of the main site (the real site is hidden at this point, using yet another sneaky and totally obvious-once-you-know-it technique I'll reveal in a moment), and the code removes the same number of blocks (remembering that you have 10 × 10 blocks = 100 blocks total, so each block can be equated to 1% loaded).

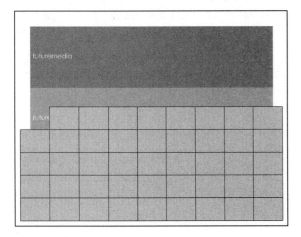

Because the blocks are very close to the background color, it doesn't look like the blocks are disappearing, but more like the site is *appearing*.

Once all the blocks have loaded, you have your dummy site fully revealed. The trouble is that it's a turkey. It doesn't work.

But wait! You have a fully revealed site only when the *real site is 100% loaded*. So here's what you do: you *switch the two sites*. The nonworking dummy is discarded, and the real site is made to appear in its place. The user will see none of this—the user will think it was the real site loading all along.

Now, you could have used the preloader component that comes with Flash, but to be honest, loading a component that is 30KB worth of extra file size (so you end up needing a preloader to load your preloader!) seems a little tame when you can instead do a bit of thinking and perform your grand con with a fraction of the file size.

I'll leave you to have a look at the code in the `index.fla` file, but the following pointers should aid your understanding of it:

- The fading effect is *not* caused by the site fading in, but by the individual blocks fading *out*. You can see this if you look in the Library for `index.fla` and examine the `mc.block` clip. It consists of a simple tween that goes from 100% alpha to 0% alpha. By stopping all the blocks at the start and running each in turn, you achieve the fade-in effect.

- In the code, `_level0` refers to the preloader SWF, and `_level1` refers to the main (real) Futuremedia site SWF.

- The last thing the preloader does is a `_level1.play()`. This causes the by now fully loaded Futuremedia site timeline to start playing.

All you need to do now is that "hide the real Futuremedia site" trick. The clue to your final bit of magician's misdirection is in the last bullet point. You'll add a new keyframe to the main site, and leave this empty and with a `stop()` action on it. While the main site loads, it's stuck on this blank keyframe and therefore doesn't show up. The code in `index.fla` makes the main site play when the main site is fully loaded, and it's this action that reveals the real site.

The main timeline in `futuremedia_code05.fla` looks like this:

The final site file, `main.fla`, looks like this:

The only differences are as follows:

■ All the keyframes have been moved from frame 1 to frame 2. You can do this to your own work-in-progress file by selecting each keyframe currently on frame 1 (first image), and then click-dragging it (second image) and dropping it over frame 2 (third image).

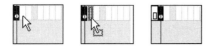

■ The new frame 1 has a single `stop()` in the new empty frame 1 (layer actions).

If you run `main.fla` on its own, you'll see a blank stage. Right-click/*CTRL*-click the blank stage of a running SWF and select Play to force the site to go to frame 2. Alternatively, run `index.fla` after compiling `main.swf` (that is, testing `main.swf` at least once to create a SWF).

And that's it. You now have a fully functioning UI. What you *don't* have is the content to populate it. In the download for this book, you'll find one final download file, `Futuremedia_complete.zip`. This file contains the complete UI and associated content SWFs and Library items. All additions between this empty UI and the final Futuremedia site are fully commented.

Parting shots

One of the biggest problems, if not *the* biggest problem, I had when starting out in Flash ActionScript was that I had no examples to look at. That blank Flash stage didn't seem to want to end up like the sort of things other people were creating. I just didn't *get it.*

Sure, there were examples available on the Web that showed how to do this month's how-do-they-do-that trick or some tutorials showing how to use the new features of the latest version of Flash. What *none* of them seemed to want to tell me was how to build a *complete* ActionScript site *of my own.* Years later, I now know that there were three missing pieces I needed as a beginner to move further in ActionScript:

■ There was the problem of working out how to start. How do you begin coding that first line in a big project? I now know you don't begin by coding—you have to plan the idea, not the code. That's why you spent so long working out how the site should work earlier in the book, and why the early parts of the project have very little code and lots of drawings and thinking about graphics, both of which are easier to change than code.

■ The ActionScript language is huge, but in normal web design, you'll use not much more than 10% of it 90% of the time. The problem I had was working out which 10% is important. This book project has tried to address that issue by relentlessly concentrating only on that 10%. Little things like the inertia effect in the space invaders game might have made you think "That's cool, but it's only one trick—why is he spending so much time on it?"

Well, you probably now appreciate that it's one of the most used tricks in ActionScript animation because it provides smooth animation. It's part of that all-important 10% core package.

■ The final missing piece was seeing it done by someone else *all the way through*. In the Futuremedia project, I've tried to give you the example I needed way back then—something to fill the blank stage over time, and in the correct order.

What you should have at the end of this book is a foundation in ActionScript and the correct *mind-set* to advance further. You now have a basic framework for filling that blank stage with ActionScript that's controlling *your* design ideas rather than mine.

Now that you have the finished first ActionScript site with help from me, the real journey—building your first ActionScript-heavy site—has just begun. You can base your site on the Futuremedia site, or you can even have a look at earlier versions of the stun:design site (the book project in the Flash 5 and MX editions of this book), which are available from the downloads section of the friends of ED site.

Remember, the good thing about the friends of ED policy of web downloads as opposed to the book plus CD format is that you don't have to buy a book to access the download files for a book. It's a good way to try before you buy or to look at the files for previous editions of the book.

You can now take the ideas developed in this site and make them your own. For example, you can change the look and feel of the Futuremedia site by changing the basic tricolor navigation. You can actually use a number of other geometries:

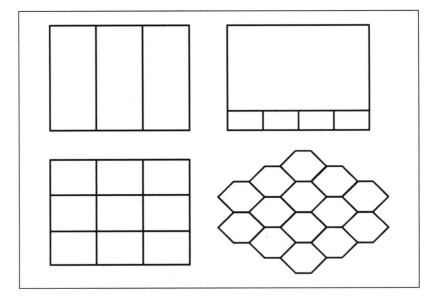

The tricolor is just one of several designs you can use. All the geometries shown in the preceding image are simply incremental changes away from the basic UI design. All you need to do is form a system whereby clicking any one shape will zoom into that shape and fade in further options

The current site uses scaling rectangles. By using the drawing API to draw the rectangles on the fly, you can add all sorts of weird and wonderful transitions. How about a single page that splits up *organically* (rather like a piece of Silly Putty being stretched until it becomes two pieces)?

Better still, have a look at a few sites and try to second-guess the behind-the-scenes tricks the designers must have used. Take the best ideas and some of your own, and start from scratch.

I've just scratched the surface here, because I don't want to put too many ideas in your head—I'd rather you came up with them yourself. Just add inspiration. After all, that's what Flash is all about.

You've come a long way, but the journey doesn't end here. In this book, you've gained the fundamental skills and understanding that will allow you to take your ActionScripting onward and upward. I hope that the book has also provided you with inspiration and excitement at the massive creative options opened up by efficient and imaginative coding. ActionScript's possibilities are limitless. It's just up to you to gotoAndPlay!

Summary

Well, it's been quite a journey. The first line of code in this book was a simple comment. Remember this?

    // My first line of ActionScript

And now look at you! You've dipped into components. (And not just simple use of components either—you've gone straight in and attached components dynamically to the stage. I didn't want to tell you at the time, but this "attaching dynamically" deal is something that the Macromedia documentation describes as advanced.) You've also looked at prototypes and ActionScript 2.0 classes, the two core advanced areas of ActionScript. After those, there's *nothing else*. You'll know it all, and you'll be able to easily understand all the other stuff you haven't looked at yet—XML and the MovieClipLoader class will be child's play.

This last chapter has been hard, and some of you will want to practice with the other stuff in the book before reading it again. Others will realize that prototypes and class-based coding aren't for them, and that's OK. The most important thing is that you've learned structured programming with ActionScript, and you've also seen how to put together a site that's almost totally controlled by ActionScript.

Of course, coding is just a tool to do the job. Now that you have the knowledge, I hope you'll start getting a feel for all the things you can do now that you couldn't before. ActionScript is just a way of putting your creative ideas down, mixing them with code, and making something cool. It's time to get some ideas and build a Futuremedia of your own—and that is the start of a whole new journey.

INDEX

(continued)